THE PUPPET AND THE DWARF

Short Circuits
Slavoj Žižek, editor

THE PUPPET AND THE DWARF

The Perverse Core of Christianity

Slavoj Žižek

THE MIT PRESS   CAMBRIDGE, MASSACHUSETTS   LONDON, ENGLAND

This book was set in Joanna MT & Copperplate 33bc by Graphic Composition, Inc., Athens, GA, and was printed and bound in the United States of America.

Library of Congress Cataloging-in-Publication Data
Zizek, Slavoj.
    The puppet and the dwarf : the perverse core of Christianity / Slavoj Zizek.
        p. cm. — (Short circuits)
    Includes bibliographical references (p.).
    ISBN 0-262-74025-7 (pbk. : alk. paper)
    ISBN-13: 978-0-262-74025-8 (pbk. : alk. paper)
        1. Christianity—Essence, genius, nature. 2. Historical materialism. I. Title.
    II. Series.
    BR121.3.Z59 2003
    230—dc21

                                                                2003051043

10 9 8 7 6 5

CONTENTS

A short circuit occurs when there is a faulty connection in the network—faulty, of course, from the standpoint of the network's smooth functioning. Is not the shock of short-circuiting, therefore, one of the best metaphors for a critical reading? Is not one of the most effective critical procedures to cross wires that do not usually touch: to take a major classic (text, author, notion), and read it in a short-circuiting way, through the lens of a "minor" author, text, or conceptual apparatus ("minor" should be understood here in Deleuze's sense: not "of lesser quality," but marginalized, disavowed by the hegemonic ideology, or dealing with a "lower," less dignified topic)? If the minor reference is well chosen, such a procedure can lead to insights which completely shatter and undermine our common perceptions. This is what Marx, among others, did with philosophy and religion (short-circuiting philosophical speculation through the lens of political economy, that is to say, economic speculation); this is what Freud and Nietzsche did with morality (short-circuiting the highest ethical notions through the lens of the unconscious libidinal economy). What such a reading achieves is not a simple "desublimation," a reduction of the higher intellectual content to its lower economic or libidinal cause; the aim of such an approach is, rather, the inherent decentering of the interpreted text, which brings to light its "unthought," its disavowed presuppositions and consequences.

And this is what "Short Circuits" wants to do, again and again. The underlying premise of the series is that Lacanian psychoanalysis is a privileged instrument of such an approach, whose purpose is to illuminate a standard text or ideological formation, making it readable in a totally new way—the long history of Lacanian interventions in philosophy, religion, the arts (from the visual arts to the cinema, music, and literature), ideology, and politics justifies this premise. This, then, is not a new series of books on psychoanalysis, but a series of "connections in the Freudian field"—of short Lacanian interventions in art, philosophy, theology, and ideology.

"Short Circuits" intends to revive a practice of reading which confronts a classic text, author, or notion with its own hidden presuppositions, and thus reveals its disavowed truth. The basic criterion for the texts that will be published is that they effectuate such a theoretical short circuit. After reading a book in this series, the reader should not simply have learned something new: the point is, rather, to make him or her aware of another—disturbing—side of something he or she knew all the time.

Slavoj Žižek

THE PUPPET AND THE DWARF

INTRODUCTION

The Puppet Called Theology

Today, when the historical materialist analysis is receding, practiced as it were under cover, rarely called by its proper name, while the theological dimension is given a new lease on life in the guise of the "postsecular" Messianic turn of deconstruction, the time has come to reverse Walter Benjamin's first thesis on the philosophy of history: "The puppet called 'theology' is to win all the time. It can easily be a match for anyone if it enlists the service of historical materialism, which today, as we know, is wizened and has to keep out of sight."

One possible definition of modernity is: the social order in which religion is no longer fully integrated into and identified with a particular cultural life-form, but acquires autonomy, so that it can survive as the same religion in different cultures. This extraction enables religion to globalize itself (there are Christians, Muslims, and Buddhists everywhere today); on the other hand, the price to be paid is that religion is reduced to a secondary epiphenomenon with regard to the secular functioning of the social totality. In this new global order, religion has two possible roles: *therapeutic* or *critical*. It either helps individuals to function better in the existing order, or it tries to assert itself as a critical agency articulating what is wrong with this order as such, a space for the voices of discontent—in this second case, religion *as such* tends toward assuming the role of a heresy. The contours of this deadlock were outlined by Hegel; sometimes, we find in his work something I am tempted to call a "downward synthesis": after the two opposed positions, the third one, the *Aufhebung* of the two, is not a higher synthesis bringing together what is worth maintaining in the other two, but a kind of negative synthesis, the lowest point. Here are three outstanding examples:

- In the "logic of judgment," the first triad of the "judgment of existence" (positive-negative-infinite judgment) culminates in the "infinite judgment": God is not red, a rose is not an elephant, understanding is not a table—these judgments are, as Hegel puts it, "accurate or true, as one calls them, but nonsensical and in bad taste."[1]
- Twice in *Phenomenology of Spirit*. First apropos of phrenology, in which the whole dialectic of the "observing Reason" culminates in the infinite judgment "the Spirit is a bone."[2]

- Then, at the end of the chapter on Reason, in the passage to Spirit as history, where we have the triad of the "law-giving Reason," the "law-testing Reason," and the Reason that accepts its impenetrable foundation. It is only by accepting the positivity of the law as its ultimate given background that we pass to history proper. The passage to history proper occurs when we assume the failure of Reason reflectively to ground the laws that regulate the life of a people.[3]

And it seems that the three modes of religion with which *Glauben und Wissen* and other early theological writings deal[4] form the same triad:

- The *"people's religion [Volksreligion]"*—in Ancient Greece, religion was intrinsically bound up with a particular people, its life and customs. It required no special reflexive act of faith: it was simply accepted.

- The *"positive religion"*—imposed dogmas, rituals, rules, to be accepted because they are prescribed by an earthly and/or divine authority (Judaism, Catholicism).

- The *"religion of Reason"*—what survives of religion when positive religion is submitted to the rational critique of Enlightenment. There are two modes: Reason or Heart—either the Kantian dutiful moralist, or the religion of pure interior feeling (Jacobi, etc.). Both dismiss the positive religion (rituals, dogmas) as superficial historically conditioned ballast. Crucial here is the inherent reversal of Kant into Jacobi, of universalist moralism into pure irrational contingence of feeling—that is to say, this immediate coincidence of opposites, this direct reversal of reason into irrational belief.

Again, the passage from one moment to the next is clear: first, (the people's) religion loses its organic *Naturwüchsigkeit*, it changes into a set of "alienated"—externally imposed and contingent—rules; then, logically, the authority of these rules is to be questioned by our Reason. . . . What, however, would constitute the step further that would break the deadlock of universalist moralism and abstract feeling converting directly into each other? There is no clear solution. Why do we need religion at all in our modern times? The standard answer is: rational philosophy or science is esoteric, confined to a small circle; it cannot replace religion in its function of capturing the imagination of the masses, and thus serving the purposes of moral and political order. But this solution is problematic in Hegel's own terms: the problem is that, in the modern times of Reason, religion can no longer fulfill this function of the organic binding force of social substance—today, religion has irretrievably lost this power not only for scientists and philosophers, but also for the wider circle of "ordinary" people. In his *Lectures on Aesthetics*, Hegel claims that in the modern age, as much as we admire art, we no longer bend the knee before it—and the same holds for religion.

Today, we live (in) the tension designated by Hegel even more than people did in Hegel's own times. When Hegel wrote: "It is a modern folly to alter a corrupt ethical system, its constitution and legislation, without changing the religion, to have a revolution without a reformation,"[5] he announced the necessity of what Mao called the "Cultural Revolution" as the condition of a successful social revolution. Is this not what we have today: (the technological) revolution without a fundamental "revolution of mores [*Revolution der Sitten*]"? The basic tension is not so much the tension of reason versus feeling, but, rather, the tension of knowledge versus the disavowed belief embodied in external ritual—the situation often described in the terms of cynical reason whose formula, the reverse of Marx's, was proposed decades ago by Peter Sloterdijk: "I know what I am doing; nonetheless, I am doing it. . . ." This formula, however, is not as unambiguous as it may appear—it should be supplemented with: ". . . because I don't know what I believe."

In our politically correct times, it is always advisable to start with the set of unwritten prohibitions that define the positions one is allowed to adopt. The first thing to note with regard to religious matters is that reference to "deep spirituality" is in again: direct materialism is out; one is, rather, enjoined to harbor openness toward a radical Otherness beyond the ontotheological God. Consequently, when, today, one directly asks an intellectual: "OK, let's cut the crap and get down to basics: do you believe in some form of the divine or not?," the first answer is an embarrassed withdrawal, as if the question is too intimate, too probing; this withdrawal is then usually explained in more "theoretical" terms: "That is the wrong question to ask! It is not simply a matter of believing or not, but, rather, a matter of certain radical experience, of the ability to open oneself to a certain unheard-of dimension, of the way our openness to radical Otherness allows us to adopt a specific ethical stance, to experience a shattering form of enjoyment. . . ." What we are getting today is a kind of "suspended" belief, a belief that can thrive only as not fully (publicly) admitted, as a private obscene secret. Against this attitude, one should insist even more emphatically that the "vulgar" question "Do you really believe or not?" matters—more than ever, perhaps. My claim here is not merely that I am a materialist through and through, and that the subversive kernel of Christianity is accessible also to a materialist approach; my thesis is much stronger: this kernel is accessible only to a materialist approach—and vice versa: to become a true dialectical materialist, one should go through the Christian experience.[6]

Was there, however, at any time in the past, an era when people directly "really believed"? As Robert Pfaller demonstrated in *Illusionen der Anderen*,[7] the direct belief in a truth that is subjectively fully assumed ("Here I stand!") is a modern phenomenon, in contrast to traditional beliefs-through-distance, like politeness or rituals. Premodern societies did not believe directly, but through distance, and this explains, for instance, why Enlightenment critics misread "primitive" myths—they first took the notion that a tribe originated from a fish or a bird as a literal direct belief, then rejected it as stupid, "fetishist," naive. They thereby imposed their own notion of belief on the "primitivized" Other. (Is this not also the paradox of Edith Wharton's *The Age of Innocence?* Newton's wife was not a naive ("innocent") believer in her husband's fidelity—she was well aware of his passionate love for Countess Olenska, she just politely ignored it, and acted as if she believed in his fidelity. . . .) Pfaller is right to emphasize how, today, we believe more than ever: the most skeptical attitude, that of deconstruction, relies on the figure of an Other who "really believes"; the postmodern need for the permanent use of the devices of ironic distantiation (quotation marks, etc.) betrays the underlying fear that, without these devices, belief would be direct and immediate—as if, if I were to say "I love you" instead of the ironic "As the poets would have put it, I love you," this would entail a directly assumed belief that I love you—that is, as if a distance is not already operative in the direct statement "I love you" . . .

And perhaps that is where we find the stake of today's reference to "culture," of "culture" emerging as the central life-world category. When it comes to religion, for example, we no longer "really believe" today, we just follow (some) religious rituals and mores as part of respect for the "lifestyle" of the community to which we belong (nonbelieving Jews obeying kosher rules "out of respect for tradition," etc.). "I don't really believe in it, it's just part of my culture" effectively seems to be the predominant mode of the disavowed/displaced belief characteristic of our times. What is a cultural lifestyle, if not the fact that, although we don't believe in Santa Claus, there is a Christmas tree in every house, and even in public places, every December? Perhaps, then, the "nonfundamentalist" notion of "culture" as distinguished from "real" religion, art, and so on, is in its very core the name for the field of disowned/impersonal beliefs— "culture" is the name for all those things we practice without really believing in them, without "taking them seriously." Is this not also why science is not part of this notion of culture—it is all too real? And is this also not why we dismiss fundamentalist believers as "barbarians," as anticultural, as a threat to culture—they dare to take their beliefs seriously? Today, we ultimately perceive as a threat to culture those who live their culture immediately, those who lack a distance toward it. Recall the outrage when, two years ago, the Taliban forces in Afghanistan destroyed the ancient Buddhist statues at Bamiyan: although none of us enlightened Westerners believe in the divinity of the Buddha, we were outraged because the Taliban Muslims did not show the appropriate respect for the "cultural heritage" of their own country and the entire world. Instead of believing through the other, like all people of culture, they really believed in their own religion, and thus had no great sensitivity toward the cultural value of the monuments of other religions—to them, the Buddha statues were just fake idols, not "cultural treasures."

One commonplace about philosophers today is that their very analysis of the hypocrisy of the dominant system betrays their naivety: why are they still shocked to see people inconsistently violate their professed values when it suits their interests? Do they really expect people to be consistent and principled? Here one should defend authentic philosophers: what surprises them is the exact opposite—not that people do not "really believe," and act upon their professed principles, but that people who profess their cynical distance and radical pragmatic opportunism secretly believe much more than they are willing to admit, even if they transpose these beliefs onto (nonexistent) "others."

Within this framework of suspended belief, three so-called "postsecular" options are permitted: one is allowed either to praise the wealth of polytheistic premodern religions oppressed by the Judeo-Christian patriarchal legacy; or to stick to the uniqueness of the Jewish legacy, to its fidelity to the encounter with radical Otherness, in contrast to Christianity. Here, I would like to make myself absolutely clear: I do not think that the present vague spiritualism, the focus on the openness to Otherness and its unconditional Call, this mode in which Judaism has become almost the hegemonic ethico-spiritual attitude of today's intellectuals, is in itself the "natural" form of what one can designate, in traditional terms, as Jewish spirituality. I am almost tempted to claim that we are dealing here with something that is homologous to the Gnostic heresy of Christianity, and that the ultimate victim of this Pyrrhic "victory" of Judaism will be the most precious elements of Jewish spirituality itself, with their focus on a unique collective experience. Who today remembers the kibbutz, the greatest proof that Jews are not "by nature" financial middlemen?

In addition to these two options, the only Christian references permitted are the Gnostic or mystical traditions that had to be excluded and repressed in order for the hegemonic figure of Christianity to install itself. Christ himself is OK if we try to isolate the "original" Christ, "the Rabbi Jesus" not yet inscribed into the Christian tradition proper—Agnes Heller speaks ironically of the "resurrection of the Jewish Jesus": our task today is to resurrect the true Jesus from the mystifying Christian tradition of Jesus (as) Christ.[8] All this makes a positive reference to Saint Paul a very delicate issue: is he not the very symbol of the establishment of Christian orthodoxy? In the last decade, nonetheless, one small opening has appeared, a kind of exchange offered between the lines: one is allowed to praise Paul, if one reinscribes him back into the Jewish legacy—Paul as a radical Jew, an author of Jewish political theology. . . .

While I agree with this approach, I want to emphasize how, if it is taken seriously, its consequences are much more catastrophic than they may appear. When one reads Saint Paul's epistles, one cannot fail to notice how thoroughly and terribly indifferent he is toward Jesus as a living person (the Jesus who is not yet Christ, the pre-Easter Jesus, the Jesus of the Gospels)—Paul more or less totally ignores Jesus' particular acts, teachings, parables, all that Hegel later referred to as the mythical element of the fairytale narrative, of the mere prenotional representation [Vorstellung]; never in his writings does he engage in hermeneutics, in probing into the "deeper meaning" of this or that parable or act of Jesus. What matters to him is not Jesus as a historical figure, only the fact that he died on the Cross and rose from the dead—after confirming Jesus' death and resurrection, Paul goes on to his true Leninist business, that of organizing the new party called the Christian community. Paul as a Leninist: was not Paul, like Lenin, the great "institutionalizer," and, as such, reviled by the partisans of "original" Marxism-Christianity? Does not the Pauline temporality "already, but not yet" also designate Lenin's situation in between the two revolutions, between February and October 1917? Revolution is already behind us, the old regime is out, freedom is here—but the hard work still lies ahead.

In 1956, Lacan proposed a short and clear definition of the Holy Spirit: "The Holy Spirit is the entry of the signifier into the world. This is certainly what Freud brought us under the title of death drive."[9] What Lacan means, at this moment of his thought, is that the Holy Spirit stands for the symbolic order as that which cancels (or, rather, suspends) the entire domain of "life"—lived experience, the libidinal flux, the wealth of emotions, or, to put it in Kant's terms, the "pathological." When we locate ourselves within the Holy Spirit, we are transubstantiated, we enter another life beyond the biological one. And is not this Pauline notion of life grounded in Paul's other distinctive feature? What enabled him to formulate the basic tenets of Christianity, to elevate Christianity from a Jewish sect into a universal religion (religion of universality), was the very fact that he was not part of Christ's "inner circle." One can imagine the inner circle of apostles reminiscing during their dinner conversations: "Do you remember how, at the Last Supper, Jesus asked me to pass the salt?" None of this applies to Paul: he is outside and, as such, symbolically substituting for (taking the place of) Judas himself among the apostles. In a way, Paul also "betrayed" Christ by not caring about his idiosyncrasies, by ruthlessly reducing him to the fundamentals, with no patience for his wisdom, miracles, and similar paraphernalia.

So yes, one should read Paul from within the Jewish tradition— since precisely such a reading brings home the true radicality of his break, the way he undermined the Jewish tradition from within. To use a well-known Kierkegaardian opposition: reading Saint Paul from within the Jewish tradition, as the one located in it, allows us to grasp "Christianity-in-becoming": not yet the established positive dogma, but the violent gesture of positing it, the "vanishing mediator" between Judaism and Christianity, something akin to Benjaminian law-constituting violence. In other words, what is effectively "repressed" with the established Christian doxa is not so much its Jewish roots, its indebtedness to Judaism, but, rather, the break itself, the true location of Christianity's rupture with Judaism. Paul did not simply pass from the Jewish position to another position; he did something with, within, and to the Jewish position itself—what?

CHAPTER 1

WHEN EAST MEETS WEST

A proper starting point would have been to ask the Schellingian question: what does the becoming-man of God in the figure of Christ, His descent from eternity to the temporal realm of our reality, mean for God Himself? What if that which appears to us, finite mortals, as God's descent toward us, is, from the standpoint of God Himself, an ascent? What if, as Schelling implied, eternity is less than temporality? What if eternity is a sterile, impotent, lifeless domain of pure potentialities, which, in order fully to actualize itself, has to pass through temporal existence? What if God's descent to man, far from being an act of grace toward humanity, is the only way for God to gain full actuality, and to liberate Himself from the suffocating constraints of Eternity? What if God actualizes Himself only through human recognition?[1]

We have to get rid of the old Platonic *topos* of love as Eros that gradually elevates itself from love for a particular individual, through love for the beauty of a human body in general and the love of the beautiful form as such, to love for the supreme Good beyond all forms: true love is precisely the opposite move of *forsaking the promise of Eternity itself for an imperfect individual*. (This lure of eternity can take many forms, from postmortal Fame to fulfilling one's social role.) What if the gesture of choosing temporal existence, of giving up eternal existence for the sake of love—from Christ to Siegmund in Act II of Wagner's *Die Walküre*, who prefers to remain a common mortal if his beloved Sieglinde cannot follow him to Valhalla, the eternal dwelling-place of dead heroes—is the highest ethical act of them all? The shattered Brünnhilde comments on this refusal: "So little do you value everlasting bliss? Is she everything to you, this poor woman who, tired and sorrowful, lies limp in your lap? Do you think nothing less glorious?" Ernst Bloch was right to observe that what is lacking in German history are more gestures like Siegmund's.

We usually claim that time is the ultimate prison ("no one can jump outside of his/her time"), and that the whole of philosophy and religion circulates around one aim: to break out of this prison-house of time into eternity. What, however, if, as Schelling implies, eternity is the ultimate prison, a suffocating closure, and it is only the fall into time that introduces Opening into human experience? Is Time not the name for the ontological opening? The Event of "incarnation" is thus not so much the time when ordinary temporal reality touches Eternity, but, rather, the time when Eternity reaches into time. This same point has been made very clearly by intelligent conservatives like G. K. Chesterton (like Hitchcock, an English Catholic), who wrote, apropos of the fashionable claim about the "alleged spiritual identity of Buddhism and Christianity":

> Love desires personality; therefore love desires division. It is the instinct of Christianity to be glad that God has broken the universe into little pieces. . . . This is the intellectual abyss between Buddhism and Christianity; what for the Buddhist or Theosophist personality is the fall of man, for the Christian is the purpose of God, the whole point of his cosmic idea. The world-soul of the Theosophists asks man to love it only in order that man may throw himself into it. But the divine centre of Christianity actually threw man out of it in order that he might love it. . . . All modern philosophies are chains which connect and fetter; Christianity is a sword which separates and sets free. No other philosophy makes God actually rejoice in the separation of the universe into living souls.[2]

And Chesterton is fully aware that it is not enough for God to separate man from Himself so that mankind will love Him—this separation has to be reflected back into God Himself, so that God is abandoned by himself:

> When the world shook and the sun was wiped out of heaven, it was not at the crucifixion, but at the cry from the cross: the cry which confessed that God was forsaken of God. And now let the revolutionists choose a creed from all the creeds and a god from all the gods of the world, carefully weighing all the gods of inevitable recurrence and of unalterable power. They will not find another god who has himself been in revolt. Nay (the matter grows too difficult for human speech), but let the atheists themselves choose a god. They will find only one divinity who ever uttered their isolation; only one religion in which God seemed for an instant to be an atheist.[3]

Because of this overlapping between man's isolation from God and God's isolation from himself, Christianity is

> terribly revolutionary. That a good man may have his back to the wall is no more than we knew already; but that God could have His back to the wall is a boast for all insurgents for ever. Christianity is the only religion on earth that has felt that omnipotence made God incomplete. Christianity alone has felt that God, to be wholly God, must have been a rebel as well as a king.[4]

Chesterton is fully aware that we are thereby approaching "a matter more dark and awful than it is easy to discuss . . . a matter which the greatest saints and thinkers have justly feared to approach. But in that terrific tale of the Passion there is a distinct emotional suggestion that the author of all things (in some unthinkable way) went not only through agony, but through doubt."[5] In the standard form of atheism, God dies for men who stop believing in Him; in Christianity, God dies for Himself. In his "Father, why hast thou forsaken me?," Christ himself commits what is, for a Christian, the ultimate sin: he wavers in his Faith.

This "matter more dark and awful than it is easy to discuss" concerns what cannot but appear as the hidden perverse core of Christianity: if it is prohibited to eat from the Tree of Knowledge in Paradise, why did God put it there in the first place? Is it not that this was a part of His perverse strategy first to seduce Adam and Eve into the Fall, in order then to save them? That is to say: should one not apply Paul's insight into how the prohibitive law creates sin to this very first prohibition also? A similar obscure ambiguity surrounds the role of Judas in Christ's death: since his betrayal was necessary to his mission (to redeem humanity through his death on the Cross), did Christ not need it? Are his ominous words during the Last Supper not a secret injunction to Judas to betray him? "Judas, who betrayed him, said, 'Surely not I, Rabbi?' He replied, 'You have said so'" (Matthew 26:25). The rhetorical figure of Christ's reply is, of course, that of disavowed injunction: Judas is interpellated as the one who will hand Christ over to the authorities—not directly ("You are the one who will betray me!"), but so that the responsibility is put onto the other. Is Judas not therefore the ultimate hero of the New Testament, the one who was ready to lose his soul and accept eternal damnation so that the divine plan could be accomplished?[6]

In all other religions, God demands that His followers remain faithful to Him—only Christ asked his followers to betray him in order to fulfill his mission. Here I am tempted to claim that the entire fate of Christianity, its innermost kernel, hinges on the possibility of interpreting this act in a nonperverse way. That is to say: the obvious reading that imposes itself is a perverse one—even as he lamented the forthcoming betrayal, Christ was, between the lines, giving the injunction to Judas to betray him, demanding of him the highest sacrifice—the sacrifice not only of his life, but also of his "second life," of his posthumous reputation. The problem, the dark ethical knot in this affair, is thus not Judas, but Christ himself: in order to fulfill his mission, was he obliged to have recourse to such obscure, arch-Stalinist manipulation? Or is it possible to read the relationship between Judas and Christ in a different way, outside this perverse economy?

In January 2002, a weird Freudian slip occurred in Lauderhill, Florida: a plaque, prepared to honor the actor James Earl Jones at a celebration of Martin Luther King, instead bore this inscription: "Thank you James Earl Ray for keeping the dream alive"—a reference to King's famous "I have a dream" speech. It is common knowledge that Ray was the man convicted of assassinating King in 1968. Of course, this was in all probability a rather elementary racist slip—however, there is a strange truth in it: Ray, in effect, contributed to keeping the King dream alive, on two different levels. First, part of the heroic larger-than-life image of Martin Luther King is his violent death: without this death, he would definitely not have become the symbol that he is now, with streets named after him and his birthday a national holiday. Even more concretely, one can argue that King died at exactly the right moment: in the weeks before his death, he moved toward a more radical anticapitalism, supporting strikes by black and white workers—had he moved further in this direction, he would definitely have become unacceptable as a member of the pantheon of American heroes.

Thus King's death follows the logic elaborated by Hegel apropos of Julius Caesar: Caesar-the-individual had to die in order for the universal notion to emerge. Nietzsche's notion of a "noble betrayal" modeled on Brutus remains the betrayal of the individual for the sake of the higher Idea (Caesar has to go in order to save the Republic), and, as such, it can be taken into account by the historical "cunning of reason" (the Caesar-name returned with a vengeance as a universal title, "caesar"). It seems that the same holds for Christ: betrayal was part of the plan, Christ ordered Judas to betray him in order to fulfill the divine plan; that is, Judas' act of betrayal was the highest sacrifice, the ultimate fidelity. However, the contrast between the death of Christ and that of Caesar is crucial: Caesar was first a name, and he had to die as a name (the contingent singular individual) in order to emerge as a universal concept-title (caesar); Christ was first, before his death, a universal concept ("Jesus the Christ-Messiah"), and, through his death, he emerged as the unique singular, "Jesus Christ." Here universality is *aufgehoben* in singularity, not the other way round.

So what about a more Kierkegaardian betrayal—not of the individual for the sake of the universality, but of the universality itself for the sake of the singular point of exception (the "religious suspension of the ethical")? Furthermore, what about "pure" betrayal, betrayal out of love, betrayal as the ultimate proof of love? And what about self-betrayal: since I am what I am through my others, the betrayal of the beloved other is the betrayal of myself. Is not such a betrayal part of every difficult ethical act of decision? One has to betray one's innermost core; as Freud did in *Moses and Monotheism*, where he deprives the Jews of their founding figure.

Judas is the "vanishing mediator" between the original circle of the Twelve Apostles and Saint Paul, founder of the universal Church: Paul literally replaces Judas, taking his absent place among the Twelve in a kind of metaphoric substitution. And it is crucial to bear in mind the necessity of this substitution: only through Judas' "betrayal" and Christ's death could the universal Church establish itself—that is to say, the path to universality goes through the murder of the particularity. Or, to put it in a slightly different way: in order for Paul to ground Christianity from the outside, as the one who was *not* a member of Christ's inner circle, this circle had to be broken from within by means of an act of terrifying betrayal. And this does not apply only to Christ—a hero as such *has* to be betrayed to attain universal status: as Lacan put it in *Seminar VII*, the hero is the one who can be betrayed without any damage being done to him.

John Le Carré's formula from *The Perfect Spy*, "love is whatever you can still betray," is much more apposite than it may appear: who among us has not experienced, when fascinated by a beloved person who puts all his trust in us, who relies on us totally and helplessly, a strange, properly perverse urge to betray this trust, to hurt him badly, to shatter his entire existence? This "betrayal as the ultimate form of fidelity" cannot be explained away by a reference to the split between the empirical person and what this person stands for, so that we betray (let fall) the person out of our very fidelity to what he or she stands for. (A further version of this split is betrayal at the precise moment when one's impotence would have been publicly displayed: in this way, the illusion is sustained that, had one survived, things would have turned out all right. The only true fidelity to Alexander the Great, for example, would have been to kill him when he actually died—had he lived a long life, he would have been reduced to an impotent observer of the decline of his empire.) There is a higher Kierkegaardian necessity at work here: to betray (ethical) universality itself. Beyond "aesthetic" betrayal (betrayal of the universal for the sake of "pathological" interests—profit, pleasure, pride, desire to hurt and humiliate: pure vileness) and "ethical" betrayal (the betrayal of the person for the sake of universality—like Aristotle's famous "I am a friend of Plato, but I am an even greater friend of truth"), there is "religious" betrayal, betrayal out of love—I respect you for your universal features, but I love you for an X beyond these features, and the only way to discern this X is betrayal. I betray you, and then, when you are down, destroyed by my betrayal, we exchange glances—if you understand my act of betrayal, and only if you do, you are a true hero. Every true leader, religious, political, or intellectual, has to provoke such a betrayal among the closest of his disciples. Is this not how one should read the address of Lacan's late public proclamations: "A ceux qui m'aiment . . . ," to those who love me—that is to say, who love me enough to betray me. The temporary betrayal is the only way to eternity—or, as Kierkegaard put it apropos of Abraham, when he is ordered to slaughter Isaac, his predicament "is an ordeal such that, please note, the ethical is the temptation."[7]

In what precise sense, then, was Christ not playing with Judas a perverse game of manipulating his closest disciple into the betrayal that was necessary for the accomplishment of his mission? Perhaps a detour through the best (or worst) of Hollywood melodrama can be of some help here. The basic lesson of King Vidor's Rhapsody is that the man, in order to gain the beloved woman's love, has to prove that he is able to survive without her, that he puts his mission or profession before her. There are two immediate choices: (1) my professional career is what matters most to me; the woman in my life is just an amusement, a distracting affair; (2) she is everything to me; I am ready to humiliate myself, to sacrifice all my public and professional dignity for her. Both are false; they lead to the man being rejected by the woman. The message of true love is thus: even if you are everything to me, I can survive without you, I am ready to forsake you for my mission or profession. The proper way for the woman to test the man's love is thus to "betray" him at a crucial moment in his career (the first public concert, as in Rhapsody; in the key exam; the business negotiation which will decide his future)—only if he can survive the ordeal, and accomplish his task successfully, although he is deeply traumatized by her desertion, will he deserve her, and she will return to him. The underlying paradox is that love, precisely as the Absolute, should not be posited as a direct goal—it should retain the status of a byproduct, of something we get as an undeserved grace. Perhaps there is no greater love than that of a revolutionary couple, where each of the two lovers is ready to abandon the other at any moment if revolution demands it. It is along these lines that we should look for the nonperverse reading of Christ's sacrifice, of his message to Judas: "Prove to me that I am everything to you, so *betray me* for the sake of the revolutionary mission of both of us!"

Chesterton also correctly linked this dark core of Christianity to the opposition between Inside (the immersion in inner Truth) and Outside (the traumatic encounter with Truth): "The Buddhist is looking with a peculiar intentness inwards. The Christian is staring with a frantic intentness outwards."[8] Here he is referring to the well-known difference between the way the Buddha is represented in paintings and statues, with his benevolently peaceful gaze, and the way Christian saints are usually represented, with an intense, almost paranoiac, ecstatically transfixed gaze. This "Buddha's gaze" is often evoked as a possible antidote to the Western aggressive-paranoiac gaze, a gaze which aims at total control, and is always alert, on the lookout for some lurking threat: in the Buddha, we find a benevolently withdrawn gaze which simply lets things be, abandoning the urge to control them. However, although the message of Buddhism is one of inner peace, an odd detail in the act of consecration of the Buddha's statues throws a strange light on this peace. This act of consecration consists of painting the eyes of the Buddha. While painting these eyes,

> the artist cannot look the statue in the face, but works with his back to it, painting sideways or over his shoulder using a mirror, which catches the gaze of the image he is bringing to life. Once he has finished his work, he now has a dangerous gaze himself, and is led away blindfolded. The blindfold is removed only after his eyes can fall on something that he then symbolically destroys. As Gombrich dryly points out, "The spirit of this ceremony cannot be reconciled with Buddhist doctrine, so no one tries to do so." But isn't the key precisely this bizarre heterogeneity? The fact that for the temperate and pacifying reality of the Buddhist universe to function, the horrifying, malevolent gaze has to be symbolically excluded. The evil eye has to be tamed.[9]

Is not this ritual an "empirical" proof that the Buddhist experience of the peace of nirvana is not the ultimate fact, that *something has to be* excluded in order for us to attain this peace, namely, the Other's gaze?[10] Another indication that the "Lacanian" evil gaze posing a threat to the subject is not just an ideological hypostasis of the Western attitude of control and domination, but something that is operative also in Eastern cultures. This excluded dimension is ultimately that of the *act*. What, then, is an act, grounded in the abyss of a free decision? Recall C. S. Lewis's description of his religious choice from *Surprised by Joy*—what makes it so irresistibly delicious is the author's matter-of-fact "English" skeptical style, far removed from the usual pathetic narratives of mystical rapture. C. S. Lewis's description of the act thus deftly avoids any ecstatic pathos in the usual style of Saint Teresa, any multiple-orgasmic penetrations by angels or God: it is not that, in the divine mystical experience, we step out (in ex-stasis) of our normal experience of reality: it is this "normal" experience which is "ex-static" (Heidegger), in which we are thrown outside into entities, and the mystical experience signals the withdrawal from this ecstasy. Thus Lewis refers to the experience as the "odd thing"; he mentions its ordinary location: "I was going up Headington Hill on the top of a bus." He qualifies it: "in a sense," "what now appears," "or, if you like," "you could argue that . . . but I am more inclined to think . . . ," "perhaps," "I rather disliked the feeling":

> The odd thing was that before God closed in on me, I was in fact offered what now appears a moment of wholly free choice. In a sense. I was going up Headington Hill on the top of a bus. Without words and (I think) almost without images, a fact about myself was somehow presented to me. I became aware that I was holding something at bay, or shutting something out. Or, if you like, that I was wearing some stiff clothing, like corsets, or even a suit of armour, as if I were a lobster. I felt myself being, there and then, given a free choice. I could open the door or keep it shut; I could unbuckle the armour or keep it on. Neither choice was presented as a duty; no threat or promise was attached to either, though I knew that to open the door or to take off the corset meant the incalculable. The choice appeared to be momentous but it was also strangely unemotional. I was moved by no desires or fears. In a sense I was not moved by anything. I chose to open, to unbuckle, to loosen the rein. I say, "I chose,"

yet it did not really seem possible to do the opposite. On the other hand, I was aware of no motives. You could argue that I was not a free agent, but I am more inclined to think this came nearer to being a perfectly free act than most that I have ever done. Necessity may not be the opposite of freedom, and perhaps a man is most free when, instead of producing motives, he could only say, "I am what I do." Then came the repercussion on the imaginative level. I felt as if I were a man of snow at long last beginning to melt. The melting was starting in my back—drip-drip and presently trickle-trickle. I rather disliked the feeling.[11]

In a way, everything is here: the decision is purely formal, ultimately a decision to decide, without a clear awareness of what the subject is deciding about; it is a nonpsychological act, unemotional, with no motives, desires, or fears; it is incalculable, not the outcome of strategic argumentation; it is a totally free act, although he couldn't do otherwise. It is only *afterward* that this pure act is "subjectivized," translated into a (rather unpleasant) psychological experience. There is only one aspect which is potentially problematic in Lewis's formulation: the act as conceived by Lacan has nothing to do with the mystical suspension of ties which bind us to ordinary reality, with attaining the bliss of radical indifference in which life or death and other worldly distinctions no longer matter, in which subject and object, thought and act, fully coincide. To put it in mystical terms, the Lacanian act is, rather, the exact opposite of this "return to innocence": Original Sin itself, the abyssal disturbance of primeval Peace, the primordial "pathological" Choice of unconditional attachment to some specific object (like falling in love with a specific person who, thereafter, matters to us more than anything else).

In Buddhist terms, the Lacanian act is the exact structural obverse of Enlightenment, of attaining nirvana: the very gesture by means of which the Void is disturbed, and Difference (and, with it, false appearance and suffering) emerges in the world. The act is thus close to the gesture of Bodhisattva who, having reached nirvana, out of compassion—that is, for the sake of the common Good—goes back to phenomenal reality in order to help all other living beings to achieve nirvana. The distance from psychoanalysis resides in the fact that, from the latter's standpoint, Bodhisattva's sacrificial gesture is false: in order to arrive at the act proper, one should erase any reference to the Good, and do the act just for the sake of it. (This reference to Bodhisattva also enables us to answer the "big question": if, now, we have to strive to break out of the vicious cycle of craving into the blissful peace of nirvana, how did nirvana "regress" into getting caught in the wheel of craving in the first place? The only consistent answer is: Bodhisattva *repeats* this primordial "evil" gesture. The fall into Evil was accomplished by the "original Bodhisattva"—in short, the ultimate source of Evil is compassion itself.)

Bodhisattva's compassion is strictly correlative to the notion that the "pleasure principle" regulates our activity when we are caught in the wheel of Illusion—that is to say, that we all strive toward the Good, and the ultimate problem is epistemological (we misperceive the true nature of the Good)—to quote the Dalai Lama himself, the beginning of wisdom is "to realize that all living beings are equal in not wanting unhappiness and suffering and equal in the right to rid themselves of suffering."[12] The Freudian drive, however, designates precisely the paradox of "wanting unhappiness," of finding excessive pleasure in suffering itself—the title of a Paul Watzlawik book (*The Pursuit of Unhappiness*) expresses this fundamental self-blockade of human behavior perfectly. The Buddhist ethical horizon is therefore still that of the Good—that is to say, Buddhism is a kind of negative of the ethics of the Good: aware that every positive Good is a lure, it fully assumes the Void as the only true Good. What it cannot do is to pass "beyond nothing," into what Hegel called "tarrying with the negative": to return to a phenomenal reality which is "beyond nothing," to a Something which gives body to the Nothing. The Buddhist endeavor to get rid of the illusion (of craving, of phenomenal reality) is, in effect, the endeavor to get rid of the Real of/in this illusion, the kernel of the Real that accounts for our "stubborn attachment" to the illusion.

The political implications of this stance are crucial. Recall the widespread notion that aggressive Islamic (or Jewish) monotheism is at the root of our predicament—is the relationship between polytheism and monotheism, however, really that of the multitude and its oppressive "totalization" by the ("phallic") exclusionary One? What if, on the contrary, it is polytheism which presupposes the commonly shared (back)ground of the multitude of gods, while it is only monotheism which renders thematic the gap as such, the gap in the Absolute itself, the gap which not only separates (the one) God from Himself, but is this God? This difference is "pure" difference: not the difference between positive entities, but difference "as such." Thus monotheism is the only logical theology of the Two: in contrast to the multitude which can display itself only against the background of the One, its neutral ground, like the multitude of figures against the same background (which is why Spinoza, the philosopher of the multitude, is, quite logically, also the ultimate monist, the philosopher of the One), radical difference is the difference of the One with regard to itself, the noncoincidence of the One with itself, with its own place. This is why Christianity, precisely because of the Trinity, is the only true monotheism: the lesson of the Trinity is that God fully coincides with the gap between God and man, that God is this gap—this is Christ, not the God of beyond separated from man by a gap, but the gap as such, the gap which simultaneously separates God from God and man from man. This fact also allows us to pinpoint what is false about Levinasian-Derridean Otherness: it is the very opposite of this gap in the One, of the inherent redoubling of the One—the assertion of Otherness leads to the boring, monotonous sameness of Otherness itself.

In an old Slovene joke, a young schoolboy has to write a short composition entitled "There is only one mother!," in which he is expected to illustrate, apropos of a specific experience, the love which links him to his mother; this is what he writes: "One day I came home from school earlier than usual, because the teacher was ill; I looked for my mother, and found her naked in bed with a man who was not my father. My mother shouted at me angrily: 'What are you staring at like an idiot? Why don't you run to the fridge and get us two cold beers!' I ran to the kitchen, opened the fridge, looked in-

side, and shouted back to the bedroom: 'There's only one, Mother!'"
Is this not a supreme case of interpretation which simply adds one
diacritical sign that changes everything, as in the well-known parody
of the first words of *Moby-Dick*: "Call me, Ishmael!" We can discern
the same operation in Heidegger (the way he reads "Nothing is
without reason [*nihil est sine ratione*]," by shifting the accent to "Nothing[ness] IS without reason"), or in the superego displacement of
the prohibitive injunction of the symbolic law (from "Don't kill!" to
"Don't!" . . . "Kill!"). Here, however, we should risk a more detailed
interpretation. The joke stages a Hamlet-like confrontation of the son
with the enigma of the mother's excessive desire; in order to escape
this deadlock, the mother, as it were, takes refuge in [the desire for]
an external partial object, the beer, destined to divert the son's attention from the obscene Thing of her being caught naked in bed with
a man—the message of this demand is: "You see, even if I am in bed
with a man, my desire is for something else that you can bring me,
I am not excluding you by getting completely caught in the circle of
passion with this man!" The two beers (also) stand for the elementary signifying dyad, like Lacan's famous two restroom doors observed by two children from the train window in his "Instance of the
letter in the unconscious"; from this perspective, the child's repartee
is to be read as teaching the mother the elementary Lacanian lesson:
"Sorry, Mother, but there is only one signifier, for the man only, there
is no binary signifier (for the woman), this signifier is ur-*verdrängt*,
primordially repressed!" In short: you are caught naked, you are not
covered by the signifier. . . . And what if this is the fundamental message of monotheism—not the reduction of the Other to the One,
but, on the contrary, the acceptance of the fact that the binary signifier is always-already missing? This imbalance between the One and
its "primordially repressed" counterpart is the radical difference, in
contrast to the big cosmological couples (*yin* and *yang*, etc.) which
can emerge only within the horizon of the undifferentiated One
(*tao*, etc.). And are not even attempts to introduce a balanced duality
into the minor spheres of consumption, like the couple of small blue
and red bags of artificial sweetener available in cafés everywhere,

yet further desperate attempts to provide a symmetrical signifying couple for the sexual difference (blue "masculine" bags versus red "feminine" bags)? The point is not that sexual difference is the ultimate signified of all such couples, but that the proliferation of such couples, rather, displays an attempt to supplement the lack of the founding binary signifying couple that would stand directly for sexual difference.

Furthermore, is not so-called exclusionary monotheist violence secretly polytheist? Does not the fanatical hatred of believers in a different god bear witness to the fact that the monotheist secretly thinks that he is not simply fighting false believers, but that his struggle is a struggle between different gods, the struggle of his god against "false gods" who exist as gods? Such a monotheism is effectively exclusive: it has to exclude other gods. For that reason, true monotheists are tolerant: for them, others are not objects of hatred, but simply people who, although they are not enlightened by the true belief, should nonetheless be respected, since they are not inherently evil.

The target on which we should focus, therefore, is the very ideology which is then proposed as a potential solution—for example, Oriental spirituality (Buddhism), with its more "gentle," balanced, holistic, ecological approach (all the stories about how Tibetan Buddhists, for instance, when they dig the foundations of a house, are careful not to kill any worms). It is not only that Western Buddhism, this pop-cultural phenomenon preaching inner distance and indifference toward the frantic pace of market competition, is arguably the most efficient way for us fully to participate in capitalist dynamics while retaining the appearance of mental sanity—in short, the paradigmatic ideology of late capitalism. One should add that it is no longer possible to oppose this Western Buddhism to its "authentic" Oriental version; the case of Japan provides the conclusive evidence. Not only do we have today, among top Japanese managers, a widespread "corporate Zen" phenomenon; for the whole of the last 150 years, Japan's rapid industrialization and militarization, with its ethics of discipline and sacrifice, have been sustained by the large majority of Zen thinkers—who, today, knows that D. T. Suzuki himself, the high guru of Zen in the America of the 1960s, supported in his youth, in 1930s Japan, the spirit of utter discipline and militaristic expansion?[13] There is no contradiction here, no manipulative perversion of the authentic compassionate insight: the attitude of total immersion in the selfless "now" of instant Enlightenment, in which all reflexive distance is lost, and "I am what I do," as C. S. Lewis put it—in short: in which absolute discipline coincides with total spontaneity—perfectly legitimizes subordination to the militaristic social machine. Here we can see how wrong Aldous Huxley was when, in *The Grey Eminence*, he blamed the Christian focus on Christ's suffering for its destructive social misuse (the Crusades, etc.), and opposed it to benevolent Buddhist disengagement.

The crucial feature here is how militaristic Zen justifies killing in two ultimately inconsistent ways. First, there is the standard teleological narrative that is also acceptable to Western religions: "Even though the Buddha forbade the taking of life, he also taught that until all sentient beings are united together through the exercise of infinite compassion, there will never be peace. Therefore, as a means of bringing into harmony those things which are incompatible, killing and war are necessary."[14] It is thus the very force of compassion which wields the sword: a true warrior kills out of love, like parents who hit their children out of love, to educate them and make them happy in the long term. This brings us to the notion of a "compassionate war" which gives life to both oneself and one's enemy—in it, the sword that kills is the sword that gives life. (This is how the Japanese Army perceived and justified its ruthless plundering of Korea and China in the 1930s.)

Of course, all things are ultimately nothing, a substanceless Void; however, one should not confuse this transcendent world of formlessness (*mukei*) with the temporal world of form (*yukei*), thus failing to recognize the underlying unity of the two. That was socialism's mistake: socialism wanted to realize the underlying unity directly in temporal reality ("evil equality"), thus causing social destruction. This solution may sound similar to Hegel's critique of the revolutionary Terror in his *Phenomenology*—and even the formula proposed by some Zen Buddhists ("the identity of differentiation and equality"[15]) cannot fail to remind us of Hegel's famous speculative assertion of the "identity of identity and difference." Here, however, the difference is clear: Hegel has nothing to do with such a pseudo-Hegelian vision (espoused by some conservative Hegelians like Bradley and McTaggart) of society as an organic harmonious Whole, within which each member asserts his or her "equality" with others through performing his or her particular duty, occupying his or her particular place, and thus contributing to the harmony of the Whole. For Hegel, on the contrary, the "transcendent world of formlessness" (in short: the Absolute) is at war *with itself*, which means that the (self-)destructive formlessness (the absolute, self-relating, negativity) must appear as such in the realm of finite reality—the point of Hegel's notion of the revolutionary Terror is precisely that it is a *necessary* moment in the deployment of freedom.

However, back to Zen: this "teleological" justification (war is a necessary evil performed to bring about the greater good: "battle is necessarily fought in anticipation of peace"[16]) is accompanied by a more radical line of reasoning in which, much more directly, "Zen and the sword are one and the same."[17] This reasoning is based on the opposition between the reflexive attitude of our ordinary daily lives (in which we cling to life and fear death, strive for egotistic pleasure and profit, hesitate and think, instead of directly acting) and the enlightened stance in which the difference between life and death no longer matters, in which we regain the original selfless unity, and *are* directly our act. In a unique short circuit, militaristic Zen masters interpret the basic Zen message (liberation lies in losing one's Self, in immediately uniting with the primordial Void) as identical to utter military fidelity, to following orders immediately, and performing one's duty without consideration for the Self and its interests. The standard antimilitaristic cliché about soldiers being drilled to attain a state of mindless subordination, and carry out orders like blind puppets, is here asserted to be identical to Zen

Enlightenment. This is how Ishihara Shummyo made this point in almost Althusserian terms of direct, nonreflected interpellation:

> Zen is very particular about the need not to stop one's mind. As soon as flint stone is struck, a spark bursts forth. There is not even the most momentary lapse of time between these two events. If ordered to face right, one simply faces right as quickly as a flash of lightning. . . . If one's name were called, for example, "Uemon," one should simply answer "Yes," and not stop to consider the reason why one's name was called. . . . I believe that if one is called upon to die, one should not be the least bit agitated.[18]

Insofar as subjectivity as such is hysterical, insofar as it emerges through the questioning of the interpellating call of the Other, we have here the perfect description of a perverse desubjectivization: the subject avoids its constitutive splitting by positing itself directly as the instrument of the Other's Will.[19] And what is crucial in this radical version is that it explicitly rejects all the religious rubble usually associated with popular Buddhism, and advocates a return to the original down-to-earth atheist version of the Buddha himself: as Furakawa Taigo emphasizes,[20] there is no salvation after death, no afterlife, no spirits or divinities to assist us, no reincarnation, just this life which is directly identical with death. Within this attitude, the warrior no longer acts as a person, he is thoroughly desubjectivized—or, as D. T. Suzuki himself put it: "it is really not he but the sword itself that does the killing. He had no desire to do harm to anybody, but the enemy appears and makes himself a victim. It is as though the sword performs automatically its function of justice, which is the function of mercy."[21] Does not this description of killing provide the ultimate illustration of the phenomenological attitude which, instead of intervening in reality, just lets things appear as they are? It is the sword itself which does the killing, it is the enemy himself who just appears, and makes himself a victim—I am not responsible, I am reduced to the passive observer of my own acts. Attitudes like these indicate how the famous "Buddha's gaze" could well function as the support of the most ruthless killing machine—

so, perhaps, the fact that Ben Kingsley's two big movie roles are Gandhi and the excessively aggressive English gangster in *Sexy Beast* bears witness to a deeper affinity: what if the second character is the full actualization of the hidden potential of the first? The paradoxical Pascalian conclusion of this radically atheist version of Zen is that, since there is no inner substance to religion, the essence of faith is proper decorum, obedience to ritual as such.[22] What, then, is the difference between this "warrior Zen" legitimization of violence and the long Western tradition, from Christ to Che Guevara, which also extols violence as a "work of love," as in the famous lines from Che Guevara's diary?

> Let me say, with the risk of appearing ridiculous, that the true revolutionary is guided by strong feelings of love. It is impossible to think of an authentic revolutionary without this quality. This is perhaps one of the greatest dramas of a leader; he must combine an impassioned spirit with a cold mind and make painful decisions without flinching one muscle. Our vanguard revolutionaries . . . cannot descend, with small doses of daily affection, to the places where ordinary men put their love into practice.[23]

Although we should be aware of the dangers of the "Christification of Che," turning him into an icon of radical-chic consumer culture, a martyr ready to die for his love for humanity,[24] we should perhaps take the risk of accepting this move, radicalizing it into a "Cheization" of Christ himself—the Christ whose "scandalous" words from Saint Luke's gospel ("if anyone comes to me and does not hate his father and his mother, his wife and children, his brothers and sisters—yes, even his own life—he cannot be my disciple" (14:26)) point in exactly the same direction as Che's famous quote: "You may have to be tough, but do not lose your tenderness. You may have to cut the flowers, but it will not stop the Spring."[25] So, again, if Lenin's acts of revolutionary violence were "works of love" in the strictest Kierkegaardian sense of the term, in what does the difference from "warrior Zen" consist? There is only one logical answer: it is not that, in contrast to Japanese military aggression, revolutionary violence "really" aims at establishing a nonviolent harmony; on the contrary, authentic revolutionary liberation is much more directly identified with violence—it is violence as such (the violent gesture of discarding, of establishing a difference, of drawing a line of separation) which liberates. Freedom is not a blissfully neutral state of harmony and balance, but the very violent act which disturbs this balance.[26]

Nonetheless, it is all too simple either to say that this militaristic version of Zen is a perversion of the true Zen message, or to see in it the ominous "truth" of Zen: the truth is much more unbearable—what if, in its very kernel, Zen is ambivalent, or, rather, utterly indifferent to this alternative? What if—a horrible thought—the Zen meditation technique is ultimately just that: a spiritual *technique*, an ethically neutral instrument which can be put to different sociopolitical uses, from the most peaceful to the most destructive? (In this sense, Suzuki was right to emphasize that Zen Buddhism can be combined with any philosophy or politics, from anarchism to Fascism.[27]) So the answer to the tortuous question "Which aspects of the Buddhist tradition lend themselves to such a monstrous distortion?" is: exactly the same ones that emphasize passionate compassion and inner peace. No wonder, then, that when Ichikawa Hakugen, the Japanese Buddhist who elaborated the most radical self-criticism after Japan's shattering defeat in 1945, listed the twelve characteristics of the Buddhist tradition which prepared the ground for the legitimization of aggressive militarism, he had to include practically all the basic tenets of Buddhism itself: the Buddhist doctrine of dependent co-arising or causality, which regards all phenomena as being in a constant state of flux, and the related doctrine of no-self; the lack of firm dogma and a personal God; the emphasis on inner peace rather than justice. . . .[28] This is how, in the *Bhagavad-Gita*, along similar lines, the God Krishna answers Arjuna, the warrior-king who hesitates to enter a battle, horrified at the suffering his attack will cause—an answer that is worth quoting in full:

> He who thinks it to be the killer and he who thinks it to be killed, both know nothing. The self kills not, and the self is not killed. It is

not born, nor does it ever die, nor, having existed, does it exist no more. Unborn, everlasting, unchangeable, and primeval, the self is not killed when the body is killed.

O son of Pritha, how can that man who knows the self to be indestructible, everlasting, unborn, and inexhaustible, how and whom can he kill, whom can he cause to be killed? As a man, casting off old clothes, puts on others and new ones, so the embodied self, casting off old bodies, goes to others and new ones. Weapons do not divide the self into pieces; fire does not burn it; waters to not moisten it; the wind does not dry it up. It is not divisible; it is not combustible; it is not to be moistened; it is not to be dried up. It is everlasting, all-pervading, stable, firm, and eternal. It is said to be unperceived, to be unthinkable, to be unchangeable. . . . Therefore you ought not to grieve for any being.

Having regard to your own duty also, you ought not to falter, for there is nothing better for a Kshatriya than a righteous battle. . . . Killed, you will obtain heaven; victorious, you will enjoy the earth. Therefore arise, O son of Kunti, resolved to engage in battle. Looking alike on pleasure and pain, on gain and loss, on victory and defeat, then prepare for battle, and thus you will not incur sin.[29]

Again, the conclusion is clear: if external reality is ultimately just an ephemeral appearance, then even the most horrifying crimes eventually do not matter. This is the crux of the doctrine of noninvolvement, of disinterested action: act as if it doesn't matter, as if you are not the agent, but things, including your own acts, just happen in an impersonal way. Here it is difficult to resist the temptation to paraphrase this passage as the justification for the burning of Jews in the gas chambers to their executioner, caught in a moment of doubt: since "he who thinks it to be the killer and he who thinks it to be killed, both know nothing," since "the self kills not, and the self is not killed," therefore "you ought not to grieve for any" burned Jew, but, "looking alike on pleasure and pain, on gain and loss, on victory and defeat," do what you were ordered to do. No wonder the *Bhagavad-Gita* was Heinrich Himmler's favorite book: it is reported that he always carried a copy in his uniform pocket.[30]

This means that Buddhist (or Hindu, for that matter) all-encompassing Compassion has to be opposed to Christian intolerant, violent Love. The Buddhist stance is ultimately one of Indifference, of quenching all passions that strive to establish differences; while Christian love is a violent passion to introduce a Difference, a gap in the order of being, to privilege and elevate some object at the expense of others. Love is violence not (only) in the vulgar sense of the Balkan proverb "If he doesn't beat me, he doesn't love me!"— violence is already the love choice as such, which tears its object out of its context, elevating it to the Thing. In Montenegrin folklore, the origin of Evil is a beautiful woman: she makes the men around her lose their balance, she literally destabilizes the universe, colors all things with a tone of partiality.[31] This same theme is one of the constants of Soviet pedagogy from the early 1920s onward: sexuality is inherently patho-logical, it contaminates cold, balanced logic with a particular pathos—sexual arousal is the disturbance associated with bourgeois corruption, and in the Soviet Union of the 1920s there were numerous psycho-physiological "materialist" researchers trying to demonstrate that sexual arousal is a pathological state.[32] Such antifeminist outbursts are much closer to the truth than the aseptic tolerance of sexuality.

CHAPTER 2

THE "THRILLING ROMANCE OF ORTHODOXY"

Chesterton's basic matrix is that of the "thrilling romance of ortho-doxy": in a properly Leninist way, he asserts that the search for true orthodoxy, far from being boring, humdrum, and safe, is the most daring and perilous adventure (exactly like Lenin's search for the au-thentic Marxist orthodoxy—how much less risk and theoretical effort, how much more passive opportunism and theoretical lazi-ness, is in the easy revisionist conclusion that the changed historical circumstances demand some "new paradigm"!): "People have fallen into a foolish habit of speaking of orthodoxy as something heavy, humdrum, and safe. There never was anything so perilous or so ex-citing as orthodoxy."[1]

Take today's deadlock of sexuality or art: is there anything more dull, opportunistic, and sterile than to succumb to the superego in-junction of incessantly inventing new artistic transgressions and provocations (the performance artist masturbating on stage, or mas-ochistically cutting himself; the sculptor displaying decaying an-imal corpses or human excrement), or to the parallel injunction to engage in more and more "daring" forms of sexuality? And it is im-possible not to admire Chesterton's consistency: he deploys the same conceptual matrix—that of asserting the truly subversive, even rev-olutionary, character of orthodoxy—in his famous "Defense of De-tective Stories," in which he observes how the detective story

> keeps in some sense before the mind the fact that civilization itself is the most sensational of departures and the most romantic of re-bellions. When the detective in a police romance stands alone, and somewhat fatuously fearless amid the knives and fists of a thief's kitchen, it does certainly serve to make us remember that it is the agent of social justice who is the original and poetic figure, while the burglars and footpads are merely placid old cosmic conservatives, happy in the immemorial respectability of apes and wolves. [The po-lice romance] is based on the fact that morality is the most dark and daring of conspiracies.[2]

It is not difficult to recognize here the elementary matrix of the Hegelian dialectical process: the external opposition (between Law and its criminal transgression) is transformed into the opposition, internal to the transgression itself, between particular transgressions and the absolute transgression that appears as its opposite, as the universal Law.[3] One can thus effectively claim that the subversive sting of Chesterton's work is contained in the endless variation of one and the same matrix of the Hegelian paradoxical self-negating reversal— Chesterton himself mockingly characterizes his work as variations on a "single tiresome joke."[4] And what if, in our postmodern world of ordained transgression, in which the marital commitment is perceived as ridiculously out of date, those who cling to it are the true subversives? What if, today, straight marriage is "the most dark and daring of all transgressions"? This, precisely, is the underlying premise of Ernst Lubitsch's *Design for Living* (1933, based on a Noël Coward play): a woman leads a calm, satisfied life with two men; as a dangerous experiment, she tries marriage; however, the attempt fails miserably, and she returns to the safety of living with two men.

In the very last pages of *Orthodoxy*, Chesterton deploys the fundamental Hegelian paradox of the pseudo-revolutionary critics of religion: they start by denouncing religion as the force of oppression that threatens human freedom; in fighting religion, however, they are compelled to forsake freedom itself, thus sacrificing precisely that which they wanted to defend—the ultimate victim of the atheist theoretical and practical rejection of religion is not religion (which, unperturbed, continues its life), but freedom itself, allegedly threatened by it: the atheist radical universe, deprived of religious reference, is the gray universe of egalitarian terror and tyranny:

> Men who begin to fight the Church for the sake of freedom and humanity end by flinging away freedom and humanity if only they may fight the Church. . . . I know a man who has such a passion for proving that he will have no personal existence after death that he falls back on the position that he has no personal existence now. . . . I have known people who showed that there could be no divine judgment by showing that there can be no human judgment. . . . We do not admire, we hardly excuse, the fanatic who wrecks this world for love of the other. But what are we to say of the fanatic who wrecks this world out of hatred for the other? He sacrifices the very existence of humanity to the non-existence of God. He offers his victims not to the

altar, but merely to assert the idleness of the altar and the emptiness of the throne. . . . With their oriental doubts about personality they do not make certain that we shall have no personal life hereafter; they only make certain that we shall not have a very jolly or complete one here. . . . The secularists have not wrecked divine things; but the secularists have wrecked secular things, if that is any comfort to them.[5]

The first thing we should add to this today is that the same goes for advocates of religion themselves: how many fanatical defenders of religion started by ferociously attacking contemporary secular culture and ended up forsaking religion itself (losing any meaningful religious experience)? And is it not a fact that, in a strictly analogous way, liberal warriors are so eager to fight antidemocratic fundamentalism that they will end up flinging away freedom and democracy themselves, if only they can fight terror? They have such a passion for proving that non-Christian fundamentalism is the main threat to freedom that they are ready to fall back on the position that we have to limit our own freedom here and now, in our allegedly Christian societies. If the "terrorists" are ready to wreck this world for love of the other, our warriors on terror are ready to wreck their own democratic world out of hatred for the Muslim other. Jonathan Alter and Alan Dershowitz love human dignity so much that they are ready to legalize torture—the ultimate degradation of human dignity—to defend it.

When Alan Dershowitz[6] not only condemns what he perceives as the international community's reluctance to oppose terrorism, but also provokes us to "think the unthinkable," like legalizing torture—that is to say, changing the laws so that, in exceptional situations, courts will have the right to issue "torture warrants"—his argumentation is not as easy to counter as it may appear. First, is torture "unthinkable"? Is it not going on all the time, everywhere? Secondly, if one follows Dershowitz's utilitarian line of argumentation, could one not also argue for the legitimacy of terror itself? Just as one should torture a terrorist whose knowledge could prevent the death of many more innocent people, should one not fully condone terror, at least against military and police personnel waging an unjust war of occupation, if it could prevent violence on a much larger scale? Here, then, we have a nice case of the Hegelian opposition of In-itself and For-itself: "for itself," with regard to his explicit goals, Dershowitz is, of course, ferociously attacking terrorism—"in itself or for us," however, he is succumbing to the terrorist lure, since his argumentation against terrorism already endorses terrorism's basic premise.

More generally, does not the same apply to the postmodern disdain for great ideological Causes—to the notion that, in our post-ideological era, instead of trying to change the world, we should reinvent ourselves, our whole universe, by engaging in new forms of (sexual, spiritual, aesthetic . . .) subjective practices? As Hanif Kureishi put it in an interview about his novel Intimacy: "twenty years ago it was political to try to make a revolution and change society, while now politics comes down to two bodies in a basement making love who can re-create the whole world." When we are confronted with statements like this, we cannot help recalling the old lesson of Critical Theory: when we try to preserve the authentic intimate sphere of privacy against the onslaught of instrumental/objectivized "alienated" public exchange, it is privacy itself that changes into a totally objectivized "commodified" sphere. Withdrawal into privacy today means adopting formulas of private authenticity propagated by the modern culture industry—from taking lessons in spiritual enlightenment, and following the latest cultural and other fashions, to taking up jogging and bodybuilding. The ultimate truth of withdrawal into privacy is the public confession of intimate secrets on TV—against this kind of privacy, one should emphasize that, today, the only way of breaking out of the constraints of "alienated" commodification is to invent a new collectivity. Today, more than ever, the lesson of Marguerite Duras's novels is pertinent: the way—the only way—to have an intense and fulfilling personal (sexual) relationship is not for the couple to look into each other's eyes, forgetting about the world around them, but, while holding hands, to look together outside, at a third point (the Cause for which both are fighting, to which both are committed).

The ultimate result of globalized subjectivization is not that "objective reality" disappears, but that our subjectivity itself disappears, turns into a trifling whim, while social reality continues its course. Here I am tempted to paraphrase the interrogator's famous answer to Winston Smith, who doubts the existence of Big Brother ("It is YOU who doesn't exist!"): the proper reply to the postmodern doubt about the existence of the ideological big Other is that it is the subject itself who doesn't exist. No wonder that our era, whose basic stance is best encapsulated by the title of Phillip McGraw's recent bestseller *Self Matters*, which teaches us how to "create your life from the inside out," finds its logical complement in books with titles like *How to Disappear Completely*—manuals about how to erase all traces of one's previous existence, and "reinvent" oneself completely.[7] It is here that we should locate the difference between Zen proper and its Western version: the proper greatness of Zen is that it cannot be reduced to an "inner journey" into one's "true Self"; the aim of Zen meditation is, quite on the contrary, a total voiding of the Self, the acceptance that there is no Self, no "inner truth" to be discovered. What Western Buddhism is not ready to accept is thus that the ultimate victim of the "journey into one's Self" is this Self itself. And, more generally, is this not the lesson of Adorno and Horkheimer's *Dialectic of Enlightenment*? The ultimate victims of positivism are not confused metaphysical notions, but facts themselves; the radical pursuit of secularization, the turn toward our worldly life, transforms this life itself into an "abstract" anemic process—and nowhere is this paradoxical reversal more evident than in the work of de Sade, where the unconstrained assertion of sexuality deprived of the last vestiges of spiritual transcendence turns sexuality itself into a mechanical exercise devoid of any authentic sensual passion. And is not a similar reversal clearly discernible in the deadlock of today's Last Men, "postmodern" individuals who reject all "higher" goals as terrorist, and dedicate their life to a survival replete with more and more refined and artificially excited/aroused small pleasures?

In psychoanalysis, perhaps the supreme case of such a reversal is the emergence of the so-called "anal character": what begins when the small child refuses to cede his excrement on demand, preferring to keep it for himself, since he does not want to be deprived of the surplus-enjoyment of doing it on his own terms, ends in the grown-up figure of the miser, a subject who dedicates his life to hoarding his treasure, and pays the price of an infinitely stronger renunciation: he is allowed no consumption, no indulging in pleasures; everything must serve the accumulation of his treasure. The paradox is that, when the small child refuses "castration" (ceding of the privileged detachable object), he takes the path that will end in his total self-castration in the Real; that is to say, his refusal to cede the surplus-object will condemn him to the prohibition on enjoying any other object. In other words, his rejection of the demand of the real parental Other (to behave properly on the toilet) will result in the rule of an infinitely more cruel internalized superego Other that will totally dominate his consumption. And this brings us to Chesterton's principle of Conditional Joy: by refusing the founding exception (the ceding of the excessive object), the miser is deprived of *all* objects.

Perhaps the ultimate example of this paradoxical reversal in Chesterton is the one between magic and reality: for Chesterton, reality and magic are far from being simply opposed—the greatest magic is that of reality itself, the fact that there really is such a wonderful rich world out there. And the same goes for the dialectical tension between repetition and creativity: we should discard the mistaken notion that repetition means death, automatic mechanical movement, while life means diversity, surprising twists. The greatest surprise, the greatest proof of divine creativity, is that the *same* thing gets repeated again and again:

> The sun rises every morning. I do not rise every morning; but the variation is due not to my activity, but to my inaction. . . . It might be true that the sun rises regularly because he never gets tired of rising. His routine might be due, not to a lifelessness, but to a rush of life. . . . A child kicks his legs rhythmically through excess, not absence, of life. Because children have abounding vitality, because they are in spirit fierce and free, therefore they want things repeated and unchanged. They always say, "Do it again"; and the grown-up person does it again until he is nearly dead. But, perhaps, God is strong enough to exult in monotony. It is possible that God says every morning, "Do it again" to the sun.[8]

This is what Hegel calls the dialectical coincidence of opposites: monotony is the highest idiosyncrasy; repetition demands the highest creative effort. Does Chesterton not thereby provide the clue to the strange Aztec ritual of offering human sacrifices so that the sun will rise again the next day? This attitude becomes comprehensible the moment we are able to perceive the infinite effort that has to sustain such an endless repetition. Perhaps the fact that, apropos of this miracle of continuous repetition, he inadvertently uses the term "gods"[9] is crucial: is not this attitude of perceiving repetition not as a blind automatism, but as a miracle of the highest effort of the will, profoundly pagan? On a different level, the same point was made long ago by intelligent Marxists: in the "natural" course of events, things change, so the truly difficult thing to explain is not social change but, on the contrary, stability and permanence—not why this social order collapsed, but how it succeeded in stabilizing itself and persisting in the midst of general chaos and change. For example, how it is that Christianity, the hegemonic ideology of medieval times, survived the rise of capitalism? And does the same not hold for anti-Semitism? The true mystery to be explained is its persistence through so many different societies and modes of production—we find it in feudalism, capitalism, socialism. . . .

For Chesterton, the basic Christian lesson of fairytales is contained in what he mockingly calls the "Doctrine of Conditional Joy": "You may live in a palace of gold and sapphire, if you do not say the word 'cow'; or 'You may live happily with the King's daughter, if you do not show her an onion.' The vision always hangs upon a veto."[10] Why, then, does this seemingly arbitrary single condition always limit the universal right to happiness? Chesterton's profoundly Hegelian solution is: to "extraneate" the universal right/law itself, to remind us that the universal Good to which we gain access is no less contingent, that it could have been otherwise: "If Cinderella says: 'How is it that I must leave the ball at twelve?' her godmother might answer, 'How is it that you are going there till twelve?'"[11] The function of the arbitrary limitation is to remind us that the object itself, access to which is thus limited, is given to us through an inexplicable arbitrary miraculous gesture of divine gift, and thus to sustain the magic of being allowed to have access to it: "Keeping to one woman is a small price for so much as seeing one woman. . . . Oscar Wilde said that sunsets were not valued because we could not pay for sunsets. But Oscar Wilde was wrong; we can pay for sunsets. We can pay for them by not being Oscar Wilde."[12]

Here Chesterton approaches the renunciation that is necessary to happiness. When, exactly, can people be said to be happy? In a country like Czechoslovakia in the late 1970s and 1980s, people were, in a way, actually happy: three fundamental conditions of happiness were fulfilled. (1) Their material needs were basically satisfied—not too satisfied, since the excess of consumption can in itself generate unhappiness. It is good to experience a brief shortage of some goods on the market from time to time (no coffee for a couple of days, then no beef, then no TV sets): these brief periods of shortage functioned as exceptions that reminded people that they should be glad that these goods were generally available—if everything is available all the time, people take this availability as an evident fact of life, and no longer appreciate their luck. So life went on in a regular and predictable way, without any great efforts or shocks; one was allowed to withdraw into one's private niche. (2) A second extremely important feature: there was the Other (the Party) to blame for everything that went wrong, so that one did not feel really responsible—if there was a temporary shortage of some goods, even if stormy weather caused great damage, it was "their" fault. (3) And, last but not least, there was an Other Place (the consumerist West) about which one was allowed to dream, and one could even visit it sometimes—this place was at just at the right distance: not too far away, not too close. This fragile balance was disturbed—by what? By desire, precisely. Desire was the force that compelled the people to move on—and end up in a system in which the great majority are definitely less happy.

Happiness is thus, to put it in Badiou's terms, not a category of truth, but a category of mere Being, and, as such, confused, indeterminate, inconsistent (recall the proverbial answer of a German immigrant to the United States who, when asked "Are you happy?," answered: "Yes, yes, I am very happy, *aber glücklich bin ich nicht . . .*"). It is a *pagan* category: for pagans, the goal of life is to live a happy life (the idea of living "happily ever after" is a Christianized version of paganism), and religious experience or political activity themselves are considered a higher form of happiness (see Aristotle)—no wonder the Dalai Lama himself has had such success recently preaching the gospel of happiness around the world, and no wonder he is finding the greatest response precisely in the United States, the ultimate empire of (the pursuit of) happiness. . . . In short, "happiness" is a category of the pleasure principle, and what undermines it is the insistence of a Beyond of the pleasure principle.[13]

In the strict Lacanian sense of the term, one should thus posit that "happiness" relies on the subject's inability or unreadiness fully to confront the consequences of its desire: the price of happiness is that the subject remains stuck in the inconsistency of its desire. In our daily lives, we (pretend to) desire things that we do not really desire, so that, ultimately, the worst thing that can happen is for us to get what we "officially" desire. Happiness is thus inherently hypocritical: it is the happiness of dreaming about things we do not really want. When today's Left bombards the capitalist system with demands that it obviously cannot fulfill (Full employment! Retain the welfare state! Full rights for immigrants!), it is basically playing a game of hysterical provocation, of addressing the Master with a demand that will be impossible for him to meet, and will thus expose his impotence. The problem with this strategy, however, is not only that the system cannot meet these demands, but that those who voice them do not *really* want them to be satisfied. When, for example, "radical" academics demand full rights for immigrants and the opening of borders to them, are they aware that the direct implementation of this demand would, for obvious reasons, inundate the developed Western countries with millions of newcomers, thus provoking a violent racist working-class backlash that would then endanger the privileged position of these very academics? Of course they are, but they count on the fact that their demand will not be met—in this way, they can hypocritically retain their clear radical conscience while continuing to enjoy their privileged position.

In 1994, when a new wave of emigration to the United States was in the making, Fidel Castro warned the USA that if they did not stop encouraging Cubans to emigrate, Cuba would no longer prevent them from doing so—and the Cuban authorities actually carried out this threat a couple of days later, embarrassing the United States with thousands of unwanted newcomers. Is this not like the proverbial woman who snaps back at the man making macho advances to her: "Shut up, or you'll have to do what you're boasting about!" In both cases, the gesture is that of calling the other's bluff, counting on the fact that what the other really fears is that one will fully meet his or her demand. And would not the same gesture also throw our radical academics into a panic? Here the old '68 motto "*Soyons réalistes, demandons l'impossible!*" acquires a new cynical-sinister meaning which, perhaps, reveals its truth: "Let's be realistic: we, the academic Left, want to appear critical, while fully enjoying the privileges the system offers us. So let's bombard the system with impossible demands: we all know that such demands won't be met, so we can be sure that nothing will actually change, and we'll maintain our privileged status quo!" If you accuse a big corporation of particular financial crimes, you expose yourself to risks that can go even as far as murder attempts; if you ask the same corporation to finance a research project on the link between global capitalism and the emergence of hybrid postcolonial identities, you stand a good chance of getting hundreds of thousands of dollars.

Conservatives are therefore fully justified in legitimizing their opposition to radical knowledge in terms of happiness: ultimately, knowledge makes us unhappy. Contrary to the notion that curiosity is innate to humans, that there is deep within each of us a *Wissenstrieb*, a drive to know, Jacques Lacan claims that the spontaneous attitude of a human being is that of "I don't want to know about it"—a fundamental resistance against knowing too much. All true progress in knowledge has to be bought at the price of a painful struggle against our spontaneous propensities—is today's biogenetics not the clearest proof of these limits of our readiness to know? The gene responsible for Huntington's chorea is isolated, so that each of us can learn precisely not only if he will get Huntington's, but also when he will get it. The onset of the disease depends on a genetic transcription mistake—the stuttering repetition of the "word" CAG in the middle of the gene: the age at which the madness will appear depends strictly and implacably on the number of repetitions of CAG in one place in this gene (if there are forty repetitions, you will get the first symptoms at fifty-nine; if forty-one, at fifty-four . . . if fifty, at twenty-seven). Good living, physical fitness, the best medicine, healthy food, family love and support can do nothing about it—it is pure destiny, undiluted by environmental variability. There is as yet no cure, we can do nothing about it.[14] So what should we do when we know that we can submit ourselves to a test, and thus acquire knowledge that, if it is positive, tells us exactly when we will go mad and die? Is it possible to imagine a clearer confrontation with the meaningless contingency that rules our life?

Thus Huntington's chorea confronts us with a disturbing alternative: if there is a history of this disease in my family, should I take the test that will tell me if (and when) I will inevitably get the disease, or not? What is the answer? If I cannot bear the prospect of knowing when I will die, the (more fantasmatic than realistic) ideal solution may seem to be the following one: I authorize another person or institution whom I trust completely to test me, and *not to tell me the result*, simply to kill me unexpectedly and painlessly in my sleep just before the onslaught of the fatal illness, if the result was positive. The problem with this solution, however, is that I *know that the Other knows* (the truth about my potential illness), and this ruins everything, exposing me to horrifying gnawing suspicion.

Lacan drew attention to the paradoxical status of this *knowledge about the Other's knowledge*. Recall the final reversal of Wharton's *Age of Innocence*, mentioned above, in which the husband, who harbored an illicit passionate love for Countess Olenska for many years, learns that his young wife knew about his secret passion all the time. Perhaps this would also be a way of redeeming the unfortunate *Bridges of Madison County*: if, at the end of the film, the dying Francesca were to learn that her apparently simple, down-to-earth husband knew all the time about her brief passionate affair with the *National Geographic* photographer, and how much this meant to her, but kept silent about it in order not to hurt her. That is the enigma of knowledge: how is it possible that the whole psychic economy of a situation changes radically not when the hero directly learns something (some long-repressed secret), but when he *gets to know that the other* (whom he mistook for ignorant) *also knew it all the time,* and just pretended not to know in order to keep up appearances—is there anything more humiliating than the situation of a husband who, after a long secret love affair, learns all of a sudden that his wife knew about it all the time, but kept silent about it out of politeness or, even worse, out of love for him?

Is the ideal solution, then, the opposite one: if I suspect that my child may have the disease, I test him *without him knowing it,* then kill him painlessly just before the onslaught? The ultimate fantasy of happiness here would be that of an anonymous state institution doing this for all of us without our knowledge—but, again, the question crops up: do we know about it (about the fact that the other knows), or not? The path to a perfect totalitarian society is open. . . . There is only one way out of this conundrum: what if what is false here is the underlying premise, the notion that the ultimate ethical duty is that of protecting the Other from pain, of keeping him or her in protective ignorance? So when Habermas advocates constraints on biogenetic manipulations with reference to the threat they pose to human autonomy, freedom, and dignity,[15] he is philosophically "cheating," concealing the true reason why his line of argumentation appears convincing: what he is really referring to is not autonomy and freedom, but happiness—it is on behalf of happiness that he, the great representative of the Enlightenment tradition, ended up on the same side as conservative advocates of blessed ignorance.

It is in this sense that the Christian doctrine "not only discovered the law, but it foresaw the exceptions":[16] it is only the exception that allows us to perceive the miracle of the universal rule. And, for Chesterton, the same goes for our rational understanding of the universe:

The whole secret of mysticism is this: that man can understand everything by the help of what he does not understand. The morbid logician seeks to make everything lucid, and succeeds in making everything mysterious. The mystic allows one thing to be mysterious, and everything else becomes lucid. . . . The one created thing which we cannot look at is the one thing in the light of which we look at everything. Like the sun at noonday, mysticism explains everything else by the blaze of its own victorious invisibility.[17]

Chesterton's aim is thus to *save reason through sticking to its founding exception*: deprived of this, reason degenerates into blind self-destructive skepticism—in short: into total *irrationalism*. This was Chesterton's basic insight and conviction: that the irrationalism of the late nineteenth century was the necessary consequence of the Enlightenment rationalist attack on religion:

The creeds and the crusades, the hierarchies and the horrible persecutions were not organized, as is ignorantly said, for the suppression of reason. They were organized for the difficult defense of reason. Man, by a blind instinct, knew that if once things were wildly questioned, reason could be questioned first. The authority of priests to absolve, the authority of popes to define the authority, even of inquisitors to terrify: these were all only dark defenses erected round one central authority, more undemonstrable, more supernatural than all—the authority of a man to think. . . . In so far as religion is gone, reason is going.[18]

The problem here is: is this "Doctrine of Conditional Joy" (or, to put it in Lacanese: the logic of *symbolic castration*) effectively the ultimate horizon of our experience? Is it that, in order to enjoy a limited scope of actual freedom, we have to endorse a transcendental limitation to our freedom? Is the only way to safeguard our reason to admit to an island of unreason at its very heart? Can we love another person only if we are aware that we love God more? It is to Chesterton's credit that he spelled out the properly *perverse* nature of this solution apropos of paganism; he turns around the standard (mis)perception according to which the ancient pagan attitude is that of the joyful assertion of life, while Christianity imposes a somber order of guilt and renunciation. It is, on the contrary, the pagan stance that is deeply melancholic: even if it preaches a pleasurable life, it is in the mode of "enjoy it while it lasts, because, at the end, there is always death and decay." The message of Christianity, on the contrary, is that of infinite joy beneath the deceptive surface of guilt and renunciation: "The outer ring of Christianity is a rigid guard of ethical abnegations and professional priests; but inside that inhuman guard you will find the old human life dancing like children, and drinking wine like men; for Christianity is the only frame for pagan freedom."[19]

Is not Tolkien's Lord of the Rings the ultimate proof of this paradox? Only a devout Christian could have imagined such a magnificent pagan universe, thereby confirming that paganism is the ultimate Christian dream. This is why the conservative Christian critics who recently expressed their concern at how books and movies like Lord of the Rings or the Harry Potter series undermine Christianity through their message of pagan magic miss the point, that is, the perverse conclusion that is unavoidable here: You want to enjoy the pagan dream of pleasurable life without paying the price of melancholic sadness for it? Choose Christianity! We can discern traces of this paradox right up to the well-known Catholic figure of the Priest (or Nun) as the ultimate bearer of sexual wisdom. Take what is arguably the most powerful scene in The Sound of Music: after Maria escapes from the von Trapp family back to the convent, unable to deal with her sexual attraction toward Baron von Trapp, she cannot find peace there, since she is still longing for the baron; in a memorable scene, the Mother Superior summons her and advises her to return to the von Trapp family, and try to sort out her relationship with the baron. She delivers this message in a weird song, "Climb Every Mountain!," whose surprising theme is: Do it! Take the risk, and try everything your heart desires! Do not allow petty considerations to stand in your way! The uncanny power of this scene lies in its unexpected display of the spectacle of desire, which makes the scene literally embarrassing: the very person whom one would expect to preach abstinence and renunciation turns out to be the agent of fidelity to one's desire.[20]

Significantly, when *The Sound of Music* was shown in (still Socialist) Yugoslavia in the late 1960s, this scene—the three minutes of this song—was the only part of the film which was censored (cut). The anonymous Socialist censor thereby displayed his profound sense of the truly dangerous power of Catholic ideology: far from being the religion of sacrifice, of the renunciation of earthly pleasures (in contrast to the pagan affirmation of the life of the passions), Christianity offers a devious stratagem for indulging our desires *without having to pay the price for them*, for enjoying life without the fear of decay and debilitating pain awaiting us at the end of the day. If we go to the limit in this direction, it would even be possible to maintain that this is the ultimate message of Christ's sacrifice: *you can indulge in your desires, and enjoy; I took the price for it upon myself!* There is thus an element of truth in a joke about a young Christian girl's ideal prayer to the Virgin Mary: "O thou who conceived without having sinned, let me sin without having to conceive!"—in the perverse functioning of Christianity, religion is, in effect, evoked as a safeguard allowing us to enjoy life with impunity.

The impression that we do not have to pay the price is, of course, misleading here: in effect, the price we pay is desire itself—that is to say, in succumbing to this perverse call, we compromise our desire. We all know the feeling of tremendous relief when, after a long period of tension or abstention, we are finally allowed to "let go," to indulge in hitherto forbidden pleasures—this relief, when one can finally "do what one wants," is perhaps the very model (not of realizing, but) of compromising one's desire. That is to say: for Lacan, the status of desire is inherently ethical: "not to compromise one's desire" ultimately equals "do your duty." And this is what the perverse version of Christianity entices us to do: betray your desire, compromise with regard to the essential, to what really matters, and you are welcome to have all the trivial pleasures you are dreaming about deep in your heart! Or, as they would put it today: renounce marriage, become a priest, and you can have all the little boys you want. . . . The fundamental structure here is not so much that of "Conditional Joy" (you can have "it" on condition of some "irrational" contingent exception/prohibition), but, rather, that of fake sacrifice, of pretending not to have "it," to renounce "it," in order to deceive the big Other, to conceal from it the fact that we do have it.

Let us take the example of Jeannot Szwarc's *Enigma* (1981), one of the better variations on what is arguably the basic matrix of Cold War spy thrillers with artistic pretensions à la John Le Carré; it tells the story of a dissident journalist-turned-spy who emigrates to the West, and is then recruited by the CIA and sent to East Germany to get hold of a scrambling/descrambling computer chip whose possession enables the owner to read all communications between KGB headquarters and its outposts. However, small clues tell the spy that there is something wrong with his mission: that is, that the East Germans and the Russians were informed of his arrival in advance—so what is going on? Is it that the Communists have a mole in CIA headquarters who informed them of this secret mission? As we learn toward the end of the film, the solution is much more ingenious: the CIA already possesses the scrambling chip, but, unfortunately, the Russians suspect this fact, so they have temporarily stopped using this computer network for their secret communications. The true aim of the operation was the CIA attempt to convince the Russians that they did not possess the chip: they sent an agent to get it and, at the same time, deliberately let the Russians know that there was an operation going on to get the chip; of course, the CIA is counting on the fact that the Russians will arrest the agent. The ultimate result will thus be that, by successfully preventing the mission, the Russians will be convinced that the Americans do not possess it, and that it is therefore safe to use this communication link. . . . The tragic aspect of the story, of course, is that the mission's failure is taken into account: the CIA wants the mission to fail, that is, the poor dissident agent is sacrificed in advance for the higher goal of convincing the opponent that one doesn't possess his secret. The strategy here is to stage a search operation in order to convince the Other (the enemy) that one does not already possess what one is looking for—in short, one feigns a lack, a want, in order to conceal from the Other that one already possesses the *agalma*, the Other's innermost secret.

Is this structure not somehow connected with the basic paradox of symbolic castration as constitutive of desire, in which the object has to be lost in order to be regained on the inverse ladder of desire regulated by the Law? Symbolic castration is usually defined as the loss of something that one never possessed, that is to say, the object-cause of desire is an object that emerges through the very gesture of its loss/withdrawal; however, what we encounter here, in the case of *Enigma*, is the obverse structure of feigning a loss. Insofar as the Other of the symbolic Law prohibits *jouissance*, the only way for the subject to enjoy is to pretend that he lacks the object that provides *jouissance*, that is, to conceal its possession from the Other's gaze by staging the spectacle of a desperate search for it. This also casts new light on the topic of sacrifice: one sacrifices not in order to get something from the Other, but in order to dupe the Other, in order to convince him or it that one is still missing something, that is, *jouissance*. This is why obsessional neurotics experience the compulsion repeatedly to ac-complish their compulsive rituals of sacrifice—in order to disavow their *jouissance* in the eyes of the Other. And does not the same apply, on a different level, to the so-called "woman's sacrifice," to the woman who adopts the role of remaining in the shadows, and sac-rifices herself for her husband or family? Is this sacrifice not also false in the sense of serving to dupe the Other, of convincing it that, through this sacrifice, the woman is, in effect, desperately craving something she lacks? In this precise sense, sacrifice and castration are to be opposed: far from involving the voluntary acceptance of cas-tration, sacrifice is the most refined way of disavowing it, that is, of acting as if I really do possess the hidden treasure that makes me a worthy object of love.

Is the way out of this predicament then, to pass from the Doctrine of Conditional Joy to the Doctrine of *Unconditional* Joy as exemplified by the mystical experience? And what is the exact status of this un-conditional *jouissance?* Is it only presupposed, imputed by the hysteric to the perverse Other, the "subject supposed to enjoy", or is it ac-cessible in moments of mystical encounters with the Real? The cru-cial question here is: how does this "Doctrine of Conditional Joy" relate to the Pauline suspension of our full commitment to earthly social obligations (live your life in the *as if* mode—"from now on, let even those who have wives be as though they had none, and those who mourn as though they were not mourning, and those who rejoice as though they were not rejoicing, and those who buy as though they had no possessions")? Are they two versions of the same principle? Are they not, rather, two *opposed* principles? In the "Doctrine of Conditional Joy," the Exception (be home by midnight, etc.) allows us fully to rejoice, while the Pauline *as if* mode deprives us of the ability fully to rejoice by displacing the external limit into an internal one: the limit is no longer the one between rejoicing in life and its exception (renunciation), it runs in the midst of rejoicing, that is, we have to rejoice *as if we are not rejoicing*. The limit of Chesterton is clearly perceptible in his insistence on the need for firm eternal standards: he ferociously opposes the "false theory of progress, which maintains that we alter the test instead of trying to pass the test."[21] In his usual way, in order to prove his point, Chesterton enumerates a series of brilliant examples of the self-refuting inconsistency of modern critical intellectuals:

> A man denounces marriage as a lie, and then denounces aristocratic profligates for treating it as a lie. He calls a flag a bauble, and then blames the oppressors of Poland or Ireland because they take away that bauble. The man of this school goes first to a political meeting, where he complains that savages are treated as if they were beasts; then he takes his hat and umbrella and goes on to a scientific meeting, where he proves that they practically are beasts.[22]

Here, in effect, we jump from establishing that a concrete example fails the test (savages are treated like beasts, not as men; aristocrats treat marriage as a lie) to the universal conclusion that the very notion that enabled us to measure the falsity of a particular case is in itself already false (man as such is a beast, an animal species; marriage as such is a lie). In rejecting this universalization, Chesterton implicitly rejects the Hegelian self-negation that is also the fundamental procedure of the Marxian critique of ideology—recall Brecht's famous "What is the robbery of a bank compared to the founding of a new bank?," or the good old "property is theft" (that is, the passage from the theft of some particular property to the notion that property as such is already theft). Similar reversals abound in the first chapter of *The Communist Manifesto*: from prostitution as opposed to marriage to the notion of (the bourgeois) marriage itself as a form of prostitution; and so on. In all these cases, Marx applies Hegel's insight (first articulated in the Introduction to the *Phenomenology of Spirit*) according to which, when the particular does not fit its universal measure, one should change the measure itself: the gap between the universal normative notion and its particular cases is to be reflected back into this notion itself, as its inherent tension and insufficiency—however, does Chesterton's basic matrix not involve the same gesture of self-negating universalization? Is not the "truth" of the opposition between Law and its particular transgressions that the Law itself is the highest transgression?

That is not only the limit of Chesterton, but, more radically, the limit of the perverse solution that forms the very core of "really existing Christianity": with modernity proper, we can no longer rely on the preestablished Dogma to sustain our freedom, on the preestablished Law/Prohibition to sustain our transgression—this is one way of reading Lacan's thesis that the big Other no longer exists. Perversion is a double strategy to counteract this nonexistence: an (ultimately deeply conservative, nostalgic) attempt to install the law artificially, in the desperate hope that we will then take this self-posited limitation "seriously," and, in a complementary way, a no less desperate attempt to codify the very transgression of the Law. In the perverse reading of Christianity, God first threw humanity into Sin in order to create the opportunity for saving it through Christ's sacrifice; in the perverse reading of Hegel, the Absolute plays a game with itself—it first separates itself from itself, introduces a gap of self-misrecognition, in order to reconcile itself with itself again. This is why today's desperate neoconservative attempts to reassert "old values" are also ultimately a failed perverse strategy of imposing prohibitions that can no longer be taken seriously. More precisely: when, exactly, did prohibitions lose their power? The answer is very clear: with Kant. No wonder Kant is the philosopher of freedom: with him, the deadlock of freedom emerges. That is to say, with Kant, the standard Chestertonian solution—the reliance on the preestablished Obstacle against which we can assert our freedom—is no longer viable; our freedom is asserted as autonomous, every limitation/constraint is thoroughly self-posited. This is also why we should be very attentive in reading Kant avec Sade: Lacan's ultimate thesis[23] is not that the Sadean perversion is the "truth" of Kant, more "radical" than Kant, that it draws out the consequences Kant himself did not have the courage to confront; on the contrary, the Sadean perversion emerges as the result of the Kantian compromise, of Kant's avoiding the consequences of his breakthrough.

Far from being the seminar of Lacan, his Ethics of Psychoanalysis is, rather, the point of deadlock at which Lacan comes dangerously close to the standard version of the "passion for the Real."[24] Do not the unexpected echoes between this seminar and the thought of Georges Bataille—the philosopher of the passion for the Real, if ever there was one—point unambiguously in this direction? Is not Lacan's ethical maxim "do not compromise your desire" (which, we should always bear in mind, was never used again by Lacan in his later work) a version of Bataille's injunction "to think everything to a point that makes people tremble,"[25] to go as far as possible—to the point at which opposites coincide, at which infinite pain turns into the joy of the highest bliss (discernible in the photograph of the Chinese submitted to the terrifying torture of being slowly cut to pieces), at which the intensity of erotic enjoyment encounters death, at which sainthood overlaps with extreme dissolution, at which God Himself is revealed as a cruel Beast? Is the temporal coincidence of Lacan's seminar on the ethics of psychoanalysis and Bataille's Eroticism more than a mere coincidence? Is Bataille's domain of the Sacred, of the "accursed part," not his version of what, apropos of Antigone, Lacan deployed as the domain of ate?

Does not Bataille's opposition of "homogeneity," the order of exchanges, and "heterogeneity," the order of limitless expenditure, echo Lacan's opposition of the order of symbolic exchanges and the excess of the traumatic encounter with the Real? "Heterogeneous reality is that of a force or shock."[26] And how can Bataille's elevation of the dissolute woman to the status of God fail to remind us of Lacan's claim that Woman is one of the names of God? Not to mention Bataille's term for the experience of transgression—impossible—that is Lacan's qualification of the Real . . . It is this urge to "go to the very end," to the extreme experience of the Impossible as the only way of being authentic, which makes Bataille the philosopher of the passion for the Real—no wonder he was obsessed with Communism and Fascism, those two excesses of life, against democracy, which was "a world of appearances and of old men with their teeth falling out."[27]

Bataille was fully aware of how this transgressive "passion for the Real" *relies on prohibition*; that is why he was explicitly opposed to the "sexual revolution," to the rise of sexual permissiveness, which began in his last years:

> In my view, sexual disorder is accursed. In this respect and in spite of appearances, I am opposed to the tendency which seems today to be sweeping it away. I am not among those who see the neglect of sexual interdictions as a solution. I even think that human potential depends on these interdictions: we could not imagine this potential without these interdictions.[28]

Bataille thus brought to its climax the dialectical interdependence between law and its transgression—"system is needed and so is excess," as he liked to repeat: "Often, the criminal himself wants death as the answer to the crime, in order finally to impart the sanction, without which the crime would be *possible* instead of being *what it is, what the criminal wanted.*"[29] This, also, was why he ultimately opposed Communism: he was for the excess of the revolution, but feared that the revolutionary spirit of excessive expenditure would afterward be contained in a new order, even more "homogeneous" than the capitalist one: "the idea of a revolution is intoxicating, but what happens afterward? The world will remake itself and remedy what oppresses us today to take some other form tomorrow."[30]

This, perhaps, is why Bataille is strictly *premodern*: he remains stuck in this dialectic of the law and its transgression, of the prohibitive law as generating the transgressive desire, which forces him to the debilitating perverse conclusion that one has to install prohibitions in order to be able to enjoy their violation—a clearly unworkable pragmatic paradox. (And, incidentally, was not this dialectic fully explored by Saint Paul in Romans, in the famous passage on the relationship between Law and sin, on how Law engenders sin, that is, the desire to transgress it?) What Bataille is unable to perceive are simply the consequences of the Kantian philosophical revolution: the fact that *the absolute excess is that of the Law itself*—the Law intervenes in the "homogeneous" stability of our pleasure-oriented life as the shattering force of absolute destabilizing "heterogeneity." On a different level, but no less radically, late-capitalist "permissive" society in the thrall of the superego injunction "Enjoy!" elevates excess into the very principle of its "normal" functioning, so that I am tempted to propose a paraphrase of Brecht: "What is a poor Bataillean subject engaged in his transgressions of the system compared to the late-capitalist excessive orgy of the system itself?" (And it is interesting to note how this very point was made by Chesterton: orthodoxy itself is the highest subversion; serving the Law is the highest adventure.)

It is only in this precise sense that the otherwise journalistic designation of our age as the "age of anxiety" is appropriate: what causes anxiety is the elevation of transgression into the norm, the lack of the prohibition that would sustain desire. This lack throws us into the suffocating proximity of the object-cause of desire: we lack the breathing space provided by the prohibition, since, even before we can assert our individuality through our resistance to the Norm, the Norm enjoins us in advance to resist, to violate, to go further and further. We should not confuse this Norm with regulation of our intersubjective contacts: perhaps there has been no period in the history of humankind, when interactions were so closely regulated; these regulations, however, no longer function as the symbolic prohibition—rather, they regulate modes of transgression themselves. So when the ruling ideology enjoins us to enjoy sex, not to feel guilty

about it, since we are not bound by any prohibitions whose viola-
tions should make us feel guilty, the price we pay for this absence of
guilt is anxiety. It is in this precise sense that—as Lacan put it, following Freud—anxiety is the only emotion that does not deceive: all
other emotions, from sorrow to love, are based on deceit. Again, back
to Chesterton: when he writes that "Christianity is the only frame for
pagan freedom," this means that, precisely, this frame—the frame of
prohibitions—is the only frame within which we can enjoy pagan
pleasures: the feeling of guilt is a fake enabling us to give ourselves
over to pleasures—when this frame falls away, anxiety arises.

It is here that one should refer to the key distinction between the
object of desire and its object-cause. What should the analyst do in the
case of a promiscuous woman who has regular one-night stands,
while complaining all the time how bad and miserable and guilty she
feels about it? The thing not to do, of course, is to try to convince her
that one-night stands are bad, the cause of her troubles, signs of some
libidinal deadlock—in this way, one merely feeds her symptom,
which is condensed in her (misleading) dissatisfaction with one-
night stands. That is to say, it is obvious that what gives the woman
true satisfaction is not promiscuity as such, but the very accompanying feeling of being miserable—that is the source of her "masochis-
tic" enjoyment. The strategy should thus be, as a first step, not to
convince her that her promiscuity is pathological, but, on the contrary, to convince her that there is nothing to feel bad or guilty about:
if she really enjoys one-night stands, she should continue to have
them without any negative feelings. The trick is that, once she is confronted with one-night stands without what appears to be the obstacle
preventing her from fully enjoying them, but is in reality the *objet petit
a*, the feature that allows her to enjoy them, the feature through which
she can only enjoy them, one-night stands will lose their attraction
and become meaningless. (And if she still goes on with her one-night
stands? Well, why not? Psychoanalysis is not a moral catechism: if this
is her path to enjoyment, why not?) It is this gap between object and
object-cause that the subject has to confront when the prohibition
falls away: is she ready to desire the obstacle directly as such?[31]

CHAPTER 3

THE SWERVE OF THE REAL

The *Fort-Da* story from Freud's *Beyond the Pleasure Principle* can perhaps serve as the best test to detect the level of understanding of Freud. According to the standard version, Freud's grandson symbolizes the departure and return of his mother by throwing away a spool— "*Fort!*"—and retrieving it—"*Da!*" The situation thus seems clear: traumatized by the mother's absence, the child overcomes his anxiety, and gains mastery over the situation, by symbolizing it: through the substitution of the spool for the mother, he himself becomes the stage-director of her appearance and disappearance. Anxiety is thus successfully "sublated [*aufgehoben*]" in the joyful assertion of mastery.

However, are things really so clear? What if the spool is not a stand-in for the mother, but a stand-in for what Jacques Lacan called *objet petit a*, ultimately the object in me, that which my mother sees in me, that which makes me the object of *her* desire? What if Freud's grandson is staging *his own* disappearance and return? In this precise sense, the spool is what Lacan called a "biceptor": it properly belongs neither to the child nor to his mother; it is in-between the two, the excluded intersection of the two sets. Take Lacan's famous "I love you, but there is something in you more than yourself that I love, *objet petit a*, so I destroy you"—the elementary formula of the destructive passion for the Real as the endeavor to extract from you the real kernel of your being. This is what gives rise to anxiety in the encounter with the Other's desire: what the Other is aiming at is not simply myself but the real kernel, that which is in me more than myself, and he is ready to destroy me in order to extract that kernel. . . . Is not the ultimate cinematic expression of the ex-timate character of the *objet petit a* in me that of the "alien" in the film of the same name, which is quite literally what is "in me more than myself," a foreign body at the very heart of myself, and can therefore be extracted from me only at the price of my destruction?

Consequently, we should *invert* the standard constellation: the true problem is the mother who *enjoys* me (her child), and the true stake of the game is to escape this closure. The true anxiety is this being-caught in the Other's *jouissance*. So it is not that, anxious about losing my mother, I try to master her departure/arrival; it is that, anxious about her overwhelming *presence*, I try desperately to carve out a space where I can gain a distance toward her, and so become able to sustain my desire. Thus we obtain a completely different picture: instead of the child mastering the game, and thus coping with the trauma of his mother's absence, we get the child trying to escape the suffocating embrace of his mother, and construct an open space for desire; instead of the playful exchange of Fort and *Da*, we get a desperate oscillation between the two poles, neither of which brings satisfaction—or, as Kafka wrote: "I cannot live with you, and I cannot live without you." And it is this most elementary dimension of the Fort-*Da* game that is missed in the cognitivist science of the mind. A recent cognitivist textbook tells us: "If someone were to claim that, for *the sake of his desire* for an object, he moved away from this object, then we would surmise that he is either a madman or he does not know the meaning of the term 'desire'."[1] Is not such an avoiding of the object for the sake of our very desire for it, however, the very paradox of courtly love? Is it not a feature of desire as such, at its most fundamental? So, perhaps, we, psychoanalysts, are a species of madmen. That is to say, is not such an avoiding of the object for the sake of our very desire for it—such a persisting Fort in the very heart of *Da*—the very paradox of desire as such, at its most fundamental? What about the eternal deferral of finally meeting "the distant beloved [*die ferne Geliebte*]"?[2] In the same cognitivist vein, Douglas Lenat tries to construct a computer that would possess human common sense, filling its memory with millions of "obvious" rules like: *Nothing can be in two places at the same time. When humans die, they are not born again. Dying is undesirable. Animals do not like pain. Time advances at the same rate for everyone. When it rains, people get wet. Sweet things taste good.*[3] However, are these rules really so obvious? What about the same thought shared by two people? What about people who believe in reincarnation? What about desperate people who long to die? What about masochists who like pain? What about our thrilling experiences when time seems to run faster than usual? What about people with umbrellas who do not get wet? What about those among us who prefer dark, "bitter" chocolate to sweet chocolate?

It is against this background that one should conceptualize the difference between desire of the Other and *jouissance* of the Other; this difference is often described as the threshold of symbolic castration: while desire of the Other (*genitivus subjectivus* and *objectivus*) can thrive only insofar as the Other remains an undecipherable abyss, the Other's *jouissance* indicates its suffocating overproximity. Here we should recall the two meanings of the French *jouir*: "enjoy" plus "the right to enjoy something [even if one does not own it]," the so-called *usufruit* (for example, when the owner of a big house leaves the house to his children, but gives his faithful old servant the right to stay in his apartment in the house rent-free until his death—the servant is free to "enjoy" his apartment).The Other's enjoyment is thus its right to "enjoy me" as a sexual object—this is what is at stake in what Lacan reconstructs as the Kantian imperative of the work of de Sade: "Anyone can tell me: 'I have the full right to enjoy any part of your body in any way that brings pleasure to me. . . .'" Although this seems to be a "feminine position" (women as the *usufruit* of men), this Other is ultimately the pre-Oedipal Mother (this is why Lacan draws attention to the fact that in de Sade's universe, with all its "perversity," the mother remains prohibited). Through symbolic castration, this overwhelming *jouissance* of the (M)Other is then sublated (in the precise Hegelian sense of *Aufhebung*) into the localized phallic *jouissance* that, precisely, is *jouissance* under the condition of desire, that is, as it appears after symbolic castration. When Lacan speaks of "phallic *jouissance*," we should always bear in mind that the phallus is the signifier of castration—phallic *jouissance* is therefore *jouissance* under the condition of symbolic castration that opens up and sustains the space of desire.

Along these lines, Richard Boothby interprets the Lacanian *objet petit a* as the remainder of the Maternal Thing within the domain of the paternal symbolic Law: once the direct confrontation with the Maternal Thing, her terrifying desire, is screened through the paternal Law, "each incarnation of the *objet a* allows the subject, not to provide any final answer to the question of the Other's desire, the unthinkable dimension of the imaginary other that emerges primitively as *das Ding*, but to pass that question into the unfolding of a symbolic process."[4] The problem with Boothby is that he endorses this Oedipalization—more precisely, he reads Lacan as endorsing it: "The function of the paternal metaphor is to submit the desire of the Mother (which is of the order of the Thing) to the law of the Father (which comprises the totality of the signifying system, the structure of the symbolic order)."[5] For Boothby, the original fact is the gap between the Real of the bodily passions, their mobility, and the fixity of imaginary identifications that coordinate the subject's identity; there are two ways of dealing with the excess of the Real, the terrifying abyss of what is in the image beyond the image: either one confronts it directly, or one mediates it through the symbolic order. Here, however, he takes the problematic step of identifying the Real with the open horizon of meaning, with the elusive unspeakable kernel of the potentiality of meaning, with the true focus of what we want to say that can never be fully explicated: "The real is the dimension of *das Ding*, of what is in the other more than the other. It is this dimension that is unassimilable in the image and is implicitly animated in every registration of the signifier, in the overflow of meaning by virtue of which every utterance says more than it means to say."[6]

Instead of the traumatic intractable Thing with which no exchange is possible, we thus enter the domain of symbolic exchanges within which the Real appears as the elusive missing ultimate point of reference that sets in motion the indefinite sliding (*dérive*) of signifiers. Consequently, Boothby identifies the Real with the phallus *qua* Master-Signifier: as a signifier, the phallus stands for the "overflow of meaning," for the potentiality of meaning that eludes every determinate signification. There is, however, a problem with this version: it implies that Lacan preaches phallic *jouissance* as the symbolization/normalization of the presymbolic excessive (M)Other's *jouissance*—however, is this really Lacan's position? Is symbolic castration the ultimate horizon of his thought, beyond which there is only the inaccessible abyss of the (M)Other, the Real of the ultimate Night that dissolves all distinctions? In order to approach this question properly, we must elaborate the concept of the Real.

Alain Badiou identified as the key feature of the twentieth century the "passion for the Real [*la passion du réel*]": in contrast to the nineteenth century of utopian or "scientific" projects and ideals, plans for the future, the twentieth century aimed at delivering the thing itself, at directly realizing the longed-for New Order—or, as Fernando Pessoa puts it: ". . . do not crave to construct in the space / which appears to lie in the future, / and to promise you some kind of tomorrow. Realize yourself today, do not wait. / You alone are your life." The ultimate and defining experience of the twentieth century was the direct experience of the Real as opposed to everyday social reality—the Real in its extreme violence as the price to be paid for peeling off the deceptive layers of reality.[7] In the trenches of World War I, Ernst Jünger was celebrating face-to-face combat as the authentic intersubjective encounter: authenticity lies in the act of violent transgression, from the Lacanian Real—the Thing Antigone confronts when she violates the order of the City—to the Bataillean excess.

What this passion for the Real confronts us with is the properly *ontological* impossibility of locating within the same space of reality our normal daily interactions side by side with scenes of intense enjoyment—here is Bataille's formulation:

A madness suddenly takes possession of a person. That madness is well known to us but we can easily picture the surprise of anyone who did not know about it and who by some device witnesses unseen the passionate lovemaking of some woman who had struck him as particularly distinguished. He would think she was sick, just as mad dogs are sick. Just as if some bitch had usurped the personality of the dignified hostess.[8]

And the fact that this dimension is that of the sacred is attested to by the minor scandal created a couple of years ago by an English writer who began his novel with: "There are women for whom it holds that, in order to be allowed to fuck them freely and repeatedly, one would be ready to calmly observe one's own wife and small child drowning in cold water." Is this not an extreme formulation of the "religious" status of sexual passion, beyond the pleasure principle and involving the teleological suspension of the ethical?

There is, however, another way of approaching the Real—that is to say, the twentieth-century passion for the Real has two sides: that of purification and that of subtraction. In contrast to purification, which endeavors to isolate the kernel of the Real through a violent peeling off, subtraction starts from the Void, from the reduction ("subtraction") of all determinate content, and then tries to establish a minimal difference between this Void and an element that functions as its stand-in. Apart from Badiou himself, it was Jacques Rancière who developed this structure as that of the politics of the "empty set," of the "supernumerary" element that belongs to the set but has no distinctive place in it. What, for Rancière, is politics proper?[9] A phenomenon that appeared for the first time in Ancient Greece, when the members of demos (those with no firmly determined place in the hierarchical social edifice) not only demanded that their voice be heard against those in power, those who exerted social control—that is to say, they not only protested the wrong (le tort) they suffered, and wanted their voice to be heard, to be recognized as included in the public sphere, on an equal footing with the ruling oligarchy and aristocracy; even more, they, the excluded, those with no fixed place within the social edifice, presented themselves as the representatives, the stands-in, for the Whole of Society, for the true Universality ("we—the 'nothing,' not counted in the order—are the people, we are All against others who stand only for their particular privileged interest"). In short, political conflict designates the tension between the structured social body, in which each part has its place, and "the part with no-part" that unsettles this order for the sake of the empty principle of universality, of what Balibar calls égaliberté, the principled equality of all men qua speaking beings—right down to the liumang, "hoodlums," in present-day feudal-capitalist China, those who (in terms of the existing order) are displaced, and float freely, lacking work-and-residence, but also cultural or sexual, identity and registration. Politics proper thus always involves a kind of short circuit between the Universal and the Particular: the paradox of a "universal singular," of a singular that appears as the stand-in for the Universal, destabilizing the "natural" functional order of relations in the social body.

This identification of the non-part with the Whole, of the part of society with no properly defined place within it (or resisting the allocated subordinated place within it) with the Universal, is the elementary gesture of politicization, discernible in all great democratic events from the French Revolution (in which *le troisième état* proclaimed itself identical to the Nation as such, against the aristocracy and the clergy) to the demise of ex-European Socialism (in which dissident "forums" proclaimed themselves representative of the whole society against the Party nomenklatura). In this precise sense, politics and democracy are synonymous: the basic aim of antidemocratic politics, always and by definition, is and was depoliticization, that is, the unconditional demand that "things should return to normal," with each individual doing his or her particular job. The same point can also be made in anti-Statist terms: those who are subtracted from the grasp of the State are not accounted for, counted in—that is to say, their multiple presence is not properly represented in the One of the State. In this sense, the "minimal difference" is the difference between the set and this surplus-element that belongs to the set, but lacks any differential property that would specify its place within its edifice: it is precisely this lack of specific (functional) difference that makes it an embodiment of the pure difference between the place and its elements.[10] This "supernumerary" element is thus a kind of "Malevich in politics," a square on a surface marking the minimal difference between the place and what takes place, between background and figure. Or, in the terms of Laclau and Mouffe, this "supernumerary" element emerges when we pass from *difference* to *antagonism*: since, in it, all qualitative differences inherent to the social edifice are suspended, it stands for the "pure" difference as such, for the nonsocial within the field of the social.[11] Or—to put it in the terms of the logic of the signifier—in it, the Zero itself is counted as One.

And is not this shift from purification to subtraction also the shift from Kant to Hegel? From tension between phenomena and Thing to an inconsistency/gap between phenomena themselves? The standard notion of reality is that of a hard kernel that resists the conceptual grasp—what Hegel does is simply to take this notion of reality more literally: nonconceptual reality is something that emerges when notional self-development gets caught in an inconsistency, and becomes nontransparent to itself. In short, the limit is transposed from exterior to interior: there is Reality because and insofar as the Notion is inconsistent, doesn't coincide with itself. The multiple perspectival inconsistencies between phenomena are not an effect of the impact of the transcendent Thing—on the contrary, this Thing is nothing but the ontologization of the inconsistency between phenomena. The logic of this reversal is ultimately the same as the passage from the special to the general theory of relativity in Einstein. While the special theory already introduces the notion of curved space, it conceives of this curvature as the effect of matter: it is the presence of matter that curves space—that is to say, only empty space would have been noncurved. With the passage to the general theory, the causality is reversed: far from *causing* the curvature of space, matter is its *effect*. In the same way, the Lacanian Real—the Thing—is not so much the inert presence that "curves" the symbolic space (introducing gaps and inconsistencies in it), but, rather, the effect of these gaps and inconsistencies.

The Real as the terrifying primordial abyss that swallows everything, dissolving all identities, well known in literature in its multiple guises, from Poe's maelstrom and Kurtz's "horror" at the end of Conrad's *Heart of Darkness* to Pip from Melville's *Moby-Dick* who, cast to the bottom of the ocean, experiences the demon God—

> Carried down alive to wondrous depths, where strange shapes of the unwarped primal world glided to and fro before his passive eyes . . . Pip saw the multitudinous, God-omnipresent, coral insects, that out of the firmament of waters heaved the colossal orbs. He saw God's foot upon the treadle of the loom, and spoke to it; and therefore his shipmates called him mad.

—this Real is precisely the ultimate lure that, as Richard Kearney was right to emphasize,[12] lends itself easily to New Age appropriation, as in Joseph Campbell's notion of the monstrous God:

> By monster I mean some horrendous presence or apparition that explodes all your standards for harmony, order and ethical conduct. . . . That's God in the role of destroyer. Such experiences go past ethical judgments. This is wiped out . . . God is horrific.[13]

Against this notion of the Real, one should emphasize that the Lacanian Real is not *another* Center, a "deeper," "truer" focal point or "black hole" around which symbolic formations fluctuate; rather, it is the obstacle on account of which every Center is always displaced, missed. Or, with regard to the topic of the Thing-in-itself: the Real is not the abyss of the Thing that forever eludes our grasp, and on account of which every symbolization of the Real is partial and inappropriate; it is, rather, that invisible obstacle, that distorting screen, which always "falsifies" our access to external reality, that "bone in the throat" which gives a pathological twist to every symbolization, that is to say, on account of which every symbolization misses its object. Or, with reference to the notion of the Thing as the ultimate traumatic unbearable Referent that we are unable to confront directly, since its direct presence is too blinding: what if this very notion that delusive everyday reality is a veil concealing the Horror of the unbearable Thing is false, what if the ultimate veil concealing the Real is the very notion of the horrible Thing behind the veil?

Critics of the Lacanian Real like to point out the problematic nature of the distinction between the Symbolic and the Real: is not the very act of drawing a line between the two a symbolic act *par excellence?* This criticism, however, is based on a misunderstanding that is best explained through reference to the "feminine" logic of non-All deployed by Lacan in *Seminar XX*. According to the standard reading of this logic, the "non-All" means that not all of a woman is caught in the phallic function: there is a part of her that resists symbolic castration, inclusion in the symbolic order. However, there is a problem with this reading: how, then, are we to read the complementary formula according to which there is nothing in a woman that is not caught in the phallic function, and thus included in the symbolic order? In the volume *Reading Seminar XX*, there is an interesting divergence between Bruce Fink and Suzanne Barnard that concerns precisely this point. Fink follows the standard reading: *jouissance féminine*, that part of a woman that resists symbolization, is beyond speech; it can be experienced only in a silent mystic rapture modeled on Bernini's Saint Teresa; in other words, "there is no *jouissance* that is not phallic *jouissance*" means that feminine *jouissance* does not exist in the strict sense of symbolic existence—it is not symbolized, it just ex-sists outside speech: "it is ineffable. No words come at that moment."[14] How, then, are we to read Lacan's identification of *jouissance féminine* with the *jouissance* of speech, *jouissance* that is inherent to the act of speaking as such? It is a sign of Fink's extraordinary intellectual integrity that he openly confesses his perplexity at this point, saying that this, perhaps, is simply one example of Lacan's inconsistency, of making contradictory claims in the space of a dozen or fewer pages:

> How [*jouissance féminine* as the satisfaction of speech] is compatible with the notion that it is an ineffable experience . . . I do not profess to know. . . . Nor can I say why Lacan associates [the satisfaction of speech] specifically with women. . . . We need not assume that there is some sort of complete unity or consistency to his work.[15]

Such an inconsistency would, however, be catastrophic for Lacan, bearing in mind that this point is absolutely central to his concept of sexual difference; so, before conceding that we are dealing here with a simple inconsistency, we should try to reconcile the two statements. And does not Barnard's essay show us a way out of this deadlock when she insists on how the feminine "non-All" does not mean that there is a mysterious part of a woman outside the symbolic, but a simple absence of totalization, of the All: totalization takes place through its constitutive exception, and since, in the feminine libidinal economy, there is no Outside, no Exception to the phallic function, for that very reason a woman is immersed in the symbolic order more wholly than a man—without restraint, without exception:

. . . the feminine structure (and, hence, Other *jouissance*) is produced in relation to a "set" that *does not* exist on the basis of an external, constitutive exception. . . . However, this does not mean, in turn, that the non-whole of feminine structure is simply outside of or indifferent to the order of masculine structure. Rather, she is in the phallic function *altogether* or, in Lacan's words, "She is *not* not at all there. She is there in full.". . . By being in the symbolic "without exception" then, the feminine subject has a relation to the Other that produces another "unlimited" form of *jouissance*.[16]

Recall the famous scene, in Bergman's *Persona*, of Bibi Andersson telling of a beach orgy and passionate lovemaking in which she participated: we see no flashback pictures; nonetheless, this scene is one of the most erotic in the entire history of cinema—the excitement is in the way she tells it, and this excitement that resides in speech itself is *jouissance féminine*. And, incidentally, does not the very duality of Bibi Andersson and Liv Ullman—the hysterical-talkative "ordinary" woman and the more aristocratic Ullman, the actress who withdraws into complete silence—reproduce the two sides of *jouissance féminine*: the hysterical "overidentification" with speech, and silence, withdrawal into the ineffable? Furthermore, as many a critic has noted, does this duality not reproduce the duality of analysand and analyst in the psychoanalytic treatment? Does not Ullman, "officially" a psychiatric patient, play the role of the analyst whose silence frustrates the analysand, provoking him or her into hysterical outbursts?[17] And is not this duality (in Lacanian mathemes, $ and *a*) a further indication that the position of the analyst is fundamentally feminine, in contrast to the masculine duality of S_1 and S_2 (the Master and the servant's Knowledge)?

This means that the Real is not external to the Symbolic: the Real is the Symbolic itself in the modality of non-All, lacking an external Limit/Exception. In this precise sense, the line of separation between the Symbolic and the Real is not only a symbolic gesture *par excellence*, but the very founding gesture of the Symbolic and to step into the Real does not entail abandoning language, throwing oneself into the abyss of the chaotic Real, but, on the contrary, dropping the very allusion to some external point of reference which eludes the Symbolic. This is also why Hegel's logic is the (first case of the) *logic of the Real*—precisely because of Hegel's "absolute panlogicism," the erasure of any external reference. In short, the unnameable is strictly inherent to language—how does it emerge? It is not that we need words to designate objects, to symbolize reality, and that then, in surplus, there is some excess of reality, a traumatic core that resists symbolization—this obscurantist theme of the unnameable Core of Higher Reality that eludes the grasp of language is to be thoroughly rejected; not because of a naive belief that everything can be nominated, grasped by our reason, but because of the fact that the Unnameable is an effect of language. We have reality before our eyes well before language, and what language does, in its most fundamental gesture, is—as Lacan put it—the very opposite of designating reality: it *digs a hole in it*, it opens up visible/present reality toward the dimension of the immaterial/unseen. When I simply see you, I simply see you—but it is only by naming you that I can indicate the abyss in you beyond what I see.

What, then, is the Real? Jonathan Lear[18] has demonstrated how Freud's "pre-Socratic" turn to Eros and Thanatos as the two basic polar forces of the universe is a false escape, a pseudo-explanation generated by his inability properly to conceptualize the dimension of "beyond the pleasure principle" that he encountered in his practice. After establishing the pleasure principle as the "swerve" that defines the functioning of our psychic apparatus, Freud is compelled to take note of the phenomena (primarily repetitions of traumatic experiences) that disrupt this functioning: they form an exception that cannot be accounted for in terms of the pleasure principle. It was "at this point that Freud covers over the crucial nugget of his own insight: that the mind can disrupt its own functioning." Instead of trying to conceptualize this break (negativity) as such in its modalities, he wants to ground it in *another*, "deeper," positivity. In philosophical terms, the mistake here is the same as that of Kant, according to Hegel: once Kant discovers the inner inconsistency of our experiential reality, he feels compelled to posit the existence of another, inaccessible, true reality of Things-in-themselves, instead of accepting this inconsistency: "Freud is not in the process of discovering a new life force, he is in the process of trying to cover over a trauma to psychoanalytic theory. In this way, invoking Plato and the ancients gives a false sense of legitimacy and security." I must agree fully with Lear: far from being the name of an unbearable traumatic fact that is unacceptable to most of us (the fact that we "strive toward death"), the introduction of Thanatos as a cosmic principle (and the retroactive elevation of libido into Eros as the other cosmic principle) is *an attempt to cover the true trauma.* The apparent "radicalization" is, in effect, a philosophical domestication: the break that disrupts the functioning of the universe—its ontological fault, as it were—is transformed into one of the two positive cosmic principles, thus reestablishing the pacifying, harmonious vision of the universe as the battlefield of the two opposing principles. (And the theological implications here are also crucial: instead of thinking the subversive deadlock of monotheism through to the end, Freud regresses to pagan wisdom.)

Here Lear introduces the notion of "enigmatic terms," terms that seem to designate a determinate entity while, in reality, they simply stand for the failure of our understanding: when he mentions Thanatos, Freud "takes himself to be naming a real thing in the world but he is in fact injecting an enigmatic term into our discourse. There is no naming, for nothing has genuinely been isolated for him to name. His hope is to provide an explanation, in fact all we have is the illusion of one." Examples from the history of science abound here—from phlogiston (a pseudo-concept that simply betrayed the scientist's ignorance of how light actually travels) to Marx's "Asiatic mode of production" (which is a kind of negative container: the only true content of this concept is "all the modes of production that do not fit Marx's standard categorization of the modes of production"). However, is not Lear too dismissive of "enigmatic terms"? Are they really just indications of our failure and ignorance? Do they not play a key structural role? "Enigmatic term" fits exactly what Lacan calls the Master-Signifier (the phallus as signifier), the "empty" signifier without a signified: this signifier (the paternal metaphor) is the substitute for the mother's desire, and the encounter with the mother's desire, with its enigma (*che vuoi?*, what does she want?) is the primordial encounter with the opacity of the Other. The fact that the phallus is a *signifier*, not the signified, plays a pivotal role here: the phallic signifier does not provide an explanation for the enigma of the mother's desire, it is not its signified (it does not tell us "what the mother really wants"), it simply designates the impenetrable space of her desire. Furthermore, as it was developed by Claude Lévi-Strauss (on whom Lacan relies here), *every* signifying system necessarily contains such a paradoxical excessive element, the stand-in for the enigma that eludes it.

The analogy with Lacan goes even further: in Lacanese, is Lear's point not that the Freudian pleasure principle is "non-All": there is nothing outside it, no external limits, yet it is not all, it can break down? Why, then, do breaks occur? When does our mind disrupt its own functioning? These breaks simply occur, ungrounded in any deeper Principle: as a "blind" destructive *passage à l'acte*, when we find ourselves in a deadlock; as a traumatic encounter. Again, what Lear calls the split between the psyche's normal functioning (under the swerve of the pleasure principle) and its break perfectly fits Lacan's couple of *automaton* and *tyche* (taken from Aristotle, also Lear's great authority); when Lear describes how, "after a break, the mind tries to get itself back into the swerve-like activity of sexuality, fantasy, dreaming," he thereby clearly echoes Lacan's notion of how fantasmatic formations and symbolic fictions endeavor to patch up the intrusions of the Real. Furthermore, when Lear emphasizes that trauma is just a species, one of the modalities, of the break, is this not strictly analogous to Lacan's thesis that trauma is only one of the modalities of the Real?

Is the misunderstanding between Lacan and Lear, then, purely and simply terminological? In his critique of Freud's treatment of Dora, Lear claims that Freud repeats Herr K.'s mistake, and "assumes [Dora] is already a woman, when her problem is that she is trying to figure out how to become one. He assumes she already understands erotic life; she is trying to figure out what it is." In short, Freud interprets Dora as a sexually mature woman with clear (albeit unconscious) desires, instead of perceiving her as what she was: a girl still in search of the mystery of feminine desire, and projecting the solution of this mystery into Frau K., her "subject supposed to know (how to desire)." However, Lear seems to miss the point here, which is that being in search of this mystery is the very definition of a feminine hysterical subject: there is no woman who really knows how to desire—such a woman would be the Lacanian Woman, the woman who doesn't exist, whose existence is a fantasy.

The more general conclusion to be drawn from this concerns the location of Eros with regard to the break. Lear tends to locate Eros within the swerve of the "pleasure principle"—however, is not love, the shattering experience of falling in love, a break par excellence, the mother of all breaks, the opening up of the possibility of new possibilities? Consequently, is not love itself the supreme example of the "enigmatic term"? It refers by definition to an unknowable X, to the je ne sais quoi that makes me fall in love—the moment I can enumerate reasons why I love you, the things about you that made me fall in love with you, we can be sure that this is not love. And, mutatis mutandis, does the same not hold for sexuality? Is the child's shattering encounter with the impenetrable enigma of his or her parents' sexuality not the break which disturbs his or her narcissistic closure, and compels him or her to confront new possibilities, as Jean Laplanche would have it? The further conclusion to be drawn from this difference is that, perhaps, one cannot oppose swerve and break as simply as Lear tends to do—this is how he defines swerve:

> I call this type of mental functioning swerve because it exercises a kind of gravitational pull on the entire field of conscious mental functioning, bending it into idiosyncratic shapes. By way of analogy, we detect the existence of black holes by the way light swerves toward them. We detect this type of unconscious process by the ways our conscious reasoning, our bodily expressions, our acts and our dreams swerve toward them.

For Lacan, however, the Real (of a trauma) is also a "swerve," a black hole detectable only through its effects, only in the way it "curves" mental space, bending the line of mental processes. And is not sexuality (this Real of the human animal) also such a swerve? Here one should endorse Freud's fundamental insight according to which sexuality does *not* follow the pleasure principle: its fundamental mode of appearance is that of a break, of the intrusion of some excessive *jouissance* that disturbs the "normal," balanced functioning of the psychic apparatus.

Does this mean that Lacan repeats Freud's mistake, and again locates the cause of the break in some preexisting positive external entity, like the Thing, *das Ding*, the impenetrable substance of the Real? Since it is Lear himself who alludes to physics (black holes), we should look here once more at the general theory of relativity, in which matter, far from causing the curvature of space, is its effect. In the same way, the Lacanian Real—the Thing—is not so much the inert presence that "curves" the symbolic space (introducing breaks in it), but, rather, the effect of these breaks. In contrast to Lear, for whom swerve is the swerve of the pleasure principle, acting as the force of stability and occasionally disrupted by breaks, for Lacan, swerve is the destabilizing force whose gravitational pull disrupts the psychic *automaton*.

A reference to Lévi-Strauss's exemplary analysis, from *Structural Anthropology*, of the spatial disposition of buildings in the Winnebago, one of the Great Lakes tribes, might be of some help here. The tribe is divided into two subgroups ("moieties"), "those who are from above" and "those who are from below"; when we ask an individual to draw on a piece of paper, or on sand, the ground-plan of his or her village (the spatial disposition of cottages), we obtain two quite different answers, depending on his or her belonging to one subgroup or the other. Both perceive the village as a circle; but for one subgroup there is another circle of central houses within this circle, so that we have two concentric circles; while for the other subgroup the circle is split in two by a clear dividing line. In other words, a member of the first subgroup (let us call it "conservative-corporatist") perceives the ground-plan of the village as a ring of houses more or less symmetrically disposed around the central temple, whereas a member of the second ("revolutionary-antagonistic") subgroup perceives his or her village as two distinct heaps of houses separated by an invisible frontier.[19] The point Lévi-Strauss wants to make is that this example should in no way entice us into cultural relativism, according to which the perception of social space depends on the observer's group-belonging: the very splitting into the two "relative" perceptions implies a hidden reference to a constant—not the objective, "actual" disposition of buildings but a traumatic kernel, a fundamental antagonism the inhabitants of the village were unable to symbolize, to account for, to "internalize," to come to terms with, an imbalance in social relations that prevented the community from stabilizing itself into a harmonious whole. The two perceptions of the ground-plan are simply two mutually exclusive endeavors to cope with this traumatic antagonism, to heal its wound by means of the imposition of a balanced symbolic structure.

It is here that we can see in what precise sense the Real intervenes through anamorphosis. First we have the "actual," "objective" arrangement of the houses, and then its two different symbolizations that both distort, in an anamorphic way, the actual arrangement. The "Real" here, however, is not the actual arrangement, but the traumatic core of the social antagonism that distorts the tribe members' view of the actual antagonism. The Real is thus the disavowed X on account of which our vision of reality is anamorphically distorted. (And, incidentally, this three-level structure is exactly homologous to Freud's three-level structure of the interpretation of dreams: the real kernel of the dream is not the dream's latent thought that is displaced/translated into the explicit texture of the dream, but the unconscious desire that inscribes itself through the very distortion of the latent thought into the explicit texture.)

This means that the Lacanian Real is on the side of virtuality against "real reality." Let us take the case of pain: there is an intimate connection between the virtualization of reality and the emergence of an infinite and infinitized bodily pain, much stronger than the usual one: do not biogenetics and Virtual Reality combined open up new "enhanced" possibilities of torture, new and unheard-of horizons of extending our ability to endure pain (through increasing our sensory capacity to sustain pain, and, above all, through inventing new forms of inflicting pain by directly attacking the brain centers for pain, bypassing sensorial perception)? Perhaps, the ultimate Sadean image of an "undead" victim of torture who can sustain endless pain, without having the escape into death at his or her disposal, is also about to become reality. In such a constellation, the ultimate real/impossible pain is no longer the pain of the real body, but the "absolute" virtual–real pain caused by Virtual Reality, in which I move (and, of course, the same goes for sexual pleasure). An even more "real" approach is opened up by the prospect of the direct manipulation of our neurons: although it is not "real" in the sense of being part of the reality in which we live, this pain is impossible–real.

And does the same not go for emotions? Take Hitchcock's dream of the direct manipulation of emotions: in the future, a director will no longer have to invent intricate narratives, and shoot them in a convincingly heartbreaking way, in order to generate the proper emotional response in the viewer; he will be able to use a computer keyboard connected directly with the viewer's brain, so that, if he presses the right buttons, the viewer will experience sorrow, terror, sympathy, fear . . . he will experience them *for real*, to an extent never equaled by situations "in real life" that evoke fear or sorrow. It is especially crucial to distinguish this procedure from that of Virtual Reality: fear is aroused not by generating virtual images and sounds that provoke fear, but through a *direct* intervention that bypasses the level of perception altogether. This, not the "return to real life" from the artificial virtual environment, is the Real generated by radical virtualization itself. What we experience here at its purest is thus the gap between reality and the Real: the Real of, say, the sexual pleasure generated by direct neuronal intervention does not take place in the reality of bodily contacts, yet it is "more real than reality," more intense. This Real thus undermines the division between objects in reality and their virtual simulacra: if, in Virtual Reality, I stage an impossible fantasy, I can experience there an "artificial" sexual enjoyment that is much more "real" than anything I can experience in "real reality."

The Real is thus *simultaneously* the Thing to which direct access is not possible and the obstacle that prevents this direct access; the Thing that eludes our grasp and the distorting screen that makes us miss the Thing. More precisely, the Real is ultimately the very shift of perspective from the first standpoint to the second. Remember Adorno's well-known analysis of the antagonistic character of the notion of society: on a first approach, the split between the two notions of society (the Anglo-Saxon individualistic-nominalistic notion, and the Durkheimian organicist notion of society as a totality that preexists individuals) seems irremediable; we seem to be dealing with a true Kantian antinomy that cannot be resolved through a higher "dialectical synthesis," and elevates society into an inaccessible Thing-in-itself; on a second approach, however, we should merely take note of how this radical antinomy that seems to preclude our access to the Thing *already is the Thing itself*—the fundamental feature of today's society is the irreconcilable antagonism between Totality and the individual.

Is this shift not structurally analogous to the one in the Russian joke about Rabinovitch from the late Soviet era? Rabinovitch wants to emigrate from the Soviet Union for two reasons: "First, I'm afraid that, if the socialist order disintegrates, all the blame for the Communists' crimes will be put on us, the Jews." To the state bureaucrat's exclamation "But nothing will ever change in the Soviet Union! Socialism is here to stay, forever!," Rabinovitch calmly answers: "That's my second reason!" The very problem—obstacle—retroactively appears as its own solution, since what prevents us from accessing the Thing directly is the Thing itself. The change here lies only in the shift of perspective—and, in exactly the same way, the final twist in Kafka's parable about the Door of the Law relies on a mere shift of perspective: the man from the country, confronted with the Door of the Law preventing his access to the terrifying Thing (the Law), is told that, from the very beginning, the door has been there only for him—that is to say, he has been included in the Law from the very beginning—the Law was not just the Thing that fascinated his gaze, it always-already returned its gaze. And, to go a step further, is not exactly the same shift at the very core of the Christian experience? It is the very radical separation of man from God that unites us with God, since, in the figure of Christ, God is thoroughly separated from himself—thus the point is not to "overcome" the gap that separates us from God, but to take note of how this gap is internal to God Himself (Christianity as the ultimate version of the Rabinovitch joke).

This notion of shift also allows us a new approach to Nietzsche, who, in one and the same text (Beyond Good and Evil), seems to advocate two opposed epistemological stances:[20] on the one hand, the notion of truth as the unbearable Real Thing, as dangerous, even lethal, like the direct gaze into Plato's sun, so that the problem is how much truth a man can endure without diluting or falsifying it; on the other, the "postmodern" notion that appearance is more valuable than stupid reality: that, ultimately, there is no final Reality, just the interplay of multiple appearances, so that one should abandon the very opposition between reality and appearance—man's greatness is that he is able to give priority to brilliant aesthetic appearance over gray reality. So, in Badiou's terms, the passion for the Real versus the passion for semblance. How are we to read these two opposed stances together? Is Nietzsche simply inconsistent here, oscillating between two mutually exclusive views? Or is there a "third way"? That is to say: what if the two opposed options (passion for the Real/ passion for the semblance) illustrate Nietzsche's struggle, his failure to articulate the "right" position whose formulation eluded him? Back to our example from Lévi-Strauss: it should now be clear what his position is. Everything is not just the interplay of appearances, there is a Real—this Real, however, is not the inaccessible Thing, but the gap that prevents our access to it, the "rock" of the antagonism that distorts our view of the perceived object through a partial perspective. And, again, the "truth" is not the "real" state of things, that is, the "direct" view of the object without perspectival distortion, but the very Real of the antagonism that causes perspectival distortion. The site of truth is not the way "things really are in themselves," beyond their perspectival distortions, but the very gap, passage, that separates one perspective from another, the gap (in this case social antagonism) that makes the two perspectives radically *incommensurable*. The "Real as impossible" is the cause of the impossibility of ever attaining the "neutral" nonperspectival view of the object. There is a truth; everything is not relative—but this truth is the truth of the perspectival distortion as such, not the truth distorted by the partial view from a one-sided perspective.

So when Nietzsche affirms that truth is a perspective, this assertion is to be read together with Lenin's notion of the partisan/ partial character of knowledge (the (in)famous *partij'nost*): in a class society, "true" objective knowledge is possible only from the "interested" revolutionary standpoint. This means neither an epistemologically "naive" reliance on the "objective knowledge" available when we get rid of our partial prejudices and preconceptions, and adopt a "neutral" view, nor the (complementary) relativist view that there is no ultimate truth, only multiple subjective perspectives. Both terms have to be fully asserted: there is, among the multitude of opinions, a true knowledge, and this knowledge is accessible only from an "interested" partial position.[21]

There are two fundamentally different ways for us to relate to the Void of the Real, best captured by the paradox of Achilles and the tortoise: while Achilles can easily overtake the tortoise, he can never reach her. We either posit the Void as the impossible-real Limit of the human experience that we can approach only indefinitely, the absolute Thing toward which we have to maintain a proper distance— if we get too close to it, we get burned by the sun. . . . Our attitude toward the Void is thus thoroughly ambivalent, marked by simultaneous attraction and repulsion. Or we posit it as that through which we should (and, in a way, even always-already have) pass(ed)— therein lies the gist of the Hegelian concept of "tarrying with the negative," which Lacan illustrated in his notion of the deep connection between the death drive and creative sublimation: in order for (symbolic) creation to take place, the death drive (the Hegelian self-relating absolute negativity) has to accomplish its work of, precisely, emptying the place, and thus making it ready for creation. Instead of the old topic of phenomenal objects disappearing/dissolving in the vortex of the Thing, we get objects which are *nothing but* the Void of the Thing embodied, or, in Hegelese, objects in which negativity assumes positive existence.

In religious terms, this passage from the Impossible-Real One (Thing), refracted/reflected in the multitude of its appearances, to the Twosome is the very passage from Judaism to Christianity: the Jewish God is the Real Thing of Beyond, while the divine dimension of Christ is just a tiny grimace, an imperceptible shade, which differentiates him from other (ordinary) humans. Christ is not "sublime" in the sense of an "object elevated to the dignity of a Thing," he is not a stand-in for the impossible Thing-God; he is, rather, "the Thing itself," or, more accurately, "the Thing itself" is nothing but the rupture/gap which makes Christ not fully human. Christ is thus the ultimate *Mann ohne Eigenschaften*, the man without properties, as Robert Musil would have put it: he is "more than man"—and why should we not take the risk here of referring to Nietzsche: he is *over-man?*—precisely insofar as one can say, apropos of his figure: "Ecce homo," precisely insofar as he is a man *kat' exochen*, "as such," a man with no distinctions, no particular features. This means that Christ is a singular universal—just as, for Rancière, those without a proper place within the social order stand for humanity as such, in its universal dimension.[22] This does not mean that Christ is somehow divided between the "human" and the "divine" parts of his nature: the minimal difference which we encounter in the logic of subtraction is not the difference between two parts, but the difference between two aspects of—or, to put it in Nietzsche's terms again, two *perspectives on*—one and the same entity; it is the difference of an entity with itself. Christ is not man *and* overman: he is overman insofar as he is a man *sans phrase*, that is, what separates the two is just a shift in perspective.[23]

In other words, Christ is the very minimal difference between "man" and "overman"—what Nietzsche, that consummate and self-professed Antichrist, called "High Noon": the thin edge between Before and After, the Old and the New, the Real and the Symbolic, between God-Father-Thing and the community of the Spirit. As such, he is both at the same time: the extreme point of the Old (the culmination of the logic of sacrifice, himself standing for the extreme sacrifice, for the self-relating exchange in which we no longer pay God, but God pays for us to Himself, and thus involves us in debt indefinitely), and its overcoming (the shift of perspective) into the New. It is just a tiny nuance, an almost imperceptible shift in perspective, that distinguishes Christ's sacrifice from the atheist assertion of a life which needs no sacrifice. This, then, is, perhaps, all that happens in the passage from Judaism to Christianity: this shift from purification to subtraction.

No wonder, then, that Nietzsche's attitude toward Christ himself was far more ambivalent than his attitude toward Christianity: when Nietzsche elevates *amor fati*, the full acceptance of suffering and pain, as the only way to redemption—that is, to a full assertion of life— is he not uncannily close to Christ's message of death on the Cross as the triumph of eternal life? This means that the properly Christian Redemption is not simply the undoing of the Fall, but *stricto sensu* its repetition. The key to Saint Paul's theology is repetition: Christ as the redemptive repetition of Adam. Adam has fallen, Christ has risen again; Christ is therefore "the last Adam" (1 Corinthians 15:45–49). Through Adam, as sons of Adam, we are lost, condemned to sin and suffering; through Christ, we are redeemed. This, however, does not mean that Adam's Fall (and the subsequent instauration of the Law) was a simple contingency—that is to say, that, if Adam had chosen obedience to God, there would have been no sin and no Law: *there would also have been no love.*

Adam's first choice was thus forced: the first choice has to be that of sin. This logic was first deployed by Hegel in his opposition of abstract and concrete universality. On a first approach, things may seem clear and unambiguous: the philosopher of abstract universality is Kant (and, in Kant's steps, Fichte); in Kant's philosophy, the Universal (the moral Law) functions as the abstract *Sollen*, that which "ought to be," and which, as such, possesses a terrorist/subversive potential—the Universal stands for an impossible/unconditional demand, whose power of negativity is destined to undermine any concrete totality; against this tradition of abstract/negative universality opposed to its particular content, Hegel emphasizes how true universality is actualized in the series of concrete determinations perceived by the abstract point of view of Understanding as the obstacle to the full realization of the Universal (for example, the universal moral Duty is actualized, becomes effective, through the concrete wealth of particular human passions and strivings devalued by Kant as "pathological" obstacles). However, are matters really so simple?

Let us recall Hegel's analysis of phrenology, which closes the chapter on "Observing Reason" in his *Phenomenology of Spirit*: Hegel resorts here to an explicit phallic metaphor in order to explain the opposition of the two possible readings of the proposition "the Spirit is a bone" (the vulgar materialist "reductionist" reading—the shape of a person's skull actually and directly determines the features of his or her mind—and the speculative reading—the spirit is strong enough to assert its identity with even the most inert stuff, and to "sublate" it—that is to say, even the most inert stuff cannot escape the Spirit's power of mediation). The vulgar materialist reading is like the approach which sees in the phallus only the organ of urination, while the speculative reading is also able to discern in it the much higher function of insemination (that is, precisely, "conception" as the biological anticipation of concept). On a first approach, we are dealing here with the well-known elementary movement of *Aufhebung* ("sublation"): you must go through the lowest in order once more to reach the highest, the lost totality (you must lose immediate reality in the self-contraction of the "night of the world" in order to regain it as "posited," mediated by the symbolic activity of the subject; you must renounce the immediate organic Whole, and abandon yourself to the mortifying activity of abstract Understanding, in order to regain the lost totality at a higher, "mediated" level, as the totality of Reason). This move thus seems to offer itself as an ideal target of the standard criticism: yes, of course, Hegel recognizes the horror of the psychotic self-contraction and its "loss of reality," yes, he acknowledges the need for abstract dismemberment, but only as a step, a detour, on the triumphant path which, according to the inexorable dialectical necessity, leads us back to the reconstituted organic Whole. My contention is that such a reading misses the point of Hegel's argumentation:

> The depth which the Spirit brings forth from within—but only as far as its picture-thinking consciousness where it lets it remain—and the ignorance of this consciousness about what it really is saying, are the same conjunction of the high and the low which, in the living being, Nature naively expresses when it combines the organ of its highest fulfillment, the organ of generation, with the organ of urination. The infinite judgment, qua infinite, would be the fulfillment of life that comprehends itself; the consciousness of the infinite judgment that remains at the level of picture-thinking behaves as urination.[24]

A close reading of this passage makes it clear that Hegel's point is not that, in contrast to the vulgar empiricist mind, which sees only urination, the proper speculative attitude has to choose insemination. The paradox is that the direct choice of insemination is the sure way to miss it: it is not possible to choose the "true meaning" directly. That is, one has to begin by making the "wrong" choice (of urination)—the true speculative meaning emerges only through repeated reading, as the aftereffect (or byproduct) of the first, "wrong," reading. And the same goes for social life, in which the direct choice of the "concrete universality" of a particular ethical life-world can end only in a regression to a premodern organic society that denies the infinite right of subjectivity as the fundamental feature of modernity. Since the subject-citizen of a modern state can no longer accept his immersion in some particular social role that confers on him a determinate place within the organic social Whole, the only way to the rational totality of the modern State leads through the horror of the revolutionary Terror: one should ruthlessly tear up the constraints of premodern organic "concrete universality," and fully assert the infinite right of subjectivity in its abstract negativity. In other words, the point of Hegel's deservedly famous analysis of the revolutionary Terror in *Phenomenology* is not the rather obvious insight into how the revolutionary project involved the unilateral direct assertion of abstract Universal Reason, and was, as such, doomed to perish in self-destructive fury, since it was unable to organize the transposition of its revolutionary energy into a concrete, stable, and differentiated social order; Hegel's point is, rather, the enigma of why, despite the fact that revolutionary Terror was a historical deadlock, we have to pass through it in order to arrive at the modern rational State.

There is a clear parallel between this necessity of making the wrong choice in order to arrive at the proper result (of choosing "urination" in order to arrive at "insemination"), and the structure of the Rabinovitch joke, in which, also, the only way to arrive at the true reason is via the wrong, first reason. Surprisingly, one can learn the same lesson even from Colin Wilson's *From Atlantis to the Sphinx*, one in the endless series of New Age airport pocketbook variations on the theme of "recovering the lost wisdom of the ancient world" (the book's subtitle). In his concluding chapter, Wilson opposes two types of knowledge: the "ancient" intuitive, encompassing one, which makes us experience the underlying rhythm of reality directly ("right-brain awareness"), and the modern knowledge of self-consciousness and the rational dissection of reality ("left-brain awareness"). After all his high praise for the magic powers of ancient collective consciousness, the author acknowledges that, although this type of knowledge had enormous advantages, "it was essentially limited. It was too pleasant, too relaxed, and its achievements tended to be communal"; so it was necessary for human evolution to escape from this state to the more active attitude of rational technological domination. Today, of course, we are confronted with the prospect of reuniting the two halves, and "recovering the lost wisdom," combining it with modern achievements (the usual story of how modern science itself, in its most radical achievements—quantum physics, and so on—already points toward the self-sublation of the mechanistic view in the direction of the holistic universe dominated by a hidden pattern of the "dance of life").

Here, however, Wilson's book takes an unexpected turn: how will this synthesis occur? Wilson is intelligent enough to reject both predominant views: the directly premodern one, according to which the history of the "rationalist West" was a mere aberration, and we should simply return to the old wisdom; as well as the pseudo-Hegelian notion of a "synthesis" that would somehow maintain the balance between the two spiritual principles, enabling us to keep the best of both worlds—that is, to regain the lost Unity while maintaining the achievements based on its loss (technical progress, individualist dynamics, etc.). Against both these versions, Wilson emphasizes that the next stage, overcoming the limitations of the Western rationalist/individualist stance, must somehow emerge from within this Western stance. Wilson locates its source in the force of imagination: the Western principle of self-consciousness and individuation also brought about a breathtaking rise in our imaginative capacity, and if we develop this capacity to its uttermost, it will lead to a new level of collective consciousness, of shared imagination. So the surprising conclusion is that the longed-for next step in human evolution, the step beyond the alienation from nature and the universe as a Whole, "has already happened. It has been happening for the past 3,500 years. Now all we have to do is recognize it" (the last sentence of the book).

So what happened 3,500 years ago—that is, around 2000 BC? The decline of the Old Kingdom of Egypt, the highest achievement of ancient wisdom, and the rise of the new, violent cultures out of which modern European consciousness arose—in short, the Fall itself, the fateful forgetting of the ancient wisdom that enabled us to maintain a direct contact with the "dance of life." If we take these statements literally, the unavoidable conclusion is that the moment of the Fall (the forgetting of the ancient wisdom) coincides with its exact opposite—with the longed-for next step in evolution. Here we have the properly Hegelian matrix of development: the Fall is in itself already its own self-sublation, the wound is in itself already its own healing, so that the perception that we are dealing with the Fall is ultimately a misperception, an effect of our distorted perspective—all we have to do is to accomplish the move from In-itself to For-itself, that is, to change our perspective, and recognize how the longed-for reversal is already operative in what has been going on for a long time. The inner logic of the movement from one stage to another is not that from one extreme to the opposite extreme, and then to their higher unity; the second passage is, rather, simply the radicalization of the first passage. The problem with the "Western mechanistic attitude" is not that it forgot-repressed the ancient holistic Wisdom, but that it did not break with it thoroughly enough: it continued to perceive the new universe (of the discursive stance) from the perspective of the old one, of the "ancient wisdom," and, of course, from this perspective, the new universe cannot but appear as the catastrophic world which came "after the Fall." We rise again from the Fall not by undoing its effects, but in recognizing the longed-for liberation in the Fall itself.[25]

It is with regard to the theme of the Fall that the opposition between Gnosticism and Christianity is most conspicuous. Both share the notion of the Fall—for Gnosticism, however, we are dealing with the Fall from the pure spiritual dimension into the inert material world, with the notion that we strive to return to our lost spiritual home; while for Christianity, the Fall is not really a Fall at all, but "in itself" its very opposite, the emergence of freedom. There is no place from which we have fallen; what came before was just the stupid natural existence. The task is thus not to return to a previous "higher" existence, but to transform our lives in this world. In Saint Thomas's Gospel, we can read: "His disciples said to him: 'When will the resurrection of the dead take place, and when will the new world come?' He said to them: 'That (resurrection) which you are awaiting has (already) come, but you do not recognize it.'"[26] This is the key "Hegelian" point of Christianity: the resurrection of the dead is not a "real event" which will take place sometime in the future, but something that is already here—we merely have to shift our subjective position.

The problem with the Fall is thus not that it is in itself a Fall, but, precisely, that, in itself, it is already a Salvation which we misrecognize as a Fall. Consequently, Salvation consists not in our reversing the direction of the Fall, but in recognizing Salvation in the Fall itself. To put it in simplified narrative terms: it is not that we must first make the wrong move, introducing a split, so that we can then heal the wound, and return to a higher unity: the first move is already the right move, but we can learn this only too late. Here again, one should apply Hegel's dictum that Evil resides in the gaze which perceives Evil: the true Fall is in the very gaze which misperceives the first move as a Fall. It is not that things went wrong, downhill, first with Adam, and were then restored with Christ: Adam and Christ are *one and the same* ("Christ is Adam"—perhaps the ultimate speculative judgment); all that changes in order for us to pass from one to the other is the perspective. Here we should recall the Hegelian notion of speculative judgment, which *should be read twice*: to get at its truth, we should not go on to another judgment, but just *read the same judgment again, including in it our own position of enunciation*.

And the same goes for the relationship between "abstract" and "concrete" universality: in a first move, universality has to be asserted in its negativity, as exclusive of all particular content—that is to say, not as an all-encompassing container, but as the destructive force which undermines every particular content. One should not oppose to this violent force of abstraction, of tearing-apart the concrete fabric of reality, concrete universality as the totality which mediates all particular content within its organic Whole; on the contrary, the true Hegelian "concrete universality" is the very movement of negativity which splits universality *from within*, reducing it to one of the particular elements, one of its own species. It is only at this moment, when universality, as it were, loses the distance of an abstract container, and *enters its own frame*, that it becomes truly *concrete*.

Adam and Christ also relate as "negation" and "negation of negation," but in the above-mentioned precise meaning—Adam is

Christ "in itself," and Christ's Redemption is not the "negation" of the Fall, but its accomplishment, in exactly the same sense that, according to Saint Paul, Christ accomplishes the Law. In a wonderful alternative history essay, "Pontius Pilate Spares Jesus,"[27] Josiah Ober entertains the hypothesis that Pilate did not yield to the pressure of the mob, and spared Christ, who survived, and thrived to a very great age as a successful preacher, supported by the Roman authorities against the Jewish establishment; his sect gradually became dominant, and also became the Roman state religion, albeit in its more Jewish version, without the Cross and Redemption by Christ's death. The coincidence of Fall and Redemption makes this hypothesis *stricto sensu* beside the point.[28]

Both Christianity and Hegel transpose the gap which separates us from the Absolute into the Absolute itself. In terms of the gap that separates man from God, this means that this gap is transposed into God Himself, as the gap between Christ and the God-Father—Christ is the new, second, Job. In ethical terms, this means that we should acknowledge the positive force of Evil without regressing to Manichean dualism. The only way to do this was deployed by Schelling: Evil is not "substantially" different from Good, a positive force opposing it—Evil is *substantially the same* as Good, simply a different mode of (or perspective on) it. To put it in Kierkegaard's terms, Evil is Good "in becoming": the radically negative break, rupture, with the old substantial order as the condition of a new universality.

In a classic Bosnian joke, a guy visits his best friend, and finds him playing tennis in a backyard court—Agassi, Sampras, and other top players are waiting there for a game with him. Surprised, the guy asks his friend: "But you were never much of a tennis player! How did you manage to improve your game so fast?" The friend answers: "You see that pond behind my house? There's a magic golden fish in it; if you tell her a wish, she immediately makes it come true!" The friend goes to the pond, sees the fish, tells her that he wants his closet full of money, and runs home to check up on it. When he approaches his closet, he sees honey dripping out from it everywhere. Furious, he runs back to his friend, and tells him: "But I wanted money, not honey!" The friend replies calmly: "Oh, I forgot to tell you—the fish has impaired hearing, and sometimes misunderstands the wish. Can't you see how bored I am, running around playing this stupid game? Do you think I really asked for an outstanding tennis?" Is there not a Kafkaesque twist to this story? There is a God; He is good, and answers our requests—the origin of evil, and of our misfortunes, is just that He does not hear very well and often misunderstands our prayers.[29]

In his reading of Sylvia Plath's poem "The Other," Tim Kendall points out the limitations of "decoding" her late poems—that is, of precisely identifying the biographical details to which a poem refers: the impossibility of doing it, the way the reader gets lost in the multitude of contradictory indications concerning not only the events in question (is this a reference to that precise conflict between Sylvia and Ted recorded in her diary?); but also the fact that the very identity of the speaker (is the "I" who speaks here Sylvia, or her rival, Assia?) and the tone in which a line is meant (irony? disdain? is Assia perceived as a threat to Sylvia, or as her intimate double, part of herself? or both?), "force the reader to become implicated in this unstable world, where meaning can only be derived from the external imposition of tone and emphasis. The reader must perform the same cognitive leaps, and pursue the same hints and suspicions, as the poem's speaker."[30] In addition to all this, it is not simply that one failure overlaps with another: it is through this very failure to show its "true reference in reality" directly that a poem sublates its "pathological" idiosyncrasy, and generates its properly universal artistic impact. This shift, this sudden recognition of how the very obstacle preventing us from reaching the Thing Itself enables us to identify directly with it (with the deadlock at its heart), defines the properly Christian form of identification: it is ultimately identification with a failure—and, consequently, since the object of identification is God, God Himself must be shown to fail.

In his (unpublished) seminar on anxiety (1962–1963), Lacan explained why a certain fragment of our daily life is picked up as the element into which, in our dreams, an unconscious desire gets invested (the function of the "daily residues [*Tagesreste*]": as a rule, the selected fragment has the character of something unfinished, open (a sentence cut short, an act not brought to fruition, something which was about to happen but, due to some circumstance or other, did not happen): "*The condition of interruption, linked to the message, causes a coincidence with the structure of desire, which by definition has a dimension of lack or inconclusion.*"[31] Are we not, in the case of Christian identification, dealing with something similar? In our very failure, we identify with the divine failure, with Christ's confrontation with "*Che vuoi?*," with the enigma of the Other's desire ("Why are you doing this to me, Father? What do you want from me?"). In one of the most intriguing passages from 2 Corinthians, Paul defends himself against false apostles by assuming a stance of carnivalesque foolishness:

> I wish that you would bear with me in a little foolishness, but indeed you do bear with me. For such men are false apostles, deceitful workers, masquerading as Christ's apostles. And no wonder, for even Satan masquerades as an angel of light. It is no great thing therefore if his ministers also masquerade as servants of righteousness, whose end will be according to their works. I say again, let no one think me foolish. But if so, yet receive me as foolish, that I also may boast a little. That which I speak, I don't speak according to the Lord, but as in foolishness, in this confidence of boasting. Seeing that many boast after the flesh, I will also boast. For you bear with the foolish gladly, being wise. If I must boast, I will boast of the things that concern my weakness. Most gladly therefore I will rather glory in my weaknesses, that the power of Christ may rest on me. Therefore I take pleasure in weaknesses, in injuries, in necessities, in persecutions, in distresses, for Christ's sake. For when I am weak, then am I strong. I have become foolish in boasting. You compelled me, for I ought to have been commended by you, for in nothing was I inferior to the very best apostles, though I am nothing.

This reference to the carnivalesque reversal is not to be understood along the lines of "I am weak in order to make the strength of God visible," and so on. It is that, in my weakness and ridicule, when I am mocked and laughed at, I am identified with Christ, who was mocked and laughed at—Christ, the ultimate divine Fool, deprived of all majesty and dignity. In Paul's view, false apostles are mighty, taking themselves seriously, so the only way for a true prophet to behave is to mock oneself like a fool. However, it is no less wrong simply to identify Paul's stance with the Bakhtinian carnivalesque reversal of existing relations of authority: this notion is deeply pagan, it relies on the insight that hierarchical power relations are fragile, since they disturb the natural balance of the Order of Things, so, sooner or later, authority has to return to dust.

The true intervention of Eternity in Time occurs when this Lord of Misrule, the Fool-King, does not stand just for a passing carnivalesque suspension of Order, reminding us of the instability of things in their eternal circuit, of the great Wheel of Fortune ("What goes up must come down!"), but starts to function as a founding figure of a New Order. We are one with God only when God is no longer one with Himself, but abandons Himself, "internalizes" the radical distance which separates us from Him. Our radical experience of separation from God is the very feature which unites us with Him—not in the usual mystical sense that only through such an experience do we open ourselves to the radical Otherness of God, but in a sense similar to the one in which Kant claims that humiliation and pain are the only transcendental feelings: it is preposterous to think that I can identify myself with the divine bliss—only when I experience the infinite pain of separation from God do I share an experience with God Himself (Christ on the Cross).

CHAPTER 4

FROM LAW TO LOVE . . . AND BACK

The paradox of the "Higgs field" is widely discussed in contemporary particle physics. Left to their own devices in an environment to which they can pass on their energy, all physical systems will eventually assume a state of lowest energy; to put it in another way, the more mass we take from a system, the more we lower its energy level, until we reach the vacuum state at which the energy level is zero. There are, however, phenomena which compel us to posit the hypothesis that there has to be something (some substance) that *we cannot take away from a given system without raising that system's energy*—this "something" is called the Higgs field: once this field *appears* in a vessel that has been pumped empty, and whose temperature has been lowered as much as possible, its energy will be further *lowered*. The "something" that thus appears is a something that contains less energy than nothing, a "something" that is characterized by an overall negative energy—in short, what we get here is the physical version of how "something appears out of nothing."

On the philosophico-ontological level, this is what Lacan is aiming at when he emphasizes the difference between the Freudian death drive and the so-called "nirvana principle" according to which every life system tends toward the lowest level of tension, ultimately toward death: "nothingness" (the void, being deprived of all substance) and the lowest level of energy paradoxically no longer coincide, that is, it is "cheaper" (it costs the system less energy) to persist in "something" than to dwell in "nothing," at the lowest level of tension, or in the void, the dissolution of all order. It is this distance that sustains the death drive: far from being the same as the nirvana principle (the striving toward the dissolution of all life tension, the longing for the return to original nothingness), the death drive is the tension which persists and insists beyond and against the nirvana principle. In other words, far from being opposed to the pleasure principle, the nirvana principle is its highest and most radical expression. In this precise sense, the death drive stands for its exact opposite, for the dimension of the "undead," of a spectral life which insists beyond (biological) death. And, in psychoanalysis proper, does not this paradox of the Higgs field also embody the mystery of symbolic castration—*a deprivation, a gesture of taking away, which is in itself giving, productive, generating, opening up and sustaining the space in which something(s) can appear?*

Insofar as "death" and "life" designate for Saint Paul two existential (subjective) positions, not "objective" facts, we are fully justified in raising the old Pauline question: who is really alive today?[1] What if we are "really alive" only if and when we engage ourselves with an excessive intensity which puts us beyond "mere life"? What if, when we focus on mere survival, even if it is qualified as "having a good time," what we ultimately lose is life itself? What if the Palestinian suicide bomber on the point of blowing himself (and others) up is, in an emphatic sense, "more alive" than the American soldier engaged in a war in front of a computer screen hundreds of miles away from the enemy, or a New York yuppie jogging along the Hudson river in order to keep his body in shape? Or, in terms of the psychoanalytic clinic, what if a hysteric is truly alive in her permanent, excessive, provoking questioning of her existence, while an obsessional is the very model of choosing a "life in death"? That is to say, is not the ultimate aim of his compulsive rituals to prevent the "thing" from happening—this "thing" being the excess of life itself? Is not the catastrophe he fears the fact that, finally, *something will really happen* to him? Or, in terms of the revolutionary process, what if the difference that separates Lenin's era from Stalinism is, again, the difference between life and death?

There is an apparently marginal feature which clearly illustrates this point: the basic attitude of a Stalinist Communist is that of following the correct Party line against "Rightist" or "Leftist" deviation—in short, to steer a safe middle course; for authentic Leninism, in clear contrast, there is ultimately only one deviation, the Centrist one—that of "playing it safe," of opportunistically avoiding the risk of clearly and excessively "taking sides." There was no "deeper historical necessity," for example, in the sudden shift of Soviet policy from "War Communism" to the "New Economic Policy" in 1921—it was just a desperate strategic zigzag between the Leftist and the Rightist line, or, as Lenin himself put it in 1922, the Bolsheviks made "all the possible mistakes." This excessive "taking sides," this permanent imbalance of zigzag, is ultimately (the revolutionary political) life itself—for a Leninist, the ultimate name of the counterrevolutionary Right is "Center" itself, the fear of introducing a radical imbalance into the social edifice.

It is a properly Nietzschean paradox that the greatest loser in this apparent assertion of Life against all transcendent Causes is actual life itself. What makes life "worth living" is the very *excess of life*: the awareness that there is something for which we are ready to risk our life (we may call this excess "freedom," "honor," "dignity," "autonomy," etc.). Only when we are ready to take this risk are we really alive. So when Hölderlin wrote: "To live is to defend a form," this form is not simply a *Lebensform*, but the form of the excess-of-life, the way this excess violently inscribes itself into the life-texture. Chesterton makes this point apropos of the paradox of courage:

> A soldier surrounded by enemies, if he is to cut his way out, needs to combine a strong desire for living with a strange carelessness about dying. He must not merely cling to life, for then he will be a coward, and will not escape. He must not merely wait for death, for then he will be a suicide, and will not escape. He must seek his life in a spirit of furious indifference to it; he must desire life like water and yet drink death like wine.[2]

The "postmetaphysical" survivalist stance of the Last Men ends up in an anemic spectacle of life dragging on as its own shadow. It is within this horizon that we should appreciate today's growing rejection of the death penalty: what we should be able to discern is the hidden "biopolitics" which sustains this rejection. Those who assert the "sacredness of life," defending it against the threat of transcendent powers which parasitize on it, end up in a "supervised world in which we'll live painlessly, safely—and tediously,"[3] a world in which, for the sake of its very official goal—a long, pleasurable life—all real pleasures are prohibited or strictly controlled (smoking, drugs, food. . .). Spielberg's *Saving Private Ryan* is the latest example of this survivalist attitude toward dying, with its "demystifying"

presentation of war as a meaningless slaughter which nothing can really justify—as such, it provides the best possible justification for Colin Powell's "No-casualties-on-our-side" military doctrine.

On today's market, we find a whole series of products deprived of their malignant property: coffee without caffeine, cream without fat, beer without alcohol. . . . And the list goes on: what about virtual sex as sex without sex, the Colin Powell doctrine of warfare with no casualties (on our side, of course) as warfare without warfare, the contemporary redefinition of politics as the art of expert administration as politics without politics, up to today's tolerant liberal multiculturalism as an experience of the Other deprived of its Otherness (the idealized Other who dances fascinating dances, and has an ecologically sound, holistic approach to reality, while features like wife-beating remain out of sight)? Virtual Reality simply generalizes this procedure of offering a product deprived of its substance: it provides reality itself deprived of its substance, of the hard resistant kernel of the Real—just as decaffeinated coffee smells and tastes like real coffee without being the real coffee, Virtual Reality is experienced as reality without being so.

Is this not the attitude of the hedonistic Last Man? Everything is permitted, you can enjoy everything, but deprived of its substance, which makes it dangerous. (This is also the Last Man's revolution— "revolution without revolution.") Is this not one of the two versions of Lacan's anti-Dostoevsky motto "If God doesn't exist, everything is prohibited"? (1) God is dead, we live in a permissive universe, you should strive for pleasure, you should avoid dangerous excesses, so everything is prohibited if it is not deprived of its substance. (2) If God is dead, the superego enjoins you to enjoy, but every determinate enjoyment is already a betrayal of the unconditional one, so it should be prohibited. The nutritive version of this is to enjoy the Thing Itself directly: why bother with coffee? Inject caffeine directly into your bloodstream! Why bother with sensual perceptions and excitation by external reality? Take drugs which directly affect your brain! And if God does exist, then everything is permitted—to those who claim to act directly on behalf of God, as the instruments of His will; clearly, a direct link to God justifies our violation of any "merely human" constraints and considerations (as in Stalinism, where the reference to the big Other of historical Necessity justifies absolute ruthlessness).

Today's hedonism combines pleasure with constraint: it is no longer the old notion of the right balance between pleasure and constraint, but a kind of pseudo-Hegelian immediate coincidence of opposites: action and reaction should coincide; the very thing that causes damage should already be the remedy. The ultimate example is arguably a *chocolate laxative*, available in the USA, with the paradoxical injunction: Do you have constipation? Eat more of this chocolate! (that is, of the very thing that causes constipation). Do we not find here a weird version of Wagner's famous "Only the spear which caused the wound can heal it," from *Parsifal*? And is not a negative proof of the hegemony of this stance the fact that genuine unconstrained consumption (in all its forms: drugs, free sex, smoking) is emerging as the main danger? The fight against such danger is one of the principal motivations of today's biopolitics. Solutions are desperately sought that would reproduce the paradox of the chocolate laxative. The main contender is safe sex—a term which makes us appreciate the truth of the old saying "Isn't having sex with a condom like taking a shower with your raincoat on?" The ultimate goal here would be, along the lines of decaffeinated coffee, to invent opium without opium: no wonder marijuana is so popular among liberals who want to legalize it—it already is a kind of opium without opium.

In his scathing remarks on Wagner, Nietzsche diagnosed Wagner's decadence as consisting in a combination of asceticism and excessive morbid excitation: the excitation is false, artificial, morbid, hysterical, and the ensuing peace is also a fake, that of an almost medical tranquilization. This, for Nietzsche, was the universe of *Parsifal*, which embodied Wagner's capitulation to the appeal of Christianity: the ultimate fake of Christianity is that it sustains its official message of inner peace and redemption by a morbid excitation, namely, a fixation on the suffering, mutilated corpse of Christ. The very term passion here is revealing in its ambiguity: passion as suffering, passion as passion—as if the only thing that can arouse passion is the sick spectacle of passive suffering. The key question, of course, is: can Saint Paul be reduced to mixture of morbid excitation and ascetic renunciation? Is not the Pauline *agape* precisely an attempt to break out of the morbid cycle of law and sin sustaining each other?

More generally, what, exactly, is the status of the excess, the too-muchness (Eric Santner) of life with regard to itself? Is this excess generated only by the turn of life against itself, so that it actualizes itself only in the guise of the morbid undeadness of the sick passion? Or, in Lacanese: is the excess of *jouissance* over pleasure generated only through the reversal of the repression of desire into the desire for repression, of the renunciation of desire into the desire for renunciation, and so on? It is crucial to reject this version, and to assert some kind of primordial excess or too-muchness of life itself: human life never coincides with itself; to be fully alive means to be larger than life, and a morbid denial of life is not a denial of life itself, but, rather, the denial of this excess. How, then, are the two excesses related: the excess inherent to life itself, and the excess generated by the denial of life? Is it not that the excess generated by the denial of life is a kind of revenge, a return of the excess repressed by the denial of life?

A state of emergency coinciding with the normal state is the political formula of this predicament: in today's antiterrorist politics, we find the same mixture of morbid excitation and tranquilization. The official aim of Homeland Security appeals to the US population in early 2003, intended to make them ready for a terrorist attack, was to calm people down: everything is under control, just follow the rules and carry on with your life. However, the very warning that people must be ready for a large-scale attack sustained the tension: the effort to keep the situation under control asserted the prospect of a catastrophe in a negative way. The aim was to get the population used to leading their daily lives under the threat of a looming catastrophe, and thus to introduce a kind of permanent state of emergency (since, let us not forget, we were informed in the fall of 2002 that the War on Terror will go on for decades, at least for our lifetime). We should therefore interpret the different levels of the Alert Code (red, orange) as a state strategy to control the necessary level of excitation, and it is precisely through such a permanent state of emergency, in which we are interpellated to *participate* through our readiness, that the power asserts its hold over us.

In *The Others* (Alejandro Amenabar, 2001), Nicole Kidman, a mother who lives with her two young children in a haunted house on Jersey Island, discovers at the end that they are all ghosts: a couple of years before, she first strangled her children and then shot herself (it is the "intruders" who disturb their peace from time to time who are the real people, potential buyers interested in their house). The only interesting feature of this rather ineffective *Sixth Sense*-type final twist is the precise reason why Kidman returns as a ghost: she cannot assume her Medea-like act—in a way, continuing to live as a ghost (who doesn't know that she is one) symbolizes her ethical compromise, her unreadiness to confront the terrible act constitutive of subjectivity. This reversal is not simply symmetrical: instead of ghosts disturbing real people, appearing to them, it is the real people who disturb the ghosts, appearing to them. Is it not like this when— to paraphrase Saint Paul—we are not alive in our "real" lives? It is not that, in such a case, the promise of real life haunts us in a ghost-like form? Today we are like the anemic Greek philosophers who read Paul's words on the Resurrection with ironic laughter. The only Absolute acceptable within this horizon is a negative one: absolute Evil, whose paradigmatic figure today is that of the Holocaust. The evocation of the Holocaust serves as a warning of what the ultimate result of the submission of Life to some higher Goal is.

What characterizes the human universe is the complication in the relationship between the living and the dead: as Freud wrote apropos of the killing of the primordial father, the murdered father returns more powerful than ever in the guise of the "virtual" symbolic authority. What is uncanny here is the gap which opens up with the reduplication of life and death in the symbolic medium, on account of the noncoincidence of the two circles: we get people who are still alive, although symbolically they are already dead, and people who are already dead, although symbolically they are still alive. The double meaning of the term "spirit" (if we ignore the alcoholic association)—"pure" spirituality and ghosts—is thus structurally necessary: no (pure) spirit without its obscene supplement, ghosts, their spectral pseudo-materiality, the "living dead." The category of the "undead" is crucial here: those who are not dead, although they are no longer alive, and continue to haunt us. The fundamental problem here is how to prevent the dead from returning, how to put them properly to rest.

I am tempted to construct a mock Hegelian triad here: a living organism is negated first by its death (a once-living organism dies); then, more radically, in absolute negation, by something which always-already *was* dead (an inanimate thing, a stone); finally, in a "negation of negation," there emerges a mock synthesis in the guise of the apparition of the "living dead," the undead, a spectral entity which, in its death itself, as dead, continues to live. Or, to put it in the terms of the Greimasian semiotic square: the main opposition is the one between alive and dead (as inanimate, never having been alive); this couple is then redoubled by the couple of dead (as no longer alive) and undead (as alive after death).

Perhaps we should therefore add another twist to the prohibition on killing: at its most fundamental, this prohibition concerns not the living, but the dead. "Don't kill . . ." whom? *The dead.* You can kill the living—on condition that you bury them properly, that you perform the proper rites. These rites, of course, are fundamentally ambivalent: through them, you show your respect for the dead, and thereby prevent them from returning to haunt you. This ambivalence of the work of mourning is clearly discernible in the two opposed attitudes toward the dead: on the one hand, we should not ignore them, but mark their death properly, perform the proper rituals; on the other hand, there is something obscene, transgressive, in talking about the dead at all. We find the same ambivalence in the "speak no ill of the dead" motto: we should not judge the dead—yet is it not a fact that it is only the dead whom we can really adequately judge, since their life is completed?

When, in *Being and Time*, Heidegger insists that death is the only event which cannot be taken over by another subject for me—another cannot die for me, in my place—the obvious counterexample is Christ himself: did he not, in the extreme gesture of interpassivity, take over for us the ultimate passive experience of dying? Christ dies so that we are given a chance to live forever. . . . The problem here is not only that, obviously, we *don't* live forever (the answer to this is that it is the Holy Spirit, the community of believers, which lives forever), but the subjective status of Christ: when he was dying on the Cross, did he know about his Resurrection-to-come? If he did then it was all a game, the supreme divine comedy, since Christ knew his suffering was just a spectacle with a guaranteed good outcome— in short, Christ was faking despair in his "Father, why hast thou forsaken me?" If he didn't, then in what precise sense was Christ (also) divine? Did God the Father limit the scope of knowledge of Christ's mind to that of a common human consciousness, so that Christ actually thought he was dying abandoned by his father? Was Christ, in effect, occupying the position of the son in the wonderful joke about the rabbi who turns in despair to God, asking Him what he should do with his bad son, who has deeply disappointed him; God calmly answers: "Do the same as I did: write a new testament!"

What is crucial here is the radical ambiguity of the term "the faith of Jesus Christ," which can be read as subjective or objective genitive: it can be either "the faith of Christ" or "the faith / of us, believers / in Christ." Either we are redeemed because of Christ's pure faith, or we are redeemed by our faith in Christ, if and insofar as we believe in him. Perhaps there is a way to read the two meanings together: what we are called to believe in is not Christ's divinity as such but, rather, his faith, his sinless purity. What Christianity proposes is the figure of Christ as our *subject supposed to believe*: in our ordinary lives, we never truly believe, but we can at least have the consolation that there is One who truly believes (the function of what Lacan, in his seminar *Encore*, called *y'a de l'un*). The final twist here, however, is that on the Cross, Christ himself has to suspend his belief momentarily. So maybe, at a deeper level, Christ is, rather, our (believers') *subject supposed* NOT *to believe*: it is not our belief we transpose onto others, but, rather, our disbelief itself. Instead of doubting, mocking, and questioning things while believing through the Other, we can also transpose onto the Other the nagging doubt, thus regaining the ability to believe. (And is there not, in exactly the same way, also the function of the *subject supposed not to know?* Take little children who are supposed not to know the "facts of life," and whose blessed ignorance we, knowing adults, are supposed to protect by shielding them from brutal reality; or the wife who is supposed not to know about her husband's secret affair, and willingly plays this role even if she really knows all about it, like the young wife in *The Age of Innocence*; or, in academia, the role we assume when we ask someone: "OK, I'll pretend I don't know anything about this topic—try to explain it to me from scratch!") And, perhaps, the true communion with Christ, the true *imitatio Christi*, is to participate in Christ's doubt and disbelief.

There are two main interpretations of how Christ's death deals with sin: sacrificial and participatory.[4] In the first one, we humans are guilty of sin, the consequence of which is death; however, God presented Christ, the sinless one, as a sacrifice to die in our place— through the shedding of his blood, we may be forgiven and freed from condemnation. In the second one, human beings lived "in Adam," in the sphere of sinful humanity, under the reign of sin and death. Christ became a human being, sharing the fate of those "in Adam" to the end (dying on the Cross), but, having been sinless, faithful to God, he was raised from the dead by God to become the firstborn son of a new, redeemed humanity. In baptism, believers die with Christ—they die to their old life "in Adam," and become new creations, freed from the power of sin.

The first approach is legalistic: there is guilt to be paid for, and, by paying our debt for us, Christ redeemed us (and, of course, thereby forever indebted us); from the participationist perspective, on the contrary, people are freed from sin not by Christ's death as such, but by sharing in Christ's death, by dying to sin, to the way of flesh. Adam and Christ are thus, in a way, "corporate persons" in whom people live: we either live "in Adam" (under the power of sin and death), or we live "in Christ" (as children of God, freed from guilt and the dominion of sin). We die with Christ "in Adam" (as Adamesque creatures), and then we begin a new life "in Christ"— or, as Paul put it, "all of us who have been baptized into Christ Jesus were baptized into his death": "we have been buried with him by baptism into death, so that, just as Christ was raised from the dead by the glory of the Father, so we too might walk in newness of life" (Romans 6:2–4). This reading also tends to deny the direct divine nature of Christ: Christ is a man who, on account of his purity and sacrifice, after his death, "was appointed, or became, Messiah when God raised him from the dead and thus 'adopted' him as his son."[5] From this perspective, Christ's divinity is not his "natural" property, but his symbolic mandate, the title conferred on him by God—after following in his footsteps, we all become "sons of God": "For in Christ Jesus you are all sons of God, through faith. For as many of you as were baptized into Christ have put on Christ. There is no longer Jew or Greek, no longer slave or free, no longer male and female, for you are all one in Christ Jesus" (Galatians 3:26–28).

Which of these two readings, then, is the right one? Here again we encounter the structure of the forced choice: in the abstract, of course, the participationist reading is the correct one, while the sacrificial reading "misses the point" of Christ's gesture; the only way to the participationist reading, however, is through the sacrificial one, through its inherent overcoming. The sacrificial reading is the way Christ's gesture appears within the very horizon that Christ wanted to leave behind, within the horizon for which we die in identifying with Christ: within the horizon of the Law (symbolic exchange, guilt and its atonement, sin and the price to be paid for it), Christ's death cannot but appear as the ultimate assertion of the Law, as the elevation of the Law into an unconditional superego agency which burdens us, its subjects, with guilt, and with a debt we will never be able to repay. In a properly dialectical move, love and grace thus coincide with their radical opposite, with the unbearable pressure of an "irrational" Kafkaesque law. "Love" appears as the name (the mask, even) of an Infinite Law, of a Law which, as it were, self-sublates itself, of a Law which no longer imposes specific, determinate, prohibitions and/or injunctions (do this, don't do that . . .), but just reverberates as an empty tautological Prohibition: *don't* . . . , of a Law in which everything is simultaneously prohibited and permitted (i.e. enjoined).

Take a weird but crucial feature of Krzysztof Kieślowski's *Decalogue*: the rock song performed during the credits is the only place in the entire *Decalogue* series where the Ten Commandments are mentioned—*in the inverted form of injunctions to violate the Ten Commandments*—"Kill, rape, steal, beat up your mother and father. . . ." This subversion of the prohibition into the obscene injunction to transgress the Law is entailed by the very formal procedure of Kieślowski's dramatization of a law: the dramatic staging automatically cancels the (purely intellectual) negation, shifting the focus on the imposing image of the act of, say, killing, irrespective of its ethical preamble (+ or –, recommended or prohibited)—like the Freudian unconscious, the dramatic staging knows of no negation. In his famous reflections on negativity and the Decalogue, Kenneth Burke reads the Ten Commandments through the opposition between the notional level and the level of imagery: "though the injunction 'Thou shalt not kill' is in essence an idea, in its role as imagery it can but strike the resonant gong: 'Kill!'"[6] This is the Lacanian opposition between the symbolic Law and the obscene call of the superego at its purest: all the negations are powerless, and turn into mere denegations, so that what remains is the obscene intrusive reverberation of "Kill! Kill!"

This reversal of prohibitions into imperatives is a strictly tautological gesture which simply elaborates what is already contained in the prohibitions, insofar as, according to Saint Paul, the Law itself generates the desire to violate it. Along the same lines, in contrast to the Law's precise prohibitions ("You shall not kill, steal . . ."), the true superego injunction is just the truncated "You shall not!"—do what? This gap opens up the abyss of the superego: you yourself should know or guess what you should not do, so that you are put in an impossible position of always and a priori being under suspicion of violating some (unknown) prohibition. More precisely, the superego splits every determinate commandment into two complementary, albeit asymmetrical, parts—"You shall not kill!," for instance, is split into the formal-indeterminate "You shall not!" and the obscene direct injunction "Kill!" The silent dialogue which sustains this operation is thus: "You shall not!" "I shall not—what? I have no idea what is being demanded of me! *Che vuoi?*" "You shall not!" "This is driving me crazy, being under pressure to do something without knowing what, feeling guilty without knowing of what, so I'll just explode, and start killing!" Thus killing is the desperate response to the impenetrable abstract superego prohibition.

In the eyes of this "crazy" Law, we are always-already guilty, without even knowing what, exactly, we are guilty of. This Law is the meta-Law, the Law of the state of emergency in which positive legal order is suspended, the "pure" Law, the form of ordering/prohibiting "as such," the enunciation of an Injunction deprived of any content. And, in effect, does not the Stalinist regime, among others, provide clear proof of how such an "irrational" unconditional Law coincides with love? In the eyes of the Stalinist Law, anyone can be proclaimed guilty at any point (accused of counterrevolutionary activity); the very denial of guilt is considered the ultimate proof of guilt, and so on—but, simultaneously, obeying a deep structural necessity, the relationship of the Stalinist subjects to their Leader is determined as that of *love*, of infinite love for the wise Leader.

How did Stalinism function on the level of political guidelines? On a first approach, things may seem clear: Stalinism was a strictly centralized system of command, so the top leadership issued directives which had to be obeyed all the way down. Here, however, we encounter the first enigma: "how can one obey when one has not been told clearly what to do?"[7] In the collectivization drive of 1929–1930, for example, "no detailed instructions about how to collectivize were ever issued, and local officials who asked for such instructions were rebuked." All that was actually given was a sign, Stalin's speech to the Communist Academy in December 1929, where he demanded that the kulaks should be "liquidated as a class."

The lower-level cadres, eager to fulfill this command, anxious not to be accused of tolerance toward the class enemy and a lack of vigilance, naturally overfulfilled the order; it is only then that we get "the closest thing to an explicit public policy statement," Stalin's famous letter "Dizzy with success," published in Pravda on March 1, 1930, which repudiates the excesses in what had been done without precise instructions by local officials.

How, then, could these local cadres orient themselves? Were they totally at a loss, face to face with an unspecified general order? Not quite: the gap was ambiguously filled in by the so-called "signals," the key element of the Stalinist semiotic space: "important policy changes were often 'signaled' rather than communicated in the form of a clear and detailed directive." Such signals "indicated a shift of policy in a particular area without spelling out exactly what the new policy entailed or how it should be implemented." They consisted of, say, an article by Stalin discussing a minor point of cultural politics, an anonymous derogatory comment in Pravda, a criticism of a local party functionary, the unexpected praise of a provincial worker, even an explanatory note on a historical event which had taken place hundreds of years before. The message to be deciphered from such signals was mostly quantitative; it concerned the level of pure intensities more than concrete content: "faster," "slow down" (the pace of collectivization), and so on. These signals were of two basic types: the main type was the "hardline" signal to proceed faster, to crush the enemy more mercilessly, even if one violated the existing laws. In the big radicalization of the policy toward the Orthodox Church at the end of the 1920s, for instance, the signal enjoined the mass closings and destruction of the churches and the arrests of priests, acts which ran counter to the explicit existing laws (such instructions were issued to local party organizations, but treated as a secret not to be published). The advantage of such a *modus operandi* is obvious: since these signals were never explicitly stated, they were much easier to repudiate or reinterpret than explicit policy statements. The complementary opposite signal pointed in the direction of relaxation and tolerance, as a rule attributed to Stalin himself, putting the blame for the "excesses" on lower-level officials who did not understand Stalin's policy. Such a signal was also issued in an informal way—for example, Stalin personally phoned a writer (Pasternak), asking him, with feigned surprise, why he had not published a new book recently; the news circulated fast on the intelligentsia grapevine. The ambiguity was thus total: a local official, confronted by a general unspecified order, was caught in the unsolvable dilemma of how to avoid being accused of leniency, but also how to avoid being scapegoated as responsible for the "excesses." We should not forget, however, that the deadlock of the Party leadership emitting these signals was no less debilitating: with total power in their hands, they were not even able to issue explicit orders about what was to be done.

The problem (for Giorgio Agamben, among others) is how (if at all) we are to pass from this superego hyperbole of the Law to love proper: is love just the mode of appearance of this Law, is this superego hyperbole the hidden "truth" of love, is the infinite "irrational" Law thus the hidden third term, the vanishing mediator, between Law and love, or is there love also beyond the infinite-obscene Law? The text on the back cover of the French edition of Giorgio Agamben's *Le temps qui reste*, his reading of Paul's Epistle to the Romans,[8] provides such a precise résumé of the book that one can surmise that it was written by Agamben himself—it is worth quoting in full:

> If it is true that every work of the past attains its complete readability only in certain moments of its own history which one should know how to grasp, this book originates in the conviction that there is a kind of secret link, which we should not miss at any price, between Paul's letters and our epoch. From this perspective, one of the most often read and commented texts of our entire cultural tradition undoubtedly acquires a new readability which displaces and reorients the canons of its interpretation: Paul is no longer the founder of a new religion, but the most demanding representative of the Jewish messianism; no longer the inventor of universality, but the one who overcame the division of peoples with a new division and who introduced in it a remainder; no longer the proclamation of a new identity and of a new vocation, but the revoking of every identity and

of every vocation; no longer the simple critique of the Law, but its opening toward a use beyond every system of law. And, in the heart of all these motifs, there is a new experience of time which, inverting the relation between the past and the future, between memory and hope, constitutes the messianic *kairos*, not as the end of time, but as the very paradigm of the present time, of all the present times.

The first problem with this focus (not on the end of time, but) on the condensed *time to arrive at the end of time* is its more than obvious formalism: what Agamben describes as a messianic experience is the pure formal structure of such an experience without any specific determinations that would elaborate the claim that Benjamin "repeats" Paul: *why* is today's moment a unique moment which renders Paul's letters readable? Is it because the emerging New World (Dis)Order is parallel to the Roman Empire (the thesis of Negri and Hardt)? Furthermore, in defense of Alain Badiou (whose book on Paul[9] is Agamben's implicit target in the quoted passage), I am tempted to assert the fundamental equality of the statements opposed in the above résumé: what if the way to found a new religion is precisely through bringing the preceding logic (in this case, of Jewish messianism) to its end? What if the only way to invent a new universality is precisely through overcoming the old divisions with a new, more radical division which introduces an indivisible remainder into the social body? What if the proclamation of a new identity and of a new vocation can take place only if it functions as the revoking of every identity and every vocation? What if the truly radical critique of the Law equals its opening toward a use beyond every system of law? Furthermore, when Agamben introduces the triad of Whole, Part, and Remainder, is he not following the Hegelian paradox of a genus which has only one species, the other species being the genus itself? The Remainder is nothing other than the excessive element which gives body to the genus itself, the Hegelian "reflexive determination" in the guise of which the genus encounters itself within its species.

When Agamben claims that the messianic dimension is not a safe neutral universality encompassing all the species, indifferent toward their (specific) differences, but, rather, the noncoincidence of each particular element with itself, is he not thereby reinventing the central thesis of the "logic of the signifier" according to which universality acquires actual existence in a particular element that is unable to achieve its full identity? A universality "comes to itself," is posited "as such," in the gap which divides a particular element not from other elements, but *from itself*. For example, in politics, as discussed by Laclau and Rancière, the properly democratic subject is the "remainder," the element of the Whole deprived of any particular features which would give him or her a specific place within the Whole, the element whose position with regard to the Whole is that of internal exclusion. Unable to occupy its proper specific place, such a democratic subject gives body to universality as such. So when one opposes radical political universality (radical emancipatory egalitarianism) to a universality grounded in exception (for example, "universal human rights" which secretly privilege some particular groups and exclude others), the point is not simply that the latter does not cover all particulars, that there is a "rest," a remainder, while radical universality "really includes all and everyone"; the point is, rather, that *the singular agent of radical universality is the Remainder itself,* that which has no proper place in the "official" universality grounded in exception. Radical universality "covers all its particular content" precisely insofar as it is linked through a kind of umbilical cord to the Remainder—its logic is: "it is those who are excluded, with no proper place within the global order, who directly embody true universality, who represent the Whole in contrast to all others who stand only for their particular interests." Lacking any specific difference, such a paradoxical element stands for the absolute difference, for pure Difference as such. In this precise sense, Pauline universality is not mute universality as the empty neutral container of its particular content, but a "struggling universality," a universality the actual existence of which is a radical division which cuts through the entire particular content.

And when Agamben cogently describes the "Kafkaesque" dimension of the Pauline distance toward the Old Testament law, when he interprets the opposition of Law and Love as an opposition internal to the Law itself, as the opposition between a positive law with precise prescriptions and prohibitions and the Kafkaesque unconditional Law which is, as such, pure potentiality, which cannot be executed, or even translated into positive norms, but remains an abstract injunction making us all guilty precisely because we don't even know what we are guilty of,[10] does he not thereby delineate the opposition between Law and its superego excess-supplement? One should effectively correlate unconditional superego guilt and the mercy of love—two figures of the excess, the excess of guilt without proportion to what I actually did, and the excess of mercy without proportion to what I deserve for my acts. In short, the superego excess is ultimately nothing but the inscription back into the domain of the Law, the reflection-into-Law, of the Love which abolishes ("sublates") the Law. The advent of the New Pact is thus not simply a new order which leaves the old Law behind, but the Nietzschean "High Noon," the time of the cleaving in two, of the minimal, invisible difference which separates the excess of the Law itself from the Love beyond Law.

Is the relationship between law (legal justice) and mercy in fact the relationship between necessity and choice (one *has* to obey the law, while mercy is, by definition, dispensed as a free and excessive act, as something that the agent of mercy is free to do or not to do—mercy under compulsion is not mercy but, at its best, a travesty of mercy)? What if, on a deeper level, the relationship is the opposite one? What if, with regard to the law, we have the freedom to choose (to obey or violate it), while mercy is obligatory, we *have* to display it—mercy is an unnecessary excess which, as such, has to occur? (And does not the law always take this freedom of ours into account, not only by punishing us for its transgression, but by providing escapes from punishment through its ambiguity and inconsistency?) Is it not a fact that showing mercy is the only way for a Master to demonstrate his supralegal authority? If a Master were merely to guarantee the full application of the law, of legal regulations, he would be deprived of his authority, and turn into a mere figure of knowledge, the agent of the discourse of the university.[11] This applies even to Stalin himself: we should never forget that, as the (now available) minutes of the meetings of the Politburo and Central Committee from the 1930s demonstrate, Stalin's direct interventions were, as a rule, those of displaying mercy. When younger CC members, eager to prove their revolutionary fervor, demanded the instant death penalty for Bukharin, Stalin always intervened and said: "Patience! His guilt is not yet proven!" or something similar. Of course this was a hypocritical attitude—Stalin was well aware that he himself generated this destructive fervor, that the younger members were eager to please him—nonetheless, this appearance of mercy is necessary.

Here, however, we confront the crucial alternative: is Pauline love the obverse of the obscene superego Law that cannot be executed and specified into particular regulations? Are we, in effect, dealing with two sides of the same coin? Agamben focuses on the *as-if-not* stance from the famous Pauline passage in which he instructs believers in the messianic time neither to escape from the world of social obligations, nor simply to accomplish a social revolution, replacing one set of social obligations with another, but to continue to participate in the world of social obligations through an attitude of suspension ("cry *as if* you are not crying, deal with money *as if* you are without it," and so on):

> Let each of you remain in the condition in which you were called. . . . I mean, brothers and sisters, the appointed time has grown short; from now on, let even those who have wives be as though they had none, and those who mourn as though they were not mourning, and those who rejoice as though they were not rejoicing, and those who buy as though they had no possessions, and those who deal with the world as though they had no dealings with it. For the present form of this world is passing away. (1 Corinthians 7:20, 7:29–31)

Agamben is right here to emphasize that this stance has nothing to do with the legitimization of the existing power relations, in the sense of "stay what you are, what you were interpellated into (a slave, a Jew . . .), just maintain a distance toward it." It has nothing to do with the standard version of Oriental Wisdom which imposes indifference toward worldly affairs (in the sense of the *Bhagavad-Gita*: accomplish your worldly acts as if it is not you who are doing them, as if their final result does not matter): the key difference is that, in Paul, the distance is not that of a disengaged observer aware of the nullity of worldly passions, but that of a thoroughly engaged fighter who ignores distinctions that are not relevant to the struggle. It is also to be opposed to the usual *as if* attitude of philosophers of fiction, from Bentham to Vaihinger: it is not that of the fetishist disavowal which pertains to the symbolic order ("although I know very well that the judge is not an honest man, I treat him, the representative of the Law, *as if* he were . . ."), but that of the disavowal of the symbolic realm itself: I use symbolic obligations, but I am not performatively bound by them. However, Agamben reads this suspension as a purely formal gesture of distance: "faith" has no positive content, it is nothing but this distance-toward-itself, this self-suspension, of the Law. Here Agamben refers to the Hegelian notion of "sublation [*Aufhebung*]": Pauline love is not the cancellation or destructive negation of the Law, but its accomplishment in the sense of "sublation," where the Law is retained through its very suspension, as a subordinate (potential) moment of a higher actual unity. Significantly, Agamben refers here also to Carl Schmitt's notion of the "state of exception" as the negation of the rule of law which is not its destruction, but its very founding gesture—the question remains, however, if Pauline love can be reduced to this founding suspension of the Law. In short, what if Romans has to be read together with Corinthians?

What we find in Paul is a commitment, an engaged position of struggle, an uncanny "interpellation" beyond ideological interpellation, an interpellation which suspends the performative force of the "normal" ideological interpellation that compels us to accept our determinate place within the sociosymbolic edifice. Can we thus say, in reading *Paul avec Schmitt*, that love has the structure of a "state of emergency/exception" which suspends the "normal" functioning of one's emotional life? Is love not war also in this precise sense: when I fall violently and passionately in love, my balance is disturbed, the course of my life is derailed, logos turns into pathology, I lose my neutral capacity to reflect and judge; all my (other) abilities are suspended in their autonomy, subordinated to One Goal, colored by It—indeed, love is a malady? To paraphrase Paul, when we are in love, "we buy as though we have no possessions, we deal with the world as though we have no dealings with it," since all that ultimately matters is love itself.[12] Perhaps the gap which separates pleasure and *jouissance* is nowhere more palpable than in the situation when, after a long period of calm complaisant life, with its little pleasures, one all of a sudden falls passionately in love: love shatters our daily life as a heavy duty whose performance demands heavy sacrifices on the level of the "pleasure of principle"—how many things must a man renounce? "Freedom," drinks with friends, card evenings.

It is therefore crucial to distinguish between the Jewish-Pauline "state of emergency," the suspension of the "normal" immersion in life, and the standard Bakhtinian carnivalesque "state of exception" when everyday moral norms and hierarchies are suspended, and one is encouraged to indulge in transgressions: the two are opposed— that is to say, what the Pauline emergency suspends is not so much the explicit Law regulating our daily life, but, precisely, its obscene unwritten underside: when, in his series of *as if* prescriptions, Paul basically says: "obey the laws as if you are not obeying them," this means precisely that *we should suspend the obscene libidinal investment in the Law, the investment on account of which the Law generates/solicits its own transgression*. The ultimate paradox, of course, is that this is how the Jewish law, the main target of Paul's critique, functions: it is already a law deprived of its superego supplement, not relying on any obscene support. In short: in its "normal" functioning, the Law generates as the "collateral damage" of its imposition its own transgression/ excess (the vicious cycle of Law and sin described in an unsurpassable way in Corinthians), while in Judaism and Christianity, it is directly this excess itself which addresses us.

That is the ultimate alternative: is the opposition between Love and Law to be reduced to its "truth," the opposition, internal to the Law itself, between the determinate positive Law and the excessive superego injunction, the Law beyond every measure—that is to say, is the excess of Love with regard to the Law the form of appearance of a superego Law, of a Law beyond any determinate law; or is the excessive superego Law the way the dimension beyond the Law appears within the domain of the Law, so that the crucial step to be accomplished is the step (comparable to Nietzsche's "High Noon") from the excessive Law to Love, from the way Love appears within the domain of the Law to Love beyond the Law? Lacan himself struggled continuously with this same deeply Pauline problem: is there love beyond Law? Paradoxically (in view of the fact that the notion as unsurpassable Law is usually perceived as Jewish), in the very last page of *Four Fundamental Concepts*, he identifies this stance of love beyond Law as that of Spinoza, opposing it to the Kantian notion of moral Law as the ultimate horizon of our experience. In *Ethics of Psychoanalysis*, Lacan deals extensively with the Pauline dialectic of the Law and its transgression[13]—perhaps what we should do, therefore, is read this Pauline dialectic together with its corollary, Saint Paul's other paradigmatic passage, the one on love from 1 Corinthians 13:

> If I speak in the tongues of mortals and of angels, but do not have love, I am a noisy gong or a clanging cymbal. And if I have prophetic powers, and understand all mysteries and all knowledge, and if I have all faith, so as to remove mountains, but do not have love, I am nothing. If I give away all my possessions, and if I hand over my body so that I may boast [alt. trans.: to be burned], but do not have love, I gain nothing. . . .
>
> Love never ends. But as for prophecies, they will come to an end; as for tongues, they will cease; as for knowledge, it will come to an end. For we know only in part, and we prophesy only in part; but when the complete comes, the partial will come to an end. . . . For now we see in a mirror, dimly, but then we will see face to face. Now I know only in part; then I will know fully, even as I have been fully

known. And now faith, hope, and love abide, these three; and the greatest of these is love.

Crucial here is the clearly paradoxical place of Love with regard to All (to the completed series of knowledge or prophecies): first, Saint Paul claims that love is here even if we possess all of knowledge— then, in the second quoted paragraph, he claims that love is here only for incomplete beings, that is, beings who possess incomplete knowledge. When I "know fully . . . as I have been fully known," will there still be love? Although, in contrast to knowledge, "love never ends," it is clearly only "now" (while I am still incomplete) that "faith, hope, and love abide." The only way out of this deadlock is to read the two inconsistent claims according to Lacan's feminine formulas of sexuation:[14] even when it is "all" (complete, with no exception), the field of knowledge remains, in a way, non-all, incomplete—love is not an exception to the All of knowledge, but precisely that "nothing" which makes incomplete even the complete series/field of knowledge. In other words, the point of the claim that, even if I were to possess all knowledge, without love, I would be nothing, is not simply that with love, I am "something"—in love, I am also nothing, but, as it were, a Nothing humbly aware of itself, a Nothing paradoxically made rich through the very awareness of its lack.

Only a lacking, vulnerable being is capable of love: the ultimate mystery of love, therefore, is that incompleteness is, in a way, higher than completion. On the one hand, only an imperfect, lacking being loves: we love because we do not know all. On the other hand, even if we were to know everything, love would, inexplicably, still be higher than completed knowledge. Perhaps the true achievement of Christianity is to elevate a loving (imperfect) Being to the place of God, that is, of ultimate perfection. That is the kernel of the Christian experience. In the previous pagan attitude, imperfect earthly phenomena can serve as signs of the unattainable divine perfection. In Christianity, on the contrary, it is physical (or mental) perfection itself that is the sign of the imperfection (finitude, vulnerability, uncertainty) of you as the absolute person. Your physical beauty itself becomes a sign of this spiritual dimension—not the sign of your "higher" spiritual perfection, but the sign of you as a finite, vulnerable person. Only in this way do we really break out of idolatry. For this reason, the properly Christian relationship between sex and love is not the one between body and soul, but almost the opposite: in "pure" sex, the partner is reduced to a fantasy object, that is to say, pure sex is masturbation with a real partner who functions as a prop for our indulging in fantasies, while it is only through love that we can reach the Real (of the) Other. (This also accounts for the status of the Lady in courtly love: precisely because of its endless postponing of the consummation of the sexual act, courtly love remains on the level of sexual desire, not love—the proof of this is the fact that the Lady is reduced to a pure symbolic entity, indistinguishable from all others, not touched in the Real of her singularity.)

Lacan's extensive discussion of love in Encore is thus to be read in the Pauline sense, as opposed to the dialectic of the Law and its transgression: this second dialectic is clearly "masculine"/phallic, it involves the tension between the All (the universal Law) and its constitutive exception, while love is "feminine," it involves the paradoxes of the non-All.[15] Or—as Eric Santner put it in the context of Badiou's reading of Saint Paul—

> The Pauline question, in B's reformulation, is: Is all the subject within the figure of legal subjection? There are two answers to this—Lacanian answers: 1) there is a place of exception; 2) not all of the subject is within the figure of legal subjection. The key, however, as far as I can see, is to note that there is no direct path from legal subjection to "not all"; "not all" only opens up through a traversal of the fantasy of exception, which in its turn sustains the force of the figure of legal subjection. Put differently, "not all" is what you get with the traversal of fantasy.[16]

The co-dependency of law and sin (its transgression) thus obeys the Lacanian "masculine" logic of exception: "sin" is the very exception that sustains the Law. This means that love is not simply beyond the Law, but articulates itself as the stance of total immersion in the Law:

"not all of the subject is within the figure of legal subjection" eq
"there is nothing in the subject which escapes its legal subjecti
"Sin" is the very intimate resistant core on account of which the
ject experiences its relationship to the Law as that of subjection; it is
that on account of which the Law has to appear to the subject as a
foreign power crushing the subject.

This, then, is how we are to grasp the idea that Christianity
"accomplished/fulfilled" the Jewish Law: not by supplementing it
with the dimension of love, but by fully realizing the Law itself—
from this perspective, the problem with Judaism is not that it is "too
legal," but that it is not "legal" enough. A brief reference to Hegel
might be of some help here: when Hegel endeavors to resolve the
conflict between Law and love, he does not mobilize his standard
triad (the immediacy of the love link turns into its opposite, hate and
struggle, which calls for an external-alienated Law to regulate social
life; finally, in an act of magical "synthesis," Law and love are recon-
ciled in the organic totality of social life). The problem with the law
is not that it does not contain enough love, but, rather, the opposite
one: there is too much love in it—that is to say, social life appears to
me as dominated by an externally imposed Law in which I am unable to recognize myself, precisely insofar as I continue to cling to
the immediacy of love that feels threatened by the rule of Law. Consequently, Law loses its "alienated" character of an external force
brutally imposing itself on the subject the moment the subject re-
nounces its attachment to the pathological *agalma* deep within itself,
the notion that there is deep within it some precious treasure that
can only be loved, and cannot be submitted to the rule of Law. In
other words, the problem (today, even) is not how we are to supplement Law with true love (the authentic social link), but, on the contrary, how we are to accomplish the Law by getting rid of the
pathological stain of love.

Paul's negative appreciation of law is clear and unambiguous:
"For no human being will be justified in his sight by deeds pre-
scribed by the law, for through the law comes the knowledge of sin"
(Romans 3:20). "The sting of death is sin, and the power of sin is the

law" (1 Corinthians 15:56), and, consequently, "Christ redeemed us from the curse of the law" (Galatians 3:13). So when Paul says that "the letter kills, but the spirit gives life" (2 Corinthians 3:6), this letter is precisely the letter of the Law. The strongest proponents of this radical opposition between the law and the divine love moving him to grace are Lutheran theologians like Bultmann, for whom

> [t]he way of works of the Law and the way of grace and faith are mutually exclusive opposites. . . . Man's effort to achieve his salvation by keeping the Law only leads him into sin, *indeed this effort itself in the end is already sin*. . . . The Law brings to light that man is sinful, whether it be that his sinful desire leads him to transgression of the Law or that *that desire disguises itself in zeal for keeping the Law.*[17]

How are we to understand this? Why, then, did God proclaim Law in the first place? According to the standard reading of Paul, God gave Law to men in order to make them conscious of their sin, even to make them sin all the more, and thus make them aware of their need for the salvation that can occur only through divine grace—however, does this reading not involve a strange, perverse notion of God? As we have already seen, the only way to avoid such a perverse reading is to insist on the absolute identity of the two gestures: God does not first push us into Sin in order to create the need for Salvation, and then offer Himself as the Redeemer from the trouble into which He got us in the first place; it is not that the Fall is followed by Redemption: the Fall is *identical* to Redemption, it is "in itself" already Redemption. That is to say: what is "redemption"? The explosion of freedom, the breaking out of the natural enchainment—*and this, precisely, is what happens in the Fall.* We should bear in mind here the central tension of the Christian notion of the Fall: the Fall ("regression" to the natural state, enslavement to passions) is *stricto sensu* identical with the dimension from which we fall, that is, it is the very movement of the Fall that creates, opens up, what is lost in it.

We should be very precise here about the Christian "unplugging" from the domain of social mores, from the social substance of our being: the reference to the Jewish Law is crucial here—why? As Eric

Santner has pointed out, it is already the Jewish Law that relies on a gesture of "unplugging": by means of reference to the Law, Jews in diaspora maintain a distance toward the society in which they live. In short, the Jewish Law is not a social law like others: while other (pagan) laws regulate social exchange, the Jewish Law introduces a different dimension, that of divine justice which is radically heterogeneous with regard to the social law.[18] (Furthermore, this justice is different from the pagan notion of justice as reestablished balance, as the inexorable process of Fate that reestablishes the balance disturbed by human hubris: Jewish justice is the very opposite of the victorious reassertion of the right/might of the Whole over its parts—it is the vision of the final state in which all the wrongs done to individuals will be undone.) When Jews "unplug," and maintain a distance toward the society in which they live, they do not do it for the sake of their own different substantial identity—in a way, anti-Semitism is right here: the Jews are, in effect, "rootless," their Law is "abstract," it "extrapolates" them from the social Substance.

And there we have the radical gap that separates the Christian suspension of the Law, the passage from Law to love, from the pagan suspension of the social law: the highest (or, rather, deepest) point of every pagan Wisdom is, of course, also a radical "unplugging" (either the carnivalesque orgy, or direct immersion in the abyss of the primordial Void, in which all articulated differences are suspended); what is suspended here, however, is the "pagan" immanent law of the social, not the Jewish Law that already unplugs us from the social. When Christian mystics get too close to the pagan mystical experience, they bypass the Jewish experience of the Law—no wonder they often become ferocious anti-Semites. Christian anti-Semitism is, in effect, a clear sign of the Christian position's regression into paganism: it gets rid of the "rootless," universalist stance of Christianity proper by transposing it onto the Jewish Other; consequently, when Christianity loses the mediation of the Jewish Law, it loses the specific Christian dimension of Love itself, reducing Love to the pagan "cosmic feeling" of oneness with the universe. It is only reference to the Jewish Law that sustains the specific Christian notion of

Love that needs a distance, that thrives on differences, that has nothing to do with any kind of erasure of borders and immersion in
Oneness. (And within the Jewish experience, love remains on this
pagan level—that is to say, the Jewish experience is a unique combination of the new Law with pagan love, which accounts for its inner
tension.)

The trap to be avoided here is the opposition of the "external" social law (legal regulations, "mere legality") and the higher "internal" moral law, where the external social law may strike us as
contingent and irrational, while the internal law is fully assumed as
"our own": we should radically abandon the notion that external social institutions betray the authentic inner experience of the true
Transcendence of Otherness (in the guise, for example, of the opposition between the authentic "inner" experience of the divine and its
"external" reification into a religious institution in which the religious experience proper degenerates into an ideology legitimizing
power relations). If there is a lesson to be learned from Kafka, it is
that, in the opposition between internal and external, the divine dimension is on the side of the external. What can be more "divine"
than the traumatic encounter with the bureaucracy at its craziest—
when, say, a bureaucrat tells us that, legally, we don't exist? It is in
such encounters that we catch a glimpse of another order beyond
mere earthly everyday reality. There is no experience of the divine
without such a suspension of the Ethical. And far from being simply
external, this very externality (to sense, to symbolic integration)
holds us from within: Kafka's topic is precisely the obscene *jouissance*
through which bureaucracy addresses the subject on the level of the
disavowed innermost ("ex-timate," as Lacan would have put it) real
kernel of his being.

As such, bureaucratic knowledge is the very opposite of scientific
knowledge concerned with positive facts: its pervasiveness gives
birth to a certain gap best exemplified by the French "certificat d'existence," or by strange stories, reported from time to time, of how
(usually in Italy) some unfortunate individual, asking a certain favor
from a state apparatus, is informed that, according to the register, he

is officially dead or nonexistent, and that, in order to be able to make claims, he must first produce official documents that prove his existence—do we not find here the bureaucratic version of "in-between the two deaths"? When bureaucratic knowledge thus brings home the absurd discord between the Symbolic and the Real, it opens us up to the experience of an order that is radically heterogeneous to commonsense positive reality. Kafka was well aware of the deep link between bureaucracy and the divine: it is as if, in his work, Hegel's thesis on the State as the earthly existence of God is "bugged" in the Deleuzian sense of the term, given a properly obscene twist.

CHAPTER 5

SUBTRACTION, JEWISH AND CHRISTIAN

When they are dealing with an erotic-religious text like the Song of Songs, commentators hasten to warn us that its extreme and explicit erotic imagery is to be read allegorically, as a metaphor: when, for instance, the lover kisses the woman's lips, this "really means" that He imparts to the Jews the Ten Commandments. In short, what appears to be a description of a "purely human" sexual encounter symbolically conveys the spiritual communion of God and the Jewish people. However, the most perspicacious Bible scholars themselves are the first to emphasize the limits of such a metaphorical reading that dismisses the sexual content as "only a simile": it is precisely such a "symbolic" reading that is "purely human," that is to say, that persists in the external opposition of the symbol and its meaning, clumsily attaching a "deeper meaning" to the explosive sexual content. The literal reading (say, of the Song of Songs as almost pornographic eroticism) and the allegorical reading are two sides of the same operation: what they share is the common presupposition that "real" sexuality is "purely human," with no discernible divine dimension. (Of course, a question arises here: if sexuality is just a metaphor, why do we need this problematic detour in the first place? Why do we not convey the true spiritual content directly? Because, due to the limitations of our sensual finite nature, this content is not directly accessible to us?) What, however, if the Song of Songs is to be read not as an allegory but, much more literally, as the description of purely sensual erotic play? What if the "deeper" spiritual dimension is already operative in the passionate sexual interaction itself? The true task is thus not to reduce sexuality to a mere allegory, but to unearth the inherent "spiritual" dimension that forever separates human sexuality from animal coupling. Is it, however, possible to accomplish this step from allegory to full identity in Judaism? Is this not what Christianity is about, with its assertion of the direct identity of God and man?[1]

There is a further problem with the Song of Songs. The standard defense of "psychoanalytic Judaism" against Christianity involves two claims: first, it is only in Judaism that we encounter the anxiety of the traumatic Real of the Law, of the abyss of the Other's desire ("What do you want?"); Christianity covers up this abyss with love, that is, the imaginary reconciliation of God and humanity, in which the anxiety-provoking encounter with the Real is mitigated: now we know what the Other wants from us—God loves us, Christ's sacrifice is the ultimate proof of it. Second claim: do not texts like the Song of Songs demonstrate that Judaism, far from being (only) a religion of anxiety, is also and above all the religion of love, an even more intense love than Christianity? Is not the covenant between God and the Jewish people a supreme act of love? As I have just indicated, however, this Jewish love remains "metaphorical"; as such, it is itself the imaginary reconciliation of God and humanity in which the anxiety-provoking encounter with the Real is mitigated. Or—to put it in a direct and brutal way—is not the Song of Songs ideology at its purest, insofar as we conceive of ideology as the imaginary mitigating of a traumatic Real, as "the Real of the divine encounter with a human face"?

How, then, do we go from here to Christianity proper? The key to Christ is provided by the figure of Job, whose suffering prefigures that of Christ. What makes the Book of Job so provocative is not simply the presence of multiple perspectives without a clear resolution of their tension (the fact that Job's suffering involves a different perspective than that of religious reliance on God); Job's perplexity stems from the fact that he experiences God as an impenetrable Thing: he is uncertain what He wants from him in inflicting the ordeals to which he is submitted (the Lacanian "Che vuoi?"), and, consequently, he—Job—is unable to ascertain how he fits into the overall divine order, unable to recognize his place in it.

The almost unbearable impact of the Book of Job derives not so much from its narrative frame (the Devil appears as a conversational partner of God, and the two engage in a rather cruel experiment in order to test Job's faith), but in its final outcome. Far from providing some kind of satisfactory account of Job's undeserved suffering, God's appearance at the end ultimately amounts to pure boasting, a horror show with elements of farcical spectacle—a pure argument of authority grounded in a breathtaking display of power: "You see all that I can do? Can you do this? Who are you, then, to complain?" So what we get is neither the good God letting Job know that his suffering was just an ordeal destined to test his faith, nor a dark God beyond Law, the God of pure caprice, but, rather, a God who acts like someone caught in a moment of impotence—or, at the very least, weakness—and tries to escape His predicament by empty boasting. What we get at the end is a kind of cheap Hollywood horror show with lots of special effects—no wonder many commentators tend to dismiss Job's story as a remainder of the previous pagan mythology, which should have been excluded from the Bible.

Against this temptation, we should precisely locate the true greatness of Job: contrary to the usual notion of Job, he is not a patient sufferer, enduring his ordeal with a firm faith in God—on the contrary, he complains all the time, rejecting his fate (like Oedipus at Colonus, who is also usually misperceived as a patient victim resigned to his fate). When the three theologians-friends visit him, their line of argumentation is the standard ideological sophistry (if you are suffering, you must by definition have done something wrong, since God is just). Their argumentation, however, is not confined to the claim that Job must somehow be guilty: what is at stake on a more radical level is the meaning(lessness) of Job's suffering. Like Oedipus at Colonus, Job insists on the utter *meaninglessness* of his suffering—as the title of Job 27 says: "Job Maintains His Integrity."[2] In this way, the Book of Job provides what is perhaps the first exemplary case of the critique of ideology in human history, laying bare the basic discursive strategies of legitimizing suffering: Job's properly ethical dignity lies in the way he persistently rejects the notion that his suffering can have any meaning, either punishment for his past sins or the trial of his faith, against the three theologians who bombard him with possible meanings—and, surprisingly, God takes his side at the end, claiming that every word Job spoke was true, while every word the three theologians spoke was false.[3]

And it is in the context of this assertion of the meaninglessness of Job's suffering that we should insist on the parallel between Job and Christ, on Job's suffering announcing the Way of the Cross: Christ's suffering is also meaningless, not an act of meaningful exchange. The difference, of course, is that, in the case of Christ, the gap that separates the suffering, desperate man (Job) from God is transposed into God Himself, as His own radical splitting or, rather, self-abandonment. This means that we should risk a much more radical reading of Christ's "Father, why hast thou forsaken me?" than the usual one: since we are dealing here not with the gap between man and God, but with the split in God Himself, the solution cannot be for God to (re)appear in all His majesty, revealing to Christ the deeper meaning of his suffering (that he was the Innocent sacrificed to redeem humanity). Christ's "Father, why hast thou forsaken me?" is not a complaint to the omnipotent capricious God-Father whose ways are indecipherable to us, mortal humans, but a complaint that hints at an impotent God: it is rather like a child who, having believed in his father's powerfulness, discovers with horror that his father cannot help him. (To evoke an example from recent history: at the moment of Christ's Crucifixion, God-the-Father is in a position somewhat similar to that of the Bosnian father, made to witness the gang-rape of his own daughter, and to endure the ultimate trauma of her compassionate-reproachful gaze: "Father, why did you forsake me?" In short, with this "Father, why hast thou forsaken me?," it is God-the-Father who, in effect, dies, revealing His utter impotence, and thereupon rises from the dead in the guise of the Holy Spirit.)

Why did Job keep his silence after the boastful appearance of God? Is not this ridiculous boasting (the pompous battery of "Were you there when . . ." rhetorical questions: "Who is this whose ignorant words / Smear my design with darkness? / Were you there when I planned the earth, / Tell me, if you are so wise?" (Job 38:2–5)) the very mode of appearance of its opposite, to which one can answer by simply saying: "OK, if you can do all this, *why did you let me suffer in such a meaningless way?*" Do not God's thundering words make his silence, the absence of an answer, all the more palpable? What, then, if this was what Job perceived, and what kept him silent: he remained silent neither because he was crushed by God's overwhelming presence, nor because he wanted thereby to indicate his continuous resistance, that is, the fact that God avoided answering Job's question, but because, in a gesture of silent solidarity, he perceived the divine impotence. God is neither just nor unjust, simply impotent. What Job suddenly understood was that it *was not him, but God Himself, who was actually on trial in Job's calamities, and He failed* the test miserably. Even more pointedly, I am tempted to risk a radical anachronistic reading: Job foresaw God's own future suffering— "Today it's me, tomorrow it will be your own son, and there will be no one to intercede for him. What you see in me now is the prefiguration of your own Passion!"[4]

Since the function of the obscene superego supplement of the (divine) Law is to mask this impotence of the big Other, and since Christianity reveals this impotence, it is, quite logically, the first (and only) religion radically to leave behind the split between the official/public text and its obscene initiatory supplement: there is no hidden, untold story in it. In this precise sense, Christianity is the religion of Revelation: everything is revealed in it, no obscene superego supplement accompanies its public message. In Ancient Greek and Roman religions, the public text was always supplemented by secret initiatory rituals and orgies; on the other hand, all attempts to treat Christianity in the same way (to uncover Christ's "secret teaching" somehow encoded in the New Testament or found in apocryphal Gospels) amounts to its heretical reinscription into the pagan Gnostic tradition.

Apropos of Christianity as "revealed religion," we should thus ask the inevitable stupid question: what is actually revealed in it? That is to say: is it not a fact that *all* religions reveal some mystery through the prophets, who carry the divine message to humankind; even those who insist on the impenetrability of the *dieu obscur* imply that there is some secret that resists revelation, and in the Gnostic versions, this mystery is revealed to the select few in some initiatory ceremony. Significantly, Gnostic reinscriptions of Christianity insist precisely on the presence of such a hidden message to be deciphered in the official Christian text. So what is revealed in Christianity is not just the entire content, but, more specifically, that *there is nothing—no secret—behind* it to *be revealed*. To paraphrase Hegel's famous formula from *Phenomenology*: behind the curtain of the public text, there is only what we put there. Or—to formulate it even more pointedly, in more pathetic terms— what God reveals is not His hidden power, only His impotence as such,

Where, then, does Judaism stand with regard to this opposition? Is it not true that God's final appearance in the Job story, in which He boasts about the miracles and monsters He has generated, is precisely such an obscene fantasmatic spectacle destined to conceal this impotence? Here, however, matters are more complex. In his discussion of the Freudian figure of Moses, Eric Santner introduces the key distinction between symbolic history (the set of explicit mythical narratives and ideologico-ethical prescriptions that constitute the tradition of a community—what Hegel would have called its "ethical substance") and its obscene Other, the unacknowledgeable "spectral," fantasmatic secret history that actually sustains the explicit symbolic tradition, but has to remain foreclosed if it is to be operative.[5] What Freud endeavors to reconstitute in *Moses and Monotheism* (the story of the murder of Moses, etc.) is such a spectral history that haunts the space of Jewish religious tradition. One becomes a full member of a community not simply by identifying with its explicit symbolic tradition, but only when one also assumes the spectral dimension that sustains this tradition, the undead ghosts that haunt the living, the secret history of traumatic fantasies transmitted "between the lines," through the lacks and distortions of the explicit symbolic tradition—as Fernando Pessoa puts it: "Every dead man is probably still alive somewhere." Judaism's stubborn attachment to the unacknowledged violent founding gesture that haunts the public legal order as its spectral supplement enabled the Jews to persist and survive for thousands of years without land or a common institutional tradition: they refused to give up their ghost, to cut off the link to their secret, disavowed tradition. The paradox of Judaism is that it maintains fidelity to the founding violent Event precisely by *not* confessing, symbolizing it: this "repressed" status of the Event is what gives Judaism its unprecedented vitality.

Does this mean, however, that the split between the "official" texts of the Law, with their abstract legal asexual character (Torah—the Old Testament; Mishna—the formulation of the Laws; and Talmud—the commentary on the Laws, all of them supposed to be part of the divine Revelation on Mount Sinai), and Kabbalah (that set of deeply sexualized obscure insights, to be kept secret—take for instance, the notorious passages about the vaginal juices), reproduces within Judaism the tension between the pure symbolic Law and its superego supplement, the secret initiatory knowledge? A crucial line of separation is to be drawn here between the Jewish fidelity to the disavowed ghosts and the pagan obscene initiatory wisdom accompanying public ritual: the disavowed Jewish spectral narrative does not tell the obscene story of God's impenetrable omnipotence, but its exact opposite: the story of His impotence concealed by the standard pagan obscene supplements. The secret to which the Jews remain faithful is the horror of the divine impotence—and it is this secret that is "revealed" in Christianity. This is why Christianity could occur only after Judaism: it reveals the horror first confronted by the Jews. Thus it is only through taking this line of separation between paganism and Judaism into account that we can properly grasp the Christian breakthrough itself.

This means that Judaism in forcing us to face the abyss of the Other's desire (in the guise of the impenetrable God), in refusing to cover up this abyss with a determinate fantasmatic scenario (articulated in the obscene initiatic myth), confronts us for the first time with the paradox of human freedom. There is no freedom outside the traumatic encounter with the opacity of the Other's desire: freedom does not mean that I simply get rid of the Other's desire—I am, as it were, thrown into my freedom when I confront this opacity as such, deprived of the fantasmatic cover that tells me what the Other wants from me. In this difficult predicament, full of anxiety, when I know that the Other wants something from me, without knowing what this desire is, I am thrown back into myself, compelled to assume the risk of freely determining the coordinates of my desire.

According to Rosenzweig, the difference between Jewish and Christian believers is not that the latter experience no anxiety, but that the focus of anxiety is displaced: Christians experience anxiety in the intimacy of their contact with God (like Abraham?), while for Jews, anxiety arises at the level of the Jews as a collective entity without a proper land, its very existence threatened.[6] And perhaps we should establish a link here with the weak point of Heidegger's *Being and Time* (the "illegitimate" passage from individual being-toward-death, and assuming one's contingent fate, to the historicity of a collective): it is only in the case of the Jewish people that such a passage from individual to collective level would have been "legitimate."

How, then, does the Christian community differ from the Jewish one? Saint Paul conceives of the Christian community as the new incarnation of the chosen people: it is Christians who are the true "children of Abraham." What was, in its first incarnation, a distinct ethnic group is now a community of free believers that suspends all ethnic divisions (or, rather, cuts a line of separation within each ethnic group)—the chosen people are those who have faith in Christ. Thus we have a kind of "*transubstantiation*" of *the chosen people*: God kept his promise of redemption to the Jewish people, but, in the process itself, he changed the identity of the chosen people.[7] The theoretical (and political) interest of this notion of community is that it provides the first example of a collective that is not formed and held together through the mechanism described by Freud in *Totem and Taboo* and *Moses and Monotheism* (the shared guilt of the parricide)—are not further examples of this same collective the revolutionary party and the psychoanalytic society? "Holy Spirit" designates a new collective held together not by a Master-Signifier, but by fidelity to a Cause, by the effort to draw a new line of separation that runs "beyond Good and Evil," that is to say, that runs across and suspends the distinctions of the existing social body. The key dimension of Paul's gesture is thus his break with any form of communitarianism: his universe is no longer that of the multitude of groups that want to "find their voice," and assert their particular identity, their "way of life," but that of a fighting collective grounded in the reference to an unconditional universalism.

How, then, does the Christian subtraction relate to the Jewish one? That is to say: is not a kind of subtraction inscribed into the very Jewish identity? Is this not why the Nazis wanted to kill all Jews: because, among all the nations, the Jews are "the part that is no part," not simply a nation among nations, but a remainder, that which has no proper place in the "order of nations"? And, of course, that is the structural problem of the State of Israel: can one form, out of this remainder, a State like the others? It was Rosenzweig who made this point:

> But Judaism, and it alone in all the world, maintains itself by subtraction, by contraction, by the formation of ever new remnants. . . . In Judaism, man is always somehow a survivor, an inner something, whose exterior was seized by the current of the world and carried off while he himself, what is left of him, remains standing on the shore. Something within him is waiting.[8]

Thus the Jews are a remainder in a double sense: not only the remainder with regard to the other set of "normal" nations, but also, in addition, a remainder with regard to themselves, a remainder in and of themselves—the rest, that which remains and persists after all the persecutions and annihilations. These two dimensions are strictly correlated: if the Jews were to be a remainder only in the first (external) sense, they would simply constitute another self-identical ethnic group. So when the Jews are conceived of as a remainder, we should be very precise in defining this with regard to what they are a remainder of: of themselves, of course, but also of humanity as such, insofar as it was abandoned by God. It is as such, as "out of place," that the Jews hold the place of universal humanity as such. And it is only against this background that the Pauline "transubstantiation" of the Chosen People (no longer only Jews—a particular ethnic group—but anyone, irrespective of his or her origins, who recognizes himself or herself in Christ) can be properly understood: Paul, as it were, just switches back to the universality—that is, for him, the Christians are the remainder of humanity. We all, the whole of humanity, considered as redeemed, constitute a remainder—of what?

Here, we should return to the Hegelian point that every universal Whole is divided into its Part (particular species) and its Remainder. The Part (particular as opposed to universal) is the obscene element of existence—on the level of the law, for example, the obscene unwritten supplement that sustains the actual existence of universal Law, Law as an operative power. Take the tension between universal and particular in the use of the term "special": when we say "We have special funds!.," it means illegal, or at least secret funds, not just a special section of public funds; when a sexual partner says "Do you want something special?," it means a non-standard "perverted" practice; when a policeman or journalist refers to "special measures in interrogation," it means torture or other similar illegal pressures. (And were not the units in the Nazi concentration camps that were kept apart, and used for the most horrifying job of killing and cremating thousands, and disposing of the bodies, called *Sonderkommando*, special units?) In Cuba, the difficult period after the disintegration of the Eastern European Communist regimes is referred to as the "special period."

Along the same lines, we should celebrate the genius of Walter Benjamin, which shines through in the very title of his early essay "On Language in General and Human Language in Particular." The point here is not that human language is a species of some universal language "as such," which also comprises other species (the language of gods and angels? animal language? the language of some other intelligent beings out there in space? computer language? the language of DNA?): there is no actually existing language other than human language—but, in order to comprehend this "particular" language, one has to introduce a minimal difference, conceiving it with regard to the gap which separates it from language "as such" (the pure structure of language deprived of the insignia of human finitude, of erotic passions and mortality, of struggles for domination and the obscenity of power). The particular language is thus the "really existing language," language as the series of actually uttered statements, in contrast to formal linguistic structure. This Benjaminian lesson is the lesson missed by Habermas: what Habermas does is precisely what one should *not* do—he posits the ideal "language in general" (the pragmatic universals) directly as the norm of actually existing language. So, along the lines of Benjamin's title, one should describe the basic constellation of the social law as that of the "Law in general and its obscene superego underside in particular.". . . The "Part" as such is thus the "sinful" unredeemed and unredeemable aspect of the Universal—to put it in actual political terms, every politics which grounds itself in the reference to some substantial (ethnic, religious, sexual, lifestyle . . .) particularity is by definition reactionary. Consequently, the division introduced and sustained by the emancipatory ("class") struggle is not the one between the two particular classes of the Whole, but the one between the Whole-in-its-parts and its Remainder which, within the Particulars, stands for the Universal, for the Whole "as such," as opposed to its parts.

Or, to put it in yet another way, we should bear in mind here the two aspects of the notion of remnant: the rest or remainder as what remains after subtraction of all particular content (elements, specific parts of the Whole), and the rest or remainder as the ultimate result of the subdivision of the Whole into its parts, when, in the final act of subdivision, we no longer get two particular parts or elements, two Somethings, but a Something (the Rest) and a Nothing. In this precise sense, we should say that, from the perspective of Redemption (of the "Last Judgment"), the unredeemed part is irrevocably lost, thrown into nothingness—all that remains is precisely the Remainder itself. This, perhaps, is how we should read the motto of the proletarian revolution "We were nothing, we want to become All"—from the perspective of Redemption, that which, within the established order, counts as nothing, the remainder of this order, its part of no part, will become All. . . .

The structural homology between the old Jewish or Pauline messianic time and the logic of the revolutionary process is crucial here: "The future is no future without this anticipation and the inner compulsion for it, without this 'wish to bring about the Messiah before his time' and the temptation to 'coerce the kingdom of God into being'; without these, it is only a past distended endlessly and projected forward."[9] Do not these words fit perfectly Rosa Luxemburg's description of the necessary illusion which pertains to a revolutionary act? As she emphasizes against the revisionists, if we wait for the "right moment" to start a revolution, this moment will never come— we have to take the risk, and precipitate ourselves into revolutionary attempt, since it is only through a series of "premature" attempts (and their failure) that the (subjective) conditions for the "right" moment are created.[10]

Agamben maintains that Saint Paul became readable only in the twentieth century, through Walter Benjamin's "Messianic Marxism": the clue to Paul's emergency of the "end of time" approaching is provided by the revolutionary state of emergency. This state of emergency is to be strictly opposed to today's liberal-totalitarian emergency of the "war on terror": when a state institution proclaims a state of emergency, it does so by definition as part of a desperate strategy to avoid the true emergency, and return to the "normal course of things." Recall a feature of all reactionary proclamations of the "state of emergency": they were all directed against popular unrest ("confusion"), and presented as a decision to restore normalcy. In Argentina, in Brazil, in Greece, in Chile, in Turkey, the military proclaimed the state of emergency in order to curb the "chaos" of overall politicization: "This madness must stop, people should return to their everyday jobs, work must go on!"

In some sense, we can in fact argue that, today, we are approaching a kind of "end of time": the self-propelling explosive spiral of global capitalism does seem to point toward a moment of (social, ecological, even subjective) collapse, in which total dynamism, frantic activity, will coincide with a deeper immobility. History will be abolished in the eternal present of multiple narrativizations; nature will be abolished when it becomes subject to biogenetic manipulation; the very permanent transgression of the norm will assert itself as the unconditional norm. . . . However, the question "When does ordinary time get caught in the messianic twist?" is a misleading one: we cannot deduce the emergence of messianic time through an "objective" analysis of historical process. "Messianic time" ultimately stands for the intrusion of subjectivity irreducible to the "objective" historical process, which means that things can take a messianic turn, time can become "dense," *at any point.*

The time of the Event is not another time beyond and above the "normal" historical time, but a kind of inner loop within this time. Consider one of the standard plots of time-travel narratives: the hero travels into the past in order to intervene in it, and thus change the present; afterward, he discovers that the emergence of the present he wanted to change was triggered precisely through his intervention—his time travel was already included in the run of things. What we have here, in this radical closure, is thus not simply complete determinism, but a kind of absolute determinism which includes our free act in advance. When we observe the process from a distant vantage point, it appears to unfold in a straight line; what we lose from sight, however, are the subjective inner loops which sustain this "objective" straight line. This is why the question "In what circumstances does the condensed time of the Event emerge?" is a false one: it involves the reinscription of the Event back into the positive historical process. That is to say: we cannot establish the time of the explosion of the Event through a close "objective" historical analysis (in the style of "when objective contradictions reach such and such a level, things will explode"): there is no Event outside the engaged subjective decision which creates it—if we wait for the time to become ripe for the Event, the Event will never occur. Recall the October Revolution: the moment when its authentic revolutionary urgency was exhausted was precisely the moment when, in theoretical discussion, the topic of different stages of socialism, of the transition from the lower to a higher stage, took over—at this point, revolutionary time proper was reinscribed into linear "objective" historical time, with its phases and transitions between phases. Authentic revolution, in contrast, always occurs in an absolute Present, in the unconditional urgency of a Now.

It is in this precise sense that, in an authentic revolution, predestination overlaps with radical responsibility: the real hard work awaits us on the morning after, once the enthusiastic revolutionary explosion is over, and we are confronted with the task of translating this explosion into a new Order of Things, of drawing the consequences from it, of remaining faithful to it. In other words, the truly difficult work is not that of silent preparation, of creating the conditions for the Event of the revolutionary explosion; the earnest work begins *after* the Event, when we ascertain that "it is accomplished."[11]

The shift from Judaism to Christianity with regard to the Event is best encapsulated in terms of the status of the Messiah: in contrast to Jewish messianic expectation, the basic Christian stance is that the ex-

ed Messiah has already arrived, that is, that we are already redeemed: the
me of nervous expectation, of rushing precipitately toward the expected Arrival, is over; *we live in the aftermath of the Event: everything—the Big
Thing—has already happened*.[12] Paradoxically, of course, the result of this
Event is not atavism ("It has already happened, we are redeemed, so
let us just rest and wait . . ."), but, on the contrary, an extreme urge to
act: it has happened, so *now we have to bear the almost unbearable burden of living
up to it, of drawing the consequences of the Act*. . . . "Man proposes, God disposes"—man is incessantly active, intervening, but it is the divine act
which decides the outcome. With Christianity, it is the reverse—not
"God proposes, man disposes," but the order is inverted: "God (first)
disposes, (and then) man proposes." It is waiting for the arrival of the
Messiah which constrains us to the passive stance of, precisely, waiting, while the arrival functions as a signal which triggers activity.

This means that the usual logic of the "cunning of reason" (we act,
intervene, yet we can never be sure of the true meaning and ultimate
outcome of our acts, since it is the decentered big Other, the substantial symbolic Order, which decides) is also strangely turned around—
to put it in Lacanian terms, it is humanity, not God, which is the big
Other here. It was God Himself who made a Pascalian wager: by dying on the Cross, He made a risky gesture with no guaranteed final
outcome, that is, He provided us—humanity—with the empty S_1,
Master-Signifier, and it is up to humanity to supplement it with the
chain of S_2. Far from providing the conclusive dot on the i, the divine act stands, rather, for the openness of a New Beginning, and it is
up to humanity to live up to it, to decide its meaning, to make something of it. It is as in Predestination, which condemns us to frantic activity: the Event is a pure-empty sign, and we have to work to generate
its meaning. "The Messiah is here"—this summarizes the terrible risk
of Revelation: what "Revelation" means is that God took upon Himself the risk of putting everything at stake, of fully "existentially engaging Himself" by, as it were, stepping into His own picture,
becoming part of creation, exposing Himself to the utter contingency
of existence. Here I am tempted to refer to the Hegelian-Marxian opposition of formal and material subsumption: through the Event (of

Christ), we are *formally* redeemed, subsumed under Redemption, and we have to engage in the difficult work of actualizing it. The true Openness is not that of undecidability, but that of living in the aftermath of the Event, of drawing out the consequences—of what? Precisely of the new space opened up by the Event.

What this means, in theological terms, is that it is not we, humans, who can rely on the help of God—on the contrary, *we must help God*. It was Hans Jonas who developed this notion, referring to the diaries of Etty Hillesum, a young Jewish woman who, in 1942, voluntarily reported to a concentration camp in order to be of help there, and share the fate of her people: "Only this one thing becomes more and more clear to me: that you cannot help us, but that we must help you, and in so doing we ultimately help ourselves. . . . I demand no account from you; you will later call us to account."[13] Jonas links this stance to the radical idea that God is not omnipotent—the only way, according to him, to explain how God could have allowed things like Auschwitz to happen. The very notion of creation implies God's self-contraction: God had first to withdraw into Himself, constrain his omnipresence, in order first to create the Nothing out of which he then created the universe. By creating the universe, He set it free, let it go on its own, renouncing the power of intervening in it: this self-limitation is equivalent to a proper act of creation. In the face of horrors like Auschwitz, God is thus the tragic impotent observer—the only way for Him to intervene in history was precisely to "fall into it," to appear in it in the guise of His son.

Such a fall by means of which God loses His distance and becomes involved, steps into the human series, is discernible in a classic joke from the German Democratic Republic in which Richard Nixon, Leonid Brezhnev, and Erich Honecker confront God, asking Him about the future of their countries. To Nixon, God answers: "In 2000, the USA will be Communist!" Nixon turns away and starts to cry. To Brezhnev, He says: "In 2000, the Soviet Union will be under Chinese control." After Brezhnev has also turned away and started to cry, Honecker finally asks: "And how will it be in my beloved GDR?" God turns away and starts to cry. . . . And here is the ultimate version: three

Russians who share the same cell in Lubyanka prison have all been condemned for political offenses. While they are getting acquainted, the first says: "I was condemned to five years for opposing Popov." The second says: "Ah, but then the Party line changed, and I was condemned to ten years for supporting Popov." Finally, the third one says: "I was condemned for life, and I *am* Popov." (And is it necessary to add that there really was a senior Bulgarian Komintern functionary named Popov, a close collaborator of George Dimitrov himself, who disappeared in the purges of the late 1930s?) Can this not be elevated into a model for understanding Christ's suffering? "I was thrown to the lions in the arena for believing in Christ!" "I was burned at the stake for ridiculing Christ" "I died on a cross, and I *am* Christ!". . . Perhaps this moment of stepping into the line, this final reversal by means of which the founding Exception (God) falls into His own creation, as it were, is inserted into the series of ordinary creatures, is what is unique to Christianity, the mystery of incarnation, of God (not only appearing as a man, but) becoming a man.

This compels us to detach the Christian "love for one's neighbor" radically from the Levinasian topic of the Other as the impenetrable neighbor. Insofar as the ultimate Other is God Himself, I should risk the claim that it is the *epochal achievement of Christianity to reduce its Otherness to Sameness*: God Himself is Man, "one of us." If, as Hegel emphasizes, what dies on the Cross is the God of beyond itself, the radical Other, then the identification with Christ ("life in Christ") means precisely the suspension of Otherness. What emerges in its place is the Holy Spirit, which is not Other, but the community (or, rather, *collective*) of believers: the "neighbor" is a member of our collective. The ultimate horizon of Christianity is thus not respect for the neighbor, for the abyss of its impenetrable Otherness; it is possible to go beyond—not, of course, to penetrate the Other directly, to experience the Other as it is "in itself," but to become aware that there is no mystery, no hidden true content, behind the mask (deceptive surface) of the Other. The ultimate idolatry is not the idolizing of the mask, of the image, itself, but the belief that there is some hidden positive content beyond the mask.[14]

And no amount of "deconstruction" helps here: the ultimate form of idolatry is the deconstructive purifying of this Other, so that all that remains of the Other is its place, the pure form of Otherness as the Messianic Promise. It is here that we encounter the limit of deconstruction: as Derrida himself has realized in the last two decades, the more radical a deconstruction is, the more it has to rely on its inherent undeconstructible condition of deconstruction, the messianic promise of Justice. This promise is the true Derridean object of belief, and Derrida's ultimate ethical axiom is that this belief is irreducible, "undeconstructible." Thus Derrida can indulge in all kinds of paradoxes, claiming, among other things, that it is only atheists who truly pray—precisely by refusing to address God as a positive entity, they silently address the pure Messianic Otherness. Here one should emphasize the gap which separates Derrida from the Hegelian tradition:

> It would be too easy to show that, measured by the failure to establish liberal democracy, the gap between fact and ideal essence does not show up only in . . . so-called primitive forms of government, theocracy and military dictatorship. . . . But this failure and this gap also characterize, *a priori* and by definition, *all* democracies, including the oldest and most stable of so-called Western democracies. At stake here is the very concept of democracy as concept of a promise that can only arise in such a *diastema* (failure, inadequation, disjunction, disadjustment, being "out of joint"). That is why we always propose to speak of a democracy *to come*, not of a *future* democracy in the future present, not even of a regulating idea, in the Kantian sense, or of a utopia—at least to the extent that their inaccessibility would still retain the temporal form of a *future present*, of a future modality of the living *present*.[15]

Here we have the difference between Hegel and Derrida at its purest: Derrida accepts Hegel's fundamental lesson that one cannot assert the innocent ideal against its distorted realization. This holds not only for democracy, but also for religion—the gap which separates the ideal concept from its actualization is already inherent to the concept itself: just as Derrida claims that "God already contradicts Himself," that any positive conceptual determination of the divine as a pure messianic promise already betrays it, one should also say that "democracy already contradicts itself." It is also against this background that Derrida elaborates the mutual implication of religion and radical evil:[16] radical evil (politically: "totalitarianism") emerges when religious faith or reason (or democracy itself) is posited in the mode of future present.

Against Hegel, however, Derrida insists on the irreducible excess in the ideal concept which cannot be reduced to the dialectic between the ideal and its actualization: the messianic structure of "to come," the excess of an abyss which can never be actualized in its determinate content. Hegel's own position here is more intricate than it may appear: his point is not that, through gradual dialectical progress, one can master the gap between the concept and its actualization, and achieve the concept's full self-transparency ("Absolute Knowing"). Rather, to put it in speculative terms, his point is to assert a "pure" contradiction which is no longer the contradiction between the undeconstructible pure Otherness and its failed actualizations/determinations, but the thoroughly immanent "contradiction" which precedes any Otherness. Actualizations and/or conceptual determinations are not "traces of the undeconstructible divine Otherness," but simply traces marking their in-between. Or, to put it in yet another way, in a kind of inverted phenomenological *epoche*, Derrida reduces Otherness to the "to-come" of a pure potentiality, thoroughly de-ontologizing it, bracketing its positive content, so that all that remains is the specter of a promise; and what if the next step is to drop this minimal specter of Otherness itself, so that all that remains is the rupture, the gap as such, which prevents entities from attaining their self-identity? Remember the French Communist philosophers' criticism of Sartre's existentialism: Sartre threw away the entire content of the bourgeois subject, maintaining only its pure form, and the next step was to throw away this form itself—is it not that, *mutatis mutandis*, Derrida threw away all the positive ontological content of messianism, retaining nothing but the pure form of the messianic promise, and the next step is to throw away this form itself? And, again, is this not also the passage from Judaism to Christianity? Judaism reduces the promise of Another Life to a pure Otherness, a messianic promise which will never become fully present and actualized (the Messiah is always "to come"); while Christianity, far from claiming full realization of the promise, accomplishes something far more uncanny: the Messiah is here, he has arrived, the final Event has already taken place, *yet the gap (the gap which sustained the messianic promise) remains.* . . .

Here I am tempted to suggest a return to the earlier Derrida of *différance*: what if (as Ernesto Laclau, among others, has already argued[17]) Derrida's turn to "postsecular" messianism is not a necessary outcome of his initial "deconstructionist" impetus? What if the idea of infinite messianic Justice which operates in an indefinite suspension, always to come, as the undeconstructible horizon of deconstruction, already obfuscates "pure" *différance*, the pure gap which separates an entity from itself? Is it not possible to think this pure in-between prior to any notion of messianic justice? Derrida acts as if the choice is between positive onto-ethics, the gesture of transcending the existing order toward another higher positive Order, and the pure promise of spectral Otherness—what, however, if we drop this reference to Otherness altogether? What then remains is either Spinoza—the pure positivity of Being—or Lacan—the minimal contortion of drive, the minimal "empty" (self-)difference which is operative when a thing starts to function as a substitute for itself:

> What is substituted can also appear itself, in a 1:1 scale, in the role of the substitute—there only must be some feature ensuring that it is not taken to be itself. Such a feature is provided for by the threshold which separates the place of what is substituting from what is being substituted—or symbolizes their detachment. Everything that appears in front of the threshold is then assumed to be the ersatz, as everything that lies behind it is taken to be what is being substituted.
>
> There are scores of examples of such concealments that are obtained not by miniaturization but only by means of clever localization. As Freud observed, the very acts that are forbidden by religion are practiced in the name of religion. In such cases—as, for instance, murder in the name of religion—religion also can do entirely without miniaturization. Those adamantly militant advocates of human life, for example, who oppose abortion, will not stop short of actually murdering clinic personnel. Radical right-wing opponents of male homosexuality in the USA act in a similar way. They organize so-called "gay bashings" in the course of which they beat up and finally rape gays. The

ultimate homicidal or homosexual gratification of drives can therefore also be attained, if it only fulfils the condition of evoking the semblance of a counter-measure. What seems to be "opposition" then has the effect that the x to be fended off can appear itself and be taken for a non-x.[18]

What we have here, yet again, is the Hegelian "oppositional determination": in the figure of the gay-basher raping a gay, the gay encounters himself in its oppositional determination; that is to say, tautology (self-identity) appears as the highest contradiction. This threshold can also function as the foreign gaze itself: for example, when a disenchanted Western subject perceives Tibet as a solution to his crisis, Tibet loses its immediate self-identity, and turns into a sign of itself, its own "oppositional determination." In contrast with gay-bashing rape, where the homosexual desire is satisfied in the guise of its opposite, here, in the case of a Western Tibet-worshipper, the utter *rejection* of Tibet, the betrayal of Tibetan civilization, is accomplished in the guise of its opposite, of admiration for Tibet. A further example is provided by the extreme case of interpassivity, when I tape a movie instead of simply watching it on TV, and when this postponement takes a fully self-reflected form: worried that something will go wrong with the recording, I anxiously watch TV while the tape is running, just to be sure that everything is working, so that the film will be there on the tape, ready for a future viewing. The paradox here is that I *do* watch the film, even very closely, but in a kind of suspended state, without really following it—all that interests me is that everything is really there, that the recording is all right. Do we not find something similar in a certain perverse sexual economy in which I perform the act only in order to be sure that I can really perform it in the future? Even if the act is, in reality, indistinguishable from the "normal" act done for pleasure, as an end in itself, the underlying libidinal economy is totally different.

So here again we encounter the logic of reflexive determination, in which watching a movie appears as its own oppositional determination—in other words, the structure is again that of the Möbius strip: if we progress far enough on one side, we reach our starting point again (watching the movie, a gay sex act), but on the obverse side of the band. Lewis Carroll was therefore right: a country *can* serve as its own map insofar as the model/map is the thing itself in its oppositional determination, that is, insofar as an invisible screen ensures that the thing is not taken to be itself. In this precise sense, the "primordial" difference is not between things themselves, nor between things and their signs, but between the thing and the void of an invisible screen which distorts our perception of the thing so that we do not take the thing for itself. The movement from things to their signs is not that of replacement of the thing by its sign, but that of the thing itself becoming the sign of (not another thing, but) *itself*, the void at its very core.[19] This gap can also be the gap which separates a dream from reality: if, in the middle of the night, one has a dream about a heavy stone or animal sitting on one's chest, and causing pain, this dream, of course, reflects the fact that one has a real pain in one's chest—it invents a narrative to account for the pain. The trick, however, is not just to invent a narrative, but to invent a more radical one: it can happen that, while one has a pain in one's chest, one has a dream about *having a pain in one's chest*—being aware that one is dreaming, the very fact of transposing the pain into the dream, has a calming effect ("It's not a real pain, it's just a dream!").

And this paradox brings us to the relationship between man and Christ: the tautology "man is man" is to be read as a Hegelian infinite judgment, as the encounter of "man" with its oppositional determination, with its counterpart on the other side of the Möbius strip. Just as, in our everyday understanding, "law is law" means its opposite, the coincidence of the law with arbitrary violence ("What can you do? Even if it is unjust and arbitrary, the law is the law, you have to obey it!"), "man is man" indicates the noncoincidence of man with man, the properly *inhuman* excess which disturbs its self-identity—and what, ultimately, is Christ but the name of this excess inherent in man, man's ex-timate kernel, the monstrous surplus which, following the unfortunate Pontius Pilate, one of the few ethical heroes of the Bible (the other being Judas, of course), can be designated only as "*Ecce homo*"?

APPENDIX

IDEOLOGY TODAY

Repulsive anti-intellectual relatives, whom one cannot always avoid during holidays, often attack me with common provocations like "What can you, as a philosopher, tell me about the cup of coffee I'm drinking?" Once, however, when a thrifty relative of mine gave my son a Kinder Surprise egg and then asked me, with an ironic, patronizing smile: "So what would be your philosophical comment on this egg?," he got the surprise of his life—a long, detailed answer.

Kinder Surprise, one of the most popular confectionery products on sale in Europe, are empty chocolate eggshells wrapped in brightly colored paper; when you unwrap the egg and crack the chocolate shell open, you find inside a small plastic toy (or small parts from which a toy can be put together). A child who buys this chocolate egg often unwraps it nervously and just breaks the chocolate, not bothering to eat it, worrying only about the toy in the center—is not such a chocolate-lover a perfect case of Lacan's motto "I love you, but, inexplicably, I love something in you more than yourself, and, therefore, I destroy you"? And, in effect, is this toy not l'objet petit a at its purest, the small object filling in the central void of our desire, the hidden treasure, agalma, at the center of the thing we desire?

This material ("real") void at the center, of course, stands for the structural ("formal") gap on account of which no product is "really that," no product lives up to its expectations. In other words, the small plastic toy is not simply different from chocolate (the product we bought); while it is materially different, it fills in the gap in chocolate itself—that is to say, it is on the same surface as the chocolate. As we know from Marx, a commodity is a mysterious entity full of theological caprices, a particular object satisfying a particular need, but at the same time the promise of "something more," of an unfathomable enjoyment whose true location is fantasy—all advertising addresses this fantasmatic space ("If you drink X, it will not be just a drink, but also . . ."). And the plastic toy is the result of a risky strategy actually to materialize, render visible, this mysterious excess: "If you eat our chocolate, you will not just eat chocolate, but also . . . have a (totally useless) plastic toy." Thus the Kinder egg provides the formula for all the products which promise "more" ("Buy a DVD player and get five DVDs for free," or, in an even more direct form, more of the same—"Buy this toothpaste and get a third extra for free"), not to mention the standard trick with the Coca-Cola bottle ("Look on the inside of the metal cover, and you may find that you are the winner of one of our prizes, from another free Coke to a brand-new car"): the function of this "more" is to fill in the lack of a "less," to compensate for the fact that, by definition, a product never delivers on its (fantasmatic) promise. In other words, the ultimate "true" product would be the one which would not need any supplement, the one which would simply fully deliver what it promises—"you get what you paid for, neither less nor more."[1]

This reference to the void in the middle of a desert, the void enveloped by a desert, has a long history.[2] In Elizabethan England, with the rise of modern subjectivity, a difference emerged between the "substantial" food (meat) eaten in the great banqueting hall, and the sweet desserts eaten in a small separate room while the tables were being cleared ("voided") in the banqueting hall—so the small room in which these desserts were eaten was called the "void." Consequently, the desserts themselves were referred to as "voids"; furthermore, they imitated the void in their form—sugar cakes in the shape of, usually, an animal, empty in the middle. The emphasis was on the contrast between the "substantial" meal in the large banqueting hall and the insubstantial, ornamental dessert in the "void": the "void" was a "like-meat," a fake, a pure appearance—for example, a sugar peacock which looked like a peacock without being one (the key part of the ritual of consuming it was to crack the surface violently to reveal the void inside). This was the early-modern version of today's decaffeinated coffee or artificial sweeteners, the first example of a food deprived of its substance, so that, in eating it, one was, in a way, "eating nothing." And the further key feature is that this "void" was the space of deploying "private" subjectivity as opposed to the "public" space of the banqueting hall: the "void" was consumed in a place where one withdrew after the public ceremony of the official meal; in this separate place, one was allowed to drop official masks and let oneself participate in the relaxed exchange of gossip, impressions, opinions, and confessions in their entire scope, from the trivial to the most intimate. The opposition between the substantial "real thing" and the trifling ornamental appearance which enveloped only the void thus overlapped with the opposition between substance and subject—no wonder that, in the same period, the "void" also functioned as an allusion to the subject itself, the Void beneath the deceptive appearance of social masks. This, perhaps, is the first, culinary, version of Hegel's famous motto according to which one should conceive the Absolute "not only as Substance, but also as Subject": you should eat not only meat and bread, but also good desserts.

Should we not link this use of "void" to the fact that, at exactly the same historical moment, at the dawn of modernity, "zero" as a number was invented—a fact, as Brian Rotman has pointed out, linked to the expansion of commodity exchange, of the production of commodities, into the hegemonic form of production, so that the link between void and commodity is there from the beginning.[3] In his classic analysis of the Greek vase in "Das Ding," to which Lacan refers in his Ethics of Psychoanalysis, Heidegger also emphasizes how the vase as an emblematic Thing is formed around a central void, that is, serves as the container of a void[4]—so it is tempting to read the Greek vase and the Kinder chocolate egg together as designating the two moments of the Thing in the history of the West: the sacred Thing at its dawn, and the ridiculous merchandise at its end: the Kinder egg is our vase today. Perhaps, then, the ultimate image condensing the entire "history of the West" would be that of the Ancient Greeks offering to the gods, in a vase . . . a Kinder-egg plastic toy. Here we should follow the procedure, practiced by Adorno and Horkheimer in Dialectic of Enlightenment, of condensing the entire development of Western civilization into one simple line—from prehistoric magical manipulation to technological manipulation, or from the Greek vase to the Kinder egg. Along these lines, the thing to bear in mind is that the dawn of Ancient Greek philosophy occurred at the same time (and place) as the first rise of commodity production and exchange—one of the stories about Thales, the first philosopher, is that, to prove his versatility in "real life," he got rich on the market, and then returned to his philosophy. Thus the double meaning of the term "speculation" (metaphysical and financial) is operative from the very beginning. So, perhaps, one should risk the hypothesis that, historically, the Greek vase to which Heidegger refers *was already a commodity*, and that it was this fact which accounted for the void at its center, and gives this void its true resonance—it is as a commodity that a thing is not only itself, but points "beyond itself" to another dimension inscribed into the thing itself as the central void. Following Beistegui's deployment of the secret hegemony of the notion of *oikos* as closed "house" economy in Heidegger—that is, of Heidegger's ignorance of market conditions, of how the market always-already displaces the closed *oikos*[5]—one could thus say that the vase as *das Ding* is the ultimate proof of this fact.

No wonder, then, that there is a homology between the *Kinder* egg, today's "void," and the abundance of commodities that offer us "X without X," deprived of its substance (coffee without caffeine, sweetener without sugar, beer without alcohol, etc.): in both cases, we seem to get the surface form deprived of its core. More fundamentally, however, as the reference to the Elizabethan "void" indicates, is there not a clear homology between this structure of the commodity and the structure of the bourgeois subject? Do subjects—precisely insofar as they are the subjects of universal Human Rights—not also function like these *Kinder* chocolate eggs? In France, it is still possible to buy a dessert with the racist name "*la tête du nègre* [the nigger's head]": a ball-like chocolate cake with an empty interior ("like the stupid nigger's head")—the *Kinder* egg fills in this void. The lesson of it is that we *all* have a "nigger's head," with a hole in the center—would not the humanist-universalist reply to the *tête du nègre*, his attempt to deny that we all have a "nigger's head," be precisely something like a *Kinder* egg? As humanist ideologists would put it: we may be infinitely different—some of us are black, others white; some tall, others small; some women, others men; some rich, others poor, and so on—yet, deep inside us, there is the same moral equivalent of the plastic toy, the same *je ne sais quoi*, an elusive X which somehow accounts for the dignity shared by all humans—to quote Francis Fukuyama:

> What the demand for equality of recognition implies is that when we strip all of a person's contingent and accidental characteristics away, there remains some essential human quality underneath that is worthy of a certain minimal level of respect—call it Factor X. Skin, color, looks, social class and wealth, gender, cultural background, and even one's natural talents are all accidents of birth relegated to the class of nonessential characteristics. . . . But in the political realm we are required to respect people equally on the basis of their possession of Factor X.[6]

In contrast to transcendental philosophers who emphasize that this Factor X is a sort of "symbolic fiction" with no counterpart in the reality of an individual, Fukuyama heroically locates it in our "human nature," in our unique genetic inheritance. And, in effect, is not the genome the ultimate figure of the plastic toy hidden deep within our human chocolate skin? It can be white chocolate, standard milk chocolate, dark chocolate, with or without nuts or raisins—inside it, there is always the same plastic toy (in contrast to the *Kinder* eggs, which are the same on the outside, while each has a different toy hidden inside). And, to cut a long story short, what Fukuyama is afraid of is that, if we tinker too much with the production of the chocolate egg, we might generate an egg without the plastic toy inside—how? Fukuyama is quite right to emphasize that it is crucial that we experience our "natural" properties as a matter of contingency and luck: if my neighbor is more beautiful or intelligent than I am, it is because he was lucky to be born like that, and even his parents could not have planned it that way. The philosophical paradox is that if we take away this element of lucky chance, if our "natural" properties become controlled and regulated by biogenetic and other scientific manipulations, we lose the Factor X.

Of course, the hidden plastic toy can also be given a specific ideological twist—for instance, the idea that, after we get rid of the chocolate, in all its ethnic variations, we always encounter an

American (even if the toy was, in all probability, made in China). This mysterious X, the inner treasure of our being, can also reveal itself as an alien intruder, even an excremental monstrosity. The anal association here is fully justified: the *immediate* appearance of the Inner is formless shit.[7] The small child who gives his shit as a present is, in a way, giving the immediate equivalent of his Factor X. Freud's well-known identification of excrement as the primordial form of gift, of an innermost object that the small child gives to his or her parents, is therefore not as naive as it may appear: the point that is often overlooked is that this piece of myself offered to the Other oscillates radically between the sublime and (not the ridiculous, but, precisely) the excremental.

This is why, for Lacan, one of the features which distinguishes man from the animals is that, with humans, the disposal of shit becomes a problem: not because it has a bad smell, but because it issued from our innards. We are ashamed of shit because, in it, we expose/externalize our innermost intimacy. Animals do not have a problem with it because they do not have an "interior," as humans do. Here I should refer to Otto Weininger, who called volcanic lava "the shit of the earth."[8] It comes from *inside* the body, and this inside is evil, criminal: "The Inner of the body is very criminal."[9] This is the same speculative ambiguity as we encounter with the penis, organ of both urination *and* procreativity: when our innermost being is directly externalized, the result is disgusting. This externalized shit is the precise equivalent of the alien monster that colonizes the human body, penetrating it and dominating it from within, and, at the climactic moment of a science-fiction horror movie, breaks out of the body through the mouth, or directly through the chest. Perhaps a better example even than Ridley Scott's *Alien* is Jack Sholder's *Hidden*, in which the wormlike alien creature forced out of the body at the end directly evokes anal associations (a gigantic piece of shit, since the alien compels humans penetrated by It to eat voraciously, and belch in an embarrassingly disgusting way).[10]

How does Israel, one of the most militarized societies in the world, succeed in rendering this aspect practically invisible, and presenting itself as a tolerant, secular, liberal society?[11] The ideological presentation of the figure of the Israeli soldier is crucial here; it parasitizes on the more general ideological self-perception of the Israeli individual as ragged, even vulgar, but a warm and considerate human being. We can see here how the very distance toward our ideological identity, the reference to the fact that "beneath the mask of our public identity, there is a warm and frail human being, with all its weaknesses," is the fundamental feature of ideology. And the same goes for the Israeli soldier: he is efficient, ready to accomplish the necessary dirty work on the very edge of (or even beyond) legality, because this surface conceals a profoundly ethical, even sentimental, person. . . . This is why the image of the weeping soldier plays such an important role in Israel: a soldier who is ruthlessly efficient, but nonetheless occasionally breaks down in tears at the acts he is compelled to perform. In psychoanalytic terms, what we have here is the oscillation between the two sides of *objet petit a*: shit and the precious *agalma*, the hidden treasure: beneath the excremental surface (vulgar insensitivity, gluttony, stealing towels and ashtrays from hotels, etc.—all the clichés about Israelis propagated by Israeli jokes), there is a sensitive core of gold. In terms of our *Kinder* chocolate example, this means that the chocolate-brown shit is on the outside, enveloping the precious treasure hidden within it.

Factor X guarantees not only the underlying identity of different subjects, but also the continuing identity of the same subject. Twenty years ago, *National Geographic* published their famous photo of a young Afghani woman with fierce bright-yellow eyes; in 2001, the same woman was identified in Afghanistan—although her face was changed, worn out by her difficult life and heavy work, her intense eyes were instantly recognizable as the factor of continuity. Two decades ago, however, the German Leftist weekly journal *Stern* conducted a rather cruel experiment which, in a way, empirically undermined this thesis: it paid a group of destitute homeless men and women to be thoroughly washed, shaved, and then delivered to the top fashion designers and hairdressers; in one issue, the journal then published two large parallel photos of each person: as a destitute homeless man or woman, dirty and unshaven; and dressed by a top designer. The result was somewhat uncanny: although it was clear that we were looking at the same person, the effect of the different dress, and so on, was that our belief that, beneath different appearances, there is one and the same person was shaken. Not only were their appearances different: the deeply disturbing effect of these changes of appearance was that we, the spectators, somehow perceived a different personality beneath the appearances. *Stern* was bombarded with readers' letters accusing the journal of violating the homeless people's dignity, of humiliating them, submitting them to a cruel joke—what was undermined by this experiment, however, was precisely the belief in Factor X, in the kernel of identity which accounts for our dignity, and persists through any change of appearance. In short, this experiment, in a way, empirically proved that we all have a "nigger's head," that the core of our subjectivity is a void filled in by appearances.

So let us return to the scene of a small child violently tearing apart and discarding the chocolate ball in order to get at the plastic toy—is he not the emblem of so-called "totalitarianism," which also wants to get rid of the "inessential" historical contingent coating in order to liberate the "essence" of man? Is not the ultimate "totalitarian" vision that of a New Man arising out of the debris of the violent annihilation of the former corrupted humanity? Paradoxically, then, liberalism and "totalitarianism" share the belief in Factor X, the plastic toy in the midst of the human chocolate coating. The problematic point of this Factor X that makes us equal in spite of our differences is clear: beneath the deep humanist insight that, "deep within ourselves, we are all equal, the same vulnerable humans," is the cynical question "why bother to fight against surface differences when, deep down, we already *are* equal?"—like the proverbial millionaire who poignantly discovers that he feels the same passions, fears, and loves as a destitute beggar.

However, does the ontology of subjectivity as lack, the pathetic assertion that we all have "a nigger's head," really provide the final answer? Is not Lacan's basic materialist position that *the lack itself has to be sustained by a minimum of material leftover*, by a contingent, indivisible remainder which has no positive ontological consistency, but is simply a void embodied? Does not the subject need an irreducible pathological supplement? This is what the formula of fantasy ($ − a, the divided subject coupled with the object-cause of desire) indicates. Such a convoluted structure (an object emerges as the outcome of the very operation of cleansing the field of all objects) is clearly discernible in what is the most elementary rhetorical gesture of transcendental philosophy: that of identifying the essential dimension (Factor X) by erasing all contingent content. Perhaps the most seductive strategy with regard to this Factor X is to be located in a favorite twentieth-century intellectual exercise: the urge to "catastrophize" the situation: whatever the actual situation, it had to be denounced as "catastrophic," and the better it appeared, the more it encouraged this exercise—in this way, irrespective of our "merely ontic" differences, we all participate in the same ontological catastrophe. Heidegger denounced the present age as that of the highest "danger," the epoch of accomplished nihilism; Adorno and Horkheimer saw in it the culmination of the "dialectic of enlightenment" in the "administered world"; Giorgio Agamben defines the twentieth-century concentration camps as the "truth" of the entire Western political project. Recall the figure of Max Horkheimer in 1950s West Germany: while denouncing the "eclipse of reason" in the modern Western consumer society, he simultaneously defended this same society as the sole island of freedom in the sea of totalitarianisms and corrupt dictatorships all around the globe. It was as if Winston Churchill's old ironic quip about democracy (the worst political regime, but none of the others is any better) was repeated here in a serious form: Western "administered society" is barbarism in the guise of civilization, the highest point of alienation, the disintegration of the autonomous individual, and so forth—however, all other sociopolitical regimes are worse, so that, in comparison, one nonetheless has to support it. . . . I shall propose a radical reading of this syndrome: what if what these unfortunate intellectuals cannot bear is the fact that they lead a life which is basically happy, safe, and comfortable, so that, in order to justify their higher calling, they have to construct a scenario of radical catastrophe? And, in fact, Adorno and Horkheimer are oddly close to Heidegger here:

> The most violent "catastrophes" in nature and in the cosmos are nothing in the order of *Unheimlichkeit* in comparison with that *Unheimlichkeit* which man is in himself, and which, insofar as man is placed in the midst of beings as such and stands for beings, consists in forgetting being, so that for him *das Heimische* becomes empty erring, which he fills up with his dealings. The *Unheimlichkeit* of the *Unheimischkeit* lies in that man, in his very essence, is a *katastrophe*—a reversal that turns him away from the genuine essence. Man is the only catastrophe in the midst of beings.[12]

The first thing that cannot fail to strike a philosopher here is the implicit reference to the Kantian Sublime: just as, for Kant, the most violent eruptions in nature are nothing in comparison with the power of the moral Law, for Heidegger, the most violent catastrophes in nature and social life are nothing in comparison with the catastrophe which is man himself—or, as Heidegger would have put it in his other main rhetorical figure, the essence of catastrophe has nothing to do with ontic catastrophes, since the essence of catastrophe is the catastrophe of the essence itself, its withdrawal, its forgetting by man. (Does this also apply to the Holocaust? Is it possible to claim, in a nonobscene way, that the Holocaust is nothing in comparison with the catastrophe of the forgetting of being?) The (ambiguous) difference is that while, for Kant, natural violence expresses the sublime dimension of the moral Law in a negative way, for Heidegger, the other term of the comparison is the catastrophe that is man himself. The further ambiguous point is that Kant sees a positive aspect of the experience of the catastrophic natural eruptions: in witnessing them, we experience in a negative way the incomparable sublime grandeur of the moral Law; while for Heidegger, it is not clear that we need the threat (or fact) of an actual ontic catastrophe in order to experience the true catastrophe that pertains to human essence as such in a negative way. (Is this difference linked to the fact that, in the experience of the Kantian Sublime, the subject assumes the role of an observer perceiving the excessive natural violence from a safe distance, not being directly threatened by it, while this distance is lacking in Heidegger?)

It is easy to make fun of Heidegger here—there is, however, a "rational kernel" to his formulations. Although Adorno and Horkheimer would dismiss these formulations with scathing laughter, are they not caught in the same predicament? When they delineate the contours of the emerging late-capitalist "administered world [*verwaltete Welt*]," they are presenting it as coinciding with barbarism, as the point at which civilization itself returns to barbarism, as a kind of negative telos of the whole progress of Enlightenment, as the Nietzschean kingdom of the Last Men: "One has one's little pleasure for the day and one's little pleasure for the night: but one has a regard for health. 'We have invented happiness,' say the last men, and they blink."[13] At the same time, however, they nonetheless warn against more direct "ontic" catastrophes (different forms of terror, etc.). The liberal-democratic society of Last Men is thus literally the worst possible, the only problem being that all other societies are even worse, so that the choice seems to be between Bad and Worse. The ambiguity here is irreducible: on the one hand, the "administered world" is the final catastrophic outcome of the Enlightenment; on the other, the "normal" tenor of our societies is continually threatened by catastrophes, from war and terror to ecological disasters, so that while we should fight these "ontic" catastrophes, we should simultaneously bear in mind that the ultimate catastrophe is the very "normal" tenor of the "administered world" in the absence of any "ontic" catastrophe.[14] The aporia here is genuine: the solution of this ambiguity through some kind of pseudo-Hegelian "infinite judgment" asserting the ultimate coincidence between the subjects of late-capitalist consumerist society and the victims of the Holocaust ("Last Men are Muslims") clearly does not work. The problem is that no pathetic identification with the Muslims (the living dead of the concentration camps) is possible—one cannot say "We are all Muslims" in the same way as, ten years ago, we often heard the phrase "We all live in Sarajevo," things went too far in Auschwitz. (And, in the opposite sense, it would also be ridiculous to assert one's solidarity with 9/11 by claiming: "We are all New Yorkers!"—millions in the Third World would say: "Yes!" . . .)

How, then, are we to deal with actual ethical catastrophes? When, two decades ago, Helmut Kohl, in order to sum up the predicament of those Germans born too late to be involved in the Holocaust, used the phrase "the mercy of the late birth [die Gnade des späten Geburt]," many commentators rejected this formulation as a sign of moral ambiguity and opportunism, implying that today's Germans can dismiss the Holocaust as simply outside the scope of their responsibility. However, Kohl's formulation does touch a paradoxical nerve of morality baptized by Bernard Williams "moral luck."[15] Williams evokes the case of a painter, ironically called "Gauguin," who left his wife and children and moved to Tahiti in order to develop his artistic genius fully—was he morally justified in doing this, or not? Williams's answer is that we can answer this question only in retrospect, after we have learned the final outcome of his risky decision: did he develop into an artist of genius, or not? As Jean-Pierre Dupuy has pointed out,[16] we encounter the same dilemma apropos of the urgency to do something about today's threat of various ecological catastrophes: either we take this threat seriously, and decide today to do things that, if the catastrophe does not occur, will appear ridiculous, or we do nothing and lose everything in the case of the catastrophe. The worst case is here the choice of a middle ground, of taking a limited number of measures—in this case, we will fail whatever happens (that is to say, the problem is that there is no middle ground when it comes to an ecological catastrophe: either it will happen or it won't).

Such a predicament would horrify a radical Kantian: it makes the moral value of an act dependent on thoroughly "pathological" conditions, that is, on its utterly contingent outcome—in short, when I make a difficult decision that involves an ethical deadlock, I can say only: "If I'm lucky, my present act will have been ethical!" However, is not such a "pathological" support of our ethical stance an a priori necessity—and not only in the common sense that, if we (most of us, at least) are to retain our ethical composure, we should have the luck of not being exposed to excessive pressures or temptations (a large majority of us would commit the worst betrayal were we to be tortured in a horrifyingly cruel way). When, in our daily lives, we retain our ethical pride and dignity, we act under the protection of the fiction that we would remain faithful to the ethical stance even under harsh conditions; the point here is not that we should mistrust ourselves, and doubt our ethical stance, but, rather, that we should adopt the attitude of the philosopher Don Alfonso in Mozart's *Così fan tutte*, who advises the two deceived lovers: "Trust women, but do not expose them to too many temptations!"

It is easy to discern how our sense of dignity relies on the disavowal of "pathological" facts of which we are well aware, but we nonetheless suspend their symbolic efficiency. Imagine a dignified leader: if he is caught on camera in an "undignified" situation (crying, throwing up . . .), this can ruin his career, although such situations are part of the daily life of each one of us. On a slightly different level, consider the high art of skilled politicians who know how to absent themselves when a humiliating decision is to be made; in this way, they are able to keep their followers' unconscious belief in their omnipotence intact, maintaining the illusion that, had they not accidentally been prevented from being there, they would have been able to save the day. Or, on a more personal level, imagine a young couple on their first date, the boy trying to impress the girl; then they meet a strong, bullying male who harasses the girl and humiliates the boy, who is afraid to square up to the intruder. Such an incident can ruin the entire relationship—the boy will avoid ever seeing the girl again, since she will forever remind him of his humiliation.

However, beyond the Brechtian fact that "morality is for those who are lucky enough to be able to afford it," there is a more radical gray zone best exemplified by the figure of *Musulmanen* ("Muslims") in the Nazi concentration camps: they are the "zero-level" of humanity, a kind of "living dead" who even cease to react to basic animal stimuli, who do not defend themselves when attacked, who gradually even lose feelings of thirst and hunger, eating and drinking more out of blind habit than in response to some elementary animal need. For this reason, they are the point of the Real without symbolic Truth—that is to say, there is no way to "symbolize" their predicament, to organize it into a meaningful life-narrative. It is easy, however, to perceive the danger of these descriptions: they inadvertently reproduce, and thus attest, the very "dehumanization" imposed on the Muslims by the Nazis. This is why we should insist more than ever on their humanity, without forgetting that they are, in a way, dehumanized, deprived of the essential features of humanity: the line that separates "normal" human dignity and engagement from the Muslims' "inhuman" indifference is inherent to "humanity," which means that there is a kind of inhuman traumatic kernel or gap in the very midst of "humanity" itself—to put it in Lacanian terms, the Muslims are "human" in an ex-timate way. This means that, as Agamben was right to emphasize, the "normal" rules of ethics are suspended here: we cannot simply deplore their fate, regretting that they are deprived of basic human dignity, since *to be "decent," to retain "dignity," in front of a Muslim is in itself an act of utter indecency*. One cannot simply ignore the Muslim: any ethical stance that does not confront the horrifying paradox of the Muslim is by definition unethical, an obscene travesty of ethics—and once we actually confront the Muslim, notions like "dignity" are somehow deprived of their substance. In other words, "Muslim" is not simply the "lowest" in the hierarchy of ethical types ("they not only have no dignity, they have even lost their animal vitality and egotism"), but the zero-level that renders the whole hierarchy meaningless. Not to take this paradox into account is to participate in the same cynicism that the Nazis themselves practiced when they first brutally reduced the Jews to the subhuman level, and then presented this image as proof of their subhumanity—they extrapolated to the extreme the standard procedure of humiliation, in which I, say, take the belt off the trousers of a dignified person, thus forcing him to hold his trousers up with his hands, and then mock him for being undignified. In this precise sense, our moral dignity is ultimately always a fake: it depends on our being lucky enough to avoid the fate of the Muslim. This fact, perhaps, also accounts for the "irrational" feeling of guilt that haunted the survivors of the Nazi camps: what the survivors were compelled to confront at its purest was not the utter contingency of survival, but, more radically, the utter contingency of our retaining our moral dignity, the most precious kernel of our personality, according to Kant.

This, perhaps, is also the most important ethics lesson of the twentieth century: we should abandon all ethical arrogance, and humbly acknowledge how lucky we are to be able to act ethically. Or, to put it in theological terms: far from being opposed, autonomy and grace are intertwined—we are blessed by grace when we are able to act autonomously as ethical agents. And we have to rely on the same mixture of grace and courage when we are facing the prospect of a catastrophe. In his "Two Sources of Morality and Religion," Henri Bergson describes the strange sensations he experienced on August 4, 1914, when war was declared between France and Germany: "In spite of my turmoil, and although a war, even a victorious one, appeared to me as a catastrophe, I experienced what [William] James spoke about, a feeling of admiration for the facility of the passage from the abstract to the concrete: who would have thought that such a formidable event can emerge in reality with so little fuss?"[17] The crucial point here is the modality of the break between before and after: before its outbreak, the war appeared to Bergson to be "*simultaneously probable and impossible:* a complex and contradictory notion that persisted to the end";[18] afterward, it suddenly became both real *and* possible, and the paradox lies in this retroactive appearance of probability:

> I never pretended that one can insert reality into the past and thus work backwards in time. However, one can without any doubt insert there the possible, or, rather, at every moment, the possible insert itself there. Insofar as unpredictable and new reality creates itself, its image reflects itself behind itself in the indefinite past: this new reality finds itself all the time having been possible; but it is only at the precise moment of its actual emergence that it *begins to always have been,*

and this is why I say that its possibility, which does not precede its reality, will have preceded it once this reality emerges.[19]

The encounter with the Real as impossible is therefore always missed: either it is experienced as impossible but not real (the prospect of a forthcoming catastrophe that, however probable we know it is, we do not believe will really happen, and thus dismiss it as impossible), or as real but no longer impossible (once the catastrophe happens, it is "renormalized," perceived as part of the normal run of things, as always-already having been possible). And, as Dupuy makes clear, the gap that makes these paradoxes possible is the gap between knowledge and belief: we *know* the catastrophe is possible, even probable, yet we do not *believe* it will really happen.[20]

What such experiences show is the limitation of the ordinary "historical" notion of time: at each moment in time, there are multiple possibilities waiting to be realized; once one of them actualizes itself, others are cancelled. The supreme case of such an agent of historical time is the Leibnizian God who created the best possible world: before creation, He had in His mind the entire panoply of possible worlds, and His decision consisted in choosing the best one among these options. Here, possibility precedes choice: the choice is a choice among possibilities. What is unthinkable within this horizon of linear historical evolution is the notion of a choice/act that retroactively opens up its own possibility: the idea that the emergence of a radically New retroactively changes the past—not the actual past, of course (we are not in the realms of science fiction), but past possibilities, or, to put it in more formal terms, the value of modal propositions about the past—exactly what happens in the case described by Bergson.[21]

Dupuy's point is that, if we are to confront the threat of a (cosmic or environmental) catastrophe properly, we need to break out of this "historical" notion of temporality: we have to introduce a new notion of time. Dupuy calls this time the "time of a project," of a closed circuit between past and future: the future is causally produced by our acts in the past, while the way we act is determined by our anticipation of the future, and our reaction to this anticipation. This circuit, of course, generates the host of well-known paradoxes of self-realizing prophecy: if we expect X to happen, and act accordingly, X will in fact happen. More interesting are the negative versions: if we expect/predict X (a catastrophe), and act against it, to prevent it, the outcome will be the same whether or not the catastrophe actually happens. If it happens, our preventive acts will be dismissed as irrelevant ("you can't fight destiny"); if it doesn't, *it will be the same*—that is, since the catastrophe (in which we did not believe, despite our knowledge) was perceived as impossible, our preventive acts will again be dismissed as irrelevant (recall the aftermath of the Millennium Bug!). Is this second option, then, the only choice to take as a rational strategy? We envisage a catastrophe, then act to prevent it, in the hope that the very success of our preventive acts will render the prospect that prompted us to act ridiculous and irrelevant—one should heroically assume the role of excessive panic-monger in order to save humanity. . . . However, the circle is not completely closed: back in the 1970s, Bernard Brodie pointed the way out of this deadlock of the closed circle apropos of the strategy of MAD (mutually assured destruction) in the Cold War:

> It is a strange paradox of our time that one of the crucial factors which make the [nuclear] dissuasion effectively function, and function so well, is the underlying fear that, in a really serious crisis, it can fail. In such circumstances, *one does not play with fate*. If we were absolutely certain that the nuclear dissuasion is one hundred per cent efficient in its role of protecting us against a nuclear assault, then its dissuasive value against a conventional war would have dropped to close to zero.[22]

The paradox here is a very precise one: the MAD strategy works not because it is perfect, but because of its very imperfection. That is to say, a perfect strategy (if one side nukes the other, the other will automatically respond, and both sides will thus be destroyed) has a fatal flaw: what if the attacking side counts on the fact that, even after its first strike, the opponent will continue to act as a rational agent?

His choice is now: with his country mostly destroyed, he can either strike back, thus causing total catastrophe, the end of humanity, or *not strike back*, thus enabling the survival of humanity and, thereby, at least the possibility of a later revival of his own country. A rational agent would choose the second option.

What makes the strategy efficient is the very fact that we can never be sure that it will work perfectly: what if a situation spirals out of control, for a variety of easily imaginable reasons (from the "irrational" aggressivity of one side to simple technological failures or miscommunications)? It is because of this permanent threat that neither side wants to come anywhere near the prospect of MAD, *so they avoid even conventional war*: if the strategy were perfect, it would, on the contrary, endorse the attitude "Let's fight a full-scale conventional war, since we both know that neither side will risk the fateful step toward a nuclear strike!" So the actual constellation of MAD is not "If we follow the MAD strategy, the nuclear catastrophe will not take place," but: "If we follow the MAD strategy, the nuclear catastrophe will not take place, *unless there is some unforeseeable accident.*" And the same goes today for the prospect of ecological catastrophe: if we do nothing, it will happen, and if we do everything we can, it will not happen, *unless there is some unforeseeable accident*. This "unforeseeable factor *e*" is precisely the remainder of the Real that disturbs the perfect self-closure of the "time of the project"—if we write this time as a circle, it is a cut that prevents the full closure of the circle (exactly as Lacan writes *l'objet petit a*). What confirms this paradoxical status of *e* is that, in it, possibility and impossibility, positive and negative, coincide: *it renders the strategy of prevention effective precisely insofar as it hinders its full efficiency.*

So it is crucial not to perceive this "catastrophist strategy" in the old terms of linear historical causality: the reason this strategy works is not that, today, we are faced with multiple future possibilities and, within this multitude, we choose the option to act to prevent a catastrophe. Since the catastrophe cannot be "domesticated" as just another possibility, the only option is *to posit it as real*: "one has to in-scribe the catastrophe into the future in a much more radical way. One has to render it *unavoidable.*"[23]

Here we should introduce the notion of minimal "alienation" constitutive of the symbolic order and of the social field as such: although I know very well that my future fate, and that of the society in which I live, depends causally on the present activity of millions of individuals like me, I nonetheless believe in destiny, that is, I believe that the future is run by an anonymous power independent of the will and acts of any individual. "Alienation" consists in the minimal "objectivization" on account of which I abstract from my active role, and perceive historical process as an "objective" process that follows its path independently of my plans. (On a different level, the same goes for the individual agent in the market: while he is fully aware that the price of a product on the market depends (also) on his acts, his selling and buying, he nonetheless keeps the price of a product there fixed, perceiving it as a given quantity to which he then reacts.) The point, of course, is that these two levels intersect: in the present, I do not act blindly; I react to the prospect of what the future will be.

This paradox designates the symbolic order as the order of virtuality: although it is an order that has no existence "in itself," independently of individuals who relate to it—that is to say, as Hegel put it apropos of the social substance, although it is actual only in the acts of individuals—it is nonetheless their *substance*, the objective In-itself of their social existence. This is how we should understand the Hegelian "In- and For-Itself": while it is In-itself, existing independently of the subject, it is "posited" as independent by the subject, that is, it exists independently of the subject only insofar as the subject acknowledges it as such, only insofar as the subject relates to it as independent. For this reason, far from indicating simple "alienation," the reign of dead specters over living subjects, this "autonomization" is coexistent with ethics: people sacrifice their lives for this virtuality. Dupuy is therefore right to emphasize that we should reject the simplistic Marxist "critique," which aims at "sublating" this alienation, transforming society into a self-transparent body within which individuals directly realize their collective projects, without the detour of "destiny" (the position attributed to the Lukács of *History and Class Consciousness*): a minimum of "alienation" is the very condition of the symbolic order as such.

One should thus invert the existentialist commonplace according to which, when we are engaged in a present historical process, we perceive it as full of possibilities, and ourselves as agents free to choose among them; while, to a retrospective view, the same process appears as fully determined and necessary, with no room for alternatives: on the contrary, it is the engaged agents who perceive themselves as caught in a Destiny, merely reacting to it, while, retrospectively, from the standpoint of later observation, we can discern alternatives in the past, possibilities of events taking a different path. (And is not the attitude of Predestination—the fact that the theology of predestination legitimized the frantic activity of capitalism—the ultimate confirmation of this paradox?) This is how Dupuy suggests that we should confront the catastrophe: we should first perceive it as our fate, as unavoidable, and then, projecting ourselves into it, adopting its standpoint, we should retroactively insert into its past (the past of the future) counterfactual possibilities ("If we had done such and such a thing, the catastrophe we are in now would not have happened!") upon which we then act today. And is not a supreme case of the reversal of positive into negative destiny the shift from classical historical materialism into the attitude of Adorno's and Horkheimer's "dialectic of Enlightenment"? While traditional Marxism enjoined us to engage ourselves and act in order to bring about the necessity (of Communism), Adorno and Horkheimer projected themselves into the final catastrophic outcome perceived as fixed (the advent of the "administered society" of total manipulation and the end of subjectivity) in order to urge us to act against this outcome in our present.

Such a strategy is the very opposite of the US attitude in the "war on terror," that of avoiding the threat by striking preemptively at potential enemies. In Spielberg's *Minority Report*, criminals are arrested even before they commit their crime, since three humans who, through monstrous scientific experiments, have acquired the capacity to foresee the future, can exactly predict their acts—is there not a clear parallel with the new Cheney doctrine, which proclaims the policy of attacking a state or an enemy force even before this state develops the means to pose a threat to the United States, that is, already at the point when it *might* develop into such a threat?[24] And, to pursue the analogy even further, was not Gerhard Schröder's disagreement with US plans for a preemptive attack on Iraq precisely a kind of real-life "minority report," indicating his disagreement with the way others saw the future? The state in which we live now, in the "war on terror," is one of the endlessly suspended terrorist threat: the Catastrophe (the new terrorist attack) is taken for granted, yet endlessly postponed. Whatever actually happens, even if it is a much more horrific attack than that of 9/11, will not yet be "that." And it is crucial here that we accomplish the "transcendental" turn: the true catastrophe *already is* this life under the shadow of the permanent threat of catastrophe.

Terry Eagleton has drawn our attention to the two opposed modes of tragedy: the big, spectacular catastrophic Event, the abrupt irruption from some other world, and the dreary persistence of a hopeless condition, the blighted existence that goes on indefinitely, life as one long emergency.[25] This is the difference between the big First World catastrophes like September 11 and the dreary, permanent catastrophe of, say, Palestinians in the West Bank. The first mode of tragedy, the figure against the "normal" background, is characteristic of the First World; while in much of the Third World, catastrophe designates the ever-present background itself.

And this is how the September 11 catastrophe actually functioned: as a catastrophic figure that made us, in the West, aware of the blissful background of our happiness, and of the necessity to defend it against the foreigners' onslaught . . . in short, it functioned exactly according to Chesterton's principle of Conditional Joy: to the question "Why this catastrophe? Why can't we be happy all the time?," the answer is "And why should you be happy in all the time?"

September 11 served as proof that we *are* happy, and that others envy us this happiness. Along these lines, one should thus risk the thesis that, far from rousing the United States from its ideological sleep, September 11 was used as a sedative enabling the hegemonic ideology to "renormalize" itself; the period after the Vietnam War was one long, sustained trauma for the hegemonic ideology—it had to defend itself against critical doubts; the gnawing worm was continuously at work, and couldn't simply be suppressed; every return to innocence was immediately experienced as a fake . . . until September 11, when the United States was a victim, and thus allowed to reassert the innocence of its mission. In short, far from awakening us, September 11 served to put us to sleep again, to continue our dream after the nightmare of the last decades.

The ultimate irony here is that, in order to restore the innocence of American patriotism, the conservative US establishment mobilized the key ingredient of the Politically Correct ideology that it officially despises: the logic of victimization. On the basis of the idea that authority is conferred (only on) those who speak from the position of the victim, it followed the implicit reasoning: "We are victims now, and it is this fact that legitimizes us to speak (and act) from a position of authority." So when, today, we hear the slogan that the liberal dream of the 1990s is over; that, with the attacks on the World Trade Center, we were violently thrown back into the real world; that the easy intellectual games are over; we should remember that such a call to confront harsh reality is ideology at its purest. Today's "America, awake!" is a distant echo of Hitler's "Deutschland, erwache!," which, as Adorno wrote long ago, meant its exact opposite.

This regained innocence of American patriotism, however, is only one version of the standard procedure of liberals confronted with a violent conflict: the adoption of a safe distance from which all participants in the conflict are equally condemned, since "no one's hands are clean." One can always play this game, which offers the player a double advantage: that of retaining his moral superiority over those ("ultimately all the same") involved in the struggle, as well as that of being able to avoid the difficult task of committing himself, of analyzing the constellation and taking sides in it. In recent years, it has seemed as if the post–World War II anti-Fascist pact is slowly cracking: from historians-revisionists to New Right populists, taboos are disappearing. Paradoxically, those who undermine this pact refer to the very liberal universalized logic of victimization: sure, there were victims of Fascism, but what about other victims of the post–World War II expulsions? What about the Germans evicted from their homes in Czechoslovakia in 1945? Do they not also have some right to (financial) compensation?[26] This weird conjunction of money and victimization is one of the forms (perhaps even the "truth") of money fetishism today: while it is emphasized that the Holocaust was the absolute crime, everyone negotiates about appropriate *financial* compensation for it. One of the great *topoi* of the "deconstructionist" critique of ideology is that the notion of the autonomous, free, and responsible subject is a legal fiction whose function is to construct an agent to whom the responsibility for socially unacceptable acts can be attributed, thus obfuscating the need for a closer analysis of the concrete social circumstances that give rise to phenomena perceived as deplorable. When an unemployed African-American who has suffered a series of humiliations and failures steals in order to feed his family, or explodes in uncontrollable violence, is it not cynical to evoke his responsibility as an autonomous moral agent? However, the old rule about ideology applies here too: the symmetrical inversion of an ideological proposition is no less ideological—are we not dealing today with the opposite tendency to put the blame (and thus legal responsibility) on external agencies? Here is an Associated Press report from July 26, 2002:

> *Obesity Cited in Fast Food Suit*—A man sued four leading fast food chains, claiming he became obese and suffered from other serious health problems from eating their fatty cuisine. Caesar Barber, 56, filed a lawsuit Wednesday in Bronx Supreme Court, naming McDonald's, Wendy's, Burger King, and Kentucky Fried Chicken. "They said '100 percent beef.' I thought that meant it was good for you," Barber told *Newsday*. "I thought the food was OK. Those people in the advertisements don't really tell you what's in the food. It's all fat, fat and more

fat. Now I'm obese." Barber, who weighs 272 pounds, had heart attacks in 1996 and 1999 and has diabetes, high blood pressure and high cholesterol. He said he ate fast food for decades, believing it was good for him until his doctor cautioned him otherwise.

The underlying message of this complaint is clear: I am not responsible, it is not my fault, I am just a passive victim of circumstances— and since it is not my fault, there *has* to be another person who is legally responsible for my misfortune. This is also what is wrong with so-called False Memory Syndrome: the compulsive endeavor to attribute present psychic troubles to some real experience of sexual abuse in the past. Again, the true stake of this operation is the subject's refusal to accept responsibility for his sexual investments: if the cause of my disorders is the traumatic experience of harassment, then my own fantasmatic investment in my sexual *imbroglio* is secondary, and ultimately irrelevant.

The question here is: how far can we go along this path? Quite a long way, according to recent news. Is it not significant that when the Holocaust has been mentioned recently in the media, it has, as a rule, been in the context of financial compensation, the amount the victims or their descendants should get from the legal successors of the perpetrators? And, since the Jews are the wronged group par *excellence,* it is not surprising that other wronged groups emulate them, and make similar claims—take the following AP report from August 17, 2002:

> *Rally for Slave Reparations*—Hundreds of blacks rallied in front of the Capitol on Saturday to demand slavery reparations, saying that compensation is long overdue for the ills of that institution. "It seems that America owes black people a lot for what we have endured," Nation of Islam leader Louis Farrakhan told the crowd. "We cannot settle for some little jive token. We need millions of acres of land that black people can build. We're not begging white people, we are just demanding what is justly ours."

And would it not be quite logical to envisage, along the same lines, the end of class struggle: after long and arduous negotiations, representatives of the working class and the global capital should reach an agreement on how much the working class should get as compensation for the surplus-value appropriated by capitalists in the course of history? So, if there seems to be a price for everything, why should we not go to the very end, and demand from God Himself payment for botching up the job of creation, and thus causing all our misery? And what if, perhaps, He has already paid this price by sacrificing His only son, Christ? It is a sign of our times that this option has already been considered in a work of fiction: in *The Man Who Sued God*, an Australian comedy (2002), Billy Connolly plays the owner of a seaside caravan park whose boat is destroyed in a freak storm; his insurance company tell him it's an act of God, and refuse to pay up. Enter a sharp-witted lawyer (Judy Davis), who comes up with a clever argument: If God destroyed his boat, why not sue God in the form of His representatives here on earth—the churches? Such a lawsuit puts the Church leaders in a tight spot: if they deny that they are God's representatives on earth, they all lose their jobs; they can't assert that God does not exist, because that would also destroy organized religion, and, furthermore, if God does not exist, what happens to the escape route of the "Act of God" clause that lets so many insurance sharks off the hook?

This *reductio ad absurdum* also clearly reveals what is fundamentally wrong with this logic: it is not too radical; it is not radical enough. The real task is not to get compensation from those responsible, but to deprive them of the position that makes them responsible. Instead of asking for compensation from God (or the ruling class, or . . .), we should ask this question: do we really need God? This implies something much more radical than it may appear: there is no one to turn to, to address, to bear witness to, no one to receive our plea or lament. This position is extremely difficult to sustain: in modern music, Webern was the first to be able to sustain this nonexistence of the Other: even Schoenberg was still composing for a future ideal listener, while Webern accepted that there is no "proper" listener.

Contrary to all appearances, this is what happens in psychoanalysis: the treatment is over when the patient accepts the nonexistence of the big Other. The ideal addressee of our speech, the ideal listener, is the psychoanalyst, the very opposite of the Master-figure that guarantees meaning; what happens at the end of the analysis, with the dissolution of transference—that is to say, the fall of the "subject supposed to know"—is that the patient accepts the absence of such a guarantee. No wonder psychoanalysis subverts the very principle of reimbursement: the price the patient pays for the treatment is, by definition, capricious, "unjust," with no possible equivalence between it and the services rendered for it. This is also why psychoanalysis is profoundly anti-Levinasian: there is no face-to-face encounter between patient and analyst, since the patient lies on the couch and the analyst sits behind him—analysis penetrates the deepest mysteries of the subject by bypassing the face. This avoiding of the face-to-face encounter enables the patient to "lose face," and blurt out the most embarrassing details. In this precise sense, the face is a fetish: while it appears to be a manifestation of the imperfect vulnerable abyss of the person behind the object-body, it conceals the obscene real core of the subject.

Is not Christianity here, then, the very opposite of psychoanalysis? Does it not stand for this logic of reimbursement brought to its extreme: God Himself pays the price for all our sins? This is why any attempt to depict the Christian God as an undemanding entity of pure mercy whose message is "I want nothing from you!" fails miserably—we should not forget that these are the exact words used by the Priest to designate the court in Kafka's *Trial*: "The court wants nothing from you." When the falsely innocent Christlike figure of pure suffering and sacrifice for our sake tells us: "I don't want anything from you!," we can be sure that this statement conceals a qualification ". . . except *your very soul*." When somebody insists that he wants nothing that *we have*, it simply means that he has his eye on what we *are*, on the very core of our being. Or, on a more anecdotal level, is it not clear that when, in a lovers' quarrel, the woman answers the man's desperate "But what do you want from me?" with "Nothing!," this means its exact opposite, a demand for total surrender beyond any negotiated settlement?[27] "Don't look a gift horse in the mouth"—is this not precisely what we should do in order to discern if we are dealing with a genuine gift, or a secretly instrumentalized one? You are given a present, yet a close look quickly tells you that this "free" gift is aimed at putting you in a position of permanent debt—and perhaps this applies especially to the notion of gift in the recent theological turn of deconstruction, from Derrida to Marion.

The point of this book is that, at the very core of Christianity, there is another dimension. When Christ dies, what dies with him is the secret hope discernible in "Father, why hast thou forsaken me?": the hope that there is a father who has abandoned me. The "Holy Spirit" is the community deprived of its support in the big Other. The point of Christianity as the religion of atheism is not the vulgar humanist one that the becoming-man-of-God reveals that man is the secret of God (Feuerbach et al.); rather, it attacks the religious hard core that survives even in humanism, even up to Stalinism, with its belief in History as the "big Other" that decides on the "objective meaning" of our deeds.

In what is perhaps the highest example of Hegelian *Aufhebung*, it is possible today to redeem this core of Christianity only in the gesture of abandoning the shell of its institutional organization (and, even more so, of its specific religious experience). The gap here is irreducible: either one drops the religious form, or one maintains the form, but loses the essence. That is the ultimate heroic gesture that awaits Christianity: in order to save its treasure, it has to sacrifice itself—like Christ, who had to die so that Christianity could emerge.

INTRODUCTION: THE PUPPET CALLED THEOLOGY

1   G. W. F. Hegel, *Wissenschaft der Logik*, 2nd part (Hamburg: Felix Meiner Verlag, 1966), p. 285.

2   G. W. F. Hegel, *Phänomenologie des Geistes* (Hamburg: Felix Meiner Verlag, 1952), p. 254.

3   Ibid., pp. 305–312.

4   G. W. F. Hegel, *Glauben und Wissen* (Hamburg: Felix Meiner Verlag, 1987).

5   G. W. F. Hegel, *Enzyklopädie der philosophischen Wissenschaften* (Hamburg: Felix Meiner Verlag, 1959), p. 436.

6   Perhaps the link between Christianity and atheism becomes somewhat clearer if we take into account the surprising fact that the turn of Heidegger's *Being and Time*—that radical attempt to render thematic the unsurpassable finitude of the human condition—from the "reified" ontological approach to reality ("subject" perceiving "objects") toward the active engagement of being-in-the-world is grounded in his reading of Saint Paul in the early 1920s. An unexpected additional link between Heidegger and Badiou is discernible here: they both refer to Paul in the same ambiguous way. For Heidegger, Paul's turn from abstract philosophical contemplation to the committed existence of a believer indicates care and being-in-the-world, albeit only as an ontic model of what *Being and Time* deploys as the basic transcendental-ontological structure; in the same way, Badiou reads Paul as the first to deploy the formal structure of the Event and truth-procedure, although, for him, religion is not a proper

domain of truth. In both cases, the Pauline experience thus plays the same ex-timate role: it is the best exemplification ("formal indication") of the ontological structure of the Event—albeit, in terms of its positive content, a "false" example, foreign to it.

7 See Robert Pfaller, *Illusionen der Anderen* (Frankfurt: Suhrkamp, 2002).

8 Agnes Heller, *Die Auferstehung des jüdischen Jesus* (Berlin: Philo, 2002).

9 Jacques Lacan, *Le séminaire, livre IV: La relation d'objet* (Paris: Editions du Seuil, 1994), p. 48.

CHAPTER 1 WHEN EAST MEETS WEST

1 See F. W. J. Schelling, *The Ages of the World* (Albany: SUNY Press, 2000).

2 G. K. Chesterton, *Orthodoxy* (San Francisco: Ignatius Press, 1995), p. 139.

3 Ibid., p. 145.

4 Ibid.

5 Ibid.

6 See the detailed analysis in William Klassen, *Judas: Betrayer or Friend of Jesus?* (Minneapolis: Fortress Press, 1996).

7 Søren Kierkegaard, *Fear and Trembling* (Princeton: Princeton University Press, 1983), p. 115.

8 Chesterton, *Orthodoxy*, p. 138.

9 Darian Leader, *Stealing the Mona Lisa: What Art Stops Us from Seeing* (London: Faber & Faber, 2002), pp. 38–39.

10 "Then the eyes of both were opened, and they knew that they were naked" (Genesis 3:5)—what can this mean but that Adam and Eve's eyes were opened to the fact that their bodies were *gazed at?* When I know I am naked, it means I know I am *exposed to the Other's gaze.*

11 C. S. Lewis, *Surprised by Joy* (London: Fontana, 1977), pp. 174–175.

12 Quoted from Orville Schell, *Virtual Tibet* (New York: Henry Holt and Company, 2000), p. 80.

13 See Brian A. Victoria, *Zen at War* (New York: Weatherhilt, 1998).

14 Shaku Soen, quoted in ibid., p. 29.

15 Victoria, *Zen at War*, p. 50.

16 Ibid., p. 113.

17 Ibid., p. 100.

18 Quoted in ibid., p. 103.

19 When does feminine hysteria emerge? On a first approach, it may appear that it occurs when a woman feels as if she is being treated only as a means, manipulated (recall Dora's notion that she is being exploited by her father, offered to Herr K. so that, in exchange, her father can have Frau K.). What, however, if the case is exactly the opposite one? What if the hysterical question emerges precisely when a woman is treated "not only as a means, but also as an end-in-itself," to paraphrase Kant's categorical imperative? It is this "more" of the end with regard to means which gives rise to the question: what is it that you see in me, what is it that I am, which is more than just a means to satisfy some of your needs?

20 See Victoria, Zen at War, p. 103.

21 Quoted in ibid., p. 110.

22 See ibid., p. 104.

23 Quoted from Jon Lee Anderson, Che Guevara: A Revolutionary Life (New York: Grove, 1997), pp. 636–637.

24 See the two famous images—the photo of a Christlike Che, shot in Havana in 1963, and the kitschy Che with a crown of thorns on the controversial advertisement by the Anglican Church of England—reproduced on pp. 12–13 of Peter McLaren's Che Guevara, Paulo Freire, and the Pedagogy of Revolution (Oxford: Rowman & Littlefield, 2000).

25 Quoted in McLaren, Che Guevara, p. 27.

26 Consider Fredric Jameson's remark (from a private conversation) that, in a revolutionary process, violence plays a role analogous to that of wealth in the Protestant legitimization of capitalism: although it has no intrinsic value (and, consequently, should not be fetishized and celebrated for itself, as in the Fascist fascination with it), it serves as a sign of the authenticity of our revolutionary endeavor. When the enemy resists, and engages us in violent conflict, this means that we have, in effect, touched its raw nerve.

27 See Victoria, Zen at War, p. 132.

28 See ibid., pp. 171–174.

29 Bhagavad-Gita, trans. W. Johnson (Oxford: Oxford University Press, 1994), pp. 44–45.

30 It is also worth remembering what Caetano Veloso reports in Verdade tropical, his autobiographical account of his imprisonment by the Brazilian

military dictatorship: the elite military police, like many in the Brazilian counterculture, had adopted an improvised Eastern mysticism as their unofficial religion, even as the military maintained a public face of conservative Catholicism, and in fact arrested dissidents on the basis of their "anti-Catholic" iconoclasm.

31 No wonder that, until the late nineteenth century, they practiced in Montenegro a weird wedding-night ritual: on the evening after the wedding ceremony, the son gets into bed with his mother; after he has fallen asleep, the mother silently withdraws, and lets the bride take her place. After spending the rest of the night with the bride, the son has to escape from the village up into a mountain, and spend a couple of days alone there, in order to get accustomed to the shame of being married.

32 See Chapter 3 of Eric Naiman, *Sex in Public: The Incarnation of Early Soviet Ideology* (Princeton: Princeton University Press, 1997).

CHAPTER 2 THE "THRILLING ROMANCE OF ORTHODOXY"

1 G. K. Chesterton, *Orthodoxy* (San Francisco: Ignatius Press, 1995), p. 107.

2 G. K. Chesterton, "A Defense of Detective Stories," in *The Art of the Mystery Story*, ed. H. Haycraft (New York: The Universal Library, 1946), p. 6.

3 What is the (in)famous Hegelian triad? Three friends are having a drink at a bar; the first one says: "A horrible thing happened to me. At my travel agency, I wanted to say 'A ticket to Pittsburgh!,' and I said, 'A picket to Tittsburgh!'" The second one replies: "That's nothing. At breakfast, I wanted to say to my wife, 'Could you pass me the sugar, honey?,' and what I said was, 'You dirty bitch, you ruined my entire life!'" The third one concludes: "Wait till you hear what happened to me. After gathering up my courage all night, I decided to say to my wife at breakfast exactly what you said to yours, and I ended up saying, 'Could you pass me the sugar, honey?'"

4 Chesterton, *Orthodoxy*, p. 15.

5 Ibid., pp. 146–147.

6 Alan Dershowitz, *Why Terrorism Works* (New Haven: Yale University Press, 2002).

7 See Doug Richmond, *How to Disappear Completely and Never Be Found* (Secaucus, NJ: A Citadel Press Book, 1999). This book belongs to the series of how-to-do manuals which, in effect, constitute a refreshing obscene double of "official" manuals like those of Dale Carnegie: books which directly ad-

dress our publicly inacceptable desires—other titles in the series are: *Cheaters Always Prosper; Advanced Backstabbing and Mudslinging Techniques; Revenge Tactics; Spying on Your Spouse*, and so on.

8 Chesterton, Orthodoxy, pp. 65–66.

9 Ibid., p. 66.

10 Ibid., p. 60.

11 Ibid., p. 62.

12 Ibid., p. 63.

13 What we should not forget is that theories of both inscrutable divine Grace and materialism share their opposition to the notion of Providence (of the ultimate balance between virtues and happiness guaranteed by God): both Grace and materialism leave the connection between virtue and happiness to chance.

14 See Matt Ridley, *Genome* (New York: Perennial, 2000), p. 64.

15 See Jürgen Habermas, *Die Zukunft der menschlichen Natur* (Frankfurt: Suhrkamp, 2001).

16 Chesterton, Orthodoxy, p. 105.

17 Ibid., p. 33.

18 Ibid., p. 39.

19 Ibid., p. 164.

20 Years ago, an ironic review aptly characterized *The Sound of Music* as a movie about a stupid nun who would have been allowed to continue her happy convent life had her Mother Superior not invited her to her room and started to shout at her hysterically about the need to climb every mountain. . . .

21 Chesterton, Orthodoxy, p. 40.

22 Ibid., p. 47.

23 See Jacques Lacan, "Kant avec Sade," in *Ecrits* (Paris: Editions du Seuil, 1966).

24 See Jacques Lacan, *The Ethics of Psychoanalysis* (New York: Routledge, 1992).

25 Michel Surya, *Georges Bataille* (London and New York: Verso, 2002), p. 479.

26 Georges Bataille, *Visions of Excess* (Manchester: Manchester University Press, 1985), p. 154.

27 Surya, *Georges Bataille*, p. 176.

28 Georges Bataille, *Oeuvres complètes* (Paris: Gallimard, 1971–1988), vol. 3, p. 512.

29 Ibid., p. 296.

30 Ibid., p. 232.

31 Here one should refer to the distinction, found in Franz Rosenzweig, between the neighbor (*der Nächste*) and the "near/proximate thing" (*das Nächste*): the neighbor is the intriguing *object* of desire, in front of us, while "the near thing" is the (*object-)cause* of desire, that which, from within us, from behind our back, out of our sight, pushes us toward the object, making it desirable, accounting for the urgency in our approach to the object. (I owe this reference to Eric Santner, of course.)

CHAPTER 3 THE SWERVE OF THE REAL

1 Michael Pauen, *Grundprobleme der Philosophie des Geistes* (Frankfurt: Fischer Verlag, 2001), p. 203.

2 And perhaps this elementary paradox also provides the key to today's cultural-political tension in our relations with foreigners: the tolerant openness, the invitation to them to stay *Da*, and its opposite, the xenophobic demand that they remain *Fort*, at a safe distance.

3 Quoted from Michio Kaku, *Visions* (New York: Anchor Books, 1997), p. 64.

4 Richard Boothby, *Freud as a Philosopher* (New York: Routledge, 2002), p. 272.

5 Ibid., p. 264.

6 Ibid., p. 287.

7 See Alain Badiou, *Le siècle* (unpublished manuscript, 2001).

8 Georges Bataille, *Eroticism* (San Francisco: City Lights, 1987), p. 106.

9 See Jacques Rancière, *La mésentente* (Paris: Galilée, 1995).

10 What, then, is this minimal difference? In the London Aquarium, on the South Bank, there is a pool of water which at first looks empty, filled only with dirty water, full of almost transparent dusty particles. When you take a closer look, however, you notice that these dusty particles are tiny animals which live in the depths of the ocean—almost transparent, "immaterial" creatures which can survive the great pressure of the depths by

being totally open to their environment (to water), totally permeable, their entire materiality consisting of a thin layer that looks like a three-dimensional drawing of their contours, almost deprived of any material substance, floating freely in the water, offering no resistance to it.

11 See Ernesto Laclau and Chantal Mouffe, *Hegemony and Socialist Strategy* (London and New York: Verso, 1985).

12 See Richard Kearney, *Strangers, Gods and Monsters* (London: Routledge, 2003), p. 99.

13 Joseph Campbell, *The Power of Myth* (New York: Doubleday, 1988), p. 222.

14 Bruce Fink, "Knowledge and Jouissance," in *Reading Seminar XX*, ed. Suzanne Barnard and Bruce Fink (Albany: SUNY Press, 2002), p. 40.

15 Ibid.

16 Suzanne Barnard, "Tongues of Angels," in Barnard and Fink, *Reading Seminar XX*, p. 178.

17 "The nurse becomes the patient and the patient becomes the nurse. Vogler's silence forms a screen against which Alma projects what one discipline would call phantasms and another her confessions. Finally, the actress becomes a spectator and the nurse a performer" (Paisley Livingston, *Ingmar Bergman and the Rituals of Art* [Ithaca: Cornell University Press, 1982], p. 206). The use of first name and surname in this quote is fully justified: Alma, as the hysterical subject-patient, is here "personally," in name, revealing her idiosyncratic intimacy; while Elizabeth is here just as "Vogler," the impersonal screen, not as a person.

18 All unmarked quotes that follow are from Jonathan Lear, "Give Dora a Break! A Tale of Eros and Emotional Disruption," in *Erotikon: Essays on Eros, Ancient and Modern*, ed. Shadi Bartsch and Thomas Bartscherer (Chicago: University of Chicago Press, forthcoming).

19 Claude Lévi-Strauss, "Do Dual Organizations Exist?," in *Structural Anthropology* (New York: Basic Books, 1963), pp. 131–163; the drawings are on pp. 133–134.

20 Here I am drawing on Alenka Zupančič, "Truth According to Nietzsche" (intervention at the symposium *Antinomies of Postmodern Reason*, Essen, March 15, 2002).

21 It was, of course, Georg Lukács who, in *History and Class Consciousness*, fully articulated this point.

22 It was, of course, Immanuel Kant who—in the spirit of the Enlightenment's celebration of universal Humanity—deployed the notion of

Christ as the "universal individual," that is, as the individual who immediately stood for the universality of the human species, bypassing all particular qualifications.

23 Today, it may seem that nobody finds Nietzsche shocking anymore—this
holds, however, only if one reduces Nietzsche to a philosopher who professed a set of "opinions" (for example, about the origins of morality,
about religion, about the crisis of modernity . . .), and then goes on to
compare him with others (like Freud), and to argue for or against him.
What gets lost here is Nietzsche's style—not what is often misperceived
as the "pathetic" character of his writings, but, rather, the opposite, the
unbearably naive seriousness of his most excessive statements: in the
Schillerian opposition between the naive and the sentimental, Nietzsche
is thoroughly naive. It is on this level that Nietzsche remains unbearably
shocking—let us imagine that, apropos of a feminist deconstructionist close to Nietzsche, somebody were to pose questions like: "But is she
human at all? Is she a person or, rather, the name of a disease? Is she
not a hyena who poetizes on the graves of masculinity? A milch cow
drained of all milk, but with a 'fine style'?" Furthermore, let us imagine
that someone were to take a mainstream theoretician, and set him or her
against the deconstructionist (as Nietzsche did with Bizet against Wagner):
"How much more life is there in a simple statement by Martha Nussbaum
than in the deconstructionist's entire hysterical rumbling?" . . . Anyone
who finds these questions "inadmissible" (which, to avoid any misunderstanding, I do) and professes to be a Nietzschean is a complete fake.

24 G. W. F. Hegel, *Phenomenology of Spirit* (Oxford: Oxford University Press,
1977), p. 210.

25 And do we not find a similar shift in the history of hermeneutics? When,
two centuries ago, the advance of natural sciences rendered a literal reading of the Bible more and more problematic, hermeneutics emerged
as the study of how one can still understand the Bible in a meaningful
way; from then on, it expanded into the art of the proper understanding of ancient texts. As such, hermeneutics was a specific introductory
art which, later, had to give way to (philosophical) reasoning proper:
once we understand the author properly, we can start arguing with
him. Afterward, however (with Heidegger and Gadamer), hermeneutics
was elevated into the thing itself, the fundamental ontology: if, as Gadamer put it, being, insofar as it is understood, is language—that is to say,
if the way being is disclosed to us is articulated in the horizon of pre-
understanding embedded in language—then ontology itself (research
into the fundamental structure of Being) becomes a matter of hermeneutics, of bringing to light the implicit horizon of meaning within
which beings are disclosed to us. This reversal is crucial: in the course of
it, what first appeared as an introductory/preparatory step, a matter of

special science or technique or interpretive practice, turns out to be the "thing itself."

26 *The Fifth Gospel* (Harrisburg: Trinity Press International, 1998), p. 19.

27 Josiah Ober, "Pontius Pilate Spares Jesus," in *What If?*, ed. Robert Cowley (New York: Berkley Books, 2001). One can nonetheless claim that Ober's story provides an adequate answer to those (like Richard Wagner) who claim that Christ's death was not crucial to his mission, but simply the result of a Jewish betrayal: had Jesus been spared, we would have a much more "Judaized" Christianity.

28 This also makes meaningless the well-known Christian joke according to which, when, in John 8:1–11, Christ says to those who want to stone the woman taken in adultery, "Let him who is without sin among you be the first to throw a stone!," he is immediately hit by a stone, and then shouts back: "Mother! Didn't I ask you to stay at home!"

29 To anyone from ex-Yugoslavia, this joke immediately brings to mind a famous incident with Milošević: in 1989, answering a crowd of hundreds of thousands gathered in Belgrade demanding weapons to attack the Kosovo Albanians, he answered: "I can't hear you very well!" Is this, then, the origin of the post-Yugoslav war: the Leader not hearing the violent demands of the crowd properly? But, of course, as ever, what Milošević got from the crowd was his own message, which he was (not yet) ready to recognize—to assume publicly—in its true form of ethnic violence.

30 Tim Kendall, *Sylvia Plath: A Critical Study* (London: Faber & Faber, 2001), p. 95.

31 Roberto Harrari, *Lacan's Seminar "On Anxiety": An Introduction* (New York: Other Press, 2001), p. 212; original emphasis.

CHAPTER 4 FROM LAW TO LOVE . . . AND BACK

1 I owe this point to Alain Badiou (intervention at the symposium *Paul and Modernity*, UCLA, April 14–16, 2002).

2 G. K. Chesterton, *Orthodoxy* (San Francisco: Ignatius Press, 1995), p. 99.

3 Christopher Hitchens, "We Know Best," *Vanity Fair*, May 2001, p. 34.

4 In what follows I draw on David Horell, *An Introduction to the Study of Paul* (New York and London: Continuum, 2000), pp. 57–59.

5 Ibid., p. 20.

6 Kenneth Burke, *Language as Symbolic Action* (Berkeley: University of California Press, 1966), p. 431.

7   Sheila Fitzpatrick, *Everyday Stalinism* (Oxford: Oxford University Press, 1999), pp. 26–28.

8   See Giorgio Agamben, *Le temps qui reste* (Paris: Editions Payot & Rivages, 2000).

9   See Alain Badiou, *Saint Paul ou la naissance de l'universalisme* (Paris: PUF, 1998).

10 See Agamben, *Le temps qui reste*, pp. 170–171.

11 This is why even a great judge is a Master-figure: he always somehow twists the law in its application by interpreting it creatively.

12 And the link between politics and emotions would be provided by a passing, but crucial, remark by Adorno that love is the proper mode of legitimization for totalitarian and authoritarian regimes: precisely because and insofar as they are unable to offer a "rational" ideological legitimization of their exercises of power, they can appeal only to the "irrational" emotion of love, which is attached to its object not for its determinate qualities, but for its very existence.

13 See, especially, chapter 4 of Jacques Lacan, *The Ethics of Psychoanalysis* (New York: Routledge, 1992).

14 See Jacques Lacan, *Seminar XX: Encore* (New York: Norton, 1998).

15 Of course, love itself can also function in the mode of universality and its exception (you truly love someone if you do not make him or her into the direct center of your universe, if you let it be known that you are ready to drop him or her for some higher Cause). This is one of the great melodramatic themes: a man deserves a woman's love only if he is strong enough to resist the temptation of abandoning everything for her, if he lets her know that he can survive without her—if he drops everything for her, and follows her slavishly, sooner or later she will start to despise him.

16 Private communication, October 24, 2002.

17 Rudolf Bultmann, *Theology of the New Testament*, vol. 1 (London: SCM, 1952), pp. 264–265.

18 See Eric Santner, *On the Psychotheology of Everyday Life* (Chicago: University of Chicago Press, 2001).

CHAPTER 5 SUBTRACTION, JEWISH AND CHRISTIAN

1   Is not Catholic celibacy (the prohibition of marriage for priests and nuns) ultimately anti-Christian, a remainder of pagan attitudes? Is it not

based on the pagan notion that those who sacrifice earthly sexual pleasures thereby gain access to divine *jouissance?*

2   According to Jung, in the conscious suffering of Christ, God atones for the suffering of Job: "for, just as man must suffer from God, so God must suffer from man. Otherwise there can be no reconciliation between the two" (C. G. Jung, *Answer to Job* [Princeton: Bollingen, 1958, p. 39]). The framework here is still that of exchange: one suffering for the other.

3   The interest of Milton's *Paradise Regained* lies in the fact that Satan in this poem is a completely different character from Satan in *Paradise Lost*: no longer the heroic fallen Angel, but a simple agent of temptation—if anything, it is Christ himself who is the counterpart to Satan in *Paradise Lost* here. The topic of both poems is the same; how to resist temptation; and Christ succeeds where Satan fails. Christ is thus not so much the "second Adam" as *the second Satan*: he succeeds where Satan failed. This focus on the topic of fidelity and resisting temptation also links *Paradise Regained* to the Book of Job: not only is Christ's resistance to temptation parallel to Job's; one can also claim that Satan in *Paradise Regained* is a new version of the theological friends who come to comfort Job—the arguments of these "friends" are strictly correlative to Satan's four temptations: those of worldly pleasures, wealth, power, and false religious sacrifice itself (precisely sacrifice as an act of exchange, as "paying the price" for sins). In short, temptation is inherent to religion: Satan's realm is fake theology itself, theology as ideology. Just as the friends offer Job the four basic versions of ideological legitimization, Satan tempts Christ with four versions of ideology.

4   In the context of the "Jewish exception," I am tempted to risk a radical rereading of Freud, who attributed to the Jews the disavowal of the primordial crime (the parricide of Moses): what if even alternative Freudian readings, which propose the hypothesis of a displaced crime (in effect, it was Moses himself who was guilty of the "parricide," killing the Pharaoh), are wrong? What if Moses' true crime was not the murder, but the *humiliation* of the Pharaoh, the public display of his impotence? Is this not worse than a straightforward killing: after the killing, the father returns as the ideal agency of the Law, while the humiliated father merely survives as a ridiculous impotent excrement? What if this humiliation of the father was the precondition for establishing Judaism as the first great religion that, originally and most of the time, was not a state religion, but the religion of a group without a state identity? Furthermore, what if this is what makes the idea of the State of Israel problematic?

5   See Eric Santner, "Traumatic Revelations: Freud's Moses and the Origins of Anti-Semitism," in *Sexuation*, ed. Renata Salecl (Durham: Duke University Press, 2000).

6 See Franz Rosenzweig, *The Star of Redemption* (Notre Dame: University of Notre Dame Press, 1985).

7 See David Horell, *An Introduction to the Study of Paul* (New York and London: Continuum, 2000), p. 82.

8 Rosenzweig, *The Star of Redemption*, pp. 404–405. Of course, I owe this quote to Eric Santner, who developed this notion of Jewish identity in detail in his outstanding *On the Psychotheology of Everyday Life* (Chicago: University of Chicago Press, 2001). Interestingly, this notion of being a remainder is also part of the traditional Slovene national identity; the traumatic cut in Slovene history is the Counter-Reformation offensive in the late sixteenth century, as a result of which a third of all Slovenes were killed, a third emigrated to Germany in order to remain Protestants, and the remainder, the scum who compromised their fidelity, are the present-day Slovenes.

9 Rosenzweig, *The Star of Redemption*, p. 227.

10 And does not Martin Luther King make the same point in his "Letter from Birmingham Jail" (1963)?

> We know through painful experience that freedom is never voluntarily given by the oppressor; it must be demanded by the oppressed. Frankly, I have never yet engaged in a direct-action movement that was "well timed" according to the timetable of those who have not suffered unduly from the disease of segregation. For years now I have heard the word "wait." It rings in the ear of every Negro with a piercing familiarity. This "wait" has almost always meant "never." It has been a tranquilizing thalidomide, relieving the emotional stress for a moment, only to give birth to an ill-formed infant of frustration. We must come to see with the distinguished jurist of yesterday that "justice too long delayed is justice denied." We have waited for more than three hundred and forty years for our God-given and constitutional rights. The nations of Asia and Africa are moving with jetlike speed toward the goal of political independence, and we still creep at horse-and-buggy pace toward the gaining of a cup of coffee at a lunch counter. I guess it is easy for those who have never felt the stinging darts of segregation to say "wait." But when you have seen vicious mobs lynch your mothers and fathers at will and drown your sisters and brothers at whim; when you have seen hate-filled policemen curse, kick, brutalize, and even kill your black brothers and sisters with impunity; when you see the vast majority of your twenty million Negro brothers smothering in an airtight cage of poverty in the midst of an affluent society; when you suddenly find your tongue twisted and your speech stammering as you seek to explain to your six-year-old daughter why she cannot go to the public amusement park that has just been advertised on television, and see tears welling up in her little eyes when she is told that Funtown is closed to colored children, and see the depressing clouds of inferiority begin to form

in her little mental sky, and see her begin to distort her little personality by unconsciously developing a bitterness toward white people; when you have to concoct an answer for a five-year-old son asking in agonizing pathos, "Daddy, why do white people treat colored people so mean?"; when you take a cross-country drive and find it necessary to sleep night after night in the uncomfortable corners of your automobile because no motel will accept you; when you are humiliated day in and day out by nagging signs reading "white" and "colored"; when your first name becomes "nigger" and your middle name becomes "boy" (however old you are) and your last name becomes "John," and when your wife and mother are never given the respected title "Mrs."; when you are harried by day and haunted by night by the fact that you are a Negro, living constantly at tiptoe stance, never knowing what to expect next, and plagued with inner fears and outer resentments; when you are forever fighting a degenerating sense of "nobodyness"—then you will understand why we find it difficult to wait. There comes a time when the cup of endurance runs over and men are no longer willing to be plunged into an abyss of injustice where they experience the bleakness of corroding despair. I hope, sirs, you can understand our legitimate and unavoidable impatience.

11 And it is perhaps on this level that we should also approach the old question, which seems to have regained its relevance recently, of the line of separation between animal and man: at the level of positive being, there is no difference, man is just an animal with specific properties and abilities; it is only from the engaged position of being caught up in the process that the difference becomes palpable.

12 Perhaps the most succinct answer to Christianity, to the Christian notion that the Messiah is already here, was provided by Kafka's claim that the Messiah will definitely arrive, but too late, when humanity is already tired of waiting for him, and his arrival will no longer matter, and will leave people indifferent.

13 Quoted from Hans Jonas, *Mortality and Morality* (Evanston: Northwestern University Press, 1996), p. 192.

14 What goes for woman in psychoanalysis (the masquerade of femininity means that there is no inaccessible feminine X beneath the multiple layers of masks, since these masks ultimately conceal the fact that there is nothing to conceal) also goes for the neighbor: "the secrets of the Egyptians were secrets also for the Egyptians themselves."

15 Jacques Derrida, *Specters of Marx* (London: Routledge, 1994), pp. 64–65.

16 See Jacques Derrida, "Faith and Knowledge," in *Religion*, ed. Jacques Derrida and Gianni Vattimo (Stanford: Stanford University Press, 1998).

17 See Ernesto Laclau, *Emancipation(s)* (London and New York: Verso, 1995).

18 Robert Pfaller, "The Potential of Thresholds to Obstruct and to Facilitate: On the Operation of Displacement in Obsessional Neurosis and Perversion" (unpublished paper, 2002).

19 And the same goes for the relationship of masking. In December 2001, Argentinians took to the streets to protest against the current government, and especially against Cavallo, the economy minister. When the crowd gathered around Cavallo's building, threatening to storm it, he escaped wearing a mask of himself (sold in costume shops so that people could mock him by wearing his mask). It thus seems that Cavallo did at least learn something from the widespread Lacanian movement in Argentina—the fact that a thing is its own best mask. And is this also not the ultimate definition of the divinity—God also has to wear a mask of Himself? Perhaps "God" is the name for this supreme split between the absolute as the noumenal Thing and the absolute as the appearance of itself, for the fact that the two are the same, that the difference between the two is purely formal. In this precise sense, "God" names the supreme contradiction: God—the absolute irrepresentable Beyond—*has to appear as such*.

   Along the same lines, consider the scene from Spike Lee's formidable *Bamboozled*, in which black artists themselves blacken their faces in the style of Al Jolson—perhaps wearing a black mask is the only strategy for them to appear white (that is, to generate the expectation that the "true" face beneath their black mask is white) In this properly Lacanian deception, wearing a black mask is destined to conceal the fact that we *are* black—no wonder, then, that the effect of discovering black under black, when they rinse off their masks, is shocking. Perhaps as a defense against this shock, we nonetheless spontaneously perceive their "true" face beneath the mask as more black than their mask—as if attesting to the fact that the blackening of their face is a strategy for their assimilation into white culture.

APPENDIX: IDEOLOGY TODAY

1 No wonder, then, that these eggs are now banned in the USA, and have to be smuggled in from Canada (and sold at three times the price): behind the official pretext (they encourage people to buy another object, not the one advertised), it is easy to discern the deeper reason—these eggs display too openly the inherent structure of a commodity.

2 See Chapter 4 ("Consuming the Void") in Patricia Fumerton, *Cultural Aesthetics* (Chicago: University of Chicago Press, 1991).

3 See Brian Rotman, *Signifying Nothing* (London: Macmillan, 1987).

4 See Martin Heidegger, "Das Ding," in *Vorträge und Aufsetze* (Pfullingen: Neske, 1954).

5 See Miguel de Beistegui, *Heidegger and the Political* (London: Routledge, 1998).

6 Francis Fukuyama, *Our Posthuman Future* (London: Profile Books, 2002), pp. 149–150.

7 See Dominique Laporte, *History of Shit* (Cambridge, MA: MIT Press, 2000).

8 Otto Weininger, *Über die letzten Dinge* (Munich: Matthes und Seitz Verlag, 1997), p. 187.

9 Ibid., p. 188.

10 There is also, of course, the opposite way of exploiting the example of *Kinder* eggs: why not focus on the fact that the chocolate cover is always the same, while the toy in the middle is always different (which is why the name of the product is "Kinder Surprise")—is this not how it is with human beings? We may look similar, but inside, there is the mystery of our psyche; each of us hides an inner wealth of abyssal proportions. Moreover, one could use the fact that the plastic toy is composed of small parts—just as we are supposed to form our ego.

11 In what follows, I draw on a conversation with Noam Yuran, Tel Aviv.

12 Martin Heidegger, "Hölderlin's Hymne 'Der Ister,'" *Gesamtausgabe* 53 (Frankfurt: Klostermann, 1984), p. 94.

13 Friedrich Nietzsche, *Thus Spake Zarathustra*, quoted from *The Portable Nietzsche* (New York: Viking, 1968), p. 130.

14 Interestingly enough, the same goes for Heidegger's critique of psychoanalysis: what cannot fail to attract our attention are the two levels at which it operates. On the one hand, there is the easy philosophical game of transcendental dismissal (which can even be accompanied by a patronizing admission of its use for medical purposes): "Although psychoanalysis can be of clinical use, it remains an ontic science grounded in the naive physicalist and biologist presuppositions characteristic of the late nineteenth century." On the other hand, there are concrete rebuttals, concrete attempts to demonstrate its inadequacy—how Freud, for example by focusing too readily on the unconscious causal chain, misses the point of the phenomenon he is interpreting, and so on. How are these two procedures related? Is the second one just an unnecessary surplus or a necessary supplement, an implicit admission that direct philosophical rejection is not sufficient? Do we not have here, on a different level, the ambiguity of the notion of catastrophe, simultaneously an ontological fact which has always-already occurred, *and* an ontic threat?

15 See Bernard Williams, *Moral Luck* (Cambridge, UK: Cambridge University Press, 1981).

16 See Jean-Pierre Dupuy, *Pour un catastrophisme éclairé* (Paris: Editions du Seuil, 2002), pp. 124–126.

17 Henri Bergson, *Oeuvres* (Paris: PUF, 1991), pp. 1110–1111.

18 Ibid.

19 Ibid., p. 1340.

20 Dupuy, *Pour un catastrophisme éclairé*, pp. 142–143.

21 There is also, of course, an ideological way of projecting/inserting possibilities into the past. The attitude of many a libertarian Leftist about the disintegration of Yugoslavia is: "The full sovereignty of the ex-Yugoslav republics may be a legitimate goal in itself, but is it worth the price— hundreds of thousands dead, destruction . . . ?" What is false here is that the actual choice in the late 1980s is silently reformulated, as if it was: "Either disintegration of Yugoslavia into separate states—or the continuation of Tito's old Yugoslavia." With Milošević's accession to power, the old Yugoslavia was over, so the only third way with regard to the alternative "Sovereign republics or Serboslavia" was, in a true political act, to reinvent a completely new Yugoslav project; and for this there was neither the capacity nor the inclination in any part of Yugoslavia.

22 Bernard Brodie, *War and Politics* (New York: Macmillan, 1973), pp. 430– 431, quoted from Dupuy, *Pour un catastrophisme éclairé*, pp. 208–209.

23 Dupuy, *Pour un catastrophisme éclairé*, p. 164.

24 The difference between the Cold War enemy and today's terrorist, used to justify America's right to preemptive strikes, is the alleged "irrationality" of the terrorist: while the Communists were cold, rational, and calculating, caring only for their own survival, fundamentalist terrorists are irrational fanatics ready to blow up the entire world. Here, more than ever, we should insist that (as Hegel would have put it) such a figure of the "irrational" enemy is a "reflexive determination" of American's own self-adopted position as the sole hegemonic world power.

25 See Terry Eagelton, *Sweet Violence* (Oxford: Blackwell, 2003).

26 And does not the same apply to anti-abortion campaigns? Do not they, also, participate in the liberal logic of global victimization, extending it even to the unborn?

27 *The Polish Wedding*, a nice melodrama about love-life complications in a Detroit working-class Polish family, contains a scene that revolves around this formula, and thus spills out its truth: when Claire Danes's exasperated boyfriend asks her: "What do you want from me?," she answers: "I want everything!" and calmly walks away from him.

"Mommy, I'm Scared"
· ·

"Mommy, I'm Scared"

How TV and Movies Frighten Children
and What We Can Do to Protect Them

Joanne Cantor, Ph.D.

Harcourt Brace & Company

New York   San Diego   London

Requests for permission to make copies of any part of the work should be
mailed to: Permissions Department, Harcourt Brace & Company,
6277 Sea Harbor Drive, Orlando, Florida 32887-6777.

The author gratefully acknowledges the following for permission to
include previously published vignettes: Lawrence Erlbaum Associates, Inc.
(Mahwah, NJ); J. B. Weaver and R. Tamborini, editors, *Horror Films: Current
Research on Audience Preferences and Reactions;* published 1996. Sage
Publications, Inc. (Thousand Oaks, CA); Tannis MacBeth Williams, editor,
Tuning In to Young Viewers: Social Science Perspectives on Television; published
1996. *Trends in Communication* (no. 2), Boom Publishers, The Netherlands
(e-mail: Boompubl@euronet.nl).

Library of Congress Cataloging-in-Publication Data
Cantor, Joanne.
Mommy, I'm scared: how TV and movies frighten children and
what we can do to protect them/Joanne Cantor.—1st Harvest ed.
p.   cm.
"A Harvest original."
Includes bibliographical references.
ISBN 0-15-100402-1 (hc).—ISBN 0-15-600592-1 (pbk.)
1. Television and children. 2. Motion pictures and children.
3. Fear in children. I. Title.
HQ784.T4C26   1998
302.23'45'083—dc21   98-17080

Text is set in New Baskerville.
Designed by G. B. D. Smith

Printed in the United States of America
A Harvest Original
First edition 1998
F E D C B A

*All the personal experiences related in these pages, which have been taken from
research my colleagues and I have conducted, from student papers, and from
incidents described to me by parents, are real. However, the names of the participants
have been changed to protect their privacy.*

To my mother,

Elizabeth M. Cantor,

in loving memory

Contents

Preface

Every book author and every publisher struggles to find a title that will communicate what the book is about in a direct and immediate way. The title *Mommy, I'm Scared* was suggested to me by a collaborator early on, and it seems to resonate positively with many people, especially mothers. I chose this title because it's a phrase most mothers have heard, and it's also something most of us have probably uttered to our own mothers. But the title is not intended in any way to exclude the many others to whom children turn when they are frightened—especially not fathers, grandparents, and other caregivers who often play an important, comforting role in the lives of children.

Although this book is based on my own academic research, my primary audience is parents and other people who take care of children. I have therefore tried to write it in a way that these readers would find the most interesting and the most helpful. As a parent myself, I know that parents want information that will help them understand their children better and that will give them useful suggestions about how to deal with specific child-rearing problems. In this book, my discussion of children's responses to frightening mass media is based on the findings of controlled research, but I have also filled these pages with illuminating, true examples, many of these presented in a child's or a parent's own words.

In the interest of this general readership, when I talk about research, I include only those elements of a study that will be most useful to people taking care of children. I am not including the names of my coauthors or other researchers or the dates of publication in the body of the text and I am not using footnotes, because I felt all these things might be distracting.

There is a secondary audience for this book, however: other researchers, medical and mental-health professionals, teachers, college professors, and students—readers who may well want to know more about the research I'm describing and may want more concrete documentation of the arguments I am making. For them, I am including notes for each chapter at the back of the book. These notes give the full references for all the studies I am citing and direct the reader to further sources of information.

"Does Your Mother Know What You Do for a Living?"

"You show *what* to little kids in the name of science?" This question, in one form or another, has come my way many times as I make public appearances and discuss my research. And it's a very fair question. Now that I'm a parent myself, I understand the motivation behind it all the more. Any discussion of research on children, particularly when dealing with an emotion as powerful as fright, naturally arouses parental concern. Because much of this book rests on laboratory research, I would like to clarify exactly what kind of work I do with children.

One of the themes of this book is that frightening media depictions can indeed cause long-term damage. Obviously, it would be extremely unethical to try to "prove" this harm by exposing children to horrific movies in the lab and tracking their development over the years. Although this cannot, should not, and will not be done, other forms of research go a long way toward demonstrating that negative effects occur quite often. The evidence I present for intense emotional disturbances in children comes from personal accounts by people who have been exposed to frightening media not in the lab but in their everyday lives. I base these conclusions on case studies, retrospective reports, in-depth interviews, and surveys, including those of random samples of parents. Some social scientists are skeptical of effects that they cannot observe under strictly controlled conditions. However, when a child repeatedly wakes up screaming, "The Wicked Witch of the West is going to get me!" after viewing *The Wizard of Oz*, who among us would doubt that the movie prompted these nightmares?

When it comes to studying children's fright reactions in the lab, I, like any social scientist wishing to work with children, must jump a number of official hurdles put up for the child's protection, including obtaining approval by the Human Subjects Committee of my university and gaining the permission of school systems, teachers, parents, and, when appropriate, the children themselves. When requesting parents' permission, we always inform them about the media content their child might see and invite them to preview the program before giving their permission.

The goal in the experimental research we conduct is not to demonstrate harm. Rather, we try to compare the emotional reactions produced by slightly different versions of the same program or by the same program when viewed by different age groups or under different circumstances. For this purpose we need to use only relatively mild stimuli, and we normally expose children to only a brief excerpt of a scary program. We are always careful not to show children material that will be unduly terrifying or more frightening than material available in any number of widely viewed TV shows or movies. Also, we talk about the program with the children after they see it, and they have the opportunity to discuss any lingering fears they might have. To my knowledge, no child has suffered ill effects as a result of participation in this research. Certainly, no child or parent has reported any problems.

How Accurate Are Childhood Memories?

There has been a great deal of controversy among psychologists and social scientists over whether childhood memories reported in adulthood are accurate enough to be used as the basis for scientific research. Part of the controversy has arisen over news reports that adults have been encouraged or coached to dredge up memories of childhood abuse—incidents that in many cases may never have happened. Although I base my major conclusions on more well controlled surveys and experiments, I do use adults' reports of their childhood memories when investigating the lingering effects of frightening television and movies.

For those reading this book who may be skeptical, I have a few arguments in defense of the accuracy of the retrospective reports included here. Recent research on the validity of childhood memories has concluded that answers to questions regarding childhood events tend to be more accurate when people are asked to report on specific events rather than to give a general evaluation of the tenor of their childhood experiences. It has also been found that parents tend to downplay the impact of negative events relative to what their children report.

Several factors increase my trust in these retrospective reports. First, the adults who write these reports achieve no advantage from exaggerating; if anything, reporting on an intense fright response seems to produce embarrassment.

Second, most of these reports contain clear and vivid descriptions of programs and movies, accounts that turn out to be reasonably accurate when compared to the media fare in question. Third, there are great similarities between different adults' independently recalled reactions to the same programs and movies. Fourth, the age trends in these reports are generally consistent with the trends I have observed in controlled studies of immediate or short-term effects.

Finally, although it is possible that the duration of the reported effects may be overstated in some cases (what seemed like a month may have been only a week, for example), the fact that so many adults still report and reveal ongoing emotional disturbances that they trace back to these programs or movies suggests that these events produced extremely intense reactions and that we should not discount the importance of these long-term emotional memories.

—Joanne Cantor, Ph.D.

"Mommy, I'm Scared"

Is Your Home Really Your Castle?

. . . .

Confronting the Resident Monster

Remember when your first child was born and you took great pains to childproof your home? You locked away the medications and poisonous cleaning agents, hid the knives and the power tools, put safety covers over the electrical outlets, and maybe placed a gate at the top of the stairs. If you're like many parents, you may even have decorated a room especially for your new baby with cheerful, bright colors and a crib that met the latest safety standards. You probably filled your baby's room with a variety of clean, safe, and adorable toys. When you bought something that your child would see or use, you started thinking about how she would react to it. Your child was going to be brought up in an environment that was not only physically safe but also felt happy and warm and comforting. No one who might harm your child would be invited into your home, and nobody could bring unsafe or inappropriate items to your child without your knowledge or say-so. You were the gatekeeper in charge of your castle—*right?*

Unfortunately, if you are like almost 100 percent of the parents in this country and you have a television, your home is full of uninvited virtual intruders of every stripe— monsters, witches, vicious animals, rapists, child molesters, burglars, terrorists, and tornadoes, to name only a few—all ready to disturb that child-friendly environment and pounce on your child's psyche at any moment. If you're concerned about the effect of these images on your child's mental health, you have two choices: Either you get rid of your television or you learn to tame this resident monster.

Chances are, you don't want to get rid of your TV. You probably enjoy watching it yourself and realize that there are many good programs for children. In fact, research now shows that educational television programming viewed at the preschool level can really improve children's chances for success much later in life. Why should you give up on the potential positive effects of television?

This book is for parents who feel that getting rid of their television is not the best option but who want to protect their children from preventable psychological harm. We have come a long way since the fifties, when we had only three channels to choose from and our choices ranged from *Dragnet* to *Hopalong Cassidy* to *The Donna Reed*

Show. Thanks to cable and satellite transmission, we now have 36, 50, even 100 options or more at a time. As a result, today we probably have more television that can inform, entertain, and instruct our children than there was decades ago. At the same time, there is certainly a great deal more television that can unnerve, upset, and traumatize our children than previous generations ever imagined.

Television and movies, by their very nature, have the ability to introduce children to frightening images, events, and ideas, many of which they would not encounter in their entire lives without the mass media. We need to learn how our children are affected by these intruders so we can make better decisions about what they should watch and find ways to help them handle their reactions if they become inordinately troubled.

CHAPTER ONE

The Suddenly Crowded Queen-Size Bed

. . . .

A Wake-Up Call to TV and Movie Fright

Every night, in homes all around the country, parents are being confronted by children in distress. Their children are trembling and sobbing or having nightmares or climbing into their parents' bed and refusing to sleep alone. Some of them are suddenly giving up activities that they once enjoyed, feeling anxious about being alone, or refusing to go to new places.

Are these children reacting to the bully who threatened them at school? Are they worried about the child molester who tried to entice them into his car? Are they anxious about the burglar who just broke into their home? Probably not. Most of these children are reacting to something that never even happened to them. They are traumatized by something they saw on television or in a movie. It's as simple as that. What is worse, the anxiety they are experiencing may not go away in days or even weeks. Often it will last months, years, and even longer.

From my fifteen years of research on mass media and children's fears, I am convinced that TV programs and movies are the number one preventable cause of nightmares and anxieties in children. What's more, although many parents are disturbed about the problem, most don't know how to predict what will frighten their child or what to do about it. That is why I've written this book.

That Midnight Visitor

Does the following story sound like something that's happened in *your* home?

Sara was watching *Goosebumps* with her seven-year-old son, Tim, but she was called out of the room when the phone rang. By the time she returned, Tim was staring in horror at gory and grotesque images from an episode of *The X-Files*. In the program, a man had a sore on his stomach, but it wasn't really a sore; it was his twin brother [!], who would growl and be nasty during the day and murder people viciously at night. Sara made Tim turn off the program, but the damage had been done: The whole family had a terrible night. Sara reports that Tim woke up in a fit and admitted that it was the program that had scared him. For a week, he insisted on sleeping in his parents' bed. After that, they made him go to sleep in his own bed, but they'd wake up and find him back in theirs. Sara was appalled. About a month after the incident, she said Tim was still scared. He was worried that the vicious creature could get into their house.

Or maybe this excerpt from a college student's paper reminds you of something that happened to *you* as a child:

I loved every minute of Poltergeist. *It was like nothing I had ever seen. It was gory and scary and so exciting. Well, in broad daylight at least. That night at home was a completely different story. I was terrified, and I didn't know what to do. How could I tell my parents what I had done and that I was frightened from seeing a movie that they had specifically forbidden me to see? But I was in a state of emergency because the clown that was now under my bed was about to come out any minute if I didn't take immediate action. I built up my courage and successfully made it to my parents' room, constantly looking over my shoulder. I crawled in between my parents in bed, hoping that they wouldn't notice me, but they did. My mom asked me what was wrong, and I mumbled something about the clown and the tree outside my window that were trying to take me away. (By the way, there are no trees tall enough in New York City to reach a window on the seventh floor of an apartment building, and I have never even had a clown doll.) I'm sure my parents knew what I had done because they themselves had seen the movie almost a year earlier. I slept with them in their bed for two whole weeks.*

If either of these anecdotes sounds familiar, rest assured that you have a lot of company. Events like these occur all the time, although they don't receive nearly the publicity that other effects of television do.

I started studying children's fright reactions to television and films in the early eighties. At the beginning of my research career, I had looked at some of the more widely studied effects of television, such as how viewing violence makes people more aggressive. But I started thinking about fear effects after several of my graduate students began telling me about their own children's frightened responses to television—reactions they were at a loss to explain. I was reminded of my own experiences as a child. I remember the terror I felt every time I saw the Wicked Witch of the West in *The Wizard of Oz* and how uneasy listening to *Peter and the Wolf* on my record player made me feel. I remember finding it difficult to sleep at night after watching or listening to something scary, but I also remember not wanting to tell my mother about it. I still somehow wanted to see these things, and I certainly didn't want to be told I couldn't watch them—I was the youngest of three children, and, after all, I didn't want to be treated like a baby!

When I began studying children's fright reactions to media, I was mainly interested in them as an academic researcher. Having studied developmental psychology, I was examining how a child's age affects the types of things that will be frightening. I wasn't initially studying long-term effects or the psychological harm caused by media viewing because you can't study these things in controlled laboratory experiments, the method I was trained in. But because I had such vivid memories of my own, and because I was hearing again and again from others who had had similar experiences, I came to the conclusion that studying children's facial expressions as they watched a scary scene or tabulating their ratings of how scared they felt immediately after watching a five-minute film clip was not enough.

So, at the beginning of each semester, I began asking my students to write short papers about anything on television or in a film that had frightened them. I was immediately struck by how deeply disturbed and distressed my students had been by a program or film, and I was amazed by the vividness and emotionality with which they wrote about their experiences. Almost all the students in these classes were able to recall and describe an incident that disturbed them greatly. Only the rare student reported never having been scared. But looking at these papers as a researcher, I still was unsure how widespread these reactions really were. Since students were putting their names on their papers, could some of them have been elaborating their stories to please their professor?

In order to reduce my doubts, I approached the same question differently. I arranged for first-year college students to be offered extra credit for filling out a brief questionnaire. I'll call this the retrospective study. To receive credit they had to answer the following question:

> Have you ever been so frightened by a television show or movie that the emotional reaction stayed with you after the program was over?

Their choice was either to say "no," and be done with it, or to say "yes," and describe the experience in a one-page paper followed by a three-page questionnaire. Either response would earn them the same amount of credit. As I saw it, laziness or pressures from course assignments would lead many students to choose the easy "no" response. So I felt more confident that the students who took the trouble to complete the anonymous paper and questionnaire were indeed telling the truth and recounting an incident that had meant a great deal to them.

The response was overwhelming: Out of 103 students who were given this option for receiving extra credit, 96 chose the "yes" response and many of them provided graphic and emotional descriptions of the terror that had been provoked by a movie or TV show. Here are two typical excerpts from their descriptions:

> *After the movie* [Jaws], *I had nightmares for a week straight. Always the same one. I'm in a room filled with water with ducts in the walls. They would suddenly open*

*and dozens of sharks would swim out. I felt trapped with
no place to go. I would usually wake up in a sweat. Occasionally I'll still have that exact same dream. The
movie didn't just affect me at night. To this day I'm
afraid to go into the ocean, sometimes even a lake. I'm
afraid that there will be a shark even if I know deep
down that's impossible.*

*The movie that I saw that disturbed me very much
was* Friday the Thirteenth, Part 2. *I watched this
movie when I was fourteen years old and it scared me so
much that I couldn't sleep for a whole month. I was scared
of the name Jason and I hated standing under a thatched
roof. At night I needed a night-light so that I could see
everything around me. I was very conscious of the small-
est little noise. I had nightmares about knives, chain saws,
blood, screams, and hockey masks. I was very jumpy.
This kind of slaughter film still has these effects on me.*

These descriptions are very much like the hundreds
of astonishingly intense examples I've collected from students in my classes and other people I have encountered
or who have written to me. One fascinating aspect of the
student papers is how much the students seem to get out
of writing them. The memories of these incidents are
extremely clear, ten and even fifteen years after the fact,
and students find themselves using dramatic and emotional language that they rarely use elsewhere. When stu-

dents talk about these experiences in class discussions, we can often hear the residue of fear in their voices. And although students are sometimes embarrassed to admit how intense and long-lasting their fear reactions were, they are usually quite relieved to learn that so many others in the class have had the same experience. Many students have reported that being encouraged to think about this traumatic incident reignited their fear. But they have often said that writing about it and learning why it may have happened helped them work through some of their anxieties and ended up reducing their fear in the long run.

A Fear That Lingers

Although the question the students answer is about any fear that lasted beyond the time of viewing, these reactions are typically not one-night affairs. In fact, almost two-thirds of the students in the retrospective study reported that their reactions had lasted a week or more. One-fifth of the students said they had not been able to get the movie or program off their mind, and almost half of them said that what they had seen had interfered with their eating or sleeping. You may have noticed that one of the anecdotes includes the phrase "To this day" to describe a movie's lingering effects. This expression is somewhat unusual in ordinary conversation, but as you read on, you will see that it comes up time and again when people talk about their experiences of TV and movie fright. Even though most of these college students were reporting on events that happened to them in their childhood or adolescence, one-fourth of them said that they were still feeling residues of the fear that the program or movie had produced.

Some skeptics might react to all this with a shrug of the shoulders; it is true that some children can see scary movies and not be greatly upset. But this should not lead us to belittle the harm done to millions of others who are more media sensitive.

Obviously, all children are different. One child's thrill is another child's trauma. Many children, even those who suffer afterward, say they enjoy watching scary movies and TV shows. Witness the eternal popularity of horror movies and the current fad in TV shows such as *Are You Afraid of the Dark?* and *Goosebumps.* Many of us like the spine-tingling feeling of being scared as we identify with a TV or movie character who is in danger. This attitude, which I will discuss in more depth in chapter 9, is frequently seen in students' reports.

The real questions are: How much fright can a child take? When does the spine tingling cease to be fun? And when will the fun experienced while viewing come back to haunt a child in the night? And for how long? And how are children, or parents, for that matter, to know before-hand where a child's terror threshold may lie and which program or movie will cross it?

Although fright reactions to television and films have never been in the limelight of public discussion, over the years a number of psychologists and psychiatrists have claimed that these reactions may cause children to be plagued by nightmares, sleep disturbances, and bizarre fantasies. There have been several case studies in medical journals telling about young people who had to be hospitalized for several days or weeks after watching horror movies such as *The Exorcist* and *Invasion of the Body Snatchers*. One recent article reported that two children had suffered from post-traumatic stress disorder, a diagnosis usually reserved for Vietnam War veterans and victims of physical violence, as a result of watching a horror movie on television. One of the children described in the article was hospitalized for eight weeks.

Obviously these are extreme cases. But, I, too, have received reports indicating that medical attention was necessary as a result of viewing a film. Here's one example:

> *I remember the time ABC broadcast the controversial made-for-television movie* The Day After *in 1983. The show terrified me. For several weeks I was absolutely certain there would be a nuclear war. I had literally become obsessed with the concept of worldwide atomic destruction. I was obsessed to the extent where I would actually wake up around 5 A.M. every morning so frightened I would crawl into bed with my parents. I further would not leave my mother's side—not even to go to the bathroom. And I stopped eating. I became very sick after many weeks with this irrational behavior and had to be taken to the doctor.*

This anecdote came from one of the students in the retrospective study. A few years later I met him when he took my course on the effects of the mass media. At that time he told me that he actually had been hospitalized because of his reaction to *The Day After*, but that he had been too embarrassed to admit that fact earlier, even though he knew his paper was anonymous.

Another student cited *Jaws* as the source of her panic attacks. After describing how she quit the swim team in the middle of a race (in a pool, mind you!) the day after seeing the movie, she continued:

> The movie Jaws *affected me in worse ways than a fear for pools. During the summer going into my sophomore year in college, I returned to summer camp after a seven-year hiatus. On the first day, all counselors had to take a swim test in the lake. Needless to say, I refused to get in, failed my test, and haven't gotten in the lake for the past three summers. Every time my campers had swimming, every time I almost got playfully tossed in, and every time I was even near the lake, I would experience small panic-anxiety attacks. I would always have a persistent fear for the water and I could never get too close to the lake. Consequently, these panic-anxiety attacks started to take a toll on my body, eventually wearing me down until I had trouble walking up even the smallest hill. My heart would race uncontrollably fast*

and my emotions would change constantly; I was laugh-
ing one moment and crying the next. . . . I don't know
if I have overcome my phobia since I am not around
camp during the year, but because of my panic-anxiety
attacks, I get extremely claustrophobic in elevators.

Although these last two cases may be exceptional, what
I've discovered through my research is that intense and
long-lasting media-induced fears are far more common
than we think and often linger well into adulthood. There
are many, many people who admit, like two of the students
already quoted, that they are afraid to swim in oceans or
even lakes or pools since watching *Jaws*. Granted, it is not
that odd that many people think of that great white shark
whenever they swim in the ocean (I know I do!), but when
people give up swimming in lakes or pools because they
once saw a movie about a shark in the ocean, we should indeed be concerned. For these people, a few hours of entertainment has altered their lives.

Many other people suffer the enduring effects of
watching Alfred Hitchcock's *Psycho:*

My phobia of taking a shower without anyone in the
house began in October of 1973. . . . No matter how silly
and childish it may seem, five years older and wiser, I
still find myself peering around the shower curtain in
fear of seeing the beholder of my death.

Jaws and *Psycho* may be the most well-known examples, but there are many, many other shows and movies that have produced effects that won't go away:

> *For years (I'm serious) this movie* [When a Stranger Calls] *has haunted me. For the months following this experience, whenever I was home alone and the phone rang, I feared that the calls were coming from somebody upstairs in my house. A few years ago we moved to a new house where the phones have a panel to show what lines are in use. If I am home alone, I think I subconsciously check to make sure that no other line is being used whenever the phone rings.*

This student's addition of the expression "I'm serious" reflects another interesting aspect of students' papers. The writer seems to be suggesting that the duration of her response is so unreasonable or unusual that I might not believe her. Most of the students who write these papers have no idea how many others have experienced the same effects.

Quite frequently, students talk (sometimes sheepishly) about the elaborate rituals they have developed for coping with their fears. Often these procedures are maintained over long periods of time, sometimes into college. One student reported that she still "protects" herself while sleeping:

When I was around six years old I watched a horror movie about vampires and werewolves preying on innocent people. One behavior that started after this viewing experience is one I still use today. I was convinced vampires would come when I was sleeping, bite my neck, and suck out all my blood. In order to prevent this horrible way of dying, I place a special blanket partially around my neck before I go to sleep. The blanket acts as a barrier between me and the vampire's fangs.

Another student titled her paper "The Bedtime Jump." It began as follows:

To this day, I still leap into my bed from the door after I turn out the light, hoping to avoid any creepy crawly bugs, creatures, or anything else that might run across my feet in the dark. Even though I am almost positive that there really isn't anything on the floor, I do the bedtime jump rather than risk it. I think it all started with the spider movie I watched when I was five or six years old.

And then there's the perennial shower ritual derived from *Psycho:*

For almost two years this had such an impact on me that I would never take a shower unless the curtain was three-fourths open so I could see in the mirror across from

*the shower that no one else was in the bathroom. I even
locked the door at all times. But even that wasn't enough,
so I also pulled out the drawer alongside the door so in
case someone got the door unlocked, they wouldn't be able
to open the door past the drawer.*

Although some of the rituals are almost ludicrous,
some of the recollections are poignant. The following was
the entire description given by one young woman in the
retrospective study, who was told that the expected length
of the paper was about a page:

*The only movie that had any lasting impact causing
me fear was* The Wizard of Oz *when I was little. I used
to sit and cry when the mean witch came on and my parents and older siblings would laugh at me. Then I couldn't
sleep 'cause I thought the witch would come and get me.*

Another description reflects how enduring the impact
was, even though the memory of the movie itself was
vague:

*Although I don't know the name of the film or very
much else about it, I can't get the images to leave my
mind no matter how hard I try.*

Finally, here is an example of a movie that tapped into or
intensified a young man's long-term feelings of paranoia:

Silence of the Lambs has always disturbed me. It's so disturbing because there are people like this out there. They're psychotic and don't care about anything. They like to play with your mind and drive you crazy. Who knows, it may be your best friend. They are out there somewhere, and they may be coming after you or me.

We need to keep in mind here that these are not the reports of psychiatric patients or of young people in trouble. These are university students who, by making it to college, have shown themselves to be relatively successful in their life adjustment. These are not our weakest and most vulnerable young people. And still, something that they never experienced firsthand, but that reached them only via TV or in a movie, has had so profound and distressing an emotional impact. Many of the symptoms they report, such as avoidance of specific activities (especially when there is no rational basis for avoidance), high anxiety levels, recurrent obsessive thoughts, and sleep disturbances, are well-known symptoms of both phobias and post-traumatic stress disorder. Imagine the effects on children who are emotionally at risk!

Spillover Effects

"But he'll get over it," some might say. "A good scare never hurt anyone!" "So what if they worried a bit or had nightmares about a movie? There are lots of things in this world to worry about, so why not this?" As a parent of a young child, I can't really empathize with this attitude. It seems obvious to me that as parents we should want to prevent nightmares and sleep disturbances in our children if we can. And, of course, it's not just emotional distress we need to be concerned with. As some of these examples suggest, the fears induced by media exposure can spill over into everyday life and interfere with otherwise normal activities.

Because I was hearing so many stories of these spillover effects, my colleagues and I designed a study to observe them in a mild form immediately after viewing and to answer a couple of questions: Would watching typical dramatic scenes where people are seriously hurt or die make children worry that they are more likely to become victims of similar accidents? And would seeing scenes like these make children more reluctant to engage in normal activities related to what they had witnessed?

We started with an episode from *Little House on the Prairie*. Although nothing could possibly sound more harmless than the title of this program (which is still on the air in reruns), it was among the top-ten fear-producing shows according to a survey of parents my collaborators and I conducted in the early eighties. Although the series offers a sensitive portrayal of a family facing joys and hardships, it addresses an enormous array of controversial and threatening issues, such as murder, child molestation, and accidental death. The scene we chose was from an episode in which a school for the blind burns down and several people are trapped inside and die in the fire.

We showed the children in our experiment either a five-minute clip from this program or a scene from a movie in which people enjoyed cooking dinner over a campfire without any threat of danger or harm. Still other children saw film clips involving different activities. We then gave the children a questionnaire asking them about a variety of issues. We asked them, for example, how worried they were that various things would happen to them, including being injured in a fire. Lo and behold, those children who had just seen the excerpt from *Little House on the Prairie* were more worried about fires than both the children who saw the other fire scene and children who saw scenes that didn't involve fire at all. What is more telling is that when we later asked them how interested they would be in getting involved in various activities, the kids who had seen *Little House on the Prairie* were less interested than all the others in building a fire in a fireplace. We also found the same type of effect for another movie scene, which showed a drowning. Those children who had just seen that tragic event thought they were more likely to be involved in a dangerous situation in the water, and they were less interested in learning how to paddle a canoe than the other children in the study.

Obviously, what we produced in this controlled experiment was a mild effect that probably did not last very long.

We tried to make sure of this by talking to the children about any continuing fears they might have and using this opportunity to go over guidelines regarding fire and water safety. I think that the minor effect we observed in the lab is in some ways similar to the strong effects I repeatedly see in students' retrospective reports and parents' reports of their children's long-term reactions. For example, one mother I talked to reported that her daughter had learned to ski at the age of four and loved it. However, she abruptly refused to ski anymore after she saw an episode of *Rescue 911* in which a child fell from a chairlift and was shown hanging dangerously by a rope until she was rescued.

Another mother sent me this report:

> *When our youngest daughter was about five, we were traveling in the northwest. One night we watched a James Bond movie on television, containing a scene of a shark that was released into a swimming pool from a grate in the side of the pool. For several days thereafter our daughter refused to go into swimming pools, even at the insistent urging of her older brother and sister. For several years she claimed to be nervous about going into pools where it looked like an underwater shark cage could be hidden.*

The realization that a movie may have interfered with swimming is one of the most common themes in students' papers:

It hadn't occurred to me until just now, but there's probably a connection between having seen and been scared by this movie [Willy Wonka and the Chocolate Factory] *and my extreme fear of having to jump off the diving board at our local YWCA pool. I wasn't scared about the water but worried about coming too close to the grating at the bottom of the pool; I feared that if I got too close, I would get sucked in.*

Sometimes students admit their reaction caused friction with their parents:

One of two frightful experiences I had with television when I was younger was viewing A Nightmare on Elm Street. *I was probably only in second grade when I viewed it. The basic premise was that there was a killer who attacked you in your dreams, but could actually kill you by doing this. He wore a glove with knives attached, and he typically kept this in the basement, usually near the furnace.*

After this incident, I would not go down into our basement, which isn't very creepy, it's decorated. This lasted several months. Once I was willing to go downstairs in the furnished part, I was still petrified to go into the back storage pantry, where our furnace was also located. This made my mom angry because for many years I was too afraid to go in the back room to get food for her. I remember clearly the first time I was actually brave

*enough to venture there with a flashlight to see near the
furnace, and it wasn't until I was in junior high school.
To this day, I am still a bit wary of basements, not because they are creepy but because I imagine the possibility that someone really is lurking there like in the movie.*

Sometimes students express intense frustration at their
reactions:

I was so affected by this movie [Creepshow 2],
*that I was afraid of going into any of the lakes around
my house in fear that an unsuspecting group of lily pads
might turn out to be a killer blob. To tell you the truth,
since the time I saw that movie, I have honestly never
swum in a lake again nor have I gotten up the guts to
watch that segment again. If that is not a fright reaction, fifteen years of avoiding lakes because of a stupid
movie, then I don't know what is.*

What's a Parent to Do?

Why didn't the parents prevent this from happening? you
might ask. Good question. A lot of the parents probably
did not know it was happening until it was too late. A repeated theme in many students' reports is that they
watched without their parents' knowledge and that they
were hesitant to admit they'd been frightened. Our research shows that although many parents are left in the

dark, so to speak, many mothers and fathers know about their children's fears all too well, like those whose stories have been reported in this chapter.

To explore more systematically what parents know, or think they know, about children's fright reactions, my colleagues and I recently conducted a phone survey in Madison, Wisconsin, calling a random sample of close to three hundred parents who had children in kindergarten through sixth grade. Quite a sizable number (43 percent) of these parents reported that their child had been frightened by something on television and that the fear had lasted beyond the time of viewing. Given the tendency of many children to keep their fear to themselves, these parents' reports may be merely the tip of the iceberg. The stories they told revealed an array of fright reactions similar to those I see in students' papers: One child vomited and could not sleep after watching *Are You Afraid of the Dark?*; another stopped helping his mother cook, something he had previously enjoyed, after seeing a *Rescue 911* episode in which a child was burned while cooking; another refused to participate in any outdoor activity after seeing *My Girl*, a movie in which the popular child actor Macaulay Culkin plays a character who dies after being attacked by a swarm of bees; two children were so scared by TV shows that they were uncomfortable going anywhere alone; and one child began hiding inside the house after viewing *The X-Files*, fearful that someone was watching her. Night

terrors, sleep disturbances, fear of the dark, fear of going
to bed alone, and clinging to parents in tears were fairly
common responses.

The movies parents named as frightening on this survey ranged from Disney movies such as *Dumbo* and *Sleeping
Beauty* to *Ghostbusters, Kindergarten Cop,* and *Silence of the
Lambs.* Many parents were surprised by their children's intense reactions and felt powerless when it came to stem-
ming the source. One mother, for example, said it
bothered her that there were no warnings before advertisements for frightening or violent movies, which can pop
up on TV at almost any time.

What the phone survey suggests, then, is that these ad-
verse effects exist not just in the memories of college students. They are important enough and obvious enough to
have been noticed by many parents. Although many children undoubtedly keep their distress to themselves, quite
a few involve their parents in their problem either by
choice or because they can't help it.

Why There's No Easy Solution

After reading all these examples of children who have
been traumatized by such a wide variety of television and
film offerings, you might be wondering if there is any escape from these horrors, short of donating your TV to
charity. The distressing fact is, however, that even if yours
is one of the few families who don't have a TV or who

guard their children's access to it with vigilance, what your child sees is not always in your control.

For one thing, many children like to watch scary programs, and some will try to overcome parental restrictions. Students' reports are full of inventive ways they have found to see forbidden shows without their parents' knowledge.

For another, young children are often exposed to what their older brothers and sisters or baby-sitters are watching. And even the most cautious and aware parents can't always prevent their children from seeing scary shows at the homes of friends or at school or day care. Different families, teachers, and caregivers often have different attitudes about television. Many parents are hesitant to convey their restrictions to the parents of their children's friends for fear of looking old-fashioned or being perceived as controlling.

Even assuming, though, that what your child sees is largely within your control, there are still complicating issues that need to be faced. "Just don't let your children watch horror movies or scary TV shows," you might say. But it's not that simple. It is often very hard for parents to predict what will disturb their children. "I had no idea it would scare him!" is a frequent refrain. Can a parent be fairly blamed for expecting a movie called *Willy Wonka and the Chocolate Factory*—or, for that matter, *Sleeping Beauty* or *Dumbo*—to be benign? The way children see things and make sense of them is very different from the

way we adults see the world and reason about it—an idea
I will explain in detail over the course of this book.

"But my child knows what's real and what's make-
believe," you might say. Again, things are not as straightforward as they appear. As this book will explain, younger
children have a difficult time differentiating fantasy from
reality. And even when they begin to know what's real and
what's make-believe, there are many reasons why make-
believe is scary, too.

And then there's the news, which is *not* make-believe.
News stories about such horrors as the Persian Gulf War,
the Oklahoma City bombing, the abduction and murder
of children, and even tornadoes, floods, and earthquakes
have been deeply upsetting to many children. A vigilant
parent might avoid watching the news with children
around, but what about that dreaded bulletin about the
terrorist bombing of a jetliner that can crop up at any moment? Real stories such as these, that raise genuine threats
to all of us, are especially challenging for parents to help
their children handle.

Finally, entertainment fare in general has become
more graphic and horrifying. The myriad cable channels
and booming video-rental business ensure that there is
virtually no escape from at least occasional exposure to
frightening TV shows and movies. Even advertisements
for scary movies have left some children traumatized.

For all these reasons, you need advice not only on how
to prevent your child's fright reactions but also on the

best ways to help your child cope with something scary while watching it and the best strategies to deal with your child's fright once it occurs.

How This Book Can Help

I want to say at the outset that my goal in writing this book is not to launch a crusade against all potentially scary TV and movie material. I am not out to ban *Snow White*, for example, simply because some young children have nightmares about the wicked queen. Rather, by examining this long-neglected topic, I wish to accomplish four things:

Sound an alert for parents. You may not know how much frightening material your child is viewing or whether it's causing more harm than you realize. Unless you know how pervasive media-induced fright reactions are and how intense and long-lasting they can be, you probably won't know how important it is to be careful about what your child views. And you may not know the right questions to pose when he wakes up in the middle of a nightmare or suddenly refuses to engage in an activity you thought he enjoyed.

Help you predict the kind of material that is likely to scare your child. I will use concepts from developmental psychology to explain which aspects of TV shows and movies frighten children at different ages, and why. Children and adults have different ways of interpreting what

they see, and parents who wish to make sensible judgments about what their child can handle must learn to
consider material from a child's point of view. Providing
you with this knowledge will help you decide for yourself
whether a particular movie or TV show may be too scary
for your child—and reduce your need to rely on reviewers, marketing campaigns, your child's friends, or other
parents. I hope it will also give you confidence in your own
judgments and help you communicate the basis for your
choices in a way that seems reasonable to the other people
who take care of your children.

Guide you in calming your child's fears. Based on the
many studies and interviews I have conducted and on
principles of child development, I will explain different
techniques for calming fears and show how some strategies that work for older kids are ineffective for younger
ones and vice versa. In addition, by explaining the reasons
why certain techniques are appropriate for certain ages, I
hope to enable you to tailor your own coping strategies to
the specific needs of your child.

*Advise you on how best to shield your child from
traumatic content.* Your child may *want* to watch scary programs even if they produce negative side-effects. I'll explain
some of the psychological reasons for this, discuss ways to
communicate tactfully about viewing restrictions, and de-

scribe some additional resources available to parents, such as program ratings and TV-blocking technologies.

One way I believe that this book will distinguish itself from other literature you have read on children and television is that I will not just be giving advice; I will be explaining the psychology behind the advice so that you can apply these principles to new programs and in new situations. My conclusions are based not only on the findings of others but on fifteen years of my own research, including observations of children as they watch television, surveys of parents, and the vivid recollections of hundreds of young adults as they look back on their earlier fright experiences.

It is my greatest hope that parents, grandparents, teachers, and other caregivers will turn to this book for aid and comfort—and pass that on to the children in their lives.

CHAPTER TWO

Through a Child's Eyes

"I Had No Idea It Would Be So Scary"

Why is it so hard to know when your child will be frightened by TV? There are two big issues here. One is that when our children are not under our direct supervision, they see programs we might restrict them from viewing if we knew they were watching them. The other is that, even when we are aware of what our children are watching, it is difficult for most parents to predict what will frighten them.

Why We Don't Know What They're Watching

> *When I was about six or seven years old my parents went out for the evening and left me with a baby-sitter. The CBS network was carrying a movie that night which dealt with a literal swarm of tarantulas taking over a small town and biting all of the inhabitants until they*

*succumbed to the poison of the tarantulas' venom. My
parents had instructed the baby-sitter to not let me watch
this film, but the baby-sitter was watching it and I just
went into the room and sat down. She did nothing to
stop me. . . . While the scenes were a little frightening
then, the feelings have remained, and every time I see a
spider I think of this movie. . . . [O]verall, it is hard to
believe that exposure to this one film fifteen years ago
could have this lasting effect.*

An undeniable fact of family life is that most parents
do not have total control over their children's exposure to
television and films. With busy, working parents, multiple
TV sets in the home, and media available at schools, day
care, and at the houses of friends, very few parents have
the security of knowing exactly when their children are
watching TV or what they're viewing. And, even if your
child is not especially interested in watching scary material, there are many forces that make it more likely that
your child will come upon something distressing.

Our retrospective study of college students showed
that more than half of those who reported a long-term
fright reaction had not particularly wanted to see the program that had caused them to be so upset. They saw it for
other reasons. Often, we see what I have come to call the
baby-sitter effect, which was exemplified at the beginning
of this chapter.

Another frequent scenario is that older brothers and

sisters are interested in a scary movie, and the younger siblings just happen to be there. One young man reported
on his younger sister's fright response and said he still felt
responsible for what had happened to her many years
earlier:

> When Poltergeist *came out on cable in the early*
> *1980s, my brother, my younger sister, and I sat down in*
> *front of the television to watch this unexpected horror*
> *film. My brother and I were fine, but my younger sister*
> *was affected by this movie in an extreme way. My sister*
> *was around ten years old when she experienced this film*
> *and it wasn't till she was thirteen that she was able to*
> *fall asleep in her bed rather than in our mother and*
> *father's. . . . Today, I really feel terrible for my sister that*
> *she had to go through this. Is it possible that she would*
> *be a different person today if she hadn't watched the*
> *scariest movie of all time, according to her?*

Often children see frightening movies at a friend's
house. Sometimes the absence of parental restrictions is
coupled with peer pressure to be brave and macho:

> When I was seven years old, I watched (although it
> *felt like I witnessed)* Friday the Thirteenth, Part 2.
> *My family didn't have cable television or any movie*
> *channels but my friend Mark's family did. One day, just*
> *he and I watched Jason Voorhees chop up and mutilate*

a camp full of oversexed teenagers. I hadn't seen an R-rated movie before this gruesome experience. It blew me away. I stayed for the entirety of the film because I didn't want Mark to think I was a "wussy," and I was also morbidly fascinated by something I'd never been exposed to. After viewing the film, I had nightmares for weeks. I would even lie awake at night (with all the lights on) wondering how long it would take Jason and his twenty-inch blade to find me!

Even a movie promo can induce lasting fears:

When I was about eleven years old there was a movie on TV called The Burning Bed. *It was, I believe, the story of an abused wife who gets fed up and douses her husband with gasoline while he's sleeping. She starts the bed on fire and he burns to death (I assume). I never watched the movie but I saw the ad for it on TV and it scared me to death. . . . I never really worried that someone would start my bed on fire, but I was suddenly certain that we were going to have a house fire which would eventually reach my bedroom and my bed. I would lie awake as long as I could, trying to stay alert, trying to smell the smoke that I knew was going to come creeping under my door.*

Although many fright stories reveal that children's exposure to scary movies was due to chance or to the viewing choices of people around them, quite a few others tell about children who really wanted to see the movie that ultimately scared them. Many students report viewing in secret, against their parents' wishes:

> *When I was about ten years old my mother and father were planning to watch* An American Werewolf in London *on television. . . . I wanted to stay up and watch it with them. My mother explained to me that she did not feel that it would be a good idea. Needless to say, I was upset and determined to watch the man turn into a werewolf. They put me to bed and the movie started. I waited fifteen minutes and then sneaked into our living room. My parents could not see me because the couch was positioned with their backs to me.*

The young girl who confessed this intrigue watched the movie for only about a half hour and returned to her bed without getting caught. But her fright response prevented her from pulling off her caper successfully:

> *That night I had an awful dream. I dreamt that a pack of werewolves was surrounding my bed. They were all drooling blood and growling. They did not jump on my bed to eat me, so I felt safe. This allowed me to dream that I was going back to sleep again. But then I realized that I had to go to the bathroom. Here was the problem:*

If I relieved my bodily function properly, I would be eaten and slashed by many werewolves. Therefore, I could not get off my bed. This dream seemed so real to me that I actually ended up peeing in my bed. I explained to my mother what happened. I got grounded, but we remember this episode as if it happened yesterday.

Why We Can't Tell What They're "Seeing"

Perhaps many adults would expect shows like *Friday the Thirteenth* and *Poltergeist* to be scary, at least if they saw them first. Presumably if parents had been aware that their children were viewing these shows, they might not have been surprised by their reactions. But many other offerings that produce fright seem utterly harmless. *Little House on the Prairie* is a prime example of a title that sounds just too family-friendly to invite parental concern. (I've noticed that students are especially embarrassed to mention that program in class discussions of their fright, particularly because of its name and reputation.) Parents who are trying to be vigilant are often misled by titles, advertising and promotional gimmicks, the presence of a particular actor, the source or studio producing a movie, or a movie's Motion Picture Association of America (MPAA) rating. One concerned parent describes being mistakenly reassured:

My children had been wanting to see the movie Jumanji *since it starred Robin Williams and they had*

enjoyed watching other Robin Williams movies like Mrs.
Doubtfire. *It seemed, from the previews I'd seen, to be
an entertaining movie for children. It was rated PG. I
hadn't heard anything negative about it, so we rented it.
My thirteen-year-old thought it was funny and enjoyed it
immensely. My eight-year-old was a bit fearful of it but
still entertained by it. My six-year-old, who's normally
very daring and adventurous, was terrified of the ele-
phants and rhinoceroses and other huge animals chasing people through houses and refused to leave my side
the rest of the day, despite my assurances that it was just
a movie and couldn't really happen.*

This mother was facing a problem that is confronted
by most families with more than one child: the difficulty
of selecting a movie that will entertain the older children
without traumatizing the younger ones. I will return to
this problem in a later chapter because there's no easy solution to it. For a large portion of what is available in the
media, what is right for one age group is definitely wrong
for another.

In addition, this mother was relying on the MPAA rating of PG: "Parental Guidance Suggested," and she assumed that the movie would be relatively mild in its
impact. In a later chapter, I will discuss this rating system
in more detail and explain why it is so hard to rely on
movie ratings in making viewing choices for children.

Even G-rated movies, those that are supposed to be for "General Audiences," including children, often aren't that safe for young children. Most parents mistakenly assume that a G rating means there's nothing to worry about. Animated, G-rated fairy tale and adventure features provide a good example of this misunderstanding. These movies are a staple of preschooler entertainment, yet when viewed by young children, they often produce fears that last well beyond the time of viewing. I have received reports of children's persistent fears related to many of these features, from *Bambi, Dumbo,* and *Pinocchio* to *Beauty and the Beast* and *The Hunchback of Notre Dame.* Parents who report their children's reactions to these movies are often surprised by the intensity of their child's response.

Why not attack fairy tales, then, you might ask? You may have heard the argument that children's folk stories, and fairy tales, in particular, have always had scary and gruesome elements. Some well-known psychoanalysts have proposed that these stories allow children to work through "traumas that are seething in the unconscious." First, let me say that I have never seen any evidence that fairy tales have this positive effect. But even if such "unconscious" effects might occur from hearing or reading fairy tales, reading a story or being read to is very different from watching television and movies, particularly for young children.

One way in which written fairy tales differ from television and movies is in the way they are usually received by the child. Children who are old enough to read the words can pace themselves according to how much they can handle, and the story will become only as frightening as their imagination lets it be. But, in any event, most children are first exposed to fairy tales by listening to an adult read the words to them. In viewing situations, in contrast, the adult mediator is gone, and often no adult is present at all.

I remember the first time I read the book version of Disney's *Snow White and the Seven Dwarfs* to my then four-year-old son. Although I myself had seen the movie as a child, I couldn't help being unnerved as I read aloud that the wicked queen ordered the huntsman to cut out Snow White's heart because she was jealous of the girl's beauty. I found myself doing a bit of selective editing then and there, doling out the story in smaller, gentler doses, because I was sensitive to the impact it would have. I also noticed how frightening my son found some of the visual images in the book, which were stills taken from the animated Disney feature. I was very glad he was first exposed to this story with me as a "translator" and reassuring presence, rather than having the movie or video version thrust upon him full force.

Had he first seen the movie or video, he would have seen the entire story (or all that he could take!) without editing for his needs, and the visual images would not only have been larger, they would have been in motion. Illustrations in a book are generally less frightening than motion pictures because our brains are wired to react more intensely to moving images (especially threatening images that seem to be coming toward us). I particularly remember my own fear as a child watching *Snow White* when the heroine was lost in the forest. What at first looked like normal trees suddenly sprouted bright yellow eyes and took on the appearance of monsters that grabbed at her as she tried unsuccessfully to escape. Animated adventure features are especially full of grotesque, evil characters who move rapidly and threateningly toward their intended victims and seemingly toward the viewing audience as well.

One young man's memory illustrates the intensity of a child's reaction to a classic Disney film:

> *When I was seven my sister took me to a showing of* Alice in Wonderland. *Throughout the movie I felt uncomfortable with the world that Alice was blundering through. One thing that really frightened me was the grinning Cheshire Cat character. Its evil smile and hissing speech had a lasting effect on me. For years afterward I was afraid of cats and don't care for them even now. But the most intense fear that I have ever experienced was the portion of the movie where Alice is captured by the Queen and her army of "card-men." When the Queen screamed, "Off with her head!" I snapped. I started to cry*

*and hid beneath my seat, cowering from the images on the
screen. I remember being unable to sleep well for about a
week after the experience. My parents had to go to great
lengths to assure me that no one was going to behead me
while I slept. . . . One thing that I think had an impact
on the intensity of my experience was the fact that my parents were not sitting next to me. Without them I was literally at the mercy of the images on the screen.*

But why is it, you may ask, that young children respond so intensely to these apparently fun, animated, totally unrealistic movies? Don't they know (and don't we
tell them often enough) that what is shown in them is totally unreal and could never happen? Isn't it unreasonable
for children to be frightened by these movies that are intended mainly for their entertainment? What's going on
here?

What's going on here is that young children are viewing these movies through a child's eyes. What we are seeing as adults and what they are seeing as children are, for
all intents and purposes, entirely different movies. It is
difficult for parents, but extremely important, to be able
to see television and movies in the way their child will see
them.

The young man who recalled his reaction to *Alice in
Wonderland* showed some insight into this issue while trying to explain the intensity of his reaction:

A small child tends to believe what is presented to him and take it at face value. I took the Cheshire Cat and the beheading to be real and transferred it to my own life.

The Importance of Understanding Child Development

I became interested in studying children's fright reactions to television partly because of the unpredictability of these effects. I didn't find it especially odd that people were having nightmares from *Jaws* or *Psycho,* but it intrigued me that so many parents were perplexed about their children's reactions to movies and programs that they did not expect would frighten them. I also found it fascinating that children of different ages seemed to be frightened by different *types* of programs and events. It might seem logical to expect that the youngest children would be the most frightened by just about every scary image, and that as children matured, all media offerings would become less frightening. But this is not what I was observing. As children get older, some things become less frightening, but other things that have not been disturbing in the past suddenly begin to terrorize.

My approach was to turn to developmental psychology for insights. What do child psychologists know, I wondered, about how children see and reason about the world at different ages? To begin to answer this question I immersed myself in the writings of Jean Piaget, the Swiss psychologist who is generally credited with being the founder of the field of developmental psychology. Like many great researchers, Piaget stumbled onto the field that he made his life's work somewhat by accident.

Early in his career, Piaget was hired to help produce items for intelligence tests. In other words, he was developing questions that would reflect children's intellectual development. What came to fascinate Piaget more than differentiating between the smarter kids, who got the right answers, and the less smart kids, who did not, was the types of errors that young children made consistently. You might expect, for example, that up to a certain age, children would not know the right answer to a particular problem and that they therefore would be uncertain or choose a variety of wrong responses. Instead, what Piaget observed was that for some tasks, the young children who got them wrong would respond without hesitation. And not only would they be sure they were right, they would all choose the same "wrong" answer. What adults saw as the wrong answer was clearly "right" for them.

A typical task involved showing children two ball-shaped globs of clay that were the same size. After getting them to agree that both balls had the same amount of clay, Piaget would let them watch as he rolled one of the balls out into a long, thin, snake shape. Then he would ask whether they both still had the same amount of clay or whether one had more than the other. Piaget found that four- and five-year-olds usually replied without hesitation that the clay in the form of the snake had more. Nine- and ten-year-olds almost always recognized that the two globs of clay had the same amount. From observing many examples like this, Piaget became fascinated with what these younger children were seeing that their older counterparts were not, and he spent the rest of his eighty-odd years observing and chronicling how children of different ages see the world around them and make sense of it.

What, you may now be asking, does the shape of globs of clay have to do with children's fright reactions to television? Piaget did not focus on the topic of children's fears, but as I read about his research and the generalizations he made about children's thought processes, I couldn't help thinking that the types of viewing and reasoning differences Piaget observed in children would have direct effects on their emotional reactions to the images and events they received through television. What particularly fascinated me about these differences was that many of them weren't intuitively obvious. By the time we become adults, we forget many aspects of the way the world seemed to us as children.

What follows in the next few chapters is an examination of some of the major patterns that Piaget and other developmental psychologists have observed in the way children of different ages see the world and reason about it, and how these can be applied to understanding children's emotional reactions to television. In addition to explaining these concepts and giving examples, I will report

on the research I have done that confirms these principles. I will also explain how you can use this information
in guiding your children's viewing and helping them cope
with any unwanted reactions they may have.

Of Ages, Stages, and Your Uniquely Individual Child

Before getting started on the specifics of how some basic
principles of child development can help you understand
your child's reactions to television, I want to inject a few
words of caution about the use of age guidelines. One way
in which research on child development is sometimes misunderstood is that people expect age guidelines to be absolute and inflexible. As you well know, not all children
develop at exactly the same rate. Most age guidelines used
in this book should be considered broad trends around
which most children will group, but for which there may
be many exceptions. For example, the age at which a child
begins to be more frightened by real than by fantasy figures
(as discussed in chapter 5) may vary somewhat from child
to child. But it should be helpful to know that preschool
children are generally more frightened by fantasy figures,
and that by the end of elementary school most children
are more frightened by things that could really happen.

Another thing to keep in mind is that although this
book will focus on specific aspects of television programs,
one at a time, all programs contain many elements that
work together to affect the emotions of children. A fan-

tasy program may be extremely vivid or not; it may contain eerie-sounding music or not; and it may deal with an issue that is of concern to your child at the moment of viewing or the whole idea may be entirely new. For example, a girl who we might otherwise expect to be too old or too young to react intensely to a particular type of show might be frightened because it relates to something that is currently going on in her family. In short, although we will be considering various elements of programs separately, they must be thought of as part of a whole when determining whether a particular program scares a particular child.

And, of course, we must never forget that you are the person who knows your child the best, and all the advice here should be considered in the context of what you already know about your child. Your child may be outgoing and adventurous or shy and hesitant to try new things. She may love or hate roller coasters, and she may be a sound sleeper or one whose sleep is easily disturbed. She may live in a dangerous neighborhood or in peaceful surroundings. She may or may not have already been exposed to the death or severe illness of family members. And she may already love or hate to watch scary things on television.

Finally, you may have more than one child, and even children in the same family can differ dramatically. All of the guidelines I will be providing here will need to be filtered through a knowledge of each child's personality and experiences. You may have one child for whom scary programs are a problem, and another who can't seem to get enough of them. This entire book should be helpful to you in dealing with your easily frightened child, but parts will also enhance your understanding of your thrill seekers. In that particular regard, chapters 9, 10, and 11 deal with why children like scary programs and how parents can discourage them from overexposure without accidentally making these programs more tantalizing.

With these considerations in mind, let us move on to some specifics of how young children's manner of thinking and seeing makes them respond with fright to programs and movies that few adults would expect to be traumatic.

CHAPTER THREE

Appearance, Appearance, Appearance

Beauty's More Than Skin Deep

> *Even though the amazing powers of the Bionic Woman*
> *saved the day, the image of the monster stayed with me.*
> *Time and again my dreams contained at least some*
> *slow-motion footage of the creature that would cause me*
> *to wake up with a start.*

A Picture's Worth a Million Words

About the time I was beginning to look at children's fright reactions from the perspective of child development, my husband and I built an addition onto our house. Toward the beginning of the construction process, an old friend dropped by with his three-year-old son, Sam. As we sat on our deck reminiscing about old times, Sam's attention became fully fixated upon the large crater in the ground right next to where we were sitting. The sight was, objectively speaking, horrible. Right after the construction crews had dug the hole, we had had torrential rains, and the area was in complete disarray. With the demolition work that had been carried out in preparation for the construction, the yard looked more like the site of a bombing than the place where a handsome new room would soon be built. Sam repeatedly interrupted us, asking the same question over and over. "What's that hole?" he would say, and we would repeatedly answer, saying something like "That's where they're going to build our new living room." During each explanation, Sam would turn toward us and away from the hole, and then nod his head as if he understood. But the next time he turned his head and saw the hole, the explanation would evaporate from his mind, and he would anxiously ask the same question again. After repeated attempts on our part to explain what the hole was for, and after a good deal of irritation on the part of Sam's father, we simply gave up.

Although we failed to reassure Sam, my familiarity with Piaget made me realize that he was exhibiting an important characteristic of the way preschool children react to the world around them: The visual image Sam was dealing with was simply too powerful to be explained away in words.

Research shows that very young children respond to things mainly in terms of how they appear. When Piaget tried to analyze young children's reactions to different-shaped globs of clay, he reasoned that one of their problems was that the longer, thinner glob *looked* bigger. A follower of Piaget noted that young children focus on and react to whatever "clamors loudest for their attention," often ignoring other things that are available to see and hear. In the clay test, the length of the glob seems to grab children's attention more easily than its circumference.

In general, what clamors loudest for the young child's attention is whatever is the most immediately and easily perceived—whatever is the most vividly visual or makes the most intense noise and whatever needs no learning or interpretation to appreciate. Often what grabs the child's attention the most is what something looks like, but sometimes sounds that are striking or peculiar do the same thing. I'll focus first on the effect of visual appearance because we know the most about this.

If you ask preschool children to group a set of pictures according to which things go together, they will usually match items that look alike. They might pair things that are the same color or the same size or the same shape and show little concern for things that belong together for other reasons. Suppose we give preschoolers four pictures: a blue hammer, a red saw, a blue fork, and a red plate. These children are likely to match the two red things and the two blue things. But as they come closer to the age of seven or so, they are more and more likely to say that the hammer goes with the saw and the fork goes with the plate because older children give color less importance and begin to think about things belonging together that are used together or have a similar function. Color is a much more obvious visual characteristic of these items; their function is something that is learned over time.

The implications of these findings for the types of things that should frighten children on television seemed clear to me. If young children react most strongly to the appearance of things when they are asked to sort them, shouldn't looks count the most heavily in what frightens them? If this is the case, things that *look* scary should be the most frightening to preschool children. The first thing my colleagues and I did to explore this idea was to ask parents which programs and movies had frightened their children the most. We gave a written questionnaire to parents of children from eleven preschools and eight elementary schools, asking them to list the television shows or movies that had caused the most fear and distress in their child. The results suggested that I might be right. What frightened preschoolers the most according to parents? *The Incredible Hulk,* an adventure program starring a monstrous-looking superhero, and *The Wizard of Oz.* Both of these shows feature grotesque, green-faced, scary-looking characters.

We can see the importance of appearance in the retrospective reports of many college students who remember their fear of the Hulk:

I can still vividly recall every detail—the green skin,
the bulging biceps, and the gnarly black mop of hair.

Similarly, when college students talk about their nightmares from *The Wizard of Oz,* many of them emphasize the
frightening appearance of the Wicked Witch of the West.
Here are some typical examples:

For me, the thing that topped all of these was the
Wicked Witch of the West from the movie classic The
Wizard of Oz. *Her scary, screeching voice, her green*
skin, her broomstick, and her big black hat all haunted
me for years after first seeing the movie at age six.

The witches and the monkeys caused me to either
run out of the room or at least close my eyes. . . . The im-
ages are so vivid with the witch's green face and ugly fea-
tures along with that horrifying voice and laugh.

Many other memories of fright experienced by young
children also focus on visual aspects of the terror-
producing movie or TV show. Here's a typical example:

When I was five or six years old, I viewed the movie
Tarantulas. *It was a black-and-white B-rated* [sic] *film*
that would strike many people as either funny or silly if
viewed at an older age. The contents of the movie escape
my mind except that I am still left with the lingering

image of an ungodly-sized tarantula walking over a city
as mass crowds run from the forthcoming destruction. . . .
Nothing has scared me quite like that since, and I some-
times wonder if my keen dislike of spiders and spidery
things stems from my initial step past the boundaries of
reality, dealing with that tarantula.

The next example shows a college student's memory of watching *Star Trek* when he was four years old. Note the striking detail of the writer's memory and his keen emphasis on the visual images:

Throughout the entire episode, people dropped like
flies, yet watching the corpses pile up is not what truly ter-
rified me. What sent shivers up my spine was seeing what
this "salt vampire" really looked like. Ugly would have
been an understatement. This creature had deeply inset
black eyes, a large gaping mouth which sported several
sharp fangs, and was covered from head to toe with long,
unkempt, dirty gray hair. Another notable feature was the
creature's suction cup–like "salt-suckers" on its palms
and fingers, which it used to extract the victim's salt di-
rectly from their face (yeech!). I distinctly remember that
those "suckers" unnerved me more than anything else.
This was easily the scariest thing that this particular
four-year-old had ever seen. The image of this grotesquely
hideous creature kept me awake the entire night. I had

this fear that a salt vampire was going to grab me from
underneath my bed, suck out my face, and end my life.

When Appearance Competes with Other Factors

Although the anecdotes were fascinating and the survey research was encouraging, I knew I needed to study the effect of appearance more systematically. Older children and adults are also sometimes upset by gory, grotesque images. What I really wanted to know was whether young children are *more* sensitive to grotesque visual images than older children. Although we had many more examples of intense reactions to scary-looking characters in younger than in older children, my colleagues and I answered the question about how sensitive to appearance different age groups are by doing a controlled experiment.

As I explained earlier, developmental research on matching tasks shows that in addition to being more likely to respond to how things look, preschool children are less likely than older children to respond to other aspects of a situation. As children move into the middle and later elementary-school years, they give other types of information more weight—information that is not as closely tied to appearance. What we wanted to do in our research, then, was to test the idea that younger children are more sensitive to the appearance of characters than older children, and that older children are more sensitive than

younger children to other aspects of a program, such as
what the character says or does or the character's good or
evil intentions.

We produced a video in four versions so that we could
systematically vary both the appearance and the behavior
of a character while leaving the story identical in every
other respect. In our video, the main character, an old
woman, was created with two very different appearances:
She appeared either ugly and witchlike or attractive and
grandmotherly. In the story, the old woman was seen to
behave either kindly or cruelly.

The story involves two curious children who enter an
old woman's house, uninvited, to retrieve their wandering
dog. When they suddenly hear her voice, they hide under
her dining-room table and watch as she discovers a stray
cat in her front hall. In the "kind" scenario, the old
woman welcomes the cat, cuddling it in her arms, and
cheerfully feeds it a bowl of cream. In the "cruel" scenario, she yells at the cat, throws it down the basement
stairs, and threatens to starve it. The video does not have
a true ending. The tape stops just as the old woman is
about to find the children.

There were four versions of the story: one in which
the main character was ugly and kind; one in which she
was ugly and cruel; one in which she was attractive and
kind; and one in which she was attractive and cruel. In the
experiment, we showed our videos to children in three age
groups. The youngest children were between three and

five; children in the middle group were six or seven; and those in the oldest group were nine or ten. Each child saw only one of the four versions.

What we found in this experiment was just what we expected. When we asked the children to rate how nice or mean the old lady was, the youngest group was most affected by how the old woman looked and least affected by how she had behaved. On the whole, the youngest children tended to think the woman was nice when she was attractive and mean when she was ugly. As the age of the children increased, the woman's looks made less and less of a difference. At the same time, the woman's behavior became more important as the children got older. In addition, when they were asked to predict what the woman would do to the children when she found them, the youngest group was strongly affected by the way she looked. Her pleasant looks made them more likely to say she would serve the children cookies, and her ugly looks made more of them think she would lock them up in a closet! Older children's expectations were not affected by what she looked like. Only her prior behavior influenced their predictions.

It is important to note that this study did not show that appearances never affect the reactions of older children. In fact, we did a second study where we showed children pictures of the old woman and asked them how they expected her to behave in a TV program. Without information about her behavior, children in all three age groups expected the ugly woman to be mean and the attractive woman to be nice. All children, and even adults, engage in stereotyping to some extent. What the first experiment showed is that when a situation involves both vivid appearances *and* other information that is less obviously visual, younger children are more influenced by appearance and less influenced by the other information than older children are.

As a generalization, then, we can say that preschool children are more likely to be frightened by something that looks scary but is actually harmless than by something that looks attractive but is actually harmful. As children get older, they come to understand that looks and behavior may be inconsistent, and they are frightened by things that cause harm but do not necessarily have a vivid visual presence. *The Amityville Horror* is a good example of a movie with a dangerous but largely invisible evil force. In the survey we conducted in the early eighties, this movie was reported to have scared many more older children than younger ones.

The Day After is another good example of a movie that frightened older children more than younger ones because the threat it depicted was more abstract than vividly visual. This made-for-TV movie depicted a Kansas community in the aftermath of a nuclear attack. Prior to its airing, the program was described as "bringing the unwatchable to TV" and "the starkest nightmare ever broadcast."

Although some national education groups and many elementary schools urged that younger children be shielded from viewing the movie, we felt that this advice was misplaced. The movie's major theme involves the abstract threat of nuclear annihilation, with the real horror of the movie coming from the contemplation of the end of civilization as we know it. These are terrifying concepts, yet they are beyond the mental capacity of the young child and cannot be conveyed in pictures.

Contrary to general expectations, we thought the movie would be more terrifying the more the viewer had the mental capacity to grasp these abstract themes. When we conducted a random phone survey of parents the night after the movie aired, we found that children under twelve were much less disturbed by the film than were teenagers. (In fact, the parents reported being more disturbed than their children!) The very youngest children who saw the movie (three- to seven-year-olds) were not at all upset. Indeed, when parents of the youngest group of children were asked whether any TV shows or movies had scared their child more than *The Day After,* they named such apparently benign offerings as the animated movie *Charlotte's Web* and the children's show *Captain Kangaroo.* Parents of teenagers, in contrast, said that *The Day After* had been the most frightening thing their child had seen all year.

These results are not surprising when you consider the cognitive abilities of young children. Public opinion about the movie's effects was based on an adult view of the movie rather than an understanding that young children would be relatively unmoved by the film's abstract, while admittedly devastating, implications.

The Wicked Beauty and the Kindhearted Beast

The fact that preschool children react mainly on the basis of appearance is especially important when they confront situations in which physical appearance contrasts with other aspects of a character or situation. In the typical story where you have an ugly villain and a handsome hero or beautiful heroine, preschool children generally have no problem understanding the intended characterization. But they often react in unexpected ways when the hero is ugly or an evil character is beautiful.

On a personal note, this explains my puzzlement the first time I saw *Gone with the Wind* at about the age of five. I was so impressed with Scarlett O'Hara's beauty that I remember not being able to understand why everybody was criticizing her for being selfish and coldhearted. She was so beautiful, and to me she could do no wrong. It wasn't until I was much older that I could put looks aside and make any sense of the story line.

The monstrous but admirable Incredible Hulk is another good example of a hero bound to be misunderstood by young children. I have even received several retrospective reports from students who were frightened by The Count on *Sesame Street*. Although this muppet is there to teach numbers and not to frighten kids, some children are alarmed by his vampire-like appearance. And of course, there's E.T., that lovable extraterrestrial from the movie of the same name. Many parents have reported how frightened their preschoolers were of the central character of this heartwarming movie. It didn't matter to these children how kind and sweet and helpful E.T. was, nor how many times parents tried to explain the creature's lovable nature; children were still extremely upset.

In trying to predict whether a television show or movie will frighten children up to about six or seven, then, it is most important to first look at the visual images that will confront them. If these images are gory or grotesque, my advice is to wait.

The following description recounts a sad example of the impact of parents not anticipating the power of grotesque visual images:

> *When I was five years old, my parents took me to a drive-in theater to see a movie. They chose an adult-oriented film,* The Elephant Man, *because they thought that I would fall asleep in the car. They regret making that assumption to this day. Surprisingly, I stayed awake through the whole film, absorbing enough of it to be traumatized for the next couple of years. The movie is a true story based on the life of John Merrick, a nineteenth-century Englishman who was afflicted with a disease*

that left him horribly deformed. He became part of a freak show and always wore a paper bag over his head so that people couldn't see his horribly disfigured face. When I saw the Elephant Man in the movie, I thought he was the ugliest, meanest monster I had ever seen. In an attempt to ease my fears, my father would always explain that the Elephant Man wasn't a monster; he was really a nice man that everybody just misunderstood. The Elephant Man would never hurt a little girl, he said, and he couldn't help it that he had a disfiguring disease.

I don't think I or my parents slept very much during the next two years. I had terrible nightmares that the Elephant Man with a paper bag over his head was chasing after me. I would wake up screaming and crying, then I would be too afraid to close my eyes again. I was sure that he was hiding in my closet, under my bed, or behind the shower curtain in the bathroom.

This example is telling not only because of the intensity of the fear that the movie produced, but because it shows how the visual image overpowered the message of the film in this child's mind. Adults, too, might be woefully upset after viewing this movie. As adults, though, we would probably empathize with Merrick as a victim, and perhaps we would feel shame that our society so mistreats individuals whose only crime is to be unsightly. That message was lost on this young child. To her, the Elephant Man was the villain, and he appeared in her dreams as her attacker. This response is not unusual. As we will see in the next chapter, many nightmares about the Incredible Hulk involve fears of being attacked by this benevolent but grotesque creature.

Are Some Images Naturally Scary?

But why are young children so quick to consider certain images scary? Just what makes something attractive or repulsive to a child or, for that matter, to most of us? Many people have noted that beauty is often defined by the norms of a particular culture and that standards of beauty are learned, to a certain extent. There is great variation in what people find beautiful in another person, and no doubt there are great differences in what people call ugly.

But what is it that causes certain visual images to be repulsive and scary instantaneously, even to infants and very young children? Young children do not have to be taught to fear ugly witches and creepy-looking monsters; they do this automatically. And many of us have what seems to be an inbred fear of snakes. Are we born with the predisposition to recoil in terror at certain visual images?

Well, it seems that we are, and there's a good reason for this tendency. If we look at the theory of evolution, it suggests that species that are alive today are here because they had certain characteristics that helped many of them survive long enough to produce offspring. One such tendency might be an innate capacity to fear things that are likely to be harmful and to respond quickly to the sight of danger. An evolutionary view would suggest that the animals we most readily fear, even today, look similar to those that were the most threatening to the survival of our species' ancestors. Research shows that without learning, humans easily become frightened by some things that may or may not be dangerous. Certain types of animals, for example, especially snakes and spiders, more readily evoke fear than other types. Somehow a snake seems easier to fear than a bear, although the bear may well be more dangerous to us. Perhaps because of our evolutionary past, most children find certain animals repulsive and others cute, although they may adjust their reactions as they mature and get to know the animals better.

Other visual images also seem to upset and frighten us automatically. We seem predisposed to be repulsed by the graphic display of injuries. This tendency makes evolutionary sense, too, since the presence of a mutilated corpse or a severely bloodied and injured animal probably meant to our ancestors that a predator was close at hand and that they were in danger as well.

A third type of visual image that automatically repels and scares us is physical deformity. Part of our response may be due to the association of deformities with injuries and disease, and part may be due to the justifiable fear of unknown species. We automatically recoil (even if we learn to control this response as adults) at disfigured faces and deformed limbs. We also respond with distress to distortions of what we come to view as natural. We feel somehow that it is natural to be born with one head, one nose, and one mouth, but two eyes and two ears. We also expect that the head should be attached to the body between the two shoulders. A perfectly normal head attached to the stomach would indeed be disturbing. Deviations from what seems natural are scary. This is where monsters come in.

A monster is simply a distortion of the natural form of a familiar being. Monsters resemble a normal being in many ways but differ in other crucial ways: variations in size (giants and dwarfs), shape (characters with misshapen heads or hunchbacks, for example), skin color or texture (like green faces or hairy bodies), or the number of certain features (one-eyed, three-armed aliens). These things automatically scare us.

And what makes a nondeformed character look scary? Perhaps characteristics that seem likely to be used violently, such as enormous muscles, sharp teeth, and clawlike fingernails. And what makes normal facial features scary? Perhaps the facial features that scare us the most remind us of facial expressions that frighten us, such as those exhibiting anger or fear.

In sum, certain types of animals, the graphic display of injuries, distortions of natural forms, and violent-looking characters all seem designed to immediately upset and frighten us. The makers of horror movies understand this very well and they populate their films with scary images for maximum impact. Young children don't need to be taught to fear them.

What Makes Young Children So Susceptible?

Piaget argued that part of the reason young children react to things differently is biological: The brain actually needs to grow and develop before children can interpret certain things in more mature ways. Although he could not be specific about how the brain functioned or developed, recent findings in neuroscience may now be providing an explanation. Researchers have identified a small part of the brain called the amygdala as the center where innately threatening sights and sounds are received. According to recent research, this region of the brain immediately makes the body respond in fear to certain images, particularly those that signal danger. When this occurs, the body exhibits the so-called fight or flight response, and we experience fear unless or until higher-order processes in other parts of the brain tell it the equivalent of "Never mind, you're not really in danger." The cerebral cortex, where this higher-level processing goes on, is not well developed in younger children. Therefore, it will not be as effective in turning off the immediate fright response. Younger children may remain frightened by the visual image or sound because their brainpower is not sufficient to undo the automatic response. As children get older, however, it seems that their brains develop enough to begin to override their immediate response to scary images. They may still have an initial response of fear, but it goes away more quickly as they are able to put it into the perspective of what else they have come to know. The tendency to be overpowered by visual images, then, is probably a physiologically based response that must be outgrown. Up to the right age, no amount of reasoning will take it away.

Of Shrieks, Screams, and Squeaking Violins

What about young children's susceptibility to eerie sounds? Earlier, I referred to the fact that certain types of intense or peculiar noises, as well as vivid visual images, have the capacity to grab young children's attention. You may remember that the descriptions of the Wicked Witch at the beginning of this chapter referred to the sounds she made as well as her looks. Her "screeching voice" and "horrifying . . . laugh" seemed to traumatize these children as much as her pointy features and green skin. Many, many retrospective accounts of scary movies recall the sounds of bloodcurdling yells and musical soundtracks that mimic the noise of an attack or a victim's screams.

The sounds that readily terrorize young children do not come from words. They come from auditory cues that even animals respond to. Long before children learn to understand and use language, they can differentiate between an angry and a loving tone of voice. Sudden loud, unexplained noises make all of us jump before we are even consciously aware of them; the roar or growl of a predator and the shrieks and screams of victims evoke fear in animals as they do in us. Again, it seems that we must be responding to the sounds that our ancestors had to be sensitive to in order to survive.

I remember an incident that happened to my family several years ago when we visited the Milwaukee Public Museum. We were relieved to see that our one-and-a-half-year-old son was enjoying many of the static displays of large dinosaurs and stampeding buffaloes. But we weren't prepared for the terror he experienced as we neared the re-creation of a tropical rain forest. Before we even entered that area, Alex cried out in distress and begged us not to go in there. We could tell he was responding to the sounds that were emanating from these rooms. These were the alarm sounds, we figured out later, that monkeys emit when in extreme danger. The sounds did not mean much to us, but they undoubtedly spoke volumes to Alex. No amount of coaxing was able to convince him to enter that space. It seems that in many cases, soundtracks that make our hair stand on end are likely to frighten very young children even if these children don't understand anything about what's going on in the movie.

Taking Your Child's Perspective

The implications of younger children's hypersensitivity to certain sounds and images are dramatic. Young children can be traumatized by brief exposure to a single bizarre visual or auditory image. It is easy to observe this effect on Halloween, when there are many images involving creepy or vicious animals and distorted or gruesomely injured characters. The popular haunted house that children are invited to explore provides a potpourri of all the images and sounds we readily fear. Older children often find this enjoyable. The problem is that for a very young child, these images can echo vividly in their minds, which do not yet have the ability to moderate their effects.

In scary movies and television programs, we see the same thing. Your young child, up to the age of six or seven, is responding most strongly to the most striking images and sounds and is getting much less of the meaning of the story than you or I would. To view a scary program from a young child's perspective, imagine that you're sitting in the front row of a darkened movie theater, that the volume is turned way up, and the dialogue is in a language you don't understand. You are at the mercy of these vivid visual images and sounds and don't have the brainpower to tune them out or reason them away. What is more, as we will see in chapter 5, what you are seeing is real.

Of course, this all suggests being cautious about what we let young children see. But beyond that, it also argues that we should be understanding of and patient with the intensity and duration of our children's responses. They cannot help it if they are overreacting, and they cannot help it if our reassuring words are unable to dim those images. Telling them it's not real or nagging them to snap out of it will not ease their fears. Fortunately, as we will see in later chapters, there are some things that can reduce their fears. But for the reasons I've explained here, nothing we can do for them after the fact comes anywhere near the effectiveness of prevention.

CHAPTER **FOUR**

The Trouble with Transformations

*"All of a Sudden, His Eyes Would Turn
a Really Weird Shade of White . . ."*

One specific instance in which I can recall being completely and utterly mortified was watching The Incredible Hulk *at the age of about six. I can vividly remember watching the show, in the dark, on the foot of my parents' bed—scared to the point that I had to run out of the room and had a near impossible time going to bed later on. Interestingly, in retrospect,* The Incredible Hulk *was not created to be a frightening program. Whether intended to scare or not, that one instance clearly sticks out in my mind as the most scared I have ever been—even more than at horror movies in which that is the intent.*

If you're familiar with the series *The Incredible Hulk,* but were not in preschool when it aired in the early 1980s, you may be quite surprised at the intensity of this recollected reaction. However, this young child's fright was far from unusual. In fact, *The Incredible Hulk* is one of the most intensely disturbing of the shows I have studied in terms of how profoundly it affected preschool and early-elementary-school children.

Although by now I have received dozens of reports from people who were frightened by this program as children, my interest in *The Incredible Hulk* was stimulated not by reports of children's fear but by Piaget's descriptions of how children between the ages of three and seven respond to the things they see in the world around them. He named this the "preoperational" stage because it occurs before the child can perform some basic mental operations. The stage following the preoperational stage, spanning roughly ages seven to twelve, was termed "concrete operational," recognizing children's ability to perform such operations if a problem is presented in a concrete, perceptible form.

The characteristic of preoperational thought that first caught my attention was what Piaget described as the failure to understand transformations.

What Piaget was talking about was not an emotional response, nor a response to fantasy characters. He was referring to children's performance on test items like the globs-of-clay task I described in chapter 2. Piaget conducted many experiments testing children's ability to "conserve," that is, to see that objects or amounts remain the same even though their physical appearance may change. The classic conservation test began with showing children two identical glasses of water. After children agreed that there was the same amount of water in the two glasses, Piaget would tell the children to watch as he poured the water from one of the glasses into a third glass, of a different shape. Usually the new glass was a lot narrower than the first two glasses, so the water came up to a much higher level. Now Piaget would ask the child whether the new glass contained the same amount as the other glass, sitting right next to it, or whether the new glass had more or less than the other one.

As adults, we know that six ounces of water is six ounces of water, whether it's in a narrow or a wide glass. Yet children under age six or so usually do not see that the amount remains the same, even when the water is poured back and forth before their eyes. Indeed, the overwhelming majority of three- to five-year-olds routinely flunk the conservation test, saying that the narrow glass that's filled to a higher level holds more water. But by the age of nine or ten, almost all children pass this test.

Piaget noted that preschoolers had this same inability to conserve in a variety of physical areas. Not only that, he also found that it was very difficult to train them to get the answer right, even with repeated trials. When attempting to explain what was going on, Piaget proposed that the young child focuses his attention on the two end states of the process—in this case, what the water looks like in the two different glasses. What the child somehow misses is the process of transformation that links the two (the pouring of the water from one glass to the other).

As I was reading about this research, I could not help thinking that this failure to understand transformations might affect children's reactions to the many physical transformations of characters that occur on television and in films, particularly in those that are scary. How would this inability to understand transformations affect children's responses to movies like Disney's *Snow White,* where the evil queen suddenly turns into a haggard old witch, or their reactions to werewolf movies, in which normal humans turn into vicious, hairy beasts before the viewer's eyes? At the time I was thinking about these issues, *The Incredible Hulk* was at the height of its popularity. Because its plot always showed the normal-looking, attractive main character suddenly being transformed into a grotesque monster, I thought to myself, "If Piaget is right about transformations, young children should have trouble with the transformation in this program, and that ought to make it especially scary for them." At the time, I didn't know quite how scary it was.

I soon discovered how frightening young children found this program when I looked at the results of the parent survey we conducted in the spring of 1981. Although we had not suggested any titles—parents simply wrote in the names of the programs that had scared their child—we found that *The Incredible Hulk* overwhelmed all other programs and movies in the replies of parents of young children. Fully 40 percent of the parents of preschoolers listed *The Incredible Hulk* as a program that had upset their child. In addition, 24 percent of the parents of first graders named it. These were the highest percentages of parents I've ever observed naming any program or movie as scary. And the interesting thing is, *The Incredible Hulk* wasn't supposed to be a scary program. Most parents didn't realize it was scary until their young child let them know about it.

After finding that young children did indeed find this program scary, at least according to their parents, we designed a study to learn more about the reasons for this reaction. We wanted to know, specifically, whether the transformation had something to do with young children's fear.

First, we put together a short video clip based on a typical episode of the program. In the episode we used, the hero, Dr. David Banner (played by the late Bill Bixby), is visiting a hospital when an explosion occurs and a worker is trapped under debris where a fire is quickly spreading. David first tries to lift the fallen objects to free the helpless, frightened worker, but he is not strong enough. Then, a second explosion hurls David against the wall, and this sets off the transformation.

During the transformation, the camera focuses on

David's eyes as the pupils become very small, and then on his arms, shoulders, and muscles, which turn green and grow so fast that they rip out of his shirt. Then the camera shows his feet increasing in size so quickly that they burst through his shoes. Finally, the entire Hulk character is seen throwing off the remains of his tattered shirt. The Hulk (played by body-builder Lou Ferrigno) now has a green face, wild hair, and bushy eyebrows, in addition to a grotesquely muscular physique.

With his superhuman strength, the Hulk easily removes the debris that is trapping the worker, carries him out of danger, and sets him down gently. Then he races through the hospital corridor, inadvertently scaring hospital employees left and right, and exits, growling, by jumping through a plate-glass window.

Once we had put this clip together, we wanted to see whether children whom Piaget would consider preoperational would react differently from children in Piaget's concrete operational stage. So we recruited children in preschool and elementary school to watch our excerpt. The preschool group ranged in age from three to five years; the elementary-school children were nine to eleven years old.

What did we expect to happen? If Piaget was right that preschool children do not understand transformations, we expected that our younger group would not understand that when the Hulk emerges, he is still David, the good guy, and that, in spite of his appearance, he is there to help the victim of the explosion. We predicted, then, that the younger group of children would be most frightened during the portion of the program when the transformation occurred and in the period following it when the monstrous-looking Hulk was on the screen. Also, if, as Piaget led us to believe, the older children were able to understand the transformation, we expected them not to be frightened by this change. On the contrary, these children were expected to be the most frightened during the first part of the excerpt when the hospital worker was injured and when it seemed as though he would be unable to escape before the fire reached him.

We showed this excerpt to the children, one at a time. Immediately after it was over we asked the children to tell us how they had felt during each of the three critical portions of the program. We illustrated each portion for them with stills from the video. What I'll call the "David portion" showed the explosion, the man trapped beneath the debris, and David trying to rescue him. The "transformation portion" showed the Hulk's torso ripping out of his shirt, his feet breaking through his shoes, and the Hulk ripping off his tattered shirt as he emerges from the debris. Finally, the "Hulk portion" showed the Hulk carrying the worker to safety and escaping from the building.

When we looked at children's ratings of how they felt during the different portions of the program, we found exactly what we had expected. Younger children found the program the least scary during the David portion, but their fear increased somewhat during the transformation, and was at its highest during the portion in which the grotesque Hulk was shown doing his good deed and then escaping. The older children showed pretty much the opposite pattern: They were the most frightened during the David portion, when a character was in danger and no one was able to help him. Their fear was greatly reduced during both the transformation portion and the Hulk portion. These children apparently understood that David was becoming the superhuman Hulk and that he was using his powers to rescue the victim. The Hulk's grotesque appearance didn't faze them. Through further questioning, we also found that although the older children understood what was happening during the transformation, younger children generally were confused by it.

This study told us that Piaget's observations about transformations of physical form were helpful in explaining children's fright reactions to a very different type of transformation on television. The research seemed clear in isolating the transformation as a central part of young children's problem with the program. However, because of how we test children in the lab—showing them only a short scene and discussing it with them immediately afterward—the study did not give us any hint of how strongly children were reacting to this program when watching it at home.

"Tell Me When the Hulk's Gone"

Students who are undergraduates today were preschoolers when the Hulk was at its height of popularity, and I am now receiving numerous accounts of Hulk-reactions from the students in my classes and from other undergraduates participating in my research. The students' retrospective reports show reactions that were surprisingly intense. The following are recent accounts from students who chose *The Incredible Hulk* when asked to talk about a frightening TV experience:

> *I recall that whenever his eyes turned green (the first sign that the Hulk was coming), I would close my eyes, plug my ears, and go sit as close to my mother as I possibly could. I would also say, "Tell me when the Hulk's gone!"*

> *Eventually, in the middle of the show, someone would hurt David Banner and all of a sudden his eyes would turn a really weird shade of white and he would begin to transform into the Hulk. I immediately turned around and hopped on my dad's lap, practically boring a hole in his side, trying to get away from the big green monster. Even though I knew David was safe because of the monster, I was still really freaked out.*

> *Watching the metamorphosis enhanced my fear of the dark. I recall trembling as I walked down the long,*

dark hallway toward my bedroom at the end. I slowly
passed all of the open doorways of dark rooms, inching
closer to my bedroom, thankful as I passed each one that
the Hulk had not been waiting behind a door to thrash
me. Weeks and even months after watching one program,
I was still afraid of walking down the hallway at night.

One thing I find interesting about these retrospective reports is that all of these students key in on the transformation itself as the main cause of their fright reaction. Even though this knowledge didn't help them reduce their fear, they seem to have been quite aware of what it was about the program that bothered them.

What is perhaps even more surprising about these reports is the intensity with which these children responded to the transformation. Each of these students reports a level of fear that we might expect from *Jaws* or *Psycho,* not from a mild-seeming action-adventure program with few pretensions of scariness.

Breaking a Fundamental Rule: The Loss of Trust

Thinking about the intensity of these responses, it seems clear to me that a simple failure to understand transformations is not sufficient to explain how profoundly this program frightened children. Not all transformations are upsetting. No one ever noticed children becoming upset during Piaget's conservation tests; nor do children ever seem alarmed when watching a science film showing water turning into ice or a bud becoming a flower. What is it about this transformation of a nice-looking hero into a monster that's so threatening to the young child? One student's description seems to hint at an explanation:

> *After the first few opening sounds, I could sense what was coming as I ran into my parents' bedroom to hide. I became terrified as I watched this perfectly normal and calm human being become transformed into this giant monster in just a matter of seconds. It made me feel like I couldn't trust people or predict what was going to happen next in life.*

When you think about the perspective of young children, it really makes sense that they should be so sensitive to transformations of characters. Their reaction is a lot more than just failing to understand what is going on. As this student suggests, perhaps the transformation represents a breach of trust about a fundamental aspect of the way things are in the world—something they have only recently come to understand and depend on.

Tolstoy once wrote: "From the newborn baby to the child of five is an appalling distance," and he certainly was right. Think of the enormous number of important things a child learns about the world from the time she is born until the preschool years. As you may remember from the birth of your own child, the newborn's behavior is at first a bundle of reflexes and random actions. She doesn't have much sense of the world around her. She doesn't see very well at first, and she reacts only to things that she can perceive directly.

One of the many things that babies learn during the first year is called "object permanence." Show a five-month-old baby a ball and then hide it under a blanket, and to her, it's gone. Over time, the young child learns that things still exist when they can't be seen and that they don't disappear by magic. The concept of "person identity" takes a while to develop, too. Before that concept develops, the baby doesn't realize that her mother is a unique being—that is, she is one and only one person, no matter where she is seen or what she is wearing. This is one reason why parents do not usually observe separation anxiety before their baby is eight or nine months old. Without understanding this basic developmental concept, the mother of a nine-month-old might find it strange that it suddenly seems harder to drop her child off at day care than it was just a month before.

Other concepts related to identity take a long time to develop. For example, in one famous study, children between the ages of three and six were allowed to pet a tame and friendly cat, and then watched its hindquarters while a researcher placed a realistic mask of a vicious dog over the cat's face. Although the animal had never been out of their sight, many of the younger children believed that when the animal turned around, it had become a dog. As you might expect, these children showed more fear in the presence of this "new" animal than their older counterparts, who understood that the new appearance did not change who the animal was or whether it could hurt them. This study illustrates that little by little, children come to understand certain fundamental rules of the physical world. One of these is that people and animals have underlying identities that are not affected by momentary changes in their appearance.

Have you ever seen a toddler mistakenly walk up behind a woman he thinks is his mother and then recoil in horror and burst into tears when she turns around and he sees the stranger's face? If you have ever been that stranger, you may have been struck by the terror in the child's expression, and you may even have asked yourself, "OK, so I'm not his mother, but do I really look that dreadful today?"

Rest assured that you didn't look that bad. The intensity of the child's reaction was not due to any flaws in your physical appearance. To the young child who has not fully grasped the concept of person identity, you were his mother when he grabbed the back of your skirt, but his mother has just been *transformed* into a stranger before his eyes. Talk about scary!

That was the toddler . . . After a while, of course, all children grasp the notion of person identity. By four or five years old, children have learned that this cannot happen. People stay the same—they don't transform into new shapes, colors, or identities before your eyes. *Phew!* That's reassuring.

But then, there's television, where the things we see are a lot like the real world, but once in a while, the rules don't apply. A lot of things that children have spent several years learning by experience no longer work the same way all the time. Take gravity, for example. Children aren't born knowing that if they let something go, it falls to the ground, but over time, with lots of experience, they get the idea. The law that things fall if you let them go is pretty reliable. Of course, it's not always that way on television and in movies. Object permanence doesn't always work on TV, either. On TV, things that are there one second may suddenly disappear the next.

Person identity is another concept that children have come to trust by the time they're four or five. People don't suddenly transform themselves into something or someone else. A mask over someone's face is just a mask. You can pull it off, and it's still Daddy underneath. If you're walking along holding your mother's hand, you won't suddenly look up and find that she's turned into a witch.

So imagine that you're a child who has mastered this reassuring concept and you're watching television. There's a story about a very nice-looking, kind, and thoughtful man. Suddenly this character you've come to like and trust starts to grow very fast, turns green, and becomes a grotesque monster before your eyes—this *is* scary. Maybe a physical transformation like this suddenly calls into question a lot of the reassuring principles you have come to rely on. If this man can suddenly change in this way, maybe other people can, too.

As we will see in the next chapter, preschool children are likely to react as though what they are seeing on television is real. Understanding how profoundly a character transformation violates the preschooler's sense of security may help to explain the intensity of these responses.

The Return of the Hulk—and His Many Cousins

When I started working on this book I thought *The Incredible Hulk* would be useful merely as a historical example to illustrate what a transformation is and to show how a popular program that was based on a transformation had such a powerful effect on young children. But since then, I have discovered that the Hulk is back. Reruns of this program are now being shown during daytime hours on the Sci-Fi Channel, which is part of basic service on many cable systems. So today's children are likely to have the same reactions that occurred almost a generation ago.

But, of course, the Hulk is not alone. Transformations are a staple of scary movies, and we now know a bit more about why they are so upsetting to young children. Animated adventure features are full of transformations: As we saw in chapter 3, *Snow White*'s evil queen becomes the wicked witch, and normal trees turn into grasping monsters. I have received reports of children being especially frightened when the evil Jafar in *Aladdin* suddenly transforms into a vicious cobra, and when naughty little boys in *Pinocchio* grow donkey ears and tails and then bray in panic as they notice what is happening to them.

We also see many scary transformations in popular movies that are not animated. In *The Wizard of Oz*, a particularly frightening scene has Dorothy seeing her beloved auntie Em in the Wicked Witch's crystal ball. Then suddenly, the aunt's reassuring face dissolves into that of the cruelly cackling witch. In *Poltergeist*, a child's dolls and toys that comfortingly surround her during the day turn grotesque and evil as night falls. And then there are those cuddly creatures in *Gremlins*, who suddenly become creepy looking and vicious. The list seems endless.

Many students have reported that Michael Jackson's "Thriller" had especially long-lasting fear effects, in part because of the pop singer's vivid transformation into a werewolf.

> *When I was about eight years old my family had dinner at their best friends' house. After dinner at around eight P.M. my parents' friends decided to put on a video. It was the Michael Jackson "Thriller" video. The video turned out to be nothing like I expected. It was about eight minutes long, and from what I remember Michael Jackson was on a date with a girl. He was talking, singing, and dancing. They were in the woods and then all of a sudden his eyes turned yellow and he turned into*

a werewolf. The girl ran through the woods to get away from him. Then he was dancing in the streets with a group of people that also had a scary appearance.

That evening I woke up in the middle of the night from a nightmare. I was wrong in thinking that once the video had finished it would be out of my mind forever. I dreamt the vivid images of Michael Jackson turning into a werewolf. I was so terrified to go back to sleep that I woke my mother up. Although she reassured me that it was just a nightmare, I could not get those vivid images out of my mind. For the next few weeks before I went to sleep, the video ran through my head, and some of the nights I had the same nightmare. This video made a lasting impression on me. Even when I see it now, I always get a weird feeling inside of me. I remember the restless nights I sat up thinking about the video.

I have noticed that current scary television programs that are popular with young children, such as *Are You Afraid of the Dark?*, also use the transformation quite heavily. A show I recently watched was about a witch who maintained her outwardly beautiful appearance by tricking young girls, with the promise of eternal beauty, into drinking a potion that transformed them into dogs. The witch's beauty was maintained by cutting out the tongues of the newly transformed dogs and eating them. (No kidding!) At the end, when one skeptical young girl discovers the witch's secret and sends her back to her real appearance by breaking her magic mirror, we witness the entire transformation of the beautiful woman into a shrieking thousand-year-old hag, and then finally into a skeleton. Not an easy image to take at any age!

Once in a while, a transformation goes from the grotesque to the beautiful, as happens at the end of Disney's *Beauty and the Beast.* When Belle's love releases the evil curse on the Beast, we see his various parts gradually change into those of a handsome young man. While these transformations can also be unsettling for young children, clearly the most frightening transformations are the more common ones that involve the metamorphosis of an attractive, harmless-looking character into a gruesome, grotesque one. This is very understandable, given what we learned in the last chapter about young children's overresponse to grotesque visual images.

In screening programs for your young child, then, be especially on the lookout for transformations—no matter how absurd they may seem from your standpoint. Remember, your child sees things very differently, and as I'll explain in the next chapter, for very young children, the images they are seeing are not only disturbing, what they are seeing is *real.*

CHAPTER FIVE

"But It's Only Make-Believe"

Fantasy, Fiction, and Fear

An example that I will never forget is when I watched the movie Pinocchio. *I saw this movie with my mother when I was about four or five years old. I really thought that what was happening in the movie was real. In the movie, if a child misbehaved, he or she was turned into a donkey. Also, if a child lied, their nose would grow. I really believed that this would happen to me if I was bad. I remember being extremely scared even a few weeks after I had seen the movie because I thought that the same thing would happen to me if I misbehaved.*

This description serves as a vivid reminder that children often fully believe stories that we adults are quick to dismiss as fantastic or impossible. Developmental psychologists have noted that children only gradually come to understand the difference between reality and fantasy. And children learn to say that some things are real and others are make-believe long before they understand what it means to be make-believe. They will tell you that *Peter Pan*'s Captain Hook is make-believe long before they stop worrying that he will capture them and feed them to the crocodile! This lack of understanding plays a key role in the things that frighten young children. Until children understand that something that is not real cannot pose a threat, they will be just as scared by TV shows and movies portraying fantasy outcomes as by those portraying real dangers. Indeed, often the young child will be more frightened by fantasy characters, because fantasy villains are usually ugly and grotesque. As children come to understand the distinction between fantasy and reality, they better appreciate that only real threats and dangers can harm them.

Why Learning What's Make-Believe Is So Difficult

As adults, we seem to take the distinction between fantasy and reality for granted. But put yourself in the situation of the very young child, and you will realize that differentiating between what's real and what's make-believe is not an easy task. At first, maybe it does seem simple. The newborn or infant believes what he sees, feels, hears, smells, and tastes to be true—and, for the most part, it generally is. But soon the young child is exposed to things that are beyond his immediate experience. One way in which this happens is through language. Beyond seeing and feeling and hearing a dog, for example, a child can hear someone talk about a dog or have a book about a dog read to him. Through language and pictures, he learns about things that he doesn't experience directly. Over time, he comes to know that everything anyone says isn't necessarily true in the same way that something he witnesses himself is usually true. But it takes a long time to come to this realization.

Although parents often make a concerted effort to teach their children the difference between real and make-believe, we also have a few customs that undermine these efforts. Most parents make it a point to communicate the value of telling the truth, especially within the family. And yet most of us promote elaborate stories about Santa Claus, the tooth fairy, or the Easter Bunny. I'm not saying that the enjoyment of these cultural myths is inappropriate or wrong, but it does complicate the child's task of sorting out what's real and what's make-believe.

Piaget's take on this situation was to say that preschool, or preoperational, children do not distinguish play and reality as two distinct realms with different ground rules. My own family brought this issue home, so to speak, one Christmas a few years ago. We were visiting my husband's relatives, and as in millions of other families, all the young children hung their stockings on the mantel, leaving milk and cookies for Santa Claus. And like many parents, the adults warned the children to go right to bed because Santa wouldn't want to see them awake when he came to deliver their presents. By morning, of course, Santa had left presents and even drunk the milk and eaten one of the cookies. When the children were applauded for having gone right to sleep, one bright four-year-old among them replied, "I saw Santa last night! I stayed up and watched him, but he didn't see me!"

Now, how can you argue with a response like that? Was he telling an out-and-out lie? If so, he could hardly be blamed for imitating his parents' attitude toward the truth. Was he talking about a dream he had that he thought was true? Or was he playing by the ground rules he observed regarding Santa Claus? We'll never know for sure because we adults were too embarrassed to question him. But this incident illustrates one of the ways in which the border between what's real and what's make-believe becomes fuzzy.

Reality vs. Fantasy

Television is another factor that makes the distinction between fantasy and reality especially complicated. Many of the images on television and in movies are so similar to real life that it is tempting to believe, at first, that what is shown there is real. It takes a very long time for children to sort out this paradox.

The distinction, for television, is not simply one of "real" vs. "pretend." Children must learn many variations of the difference between real and make-believe. At first children believe that the things they are seeing are actually inside the television set—that if they look inside, they'll find those things and that what's in there might actually be able to come out. Research suggests that by about the age of four or so, they understand that the things they are seeing are not actually in the box, but that is just the first step toward understanding television's many realities.

By about the age of seven or eight, according to research, children come to distinguish between things that are real and those that are make-believe on television. At first they judge what is make-believe by its format, concluding that all cartoons are make-believe and all live-action shows are real. But over time, they become conscious of the fact that certain things that they see in fantasy shows are physically impossible, whether they are shown through animation or live action. They understand, for example, that people don't fly the way Peter Pan and Superman do on television and in movies. They come to judge whether something on television is real on the basis of whether the things they see in a story actually exist in the real world. A police story is real, they will say, because there are police in the real world, but stories with certain types of villains, such as witches and monsters, are not real because these characters are not found in real life.

And how do children learn to distinguish between people, animals, and events that exist in the real world and those that do not? Surprisingly, there's no simple rule.

Children just have to learn this by experience. There is no obvious distinguishing characteristic for what is plausible and what is fantastic. What is it about dragons that causes them to be make-believe, while dinosaurs are real? There's nothing in the way they look in pictures that could tip a child off. There are many things that are real that seem downright outrageous when you think about them: the fact that the pictures you see on television can come to your home invisibly through the air or the fact that planes can fly or, for that matter, the way babies are made. None of these ideas seems very realistic on the surface. Over time, we come to accept some very weird things as real, while we learn that other things are impossible. It's no wonder that children take a long time to understand what can and cannot happen.

In choosing programs for preschool children, then, you should not be reassured when a story contains scary elements that are physically impossible, such as a prince turning into a frog, a sorcerer casting evil spells, or a monster devouring a city. These outlandish happenings will not make the story any less compelling or frightening. Focus your attention on the elements of the story that were discussed in the previous two chapters: Are there dangerous-looking animals or grotesque characters? Do they make intense and disturbing sounds or threaten physical harm? Do normal-looking beings transform into hideous monsters?

Similarly, with realistic shows, what you need to look

for when screening them for preschoolers is how disturbing they are in terms of these surface features, not whether
they present realistic threats. By the time children reach
the age of eight or so, however, it will matter to them
whether programs are based on reality or not, and the real
ones will be scarier.

Research confirms that as children get older, they become less and less scared by fantasy programs and movies,
but they continue to be frightened—and sometimes become *more* frightened—by realistic portrayals. In the survey we conducted in the early eighties, in which we asked
parents of children from kindergarten through fourth
grade which programs and movies had frightened their
child, we categorized the content as either fantasy (showing impossible events, as in *The Wizard of Oz*) or fiction
(showing things that could possibly occur, as in *Jaws*). In
the parents' responses, mentions of fantasy fare decreased
as the child's age increased, and mentions of fictional offerings actually increased with age. Our more recent survey of parents of children in kindergarten, second, fourth,
and sixth grade reconfirmed the importance of the
fantasy-reality distinction in what frightens children. Although children in all grades were scared by such realistic
offerings as *Rescue 911,* only children in the younger two
groups had problems with such obviously fantastic offerings as *Peter Pan, Batman,* and *The Wizard of Oz.* When children themselves name the TV shows and movies that
frighten them, we see the same trends. Evil witches and

monsters recede in the nightmares of older elementary-school children and are replaced by dangerous animals and vicious criminals. The following two examples are typical of what frightens this older group:

One night my Girl Scout troop had a slumber party. We all got ready for bed in our sleeping bags in front of the TV and watched Creepshow. *It was a collection of short thrillers. Some were stupid, and a couple have stuck with me the rest of my life. One short story was about a man in his apartment. He had a few cockroaches; then they started to multiply. They were coming out of the drains and out of the light fixtures. Eventually they overwhelmed the man and killed him. They were all over him coming out of his nose and mouth. I believe that I have more than normal feelings of disgust when it comes to all sorts of bugs. It could be due to seeing these past images. Even today I can't sleep unless my mouth is shut. Who knows, a bug could crawl in when I was sleeping.*

One of the few television programs that I can still clearly remember as having frightened me for a long time was the show Hunter. *I was probably nine or ten years old at the time and my older brother was baby-sitting. He wanted to watch it, so I remember sitting down to watch it with him. It was an episode about a man who would kidnap little girls and then bury them alive. He had killed a number of them already when the show started and the two police detectives on the show caught him just as he was about to bury another one. They had already found the bodies of a few of the others. This was the first time that I had ever seen kidnapping on television or anywhere for that matter. I was scared for many nights after seeing the program that I would be kidnapped and buried alive by some psychopath.*

Fiction: That Frightening Middle Ground

According to research, children by about the age of ten come to grasp more than simply what's possible and impossible in the media. They come to appreciate that some programs are scripted and acted for the purpose of telling a story. Before that time, they are likely to think that a family drama shows the real activities of a real family and that a realistic adventure story shows events that actually transpired.

Once children know that dramas and comedies contain actors speaking lines that were written for them, does this knowledge prevent them from being unduly scared by most entertainment offerings? If only this were the case! Unfortunately, fiction can be very scary.

When children come to understand that most programs and almost all movies are scripted and performed by actors, they at first think that all scripted stories are untrue. But over time, they learn that there is an important category between the programs that show real events that actually happened (such as the news and documentaries) and fantasies, which portray unreal, impossible events that could never happen in the real world. That intermediate category is fiction, which is the product of someone's imagination but is based on events that can and do occur.

There are several reasons why we respond so intensely to television shows and movies, even when we know that what we're seeing is fiction. First of all, we automatically fear certain dangerous things in real life, and we have an immediate fear reaction even when we see these things on the screen. Over time, and as we grow older, we may still have that initial reaction, but it is less intense as we distinguish between the scary things that are really present and can harm us and those that are only being represented to us on video or in film. We are also naturally inclined to empathize with other people's emotions, and as we become attached to characters in a movie, we often feel emotions similar to the ones they are feeling. Again, we can keep reminding ourselves that these are not real people, but for many of us, our emotions become strongly intertwined with those of the characters we view, and we sometimes care deeply about what happens to them. We also watch TV and movies for entertainment, and often we purposely throw ourselves into the story, adopting an attitude that is sometimes referred to as "the willing suspension of disbelief."

As adults, though, it seems that we ought to be able to leave our emotions in the theater after the movie is over. Even if we cared about the fictional heroine who was stalked by the psychopathic killer, we should not still be worrying days later if we saw her escape unharmed, should we? But we often continue to feel anxious, and for good reason. Because fiction is based on things that can and do happen, watching a scary program heightens our fears of real events like those in the program. A fictional story about the kidnapping of a young child may be entirely made up by the dramatist, and yet the elements of the story are real. Watching a program about a kidnapped young child intensifies our awareness of this risk. If we feel that it could happen to us (or our child) we will feel more threatened by that possibility, and this feeling of vulnerability is likely to last as long as our memory of the program. The more a fictionalized threat is similar to things that threaten us in our own lives, the more scared we will be, not just while watching, but afterward as well. This applies to children, too.

After the movie *Jaws* came out, it was children at the beach who suffered the most obvious spillover effects. I have received dozens of reports of ruined seaside vacations:

> When the film Jaws *arrived at the movie theaters, everyone considered it a "must-see" movie. Naturally, my friends and I attended this feature. This was the first "scary" movie my parents had allowed me to see. While I was quite aware of the immediate fright reaction induced by viewing this movie, I was naive to the possibility of any long-term or lingering effects.*

About a year later, a vacation to the Florida coast caused the dreaded sensation to resurface. As we approached the shoreline, an alarm rifled through my body. I knew Jaws was circling just beyond the swimming markers. Consequently, I refused to enter the water. Subsequent vacations have yielded the same reaction. I think I was the only person in Hawaii who would not step into the ocean. I considered the surfers suicidal maniacs. Weren't they aware of the eminent risks?

It also seems that young girls just starting out on their baby-sitting careers were the most frightened by the movie *When a Stranger Calls*, which showed a baby-sitter being stalked by a psychopathic killer. The *Friday the Thirteenth* series did not make it any easier for teenagers going camping. The list goes on. You don't have to believe that any of these specific events ever really happened to feel threatened when engaging in activities similar to those of the victims in these movies. These movies heighten our awareness of dreadful possibilities.

When I was in (about) the third grade my friends and I had a slumber party, and we decided to watch a horror movie. In this movie a group of teenage girls were having a slumber party, and one by one throughout the movie they disappeared and were gruesomely murdered. The movie showed explicit details of their deaths, and one aspect that particularly affected me were the scenes of

*them pleading for their lives. I remember seeing the terror
in their eyes as they begged to be spared, and I remember
hoping each time that they would get away, and how
awful I felt when they were murdered anyway. That
night none of us could sleep, and every sound that we
heard scared all of us to a point where we would scream,
and we eventually ended up huddled together for the entire night to protect each other. We were so scared that
none of us would even get up and go to the bathroom.
Even after that night the images of the young girls beg-
ging for mercy stuck in my head. For many nights after
that I had nightmares and difficulty sleeping, every
sound I heard scared me, and I thought that some killer
was coming to get me.*

Children who find themselves in the same situation as
the fictional victim become especially frightened by a plot
that makes them acutely aware of what might happen to
them. But scary programs do more than that. These
movies contain all sorts of devices that engage our emotions more strongly than a simple reminder about possible risks. Scary movies and TV shows include a variety of
elements that usually are not there when we face real
threats in our own lives.

First, there's suspense. In the real world, when a vicious attack, major tragedy, or accident occurs, we usually
have no forewarning. These things often happen very
quickly, before the victim even realizes what is happening.

However, the television or movie producer rarely lets things occur that way. Most scary programs and movies let us know what is going to happen or what might happen, and we become anxious well in advance of the horrifying outcome. Research shows that it's much more frightening this way. Because these shows are meant to be scary, the producer dramatizes the events to evoke the most intense emotions from the audience.

> *The movie was* Friday the Thirteenth. *This particular movie was very uncomfortable because it was suspense-filled. The reason I was scared was because I knew the people were going to die, yet I did not know the exact moment it was going to happen. The actual horror of the movie did not scare me (ex.: blood, people having their heads cut off). But when I was unable to know when the person was going to be killed, or where the killer Jason was, this is what bothered me.*

Another element of frightening films that is absent when real threats occur is the musical score and other sound effects. It seems that music and sound effects dramatically affect our emotional reactions. Sudden loud noises shock and arouse us, and we automatically respond with fear to the shrieks and cries of victims.

Many retrospective reports of movie-induced fright refer to the power of sound effects and music. Here are a few examples:

. . . And the suspenseful music that accompanied the shark attacks is forever imprinted in my mind. I just have to play the [Jaws] *music in my head when I'm swimming and I can really scare myself.*

In the movie [Friday the Thirteenth] *the sound was high and loud, and the music was scary. While I was watching the movie, I knew I did not like the music and the sound because it was the signal of killing. Every time I heard this kind of sound, I would know that more people would be killed, and they could not do anything to protect themselves.*

One particular scene from the movie [Piranha] *that had a great effect on me took place at a summer camp for kids. The children in the scene were participating in various summertime activities, including swimming in the lake. There were underwater camera shots of the swimmers' feet and of the killer fish approaching for the attack. Along with these shots were terrible spine-chilling sound effects supposedly coming from the fish and a scary type of music used to create suspense. At the moment of the attack people were screaming and frantically swimming to escape from the killer fish.*

By using these dramatic devices, movies and TV shows aim to intensify our response and etch the scary scenes indelibly in our minds in a way that many real events do not.

Remember, most vicious and brutal attacks are not witnessed by anyone; even the victim may be taken by surprise. Loved ones of the victim usually only hear about the attack and are left to imagine what it must have been like. But television and movies enact these attacks in lurid detail, exposing us to horrid scenes we might never experience in our entire lives. These images will be especially riveting for children and teenagers, who have less experience with such fictional stories and a less mature understanding of how movies and TV programs use special features to manipulate their emotions. Because these elements are so vivid, children are especially susceptible to their terror-intensifying effects.

The Vulnerable Female

If there is any fictional theme that repeats and repeats itself in the horror stories I receive from college students, it's the theme of the violent victimization of young women, usually by men. Often the theme involves sexual assault, and as you would expect, the most intense reactions to these plots come from female viewers. Content analyses have shown that in horror movies, attacks against men are usually over and done with quickly, but attacks against women are longer and more drawn out, making the viewer see the female victims suffer more and show more fear. This is one theme that has an intense impact not only on young teenage girls but on women in college as well. The following example is typical:

The action that sparked my fear response was a violent, very graphic portrayal of an attempted rape with a young girl as the victim. The scene used fast cutting, close-ups, suspenseful music, and the sound of the girl crying to aid in its intensity. During the entire scene I felt tense. It was as though I didn't notice the other things around me. I was truly frightened. I experienced empathy for the victim and uncomfortable thoughts that these acts occur every day in the real world. I tried to imagine what must have been running through the young girl's head. All I could say over and over again was "That's so horrible, how awful!" The imagery of the rape scene seemed to haunt me as I sat down to begin studying. I couldn't get the scene out of my head.

This description shows that the woman who wrote it had an awareness of the various production techniques that were used to intensify her response. But she was also aware of the importance of the theme of female victimization:

The intensity of my response has to do with my close identification with the subject matter at hand. Forced sexual acts are a major concern and fear of many women in the real world. My fear response was more intense in this case because I could relate to and identify with the underlying implications of the scene. To me this was not a random act of violence; it was an issue that hit close to home.

The fact that television dramas and movies play on women's fears of victimization comes up over and over again in women's memories of their media traumas. For example:

> *One of the scariest things I have ever seen was on* Beverly Hills, 90210 *sophomore year in college. Now, I know that this sounds like the silliest thing that you have ever heard—a twenty-year-old girl being afraid of a show as bad as* 90210, *but it is true. Let me explain. Two years ago there was a plot about Donna and a stalker. Being that she was the only virgin on the show, this news was particularly surprising. Anyway, the point is that the whole episode that week revolved around this guy breaking into Donna's beautiful beachfront apartment, sneaking around in the dark, and then getting very close to raping her. Obviously, he did not get the chance to rape her since Donna's boyfriend, David, arrived in the nick of time. But he got pretty damn close—way too close for my comfort. This somewhat-normal-appearing man was walking around in her apartment with a crowbar waiting for her to come into her room on a night that he knew she was all alone. Granted, I was sitting in a room with the five other girls I lived with, but they were still all girls and at some point I knew I would be alone in the apartment.*
>
> *Now this was not the most frightening experience I have ever had, but it has stuck with me. When I am walking alone at night sometimes or I am in the house by*

myself, I am that little bit more nervous. I am no lu-
natic; I just have memories of that episode and wonder
what would happen if my David did not come to the
door at that precise moment.

The prevalence of the theme of sexual assault in young women's traumatic responses to fictional programs and movies is striking. Maybe it is due to the fact that all women are potential victims of sexual assault; in fictional plots women do not have to be involved in risky activities to become a victim. In contrast, it seems that men who are victims in fiction are typically involved in activities that make violence more likely: They are criminals, police officers, vigilantes, or soldiers. Truly random assaults seem much more rare for the male fictional character. Of course it's true that women are more vulnerable than men to sexual assault in real life, but many movies and television programs play on this fear to an extent that can cause obsessive fear reactions, particularly among younger girls who are not well equipped to put the disturbing images in context.

The Supernatural: The Gray Area
between Fantasy and Fiction

A second theme that comes up over and over again in the media-induced fears of older elementary-school children and teenagers is that of the supernatural and the occult. This area is hard to define because it seems to occupy the border between fantasy and fiction. As I said earlier, by the time children reach the age of seven or eight, they are aware that certain fantasy happenings are impossible. However, many people never seem to fully reject the possibility of such supernatural events as alien attacks and demonic possession. *The Exorcist* is a film about demonic possession that has powerful effects, even on adults. Similarly, a film like *Poltergeist,* which shows supernatural attacks on a family whose house was built over a graveyard, plays on viewers' superstitions and the ambiguous lines between what's possible and impossible. Many movies and programs play on that ambiguity. In addition, they often contain elements of real threats that even the most skeptical adults can fear. Michael Myers, the homicidal maniac in *Halloween,* keeps coming back from the dead. As adults, we know that can't happen. However, we do know that homicidal maniacs exist, so we can still feel vulnerable even if we don't believe that aspect of the plot.

Stories of the supernatural defy the reassuring laws of physics that adults and older children rely on in evaluating risks. For example, it does no good to lock all the doors if the villain can penetrate the walls. Supernatural plots are much less predictable. The older child cannot rely on his knowledge of what is real and what is make-believe. Anything can happen.

I've suffered from nightmares after watching Aliens
(around the age of twelve). The creatures themselves are

what scared me: both their gruesome appearance and their apparent intelligence. In the movie they outsmart the humans, who are no match for the aliens, even with their weapons. My room makes strange sounds at night (at least I perceive strange sounds in my room, particularly in my attic). In one scene from the movie, the humans could tell the aliens were near but had no idea where they were. It turned out the aliens were directly above them, in the ceiling. Lying awake in my bed, I could hear odd noises coming (seemingly) from my attic right above me, and I imagined an alien shifting around up there. The situation where the aliens were above the humans and came through the ceiling created an image of the same thing happening in my room. This occurred pretty frequently for about a month after viewing the movie. A couple times I even had nightmares about the creatures.

Another problem is that the credibility of occult happenings is reinforced by frequent reports of unexplained supernatural events in reality-based programs:

The film I viewed was The Exorcist. *It contained graphic scenes of a young girl possessed by the devil. I was approximately twelve years old at the time and was in a slumber-party situation. I vividly remember the stress this film caused me. I was not only extremely afraid of the devil and evil, but I became obsessed with*

the possibility of becoming possessed myself. To make mat-
ters worse, later on in the same week I came home from
school and turned on some afternoon talk show with the
subject matter consisting of "real" stories of "real" people
who were at one time possessed. That program and the
movie were enough to keep me from sleeping for two nights
straight and finally when I did fall asleep I had terrible
nightmares. I slept with my parents for the next few weeks.

Just as parents sometimes make it harder for preschoolers to distinguish fantasy and reality by promoting
the tooth fairy, our mass media make the distinction more
ambiguous for all of us by overplaying the credibility of
supernatural forces. By the teen years, most kids have
learned that certain things can't happen, but can they
be absolutely sure? And, they might well wonder, what if
they're wrong?

We turn next to a domain where there's no ambiguity
about real vs. make-believe: the news and other reports of
real events that actually happened.

CHAPTER SIX

When Reality Is a Nightmare

All the News That's Fit to Terrify

When I was about eleven years old I saw something on television that scared me enough to make me remember it vividly all of these years. It wasn't a scary movie but a newsclip of something that really happened. A young, oriental man was being held in handcuffs by two men in uniforms (of some sort). I cannot recall the greatest detail about them because that is not what has stuck in my mind all this time. It was the young fellow I cannot forget about. As he was being restrained, he looked very frightened and powerless. At the mercy of these two men, it was obvious he had no escape. Then I saw a gun go up to his temple. My mouth fell open as I thought, "They can't just shoot him!" But I was wrong. Ten seconds later a shot rang through the air and the man fell to the ground, with blood spurting out of his head. His body lay lifeless. I sat there not being able to believe what I had just seen. . . . Luckily I haven't seen many of these types of scenes on television, but the one I did see will remain in my memory forever.

How many other children were devastated by this infamous news moment during the Vietnam War? And how many more graphic incidents like that one are our children being exposed to these days? Think of the many recent upsetting stories that have been covered heavily by television news: the Rodney King beating, the Oklahoma City bombing, the shooting deaths of children at school, innumerable natural disasters, and countless stories of child molestation and murder—this list could go on and on. There is little doubt that television news is becoming more graphic and sensational. A recent study reported that local news is especially violent. Of one hundred newscasts analyzed on a single day, the average "mayhem index" was 43 percent, meaning almost half of the news in the program involved violence or disasters.

What children see on news shows really frightens them. In the survey we did in the early eighties, in which we asked parents to name the television shows and movies that had frightened their child, television news stories were in the top ten in terms of the number of parents who mentioned them. The most frequently cited news story at that time was the Atlanta child murders case, in which a serial killer repeatedly targeted young children.

A decade later, shortly after the war in the Persian Gulf, almost half of a random sample of parents my colleagues and I contacted said their child had been upset by television coverage of the war.

Age Trends in News Stories That Frighten

More recently, in the random survey of parents with children in kindergarten through sixth grade that we did in the spring of 1994, we found that 37 percent said their child had been frightened or upset by a television news story during the preceding year. In this study, we were looking for age trends in what had frightened them.

Our first expectation was that the news would become more frightening as children got older because of their emerging appreciation for the reality-fantasy distinction. As children come to know that fantasy dangers cannot harm them but real dangers can, they can become more and more attuned to the threats that television news consistently depicts. Our survey showed this to be true. There was an upward trend in the percentage of children frightened by the news, going from 26 percent of the kindergartners to 44 percent of the sixth graders. We observed the greatest increase in the scariness of news between kindergarten and second grade. You may remember that this is approximately the same time that children are becoming competent in making the distinction between fantasy and reality.

What types of news stories frightened children the most? More than one-third of the children who had been frightened by the news were scared by stories portraying criminal violence, such as shootings, muggings, and kidnappings. Almost as many children were frightened by stories about foreign wars and famine, of which there were many during the period of the survey, particularly from Bosnia, Rwanda, and Somalia.

One-fourth of the children frightened by news were scared by stories about natural disasters. Again, there were many disasters in the news during that time, including severe earthquakes and rampaging fires in California, as well as devastating floods, hurricanes, and tornadoes around the country.

Children were especially responsive to stories in which a child was the victim. Many of them explicitly told their parents that they were afraid that what they saw in the news story would happen to them, too. Girls were especially likely to be upset after viewing the victimization of children.

We also found differences in the kinds of news stories that frightened children at different ages: Older children were much more responsive than younger children to crime stories featuring violence, but younger children were a great deal more upset than older children by news coverage of natural disasters.

Why these age differences? It seems to me that these differences are in line with what we have observed regarding younger children's responsiveness to visual images.

When you think about it, news stories featuring criminal violence are usually not that explicitly visual. Rarely are crimes of violence caught on camera. When they are, as in the Rodney King beating, I would expect younger children to be as frightened by them as older children. But the typical crime story shows only the aftermath of violence, which usually is not as visually vivid as the crime itself. The most upsetting part of many crime stories, particularly when the crime is between strangers, is the notion of the viewer's own vulnerability, rather than the crime itself.

Natural disasters, in contrast, are usually dramatically visual, and television news stresses the images of devastation: Homes are shown being ripped apart by hurricanes, swept away in floods, or crushed in earthquakes, and this footage is frequently accompanied by images of frightened bystanders or sobbing victims. These events are easy for children to understand. The images are readily remembered and often cause children to worry that a similar disaster will happen to them next.

There are some trends in children's fears in general that are helpful in predicting the types of news stories that will frighten children of different ages. Dozens of studies have been conducted in which children have been asked what frightens them, and there is a large consensus regarding age trends in fears.

The research suggests that three- to eight-year-olds are most often frightened by animals; the dark; supernatural beings, such as ghosts, monsters, and witches; and by anything that looks strange or moves suddenly. These findings are very consistent with what we have observed about children's reactions to fantasy programming, but of course these things rarely appear in the news. In contrast, the fears of nine- to twelve-year-olds most often relate to personal injury and physical destruction. This category includes accidents, kidnapping, disease, and violence—the essential focus of much television news. Teenagers continue to fear personal injury, but in addition, they begin to have fears related to more abstract issues such as economic problems, global disharmony, and environmental devastation. It should be helpful to keep these trends in mind when determining which news stories may frighten your child.

Getting the Message Out

I had been working on this book for some time when I suddenly recognized the importance of spreading the information about children's reactions to news. I received a distress call from a mother on the East Coast who reported that her daughter's school had adopted the policy of showing the children news excerpts every morning. Her child, a ten-year-old, had had an intense fright reaction to the coverage of the murder of JonBenet Ramsey (the kindergarten beauty queen who was found dead in the basement of her own home). At my request, the mother wrote down and sent me her account of what her daughter had said:

"Mom, you won't believe what was on the news today! This girl was killed in her own house, Mom. In her own house! I'm sorry, Mom, but I am not going to be able to be by myself in the house ever again even in my room, and I am never going in the basement alone anymore. And you know, they showed her funeral. I never even knew her and I felt like I was at her funeral. That is something private, Mom. I shouldn't have been there. I didn't even know her and I was at her funeral."

It is not difficult to understand why children often have such intense reactions to television news. It's very normal to feel sorry and sad for a real victim who suffered a real tragedy, but more than empathy is fueling children's intense reactions. After all, the news displays many horrible things that not only *can* happen—they *did* happen. Obviously, if something did happen, it can happen again.

This possibility may provoke lasting fears:

A [television] crew was interviewing a woman when her estranged husband suddenly jumped into the picture and shot her several times. The image of this crazed man ruthlessly gunning down the woman is permanently burned into my mind. . . . I guess, in a way, that image made me lose a little trust in the people that are closest to me. It makes me think that people could snap in an instant.

If It Bleeds, It Leads

These findings on children's emotional disturbances raise the question: How much news should parents allow their children to see? Many parents who restrict entertainment fare are reluctant to limit exposure to news on the grounds that news is educational. Many television news producers respond to criticism of their policy of always choosing a bloody incident as the lead story by saying that their critics are advocating censorship. They argue that the bloody incident is there because it happened and that not to show it would infringe upon our right to know.

What these arguments ignore, of course, is that whatever makes it onto television news is there because someone decided it was newsworthy. Thousands of things happen every day that could be on the news, but only a few events can be chosen. We must remember that one primary function of television news is to sell commercial spots to advertisers. Therefore, the news must be programmed to ensure that a large audience will tune in. To be news, a story has to be different or unusual. Most planes don't crash, so a routine flight doesn't make the news, but when a crash occurs, we always hear about it. What many news programmers believe is that sensational news is what draws people to watch, and as we'll discuss in more detail in chapter 9, to some extent they are right. There is a big audience for news about violent incidents and criminal behavior.

The temptation to be sensational is strongest for television, because television puts the highest value on striking visual images. An unimportant incident that has arresting videotape has a better chance to make it onto television than something more important that is too abstract to photograph. And, as we've seen, sensational visuals are especially problematic for our youngest children.

Those Popular Police, Crime, and Rescue Shows

As if the news weren't enough, television provides us with many more opportunities to witness the horror and tragedy of violent incidents that are real. We are currently in an era in which reality-based shows such as *Rescue 911* and *Cops* and documentaries about crime and other dangers are quite popular and readily available in the early evening when many children are in the audience.

In our most recent random survey of parents, *Rescue 911* was mentioned more often than any other program (including fantasy and fiction genres) as causing fear in children. Remember the anecdotes from chapter 1 about the child who quit skiing and the child who gave up cooking as a result of watching this program? I personally observed the effect of *Rescue 911* a few years ago when my son had his slightly older friend sleep over. Although this friend had previously been a good role model for going to bed without fear, that night he repeatedly ran into our bedroom, saying he thought burglars were trying to get in

the window. Since this was so different from his usual behavior, I asked his mother the next day if she had noticed
her son having trouble sleeping. She replied that she had,
and that the problem started when he began watching
Rescue 911.

The program, it turns out, touts itself as having an educational focus: In addition to showing near misses to serious tragedies, it does give tips on how to avoid them.
Unfortunately, for many children, the brief safety instructions do little to undo the alarming effects of watching the
life-threatening incidents.

Unsolved Mysteries is another good example of a well-
intentioned program that scares kids anyway. Not only
does this program provide children with vivid re-creations
of crimes that actually happened, but the fact that the perpetrators are still on the loose makes children feel even
more vulnerable. Here's a good example of what I mean:

> *The only frightening experience that I can recall*
> *happened while I was watching* Unsolved Mysteries
> *when I was in high school. The mystery was about a*
> *teenage girl in Texas who was abducted from a car wash*
> *in the summer at dusk. At the time she had been missing*
> *six months. On the show they did a reenactment of what*
> *may have happened to her and this is the part I remem-*
> *ber the most vividly. They showed the girl leaving her*
> *house and telling her parents that she is going to the car*
> *wash. She drives there; the car wash is one of those self-*

clean ones and it looks as though it was in the middle of nowhere. It is in a rural area and there are no other people around. So, she begins to wash her car, and another car pulls up, a bearded, middle-age man gets out, grabs her, they struggle, and she is taken. Her car door's left open, radio on, with her money and identification left in the car. Her parents were the last people to see her. I think I remember this because I live in a rural area and when I go there I drive past a car wash similar to that one. I never questioned my safety there at any time until this story. I often wonder what happened to her.

Documentaries can have the same devastating effect:

As a child of about ten, I watched a television show about missing children. I saw little girls who looked just like me, that had been taken from their parents. I remember imagining all the terrible things that strangers were probably doing to the children. I remember curling up into a ball and crying for these children; yet I was still unable to call for my mom. I needed to know what happened to all of the children, if any had been rescued. I realized the same thing could happen to me. I was terrified that I would be taken from my mom. I was afraid to go anywhere alone. I could not be in the basement anymore, which was where I originally saw the show. If I had to go into the basement, I would run as fast as I could downstairs and then back up. It seems as though from that night on I knew someone was going to kidnap me. At bedtime, I would try to camouflage myself on the bed so they would not know I was there. Many nights I crept into my parents' bed to feel safe. My reaction to the show gradually disappeared over the next year.

Making Wise News Choices for Children

Let's return to the story of the mother who contacted me about her daughter's reaction to seeing the JonBenet Ramsey murder coverage at school. The reason the mother called me was to enlist my help in convincing the school to be more careful in selecting news stories to present to ten-year-olds. At first, the child's teachers did not seem to be responsive to the mother's request that the news be screened in advance. But after I sent her some reprints of the research cited in this chapter, she and her husband got the school to modify its policy. The teachers now watch the news before showing it to the children, and leave out the most violent and sensational stories, particularly those involving child victims. It is to the school's credit that they were willing to modify their policies to accommodate the emotional needs of their students when relevant research findings were brought to their attention.

I am not advocating censorship, and I don't think that children should be brought up to believe that the real world is nothing but sweetness and light. But I consider it fully legitimate to ask whether children shouldn't be shielded from the TV-news version of reality, which presents much more horrifying images of the world than they would otherwise experience. At what age should we burden children with such graphic, often gory images as victims of bombings, molestation, and murder; terminally ill AIDS patients; and parents sobbing over the deaths of their children in accidents? In my opinion, we needn't be in any rush.

Children need, of course, to be informed about specific threats to their safety. They also need to be introduced to the negative aspects of the world around them. But much of that information should be presented in small and less-threatening doses, not in the sensational fashion that television news typically employs.

My advice to parents with regard to television news and reality programming is, Beware! The nightly news is full of graphic visual images of death and destruction, and television has recently adopted a special fascination with the theme of children as victims. Children may not be interested in the news, but they will be affected by it if you watch it when they're around. If you have preschool children, the safest bet is to watch the news when they are in bed or get your news from the papers. For older elementary-school children you might watch a station with a family-friendly news broadcast if there's one in your area.

As your children reach their teens and are ready to grapple with these difficult issues, I would keep tabs on the news they are watching and be ready to discuss it with them. (See chapter 8 for advice on these discussions.)

CHAPTER **SEVEN**

When Words Won't Work

. . . .

How to Help a Frightened Preschooler

When I was five years old, I was very scared after watching the movie The Wizard of Oz. *I was terrified of the Wicked Witch of the West. I thought she was hiding in my closet or under my bed; I figured that sooner or later she would jump out and say, "I'll get you, my pretty!" and send the flying monkeys after me. My dad tried to calm me by explaining that there were no witches; furthermore, there wasn't enough room for one under my bed or in my closet. He explained that monkeys can't really fly or hurt little girls; besides, no monkey would be able to get into the house since the doors were locked. Unfortunately, although my father's arguments seem perfectly logical now, they were useless when I was five years old. I was totally unable to grasp the fact that witches were the result of a movie producer's imagination and nothing to be feared. Logical explanations were futile; I still made my dad check my closet and bed for witches before I would go to sleep.*

"You Can Talk Till You're Blue in the Face"

An early study of children and fear tells the story of the young child who sat down and classified fairy-tale characters as "real" or "unreal." It was an ambitious attempt to overcome his fear, but it didn't work. He was still scared of them regardless of their category. As we saw in chapter 5, it takes a long time for children to fully understand the true meaning of the difference between fantasy and reality. To a very young child, just because something is make-believe, it doesn't mean it can't come and get you in the night!

But many parents think telling a young child that a television story is not real helps their child overcome his fears. When my colleagues and I questioned parents of preschoolers in a survey, most of them said they used that type of explanation when coping with their child's TV fears.

The fact is, young children usually don't find such words reassuring. One way my colleagues and I verified this was to conduct an experiment. We took a scene from *The Wizard of Oz* that many children find especially scary: Dorothy is in the tower of the Wicked Witch of the West and the witch tells Dorothy that if she doesn't give up the ruby slippers, she will be dead by the time the hourglass is empty.

We showed this scene to both preschool children and nine- to eleven-year-olds. Before they saw it, some children were told to remember, while watching, that it's just a story that's make-believe, that witches are pretend, and that the witch is just a regular person dressed up in a costume. Other children were not given these instructions.

After watching the scene, the children were asked how they had felt while watching it. Did the remember-it's-not-real instructions help children feel less scared? Not the children in the preschool group. Yet the same instructions did make the older children less fearful.

One thing I find really fascinating is that many children are wiser than their parents in knowing what helps them when they are frightened. When my colleagues and I asked children to indicate how helpful different methods would be in making them feel better if they were scared by something on TV, preschoolers thought "tell yourself it's not real" would be the least effective of all the strategies, while nine- to eleven-year-olds thought it would be far and away the best strategy.

Telling yourself it's not real is one of several widely used fear-reducing strategies that are more effective for older children than for younger ones. These methods, which are based on reasoning, usually involve attempts to help the child view the frightening thing in a different light. I refer to these as "verbal strategies" because they require children to process verbal information. Most verbal strategies are ineffective for young children for two reasons. One reason is related to some of the issues I raised in chapter 3 when I talked about how young children's attention is dominated by visual images and things that are easily perceived. As we saw when studying the effect of visual images, the ability to reason about things that are less obvious is very immature in young children, so the ability to use abstract thoughts to overpower frightening images is very weak.

A mother recently told me about the difficulty she had reassuring her five-year-old son who was frightened by the movie *Ghostbusters*. When she tried to explain that ghosts could not come through walls, he replied, "But you're wrong, Mom. I saw it with my own eyes!" This mother's explanation was powerless against the force of the compelling visual images in the movie.

The other problem with verbal strategies is that they rely on the comprehension of words and sentences. Not only are younger children less familiar with the meanings of individual words; they also are less adept at combining word meanings into an overall understanding of a message. Just as we saw that younger children may focus on part of a visual image and ignore the rest of it, they sometimes respond so strongly to a single word that they miss the rest of the sentence.

Another experiment my colleagues and I conducted is a case in point. The results surprised us—and taught us something about the complexities of communicating with preschoolers. Our initial idea was that if we provided children with accurate and reassuring information about something that seemed scary in a movie, the movie would become less frightening. We used the famous snake-pit encounter in *Raiders of the Lost Ark* as our scary scene. Before watching the scene, children of different ages were shown an educational video that tried to convey the fact that most snakes are actually harmless. In the video, the narrator uses the sentence, "Although a few snakes are poisonous, most of them are not."

We expected the video to reduce older children's fear while watching the movie. We also felt it would probably not help the preschoolers because their visceral reaction to the snakes in the movie would outweigh their ability to benefit from the reassuring information. What we discovered was that when these young children heard the word "poisonous," they effectively ignored the rest of the sentence. That word struck such a responsive chord that the intended meaning of the sentence was lost. And not only was this information not helpful to preschoolers—it actually made them more scared! When confronted by the scary visuals in the movie, these children were apparently more sensitive to the danger of snakes than the other children their age who had not viewed the educational video. Our attempt to make these children feel better had the opposite effect.

This is a very good example of the way well-meaning efforts to reduce fear can backfire. What we've learned from this and other studies is how to create explanations that are more suited to a young child's needs. I'll talk in chapter 8 about making explanations more effective even for preschoolers, but in this chapter I'll focus on the techniques that younger children prefer and the ones that work best for them.

What Comforts Little Ones?—First, a Hug

As you might expect from the preceding discussion, the techniques that work for young children do not involve words or mental acrobatics. Simple strategies involving physical comfort, warmth, and closeness are probably the most effective. The same preschoolers who reported that telling themselves it's not real would be ineffective said that getting something to eat or drink or holding a blanket or cuddly toy would help them the most. And of all the techniques we asked children to rate for effectiveness, the one endorsed by the most children is sitting by mom or dad. Children of all ages like touching, holding on to, or being near a warm, caring adult when they are frightened, and this surely has already been demonstrated by the many accounts in this book of children seeking out their parents or even sleeping with them after seeing a scary movie.

An interesting experiment was recently reported in which preschoolers watched a scary television movie with or without their older sister or brother. The researchers found that more than half of the sibling pairs talked about how scary the program was while watching the movie, and more than a third of the older siblings actively tried to comfort their little sisters and brothers by offering words of reassurance, a hug, or a hand to hold. It is not surprising, then, that children who watched with their older siblings were significantly less frightened and enjoyed the program significantly more than those who watched it alone.

In the absence of other real people, young children often choose favorite blankets and cuddly toys for comfort, warmth, and even protection. Sometimes they do this to an exaggerated degree:

> *I would protect and calm myself by putting every single stuffed animal I owned on top of my bed as I slept; this meant about fifty stuffed animals on top of me.*

What our research suggests is that a glass of water, a hug, and the comforting attention of a parent or caregiver is often helpful, and you're better off simply reassuring your preschool child that nothing bad will happen and getting his mind off the topic than trying to explain the specifics of why he is not in danger. For children at this age, providing them with warmth (literally or figuratively) is the best place to start:

> *A technique I used to cope with my fears was to make hot chocolate with my mother and talk about "happy things."*

Often parents are surprised when their rational explanations are not effective with their preschoolers:

> *My mom claims that one calm warm summer night, she and my father felt like watching a scary film,* Creature from the Black Lagoon. *I must have been about four to five years old, and they figured I would have no problem watching because I was with them. Their rationale was, "Hey, he's with us, so we can explain to him that none of this is real." After maybe the first five minutes of the film, when the creature pops out of the pond, I maniacally began to cry my eyes out, and would not stop until my father turned off the television. Mother tells me that no matter how much they tried to explain to me that what was on TV was make-believe, I was still shaking. Her only option was to stay up with me all night, touching me and singing to me softly.*

On the Family Bed, and Eating Your Troubles Away

You may have noticed that some of the techniques that young children prefer are controversial, and you may worry that they risk producing unwanted side effects. For example, many people argue that if children use food to comfort themselves during stress, these habits may come back to haunt them later in terms of obesity or eating disorders. Obviously, this is not what you would want to happen. A drink or a small snack during an acute anxiety state should not be repeated endlessly. But the occasional use of food or drink in this context may be very effective in the short run. Emotions such as fear are felt more intensely on an empty stomach, the process of eating may itself be distracting and is often pleasant, and a warm drink may take the chill off that scary feeling. Of course, efforts should be made to avoid making unscheduled fear-induced snacks a regular thing.

What may be even more controversial about what young children like to do when they're scared is the issue of sleeping in their parents' bed after a nightmare. Experts differ, sometimes vehemently, on whether this should ever be allowed. The girl whose intense reaction to *The Elephant Man* was reported in chapter 3 wanted to sleep with her parents but was forbidden to do so on the advice of her pediatrician. This physician went so far as to tell her parents to leave her to cry alone in her bed so that she wouldn't become too dependent on them. She reported that neither she nor her parents slept very much for two years after the movie, but that her parents rewarded her for every night she did not wake them up, and she was eventually able to sleep through the night.

I do not believe that there is a single right or wrong answer to the question of letting your child sleep with you after a nightmare. As reports in this book show, children are joining their parents in bed much more frequently than most parents are willing to admit. Whether this is a good idea for your family depends on many things, including, of course, whether you think this is acceptable behavior and how it affects your own ability to get a good night's sleep. The risk, of course, is that it may become a habit that is difficult to break.

Although the family-bed issue is a controversial one, it seems clear that ignoring, belittling, or punishing children because of their TV-induced fears is a bad idea. Parents who acknowledge their children's fears and help manage them lay the groundwork for a sense of mutual trust and a closeness that will be of use in a variety of other emotional situations. The young woman who suffered Elephant Man nightmares offered these final thoughts:

> *My parents and I agree that they should not have followed my pediatrician's advice. Having to deal with my fears alone clearly made them worse; in retrospect, my parents wish they had been more comforting, and they told me never to leave my own children unconsoled.*

Cutting Out or Cutting Down the Stimulation

Young children who are scared will often try to get away from what's scaring them. If it's television, they may simply leave the room or turn off the TV. If it's a movie, they might scream to be taken out of the theater. That screaming in the theater serves a purpose—by disturbing other viewers, it forces you to leave the theater whether you want to or not.

Trust your crying child: Do not hesitate to remove your child from the scene (or to remove the scary scene from your child). Sometimes parents wonder whether this is a good idea. They hope that if their child will only stay to see the movie through to its happy ending, the fear will go away, and all will be well. Under certain circumstances this approach may work for older children, but there's a good reason it won't work for preschoolers. Very young children are not adept at putting sequences of scenes together in terms of cause and effect: Their fright response to the evil, grotesque monster will not necessarily be reduced by the knowledge that he was killed at the end. Their vivid visual memory may replay and replay the scary scene, whether or not they see the ending. So your best bet is to limit your child's exposure to the program or movie altogether and get him involved in something else as quickly as possible.

One advantage when dealing with preschoolers in this situation is that they are more easily distracted than older children by participation in other activities. With a smaller brain capacity, it is harder for them to keep those horrid events in mind while at the same time focusing on a new activity. Find something pleasurable and distracting to do as soon as possible, and as long as the child seems happy and comfortable, don't feel the necessity of reminding him of his trauma. In many ways, for the preschooler, out of sight is out of mind; don't hesitate to capitalize on this fact.

Another thing young children sometimes do when watching something scary on TV is to stay in the situation, but reduce their exposure to what's troubling them. Some children cover their eyes and peek through their fingers; some peek around a corner or over a pillow; some cover their ears. What they are doing here is exposing themselves to bits and pieces of the program rather than the whole thing. Research shows that these techniques can actually reduce younger children's fright while viewing scary programs. In some cases these activities simply cut down on the scary sights and sounds children receive. In others, they make them feel that they are more in control.

Gradual Exposure in Manageable Doses

Another technique that often works for younger children is referred to as "desensitization." Visual desensitization involves brief exposures to mild versions of something the child finds frightening. As the child becomes comfortable with the mildest version, he then sees a slightly stronger version, with the intensity continuing to increase gradually and only at the rate he can handle. In the experiment we did with *Raiders of the Lost Ark* we also explored whether we could make the snake scene less frightening by desensitizing children to the visual image of snakes. We created a video that showed a series of snakes—first small ones shown from a distance and then larger ones shot from close range. At first the images of snakes were taken from still photos, but as the video progressed, the snakes were shown moving more and more. Children who saw this video were less frightened by the snake-pit scene from the *Raiders* movie than children who had not been gradually exposed to snake visuals. This technique was effective for preschoolers as well as older elementary-school children. Other researchers have found similar results by allowing children to hold rubber replicas of spiders or showing them real lizards and worms before they saw scary movies involving these creatures.

My colleagues and I have also taken on *The Incredible Hulk,* using segments of a *Mister Rogers' Neighborhood* episode intended to reduce children's fear of the Hulk. After children had seen a video of actor Lou Ferrigno having his Hulk makeup applied—a much slower and more understandable transformation than the one in the program—they were less afraid while watching an *Incredible Hulk* episode.

That's fine for the laboratory, but how can parents perform visual desensitization at home? That depends on what your child was scared by. If it was an animal, there are many nature videos and realistic toys that could allow you to gradually introduce your child to the animal in an unthreatening context. A visit to a zoo or pet shop might allow your child to see the animal live—and harmless. For other frightening things, parents might consider books as a way of desensitizing. There are many picture books on the market to help children get over various fears.

Parents themselves have devised all kinds of methods. One mother reported giving her child control of the remote when he was a little scared but wanted to keep watching a video. He would fast-forward his way through parts of movies he found scary. Over time, though, he got used to those scenes and was able to view them in their entirety. Another mother said her preschooler would leave the room during the scene in *Aladdin* when the evil Jafar turns into a huge snake. The boy would remain within earshot so that he could follow the story. Gradually he began staying in the room for longer periods, and now he doesn't leave at all. Both of these stories are examples of mastering fear through desensitization.

A word of caution: Desensitization should only be used when the child really wants to see a scary program or will be exposed to it anyway. A child who is truly traumatized by a program may not be able to view even small portions of it without getting upset. Attempts to desensitize a child in this situation may well make things worse. In these cases, I would recommend avoiding the program or movie entirely. In some cases this will mean avoiding even the opening credits of the program or promos for the movie.

Magical and Mystical Remedies and Rituals

A final set of techniques that preschoolers like may seem totally irrational to the adult, although they do have their own logic in a child's mind. Here I'm talking about the various self-protective rituals children engage in to make themselves feel less vulnerable, usually when they go to bed.

First, there is the repetitive checking to see that the evil being from the television show is not hiding in the closet, under the bed, or behind the curtains. Then there is the defensive posture taken in the bed: Some children insist on facing the door for protection; others need to have their back to the door. Many children need to sleep with the light or a night-light on. Some children bring weapons of their own to bed just in case (one young man claimed to have slept with his baseball bat for years). And there's also the defensive gear, such as the blanket used to ward off vampires that was mentioned in chapter 1. Children can be very creative in selecting their methods of feeling more secure. I don't see a problem with these devices as long as they don't interfere with the child's (or his roommates') ability to get a healthy night's sleep.

Sometimes magic is invoked:

> For as long as I can remember, I have been horribly terrified of horror films. My earliest memory of fear is when I used to have my father come into my room before bedtime, and cast a "magic spell" that would keep my room safe from monsters.

There are actually products you can buy that have eased the fears of many children. Many have found Native American dream catchers helpful. These are woven circular hangings which, according to legend, catch the bad dreams before they reach the child. Many children feel secure with a dream catcher nearby and report that it does keep the bad dreams away. From time to time I have seen products on the market that advertise themselves as monster blockers or ghost resistors. Children or their parents simply spray these liquids in the closet or the corners of the room, wherever the bad guys are expected to be hiding. Many parents and children report that this type of approach does keep the demons at bay.

The principle here is that the child has to believe that the method or the ritual will keep him safe, and the parent usually has to be willing to go along with the premise. This whole approach may sound bizarre to rational parents who believe that buying into the ritual validates the fear and implies that the demon is real. But you can go along with this ritual without explicitly endorsing the reality status of the evil being. The fear is real—and it's the fear that you're dealing with. You can say, "I know there are no witches, but we can check the closet anyway if it makes you feel better."

An Ounce of Prevention

The methods I've described in this chapter are those that preschool children say they prefer and that have been shown to be effective for many children. Obviously, though, it is difficult to know which one will work best for a particular child and a particular program. Some children's fright may be so intense that these first-line techniques will not be sufficient. Sometimes, for example, the child's experience is truly traumatic or the scary aspect of a particular program comes just at the time a child is dealing with a related, troubling real-life issue. If your child's reaction does not abate over time and truly interferes with his or her day-to-day activities, don't be afraid to contact your family physician or a counselor, who can help your child deal with the problem in more depth.

Remember, too, that some of these fears will take a while to subside, but most will become manageable over time. It's good also to remember that many children hide their fright from their parents because they want to appear more grown-up or they're afraid they might suffer future restrictions. What is important is your warm and caring response. What I've noticed in the retrospective reports is that the children who have suffered the most or who have suffered the longest are those who didn't confide in their parents or whose parents derided their fears or didn't take them seriously.

Finally, it is very clear that efforts at prevention are well worth the hassle when weighed against the difficulty of reassuring a young child who has been frightened by something on TV or in a movie. As I've said throughout this book, many of these responses are remarkably intense, and they can be very hard to undo. If you happen to be there when your young child is viewing something potentially frightening, you can watch for signs of fear. Believe it or not, a child won't always say, "Mommy, I'm scared!"—but you may get a grateful nod if you ask whether you should turn the TV off now. If you're certain a show is frightening, trust your judgment and turn it off. Even if the child does not appear scared or admit to being frightened at the time, things might look different in the middle of the night . . .

CHAPTER EIGHT

Making Explanations
Child-Friendly

Reasoning That Comforts Kids

Some of the coping strategies that help preschoolers can work for older children, too, especially gradual exposure to mild versions of whatever is frightening. But as children get older, they often find that other strategies that worked when they were younger become less effective. They derive less comfort from their favorite stuffed animal, and they become more skeptical about adopting new magical rituals. Also, because older children develop the capacity to process larger amounts of information, it becomes more difficult to distract them from whatever has frightened them. The good news is that with older children you have the option of using verbal strategies. By late elementary school, kids seem to prefer techniques involving words and logical reasoning.

> *I remember having long talks with my mom when I was probably around eight years old, asking her every possible question with the need to know an exact answer in order to be happy. After watching the movie* Halloween *with my family, I was astonished to see that the bad guy, Michael Myers, had disappeared. I needed my mom to assure me that he was not coming back to life to hurt anyone else, more specifically—me. I did not go to bed until all my questions were answered in a way that assured me I would be fine. My mom would tell me that it was impossible that he could come and get me, and that it was just a movie.*

When it comes to scary fantasy shows, older children do well when told to focus on the unreality of the situation. As we saw in the previous chapter, the tell-yourself-it's-not-real strategy is a favorite of older elementary-school children. In the *Wizard of Oz* study, nine- to eleven-year-olds who were told to remember that the witch was not real showed less fear while watching her in a scene, but the same technique did not help preschoolers, who were not fully fluent in the fantasy-reality distinction. Similarly, other researchers have reported that seven- to nine-year-olds had their vampire-movie fears reduced by an explanation of how makeup made the vampires look scary, while five- to six-year-olds were not helped.

Making Verbal Strategies More Effective for Younger Children

Although verbal explanations by themselves tend to be ineffective for preschoolers, there are ways of enhancing their effectiveness. First of all, remember that for preschoolers, seeing is believing. Anything you can do to *show* them something reassuring rather than telling them about it will increase the chances that your strategy will work. For example, in a study involving *The Incredible Hulk*, my colleagues and I tried to counteract children's fears by giving them simple explanations of how the Hulk likes to help people while showing them footage of various scenes in which the Hulk rescues people in distress. This illustrated verbal explanation was effective in reducing fear even in preschool children.

At the end of another study, my colleagues and I gave children hands-on experience with the fear-reducing concept we were trying to get across. For that study, in which we used a scene from the sci-fi thriller *The Blob*, we tried to reassure children by describing the special effects that made the blob look real and letting them create their own "blobs" out of gelatin and food coloring. Talking about and *showing* how scary makeup is applied or allowing children to try on and play with ugly masks may also help them appreciate the make-believe nature of some of the visual images that scare them.

The Challenge of Downplaying Scary Things That Can Happen

Dealing with shows that are not fantasies, however, is decidedly more challenging because there are no easy reassurances. Although fiction may also be considered "make-believe" or "not real" in some sense, those phrases have a very different meaning when applied to fiction than when applied to fantasy, as I discussed in chapter 5. When it comes to reassuring older children about threats they encounter in the media, what is critical is whether what they are seeing *could* happen, not whether that specific event actually *did* happen. Because of this, reducing children's fear in response to fiction is very similar to reassuring them about something that happened in the news or was shown in a documentary.

It is important to keep in mind that the reassuring aspect of fantasy is the fact that the fantastic things we see could never happen to anyone, anywhere. Witches don't exist, and when children understand and truly accept this fact, we can use it to ease their fear. On the other hand, fiction is a form of make-believe that won't necessarily lend itself to the tell-yourself-it's-not-real strategy. Even though we can tell children, for example, that the character played by Macaulay Culkin in *My Girl* wasn't a real person and he didn't actually die from the bee stings he received in the movie, we can't honestly tell them that no child ever died from a bee sting. Making children understand that the child in that movie did not actually die might ease their sadness about his death, but it is not likely to make them less scared of bees.

It is also a good idea to remember that fantasy programs often contain realistic as well as fantastic elements. Although older children can be reassured that the witch and the flying monkeys in *The Wizard of Oz* will not come after them, many of them are just as frightened by the tornado in that movie, which can't be dismissed so easily.

Dealing with children's exposure to realistic threats and dangers, whether they arise in news reports or in fiction, is a difficult task for parents. These threats arise from sources other than exposure to the mass media, and even adults are not immune to them. One strategy for reducing fears about realistic threats is to provide an explanation that makes the danger seem more remote or less likely to occur. But that technique is difficult to apply successfully. We attempted to do this in the snake study reported in chapter 7. Telling children that most snakes are not poisonous had only a slight tendency to help second and third graders, and the technique backfired completely for children in kindergarten and first grade, making them think more about the poison in snakes than they would have without the explanation.

In the study involving *The Blob* that I referred to earlier in this chapter, we explained to a group of five- to eight-year-olds that a frightening event in a movie could *never* happen anywhere. We told others that the event was very *unlikely* to occur in the area where they lived, hoping that what was unlikely to occur would also seem non-threatening. We told a third group that the event was *highly likely* to occur where they lived. We found, unfortunately, that the children didn't differentiate very well between things that were likely and unlikely to occur. Any possibility that the scary outcome would happen made it equally scary. The only thing that reduced their fear was telling them that it was absolutely impossible.

This finding is consistent with research my colleagues and I have done on children's understanding of concepts related to probability and likelihood. For example, although children in first grade had already grasped the meaning of *definitely,* as in "this will definitely not happen," even many third graders did not understand the difference between an event that would *probably* occur and one that could *possibly* occur. So it's not that reassuring to tell an elementary-school child that the frightening thing they just witnessed is a rare event.

Children older than third grade should become more adept at using information about the small chance of bad things happening. However, research indicates that older children and even adults also overestimate the likelihood of outcomes that are intensely threatening, even when the chances of their happening are infinitesimal. If the possible outcome is catastrophic enough, the thought of any likelihood at all of the event is unacceptable. For this reason, focusing on a frightening event's low likelihood seems to be one of the least effective strategies for reducing the fears of children of any age.

The Calm, Unequivocal, Limited Truth

If minimizing the threat is not helpful, what option do you have? Saying that something that is real is totally impossible is not a good idea because your white lie may come back to haunt you when your child learns the truth elsewhere. If you lose your credibility in this area, your child may stop turning to you for reassurance and lose one of her most powerful resources for coping with fear. On the other hand, if you are not careful, the truth may be interpreted as scarier than it really is. My advice is, Don't lie when talking about realistic dangers, but don't tell your child any more than necessary about the truth. And be sure to phrase your explanation in as calming and unemotional terms as possible.

Returning to the example from the movie *My Girl*, in which a character dies after being attacked by bees, telling your child that very few people die from bee stings is not likely to be very helpful. It would be more effective to say something definite and positive like the following (unless you know it to be false): "You are not allergic to bees, so this can't happen to you."

Let me give you another example of what I mean by saying something definite, reassuring, and positive, using something that happened in my own home. A few years ago, when looking for another program, my son and I accidentally stumbled across a documentary on tornado safety. Unfortunately, as has become increasingly typical, the show was more about the dangers of tornadoes than about how to protect yourself from harm, and it included one especially frightening series of footage taken with a home video recorder during a tornado. The camera was aimed out the window of the house, while several people were heard screaming, "It's here!" "Get down!" and "Where is everybody?" Along with these screams, the camera showed the window being shattered by the high winds. I tried to change the channel, but my son was intent on seeing the program to the end. We watched it together and discussed it afterward.

The first thing Alex asked after the program was over was "Do we have tornadoes in Madison?" Based on my earlier research finding that a local danger will be scary, even if it's very unlikely, I immediately replied, "No," not remembering any that had actually touched down in the city (and, frankly, not wanting to). But my husband corrected me, reminding me of the one that had torn the roof off a car dealership a few years earlier. My next response was to say, truthfully (as far as I know), that we'd never had any tornadoes in Monona, the small suburb of Madison where we actually live. This information was extremely reassuring to Alex, and he went happily off to bed shortly thereafter. I'm sure that that explanation is what made him feel better because for a week or two after that incident, he woke up every morning saying, "I'm so glad we live in Monona." Although I did not say we could never have a tornado here, the fact that I could be so absolute about the past was very reassuring.

The story does not end here, however. As you might imagine, things got more complicated the next time we heard the tornado sirens. As I talked about going down to the basement, Alex said, "But *we* don't have to go down there since we don't have tornadoes here." Thinking quickly, I replied that although we had never had a tornado, we did sometimes get strong, damaging winds, and that it was important to protect ourselves from them as well. This explanation was enough to get him to follow me into the basement without causing him too much anxiety. "Strong damaging winds" got the point across without producing the intense emotional reaction that the idea of a tornado in our town would have produced.

The basic idea, as I see it, in reassuring children about real threats is to provide a truthful explanation that avoids emotional words and that communicates just as much as a child needs to know, but no more. Be ready to answer further questions, but don't go into more details than your child is interested in.

The problem of horrible, real threats that have a small chance of happening seems most acute when dealing with highly publicized cases of child molestation and murder, which are sensationalized on television with increasing frequency. It's bad enough that we as parents are confronted with these awful possibilities, but we also have to deal with the fears these stories produce in our children. When your child asks you how Megan Kanka or Polly Klaas (or the next highly publicized child victim) was killed, what's the best thing to say? My advice is to be truthful, yet as inexplicit as you can be. You can say, for example, that the child in question was killed by a very sick man, but spare them any of the details that they do not already know. The concept of child victimization is frightening enough that the real details—especially the part about molestation—will only make things immeasurably worse.

What If the Threat Can't Be Minimized?

If you're not successful in convincing your child that what she's concerned about won't happen, the best approach is to provide her with the information and tools that will help her prevent it from happening or at least that will make her feel more in control of the situation or its outcome. In the study I reported in chapter 1, in which we showed the schoolhouse burn down in *Little House on the Prarie,* we ended the session by giving children basic fire-safety guidelines that they could use in their own lives. These guidelines were taught with illustrations involving popular cartoon characters. Children were told, for example, to make sure their home had smoke alarms and to check to see that the batteries were fresh. They were also encouraged to have a family escape plan and to practice family fire drills. Activities such as these, carried out in the home, should be helpful in calming your child's fears of fire if they have already been aroused by a TV show or movie.

For other threats, similar simple protective strategies might be developed. If the fear is of natural disasters, you could review your plans for tornado safety, for example. If the offending movie is about burglars entering the home, you might do a tour of the home, showing how all the doors and windows are securely locked and how the particular technique that the burglar in the TV program used wouldn't work at your house. (Be sure you know this to be true in advance, or avoid the issue.) If the fear is of kidnapping, use the film as an excuse to go over your rules for dealing with strangers. It will help if the child is given an active role in the safety lessons. Going through the motions and role-playing not only the actions but the feeling of being in control of the problem should help.

During my younger years (age eight) I was frightened by daily news reports regarding a kidnapper with a white van that was stalking kids in my town. My parents would sit me down and explain to me that I was smart and that I knew not to talk to strangers and that I knew that if I saw a white van, that I should run away. These talks helped me to cope with the problem because I knew that I wouldn't be taken by surprise—I knew what to do to protect myself.

Sometimes when we try to teach self-protective behaviors to children who are unaware of specific threats, we end up scaring them more than we teach them. But when the mass media thrust these frightening possibilities on our children, we can often turn this unfortunate incident into what educators call a "teachable moment," and make the best of a bad situation.

Of course, not all accidents and disasters are preventable even with protective action, and the older your children become, the better they will understand this. How do you reassure children that nothing like the Oklahoma City bombing will ever happen again? Or that there will never be another midair explosion like the one that downed TWA 800? Or that they could protect themselves in either of these situations? You really can't provide them guarantees, but as they get older, you can stress the protections that have come out of these disasters. We now have better security at federal buildings and in airports, and planes are being redesigned to eliminate the specific causes of well-known crashes. These explanations can only go so far, of course, but your reassurances that we are learning from past mistakes may provide some help.

If All Else Fails, Just Be There and Listen

Simply talking to older children about their fears can also have a tremendously therapeutic effect. Whether the specific content of the discussion helps or not, it seems clear that parental attention, or the calming supportive pres-

ence of another thoughtful human being, is helpful.
Make sure your child knows you are there to listen to her
fright stories, even if you wish she had not seen the program that scared her.

> *The experience of actually watching a scary movie
> was not that uncomfortable for me. It was only when I
> thought about the films later in the day or before going to
> bed that I became frightened. After spending some time
> thinking about the scary images and themes of the films,
> I would be unable to sleep. Typically, I went back down-
> stairs and found my father watching television. He and
> I discussed what had scared me and I felt much better.*

As children get older and realize that there are no
guarantees of safety, the act of talking fears over with
someone who takes them seriously may be more beneficial than the actual content of the conversation. I remember a very intense emotional reaction I once had and how
the right kind of sympathetic ear was the only thing that
helped. I was already an adult and my exposure to what
frightened me was probably inevitable, although the tim-
ing could not have been worse. As I was entering my senior year in college, there was a terrible national news
story about eight student nurses who were murdered by a
man named Richard Speck. This man somehow managed
to get himself invited into the students' apartment, where
he brutally killed each of them, one by one. I think one of

them survived, actually, and lived to provide the world with the horrible details. The thought that eight women were no match for one killer was terrifying to me, but the story really hit home not only because I was moving into my first apartment (after three years in the security of the dorms) but because of the similarity of my new apartment to the one the nurses had lived in—both were garden apartments with ground-floor entrances at the front and the back.

The thought of what had happened to these nurses made me feel so vulnerable in my new apartment that I literally could not sleep for what seemed like a week or more. Any sound that I heard in the night, including that of my roommate rolling over in her bed, made me jump or cry out. My reaction was way out of proportion, and I simply couldn't calm myself down. But I had been looking forward to living in an apartment for a long time, and I was embarrassed to tell people about my newfound anxiety.

Fortunately, I soon talked about my problem to a friend who was very sympathetic. He said that if this news story was causing me so much anxiety, I should talk to a therapist about it. In those days, going to a therapist was not as common as it is today, but I thought I'd be willing to do almost anything if it would relieve me of my anxiety.

The interesting thing about this conversation is that after I had decided I would go to see a therapist, I started rehearsing in my mind what I would say to him and what he might say to me, and I suddenly felt in control of the problem. My anxiety immediately started to wane, and it eased so much that I was able to sleep. In fact, I never did make that appointment with the therapist because I had gotten the benefit of having my fears taken seriously by someone who cared. I had discovered that what I was experiencing might be considered reasonable or at least understandable under the circumstances and that there were professionals who helped people in my situation. This discovery was enough to give me back my sense of control.

Of course, solutions are not always that simple. I was lucky. But I'm also confident that a good therapist would have helped me in that situation if I had needed one to get over this trauma.

It is important that you as a parent be ready and willing to discuss your child's fears, even if you can't give her an absolute guarantee of safety. Tell your child that you understand why she's so frightened, even though you don't believe she's in danger. Tell her about this book (if she's old enough, let her read it), and about how frequently the mass media stir up people's fears to levels that are extremely hard to manage. It might help to identify the reasons why this particular program, movie, or event was so terrifying by discussing either how the events were portrayed or how they relate to her current situation. It might also be helpful to tell her about some of your own media traumas and how you succeeded in getting over them. Misery really loves company, particularly company that has been in the same place but has since moved on.

And finally, there is the option of seeking professional help if the fear remains overpowering and out of control.

Balancing Fear with Vigilance

It is true, of course, that this world can be a dangerous place, and children need to be aware of certain threats so that they can protect themselves. A certain amount of fear is necessary for survival. Children need to avoid drowning, for example, without developing a phobia of the water, and they need to protect themselves from child abuse or kidnapping without becoming socially withdrawn. One of the greatest challenges facing parents and other caregivers today lies in striking a balance between a healthy amount of fear and a level that is damaging, while allowing your child to maintain a positive outlook on life.

Of course, after your child's crisis of media-produced fear is over, if it was caused by a fictional program or movie that might have been avoided, it will be a good time to talk about being more careful about programming that makes your child particularly anxious. If your children are in the habit of seeking out the most sensational news stories or the most thrilling movies, they may benefit from your advice that they moderate or curtail their habit.

CHAPTER NINE

Why Kids Are Drawn to Scary Entertainment

—*And What If They Like It Too Much?*

A few years ago, I saw a comic strip in which teenage kids were talking about the upcoming airing of *Gremlins* on television. They were reminiscing about each vicious and gory incident in the movie, saying things like "and when the creature blows up in the microwave—awesome!" The mother of one of the kids, overhearing the conversation, sighs and thinks to herself, "I wonder whatever happened to *The Sound of Music*." To many parents, it's hard to understand why kids are flocking to so many TV programs and movies that we may find overly violent, disturbing, or downright disgusting.

The fact is, if children didn't like to watch scary programs and movies, many of the effects discussed in this book would not occur. If scary programs were not popular, there wouldn't be so many of them on television, and mysteries and horror movies would not be such a staple of the entertainment industry. Although philosophers have pondered for centuries why frightening images are popular, social scientists have only recently begun to explore this question. Most research on the issue relates to why people watch violence. Although not everything that scares children portrays violence and not all violence is scary, most of the things that produce fright relate to violence or the threat of harm in some way.

Why Is There So Much Media Violence?

Nielsen ratings consistently show that most of the Saturday-morning programs with the highest child viewership are violent. Still, there is some debate about whether children really like to watch violence, or whether violent programs are popular simply because there is very little else available for children to watch. The few experiments that have raised or lowered the violence in a program to gauge the effects on children's enjoyment have produced inconsistent results. Clearly, many things work together to determine whether violence is enjoyed, including how it is portrayed and the type of child who is watching.

There are some important economic reasons why violence is found on TV and in the movies as often as it is. One is that commercial TV programs are produced for the widest possible age range. Violent programs are easily understood even by young children, which allows them to capture a very broad audience. A second reason we have so many violent programs and movies is that it is more profitable to produce shows that can be exported to foreign countries. It is a good deal easier to translate violent programs into different languages, and other cultures understand them more readily than programs that deal with issues that are more subtle or more specific to our society.

Social Reasons for Choosing Scary Entertainment

In addition to economic factors, we often see children watching scary shows for social reasons. Scary movies seem to play a role in some sort of rite of passage for teenagers. Several of the students quoted in chapter 5 had experienced especially intense fright reactions to something they had seen at a slumber party. Obviously, slumber-party video viewing is a recent phenomenon since videos only became available about a generation ago. Perhaps it is the modern incarnation of ghost stories told around the campfire. When young people get together in groups for an overnight experience, they often turn to frightening things.

I'm not sure how to explain this tradition. Perhaps scary themes and movies are chosen for sleepovers simply to spice them up and to create an event that will be memorable and distinctly out of the ordinary. Maybe they are used to promote the bonding that often occurs when people go through a negative emotional experience together. Perhaps sleepovers present a safe way to watch the movies the teenagers wouldn't have the nerve to watch if they had to go home to bed alone. Or, watching scary videos together may be a way for youngsters to prove to themselves and to each other that they are tough, grown-up, and brave. In fact, all of these things may go into making scary movies so typical at slumber parties.

You may recall the story of the young boy who "witnessed" *Friday The Thirteenth, Part 2* because he didn't want his friend to consider him a "wussy." He's not alone; it's quite common for boys to watch scary things at the urging of their friends so that they will be considered brave or macho. One boy actually sat through *Jaws* at the age of six:

> . . . *As a result I would have fantasies and nightmares about the blood spurting out of the fisherman's mouth or the shark's teeth piercing his flesh. However, there was one positive aspect of my fright experience, and that was a sense of accomplishment. Even though I felt a little traumatized over the viewing experience, I also felt that I watched something that other people my age couldn't sit through. I would have to speculate that this is because at such a young age there is a great amount of*

competition over what one young boy can stand and what another young boy can stand. To the victor comes a sense of pride and accomplishment.

Psychological Reasons for Viewing

Beyond these economic and social reasons for the popularity of violent, scary entertainment, violence is popular because there is something about it that many people, including children, are attracted to. After reading hundreds of retrospective accounts and reviewing the available research findings, my judgment is that many people are drawn to things that frighten them—often even if they do suffer afterward. The following sentence, taken from an account of *Poltergeist*-induced nightmares, is typical:

We were scared out of our minds but we couldn't take our eyes off the screen or turn off the VCR.

Indeed, it's not hard to find children who say they like to watch violence, plain and simple. For example, when a researcher asked sixth- to eighth-grade children in Milwaukee the question: "Would you watch a television program if you knew it contained a lot of violence?" 82 percent replied "yes." What are some reasons why children, teens, and adults, for that matter, are drawn to violent, scary images? One reason seems to be what is often referred to as morbid curiosity. Even if we don't find it enjoyable or entertaining, many of us can't help joining the crowd around an accident—or, if we don't have the nerve to take a close look, we probably tune into the news that night to find out what happened. We seem to be innately fascinated with (and concerned about) the concept of death, and this seems to draw our attention to violence, death, and injury. If we take an evolutionary perspective here, it stands to reason that animals who paid attention when violence, injury, disease, and death were happening had a better chance of surviving.

Morbid curiosity leads us to want to see certain things that are associated with death. A few years back, for example, it was reported that the charred remains of the Branch Davidian compound outside Waco, Texas, where so many died in a fiery confrontation with the FBI, became such a popular tourist attraction that local officials had to put up a fence. More recently, the house where JonBenet Ramsey was found murdered has also attracted large numbers of the curious. The USA Network reports that whenever it devotes a week to shark programming, its ratings double. Morbid curiosity seems to account, in part, for the success of the "if it bleeds, it leads" philosophy of many news programs, which I talked about in chapter 6. There is something about violent injury and death that draws us in. As one student wrote:

Many people have a curiosity about what it would
be like to be in a violent situation, but never allow it to

happen for fear of personal injury. One way to fulfill this curiosity is to view a violent scene. There is no chance for personal injury and one can still get a taste of what the violent situation is like.

Although part of the reason violent portrayals are attractive is that they deal with the frightening notion of death, another part of their attraction for children seems to come from the fact that they are often full of action. Some researchers have even argued that it is action (characters moving fast) rather than violence (characters injuring each other) that attracts children's attention to violent television programs. Clearly both elements are important. Morbid curiosity by itself might lead us to be as fascinated by movies about elderly people passing away quietly or disease victims in the final stages of their illness as we are by shoot-'em-ups, dinosaur attacks, or hand-to-hand combat. But it's clear that there is a much bigger audience for action-packed mayhem than for quieter ways of dying.

One reason for the preference for action-packed violence seems to be that it is arousing. Many people, and children especially, enjoy violent, scary shows because they like the thrill of being stimulated and aroused by entertainment. Viewing violence or watching nonviolent but threatening images temporarily makes children's hearts beat faster and their blood pressure go up. Like adults, many children seek out the feelings produced by violence and suspense to stimulate them when they are bored and take them out of the humdrum of their daily lives. As one veteran of *The Incredible Hulk* put it:

> *This television program scared me to death every time I watched it, yet I tuned in with my mother and younger brother (who was also frightened) each week. I think that there may have been a part of me that enjoyed having my senses aroused. The sound of the high note and the doctor's green eyes got my heart pumping and got me out of the relaxed state in which I usually watch television.*

If there's one characteristic of children that is strongly related to whether or not they're interested in viewing violence, it's their gender. There are many, many studies that show that boys choose to watch violence more often than girls and that they generally enjoy it more. Some psychologists believe that this difference is due to the fact that we treat our little boys differently from our little girls, teaching them that violence is a male, not a female, activity. Other psychologists maintain that boys' greater interest in violence is rooted in their hormones, and that biology predisposes them to be more aggressive and to be more interested in aggressive things. Both factors probably contribute to the fact that boys are more interested than girls in violent toys, violent stories, and violent programs and movies.

It has also been shown that children who are more violent themselves are more interested in viewing violent programs. It's sometimes difficult to know which came first: whether the children became more violent because they watched so much violent programming, or whether their own violent tendencies led them to seek out violent stories to understand or justify their own behavior. The consensus of researchers is that both processes occur. Viewing violence contributes to children becoming more violent, and children who are violent are more interested in viewing violence.

Another reason many children watch violent and scary programs is that they imagine themselves in the place of the characters, and many of them enjoy the feeling of power they get when the good guy, or the character they root for, overcomes dangers and triumphs over the bad guy. One student described his enjoyment of *The Wizard of Oz* this way:

> *I waited with anticipation for each terrifying moment, and from a very early age I enjoyed the emotional buildup and release that came with each one. For me, the resolution that gave the most pleasure was when Dorothy finally killed the Wicked Witch of the West. I was far less concerned with how she got back to Kansas.*

This anecdote leads into another reason for children's attraction to violence, one that deals with fright more directly. Some research shows that watching television crime shows in which the bad guys are punished in the end actually reduces the fears of mildly anxious people. In one study, college students took a six-weeks' heavy dose of action-adventure programs featuring good triumphing over evil. This treatment not only reduced their feelings of anxiety, it increased their appetite for this type of material even after the study was over. Surveys my colleagues and I have done also suggest that some children may choose to watch mildly scary television programs to help them cope with their anxieties. In one survey of parents, for example, we found that children who had been frightened by television were especially interested in violent programs in which good triumphed over evil, but they were not particularly interested in other types of violent programming.

A few programs aimed at children seem to be especially designed to serve the function of reassuring them about their fears. The most obvious one, one that has been on television in various forms since the late sixties, began as *Scooby-Doo, Where Are You?* This animated program features a group of teenage kids and a dog or two who travel around in their van and solve mysteries involving monsters, ghosts, mummies, abominable snowmen, and the like. Scooby, the canine star, and Shaggy, one of the teenagers, are always extremely frightened by the threatening beast or monster. Their fear is dramatized humorously, with chattering teeth, trembling bodies, and cries of "Get me out of here!"

Each plot of *Scooby-Doo* is nearly identical to the others: Someone has concocted a scheme to steal something valuable by scaring everyone else. To accomplish his goal, the villain dons some sort of scary costume and arranges other special effects to convince the general public they had better stay away. In every episode, the kids figure out the mystery and confront the villain, revealing that there is a real person inside the monster costume. The kids are then praised for their heroism and their ability to solve the mystery, and they explain the very complicated set of clues that helped them discover who the villain really was. The obvious message is, Things aren't as scary as they seem, and you, too, can overcome your fear.

Although most kids don't even consider this a scary program, it seems that some children who are confronting fears turn to programs like this to work through their anxieties. The program produces a very safe level of fear that the young child can easily master and shows that other people (and even a dog!) have anxieties that they can learn to control. Other mildly scary programs that show a hero in danger but ultimately triumphing over it seem to have a similar effect.

But there's a definite limit to the effectiveness of television and movies as an anxiety reducer. I talked in chapter 7 about a fear-reducing technique called desensitization, which exposes a child to something that's feared in weak, manageable doses. It is important to note that an effective fear-reducing strategy must provide only a very mild dose of fear, one that the child can easily learn to handle. Something intensely frightening will more than likely have the opposite effect, making the child's fears even stronger and more difficult to allay.

The Anxious, Traumatized Child vs. the Jaded Kid Who Can't Get Enough

Although mildly anxious children may turn to safe levels of violence to reassure themselves, children experiencing intense anxieties generally don't enjoy watching violent television. In a study of children in inner-city Milwaukee, children who were experiencing acute anxiety symptoms from the real violence in their environment were the least interested in viewing very violent shows and were the most upset when they did watch them. Rather than helping these children cope, viewing violence made them feel worse.

But there were other children in the Milwaukee study who reacted quite differently to their violent surroundings. These children seemed to have become emotionally numb to real violence, showing very little trauma and few anxiety symptoms. It was these children who were especially interested in viewing very violent programs. Not only were these children more interested in viewing violence; they said they felt especially good when watching people on violent shows fight and hurt each other. Even more disturbing, the more interested these kids were in viewing violence on TV, the less they cared to see the bad guys get caught. These tough kids who had seen it all seemed to like violence for violence's sake. They liked the thrill of the fight and couldn't care less if the good guy won in the end.

Although children who are callous and numb may be less likely to have nightmares and other fear reactions, what is worrisome about this group is that they are more prone to other effects of witnessing violence and especially prone to the negative effects of desensitization.

The Downside of Desensitization

When I talked about desensitization as a coping strategy in chapter 7, it was in a positive context. But desensitization can be taken to an extreme when the child is exposed to large amounts of violence and other threatening images. As a result of repeated exposure to intense violence, children and adults show a lessening of their emotional response to it. They are then likely to seek out more intense levels of violence to achieve the same thrill that lower levels used to give them.

Research shows that children who watch a lot of violence become less aroused by it over time and that children become less bothered by real interpersonal aggression after watching fictionalized violence. Research also shows that repeated exposure to violence leads to less sympathy for its victims and to the adoption of violent attitudes and behaviors.

The trend for children and teenagers to become desensitized to violence is especially disturbing if we take a look at movies that are being made today. I remember how intense reactions were to such groundbreaking movies as *Bonnie and Clyde* and *The Wild Bunch* in the sixties. But in retrospect, these movies are very mild compared to popular movies of today like *Natural Born Killers*. What is worse, now that there are so many television channels, and almost all movies are available on video, teenagers who enjoy super-violent programming have a virtually unlimited supply of intense mayhem. The prevalence and easy availability of emotion-deadening viciousness makes the desensitization of large numbers of children a higher risk now than ever before.

In sum, then, there are a variety of reasons why your child may want to view violent, scary programs: Some of these are social, relating to the desire to demonstrate "manliness" or to engage in an adolescent rite of passage, some are psychological, and some may actually benefit your child—if he chooses a manageable dose of a threat that he learns to master. But heavy doses of brutality result in one of two unhealthy outcomes: either the severe fright reactions that this book describes or the deadening of emotional responsiveness and antisocial attitudes toward violence.

The fact that children may be attracted to scary programs certainly complicates the task of parents who want to shield their children from unnecessary trauma. The next chapter deals with the issue of ratings, program and movie labels that are intended to help parents make more informed decisions about what their children should watch. As we will see, not only are ratings sometimes misleading, they often make parents' jobs harder by making hazardous programs and movies more appealing.

CHAPTER **TEN**

. . . .

Ratings Roulette

. . . .

The Perils of "Parental Guidance"

A mother recently told me the following story:

> *We told our son that he would be getting a new ten-speed bike for his thirteenth birthday. But he told us he wouldn't need a new bike. He declared that he wouldn't have time to ride it after he was thirteen, since he would be spending all his free time watching PG-13 movies!*

Having read this far, I hope you're convinced of two things: First, it is extremely important to be aware of and to guide what your child sees on television, in videos, and at the movies. And second, it may be more difficult than you thought to shield your child from programs you consider inappropriate. Although you may think that your home, at least, is your castle, that castle has no moat and no fortress to protect it from the televised intruders that may disturb your children. Some of the intruders may seem harmless on the surface, but they conceal a seamier side. And to make things even more difficult, your children may be curious about these very intruders and may be eager to invite them in, despite your concerns.

I want to talk now about some practical problems of managing television in your home and selecting movies or videos for your children. Once you've decided that you want to be selective in what your children watch, how can you know in advance what will be in a program, video, or movie?

One way, of course, would be to watch every program or movie before your child sees it. Although this would perhaps be an ideal solution, no parent has the time to do it, and it's simply not feasible when we're talking about watching live television. So we have to depend on various forms of information that are provided to us. We have had movie ratings since the sixties, and now we have television ratings as well. Let's look at each of these in turn.

What You Should Know about Movie Ratings

When choosing a movie or a video for your child, the most obvious bit of information you have to go on besides its title is its Motion Picture Association of America (MPAA) rating. Most parents are familiar with this system, which puts movies into four major categories: G for "General

Audiences," PG for "Parental Guidance Suggested," PG-13 for "Parents Strongly Cautioned," and R for "Restricted." A fifth rating, NC-17, "No One 17 and Under Admitted," was recently added, but it is rarely used.

The MPAA employs a committee of parents, who screen the movies and give them ratings by majority vote. A movie producer who is unhappy with a rating can re-edit the film and resubmit it or submit the film to an appeals board, headed by MPAA president Jack Valenti, who developed the system in the 1960s.

Many parents take note of a movie's MPAA rating in making selections for their children, but these ratings have been widely criticized for being much too vague and too arbitrary. The rating system gives rough age guidelines regarding who should be allowed to see the movie, but it does not say why a movie received its rating. A PG rating, for example, indicates that many parents may consider some material unsuitable for their children, but it doesn't give any clue as to what's in the movie that makes it unsuitable.

Although the MPAA ratings do not indicate why a program received the rating it did, this information is available in other locations. Bowing to public pressure, the MPAA has provided content information for all movies that have received a rating of PG or higher since 1995. This information is usually not available in movie advertisements or on videocassette labels. However, it is often included in movie reviews, and it can be accessed through the MPAA's web site (www.mpaa.org), by subscription to the *Motion Picture Rating Directory* (at a cost of $160 per year), and by telephone in some cities.

As a researcher interested in this issue, and as a mother who finds it difficult to locate suitable movies for my own child to view, I thought it would be interesting to use the *Motion Picture Rating Directory* to determine the proportion of movies that were given the various ratings. What I found may surprise you, but it does explain why it's so hard to find movies that are obviously intended for young children. Out of some fourteen hundred movies that the MPAA rated in 1995 and 1996, only 3 percent were rated G. During that time, 14 percent were rated PG, 16 percent were rated PG-13, and a whopping 67 percent were rated R!

Because the G rating is so rare, many parents look to movies rated PG as the next best option. But without the additional content information, they are left in the dark in terms of what to expect. I became curious to know how many PG-rated movies simply had bad language, for example. I had heard members of the movie industry admit that very few producers actually want a G rating because they're afraid that only very young children will want to see their movie. (And as we'll see later in this chapter, their fears are well grounded!) Adding a few bad words is one way to avoid a G rating, and, looking at the reasons the MPAA gave for all the movies that were rated PG in 1995 and 1996, my colleagues and I found that more than one-fourth of them (26 percent) had bad language only. Many parents feel that these bad words are the lesser of the three evils that are prevalent in movies (language, sex, and violence). If only the rating would tell parents which were the ones with language!

And how helpful is the PG rating in letting us know what to expect in terms of other types of content? In addition to those with bad words, 12 percent of PG movies had violence only and another 26 percent had both violence and bad language. Eighteen percent of PG-rated movies had no violence, no sex, and no bad language. Most of these were described as having "thematic elements" that were somehow inappropriate for young children. So it's quite clear that the PG rating tells parents virtually nothing about the content to expect in a movie. If they can't access the MPAA's web site or find the content reasons in another location, they are left almost completely in the dark.

There's another little-known problem with the PG rating that I came upon in my analyses. When my colleagues and I looked at the content of a random sample of movies shown on television, there was only a whisper of a difference between movies rated PG and those rated PG-13. It was then that I was reminded that the PG-13 rating was not introduced until 1984. This rating was added in response to children's fright reactions to such movies as *Gremlins* and *Indiana Jones and the Temple of Doom*. Before that time, movies that now would be given a PG-13 rating were probably rated PG. Did you know, for example, that *Jaws*—the movie cited so many times as causing long-term fears—is rated only PG? Certainly that movie deserves more of a caution than "Parental Guidance Suggested." But it was released before the PG-13 rating existed. So, in addition to other problems with the MPAA ratings, it's important to find the date of a movie's release when interpreting the PG rating. If a PG-rated movie was released before 1984, its content may bring an especially upsetting surprise.

Can't We Even Trust the G Rating?

The G rating doesn't necessarily help us either. As one mother who answered a recent nationwide survey of ours put it:

> *As of now, I do not trust the MPAA's ratings at all. Not even G.*

The G rating is not necessarily safe for young children. The label "General Audiences: All Ages Admitted" appears comforting to most parents, although the explanation of the rating supplied by MPAA president Jack Valenti hedges a bit:

> This is a film which contains nothing in theme, language, nudity and sex, violence, etc. which would,

in the view of the Rating Board, be offensive to
parents whose younger children view the film. The
G rating is not a "certificate of approval," nor does
it signify a children's film.

The explanation goes on to say that a G-rated movie has
no nudity or sex and that "the violence is at a minimum."

If there's one type of movie where the G rating especially falls down on the job, it's the animated feature. Although most of these fairy tale or adventure movies are
rated G, many of them have a good deal more than minimal violence. For example, the G-rated *Beauty and the
Beast* is intensely violent, both in the vicious attacks by the
wolves on the Beast, and in the fierce, deadly battle between the Beast and the villain Gaston. In a story in the
Boston Globe, one mother complained that the wolves in
this movie had caused her three-year-old daughter to become terrified of dogs, and that her daughter was still
afraid of dogs three years later.

Although it may seem shocking to those who have always believed cartoon features to be designed for young
children, my own research and the frequency of parents'
reports of their children's distress lead me to conclude
that many of them are too scary for many children below
the age of six. Some parents who agree with me on this
have confided that many of their friends think they're
crazy. If animated features can't be rated G, what use is
there in the G rating at all?

This last question brings up a very good point. Animated fairy tale and adventure films seem to be rated on the basis of their target market—children—rather than the effects they have on children. A G rating is not an indication of content. And it is not very helpful to parents.

Just Let Us Know What's in the Show

To summarize some of the problems with movie ratings: We can't tell what's in the movie from the rating alone; we can't interpret PG ratings that were issued before 1984 (when PG-13 was introduced); and we can't trust the G rating to be safe for preschoolers. MPAA ratings reflect what a committee of parents think would be offensive to other parents. They do not reflect any expertise in the field of child psychology or knowledge of the impact of the media on children. These ratings are not helpful in predicting the effects a movie will have on your child.

What *would* help us make viewing decisions for our children? The answer is, an honest indication of what is in the movie. If a rating simply indicated the movie's contents, parents could ask themselves, "Is my child ready to watch this?"

Take another striking example of a G-rated animated feature, *Bambi*. In the middle of this classic movie, the sweet young fawn's mother is shot and killed by a hunter. When I went to a matinee where *Bambi* was playing, I heard interesting conversations all around me. After the hunter's shot rang out, and while Bambi was searching in vain for his mother, I heard many children asking the same question: "What happened to Bambi's mother?" I also noticed that different parents were answering in different ways—some were being honest, but others didn't want to communicate the brutality of the truthful answer. If you take your preschooler to *Bambi,* be prepared for your child to suddenly confront the thought of *you* dying. I often hear reports of preschoolers' problems with *Bambi,* yet it's hard to get the message out that it's better to wait with this movie. What could sound more innocent than a G-rated cartoon named *Bambi?* Wouldn't information about what happens in this movie serve you better than the rating?

There are scary scenes in many animated fairy tale and adventure features. In addition to the recurrent theme of the loss of the mother, there are a multitude of monstrous and grotesque villains. There are also many disturbing character transformations, and there's plenty of intense violence. This is the stuff of nightmares for two- to five-year-olds. These films are often fun for slightly older children, perhaps six or seven and up, but they can be too much for younger ones to take. My advice is not to take the safety of any so-called children's movie for granted, but to err on the side of caution if you have any doubts.

I want it to be clear that this recommendation is not an attack on the entertainment industry; nor is it intended to single out any specific producers of children's movies. This is information for parents who are seeking enjoyment—not nightmares—for their children. All children are not equally sensitive to this type of material, but enough of them respond badly that discretion is warranted.

Members of the movie industry may be alarmed at the advice I'm giving because they may see it as potentially cutting into the audience for their G-rated movies. But I am not advising you to boycott these movies; simply wait until your child is old enough to see them without trauma. Who knows, if a child's first experience with the movies is a fun thrill rather than a series of sleepless nights, maybe that child will become a more avid consumer of movies in the long run!

Making the Most of Movie Ratings

In spite of all the problems with movie ratings, they do provide *some* information. Most R-rated movies and a high proportion of those rated PG-13 have enough sex, violence, and bad language to eliminate them as an option for young children. And you can use the MPAA's web site to get some idea of the reasons why recent movies received their ratings. To me, the best use of the MPAA ratings is to rule out movies with more restrictive ratings (unless you have viewed them yourself, and know the rating to be wrongly applied). And don't be reassured by the lower-level ratings of G or PG without getting

further information about the content of the movie. (A
video guide might be a good place to start.) A table in
the appendix summarizes important features of the movie
ratings.

What About TV Ratings?

Although there are many difficulties in selecting movies
and videos for your children, the stakes are even higher
for television because TV programs come into your home
automatically. For all the channels your set receives, the
programs are there at the touch of a remote. Unless some
program-blocking technology is in place, or you are monitoring your TV at all times, their availability in your home
is out of your control.

Fortunately, we are entering a new era, one in which
parents are being given new tools to help them screen out
certain types of programs. The Telecommunications Act
of 1996 required new television sets to be manufactured
with an electronic device known as a V-chip within a specified period of time. The V-chip reads a code or rating
that is embedded in each program as it is transmitted. Parents decide which rating levels are inappropriate for their
child, and by flipping a switch, they ensure that no programs with those ratings will be shown on their TV unless
they themselves choose to override the blocking.

The concept seems simple enough, but the complicating and controversial part is how programs are rated.
Someone has to give each program a rating that parents

will find useful in deciding whether or not a program should be blocked.

The Tug-of-War over the TV Ratings: Parents vs. the Television Industry

In February of 1996, shortly after the Telecommunications Act was passed, the leaders of the broadcast, cable, and film industries agreed to come up with a rating system to apply to their programs. Many of these leaders were reluctant to provide ratings because of their fears that the ratings might lower viewership for their programs and ultimately reduce their profits. But with the threat that someone else might create a system if they did not, they set up the Ratings Implementation Group headed by MPAA president Jack Valenti. Because of the volume of programs that would need to be rated, it was assumed from the start that producers or distributors would rate their own programs rather than having a committee determine the ratings. Unfortunately, under Valenti's leadership, it was also assumed that the TV ratings would be based on the movie ratings that he developed.

Although Valenti's group publicly acknowledged that ratings were for parents, many people, myself included, were concerned that economic forces in the industry would outweigh parents' wishes in determining the type of rating system that would emerge. So, in the summer of 1996, I joined with the National PTA and the Institute for Mental Health Initiatives (IMHI) to do a nationwide survey to find out what parents wanted in a rating system. We explored whether parents preferred the MPAA approach, which gives age guidelines but doesn't specify content, or a content-based approach, which indicates the level of sex, violence, and coarse language in a program, but gives no age recommendations. This second approach is similar to a system that has been used for years on the cable channels HBO, Showtime, and Cinemax.

We sent our survey to a random sample of the PTA's national membership, and the results came back from every state in the country. These parents voted overwhelmingly for information about content: 80 percent of them chose a content-based system, while only 20 percent felt the system should give age recommendations. Our findings were echoed in two other national polls in the fall of 1996 and in several others after that.

Although the entertainment industry engaged in a very public process of consulting with researchers and child advocates while developing their rating system, they ignored our unanimous recommendations for a content-based system and came out with the TV Parental Guidelines in December of 1996, based primarily on the MPAA ratings. Instead of G, PG, PG-13, and R, the new ratings were TV-G, "General Audience"; TV-PG, "Parental Guidance Suggested"; TV-14, "Parents Strongly Cautioned"; and TV-MA, "Mature Audience Only." The new rating system also had two other levels, to be used for what the industry dubbed "children's programming": TV-Y for "All Children" and TV-Y7, "Directed to Older Children." The rating system, which is designed to be applied to all programs with the exception of news and sports, was adopted by all channels except PBS (the Public Broadcasting System) and BET (Black Entertainment Television). PBS said the ratings as designed were uninformative; BET objected to the concept of ratings per se.

Problems with the Industry's Rating System

As if the fact that American parents overwhelmingly preferred a system of content indicators rather than age guidelines wasn't sufficient evidence to force the TV industry to change its mind, there were other problems with the TV Parental Guidelines as well.

The TV rating system provided no information at all about why a program got its rating. At least with the MPAA ratings, parents now have the web site available to find out about content and we have the assurance that a committee of our peers has determined the rating a movie received. But with the TV Parental Guidelines, not only were no parents involved in determining a program's rating, none were involved in the appeals process either. In fact, no one outside the industry was permitted to sit on the Monitoring Board for the new rating system. So much for serving parents!

But the report card was even worse for the TV Parental Guidelines: Guess how this type of rating affects children!

"The cooler the movie, the higher the rating."

This spontaneous comment came from a ten-year-old girl who participated in research my colleagues and I conducted for the National Television Violence Study, an independent violence monitoring project funded by the cable TV industry. The aim of the research was to determine whether putting warning labels or restrictive ratings on violent shows would discourage children from viewing them, or whether the attempt would backfire and make children more interested in seeing them—the forbidden-fruit effect. In the study this girl participated in, which involved children between the ages of five and eleven, a child and his or her parent selected the programs the child would see. Some of the program choices the pair was given had the label "Contains some violence. Parental discretion advised." Other choices involved movies that were rated PG-13: "Parents Strongly Cautioned."

What was most interesting about this study was the difference between how parents and children talked about the programs' labels. Almost all the comments the parents made about the programs with restrictive labels were negative. In contrast, more than half of the children's comments about these programs ranged from favorable to downright enthusiastic. For example, one child said, "PG-

13. Choose that one!" Another blurted out, "Parental discretion advised—that's awesome!" These cautionary labels really added to the programs' allure for many children.

My colleagues and I also did some studies to find out how these ratings affect kids who make viewing decisions in the absence of their parents. We found that boys were more interested in a program when it was labeled "parental discretion advised" than when it came without a label. We also found that children between ten and fourteen were much more interested in a movie when they were told it was rated PG-13 or R and much less interested in the same movie if they thought it was rated G. Among younger children, those who were the most aggressive or who liked to watch TV the most also found programs with restrictive ratings more enticing. On the other hand, content-based systems like the one used by HBO and Showtime did not attract children to programs with higher violence levels.

These studies show that ratings like those the TV industry developed are the most likely to attract our children to the programs we want to shield them from! Telling a child "you're too young for this program" and telling parents "protect your child from this" makes a program much more tantalizing. Simply providing information about the content, the way HBO and Showtime do, is not nearly as provocative.

Unfortunately then, rather than helping you, TV ratings may very well make it harder for you to protect your child from inappropriate programs. Many parents have reported this problem, including a mother who said that her ten-year-old son had suddenly become so fascinated with anything rated TV-14 that it was causing immense conflict in her family. Another mother told me that her fourteen-year-old daughter, who had previously accepted her parents' restriction on *NYPD Blue*, suddenly insisted she was entitled to see it after it began being labeled TV-14. So it seems that age-based ratings can cause problems with children both under and over the recommended age minimum. At least the V-chip may allow parents to block a program without calling their child's attention to the forbidden fruit. But it may be a long time before most TV sets are equipped with blocking technology.

The Compromise Rating System: The Good, the Bad, and the Complicated

The TV industry's rating system met an unprecedented throng of opponents, who joined together in the spring and summer of 1997 to pressure for changes. The National PTA led a coalition of public health and child advocacy groups, including the American Medical Association, the American Academy of Pediatrics, the American Psychological Association, the Center for Media Education, and the Children's Defense Fund. These groups relentlessly lobbied Congress and the Federal Communications Commission (FCC), asking them to insist on a better system. The television industry countered that all the criticism was coming from these "special interest groups," as they called them, and maintained that most parents were satisfied with the ratings the industry was providing. However, after comments to the FCC and a congressional hearing in Peoria, Illinois, showed how widespread parents' opposition was, the industry started to negotiate with the child advocacy groups, and most channels agreed to a compromise rating system in July of 1997. At that time, PBS agreed to use the new system and BET maintained its refusal to rate its programs. NBC refused to adopt the compromise system and continued to use the age-based ratings.

The compromise system, which began being applied to programs on October 1, 1997, keeps the original age-based system but adds various content indicators to help parents determine what, specifically, caused the program to receive its rating. The upper three ratings (TV-PG, TV-14, and TV-MA) may now be accompanied by a V for violent content, an L for coarse language, an S for sexual content, and a D for sexual dialogue or innuendo. For children's programs, an FV may be added to the TV-Y7 rating to indicate that the program contains "fantasy violence." The amended television rating system is shown in the appendix.

The fact that the industry budged at all—Jack Valenti had warned critics that he'd see them in court "in a nanosecond" if they tried to force any changes—is a great victory for parents. This is one instance where parents' voices were heard, and we should all feel indebted to the child advocacy groups and to members of Congress, particularly Representative Ed Markey of Massachusetts and Senator John McCain of Arizona, who kept the pressure on the television industry. The additional content information will undoubtedly be helpful.

Problems with the Amended System

The bad news is that the compromise rating system keeps some unfortunate features of the original system because the industry adamantly refused to give up on its age-based rating structure. First, the fact that the age guidelines have been retained makes it likely that the forbidden-fruit effect will continue, making restricted programs more tantalizing to many children. Second, the new system does not require full disclosure when some types of content are less controversial than others within the same program. Under the compromise, the overall rating of a program is determined by its most intense content. In other words, if a program has "strong coarse language," it is rated TV-14-L; if it has "moderate violence," it is rated TV-PG-V. But if it has both of these elements, it is still rated TV-14-L, and no mention is made of its violent content. What this means is that if a movie is rated TV-14 or TV-MA, it may have lower levels of sex, violence, or coarse language that are not explicitly indicated by a content letter.

Another problem with the compromise is that the industry insisted on using euphemisms rather than describing content clearly and accurately. Although the parent groups had argued for using a V for violence, an S for sex, and an L for coarse language, the industry insisted upon adding D for situations in which sex is talked about but not shown. They also balked at using the word "violence" to refer to the mayhem that goes on in many children's shows, such as *Power Rangers* or *The X-Men*. Instead, the amended system uses the letters FV to refer to "fantasy violence." Any intense violence that occurs in children's programs is labeled fantasy violence, whether the violence is indeed of the impossible variety or whether it is quite realistic but simply appears in a children's show.

Finally, it remains to be seen whether producers will assign ratings accurately and consistently to their programs.

The compromise system is complicated, but at least it permits parents to receive some information about the type of content in a program and, importantly, the agreement added five representatives of child advocacy groups to the Monitoring Board of the rating system. If television producers assign ratings arbitrarily or irresponsibly, there are some members of the monitoring group who are beholden to families rather than to the television industry's bottom line.

Alternative Rating Systems

There are a number of groups that are dissatisfied with the TV Parental Guidelines and that have developed their own systems for rating television content. One of these groups, the Children's Television Consortium, is especially concerned that the television industry's system is not informed by the findings of medical or psychological research. They have developed a system called Our Kids TV (OKTV), based on what is known about the effects of television on children. This system will be especially helpful to parents who are concerned about their children's fright reactions because it has a separate set of ratings dealing with horror, based heavily on my research about what frightens children at different ages.

One handicap of the OKTV system is that unless the raters are provided with advance information about the content of specific episodes of programs, they may lack the important details necessary to rate them accurately. Another problem involves the public's access to the ratings: Newspapers are unlikely to provide alternative ratings in their program listings. Moreover, the television industry is not likely to embed such ratings in their program transmission, rendering them unreadable by the V-chip. Nevertheless, because these ratings will undoubtedly be much more useful to parents than the industry's system, it may well be worthwhile to take the extra effort to locate them. When the OKTV system is up and running, you will be able to obtain information about it through the web site of the American Academy of Child and Adolescent Psychiatry (www.aacap.org).

This chapter has suggested how movie and television ratings may be of value and has also pointed out some of their deficiencies. Now it's time to see how best to put what you've learned in this book into day-to-day practice. After all, it's up to you to manage your child's TV viewing and make the best of ratings and new technologies. It is also important that you speak up and be sure your opinions and needs are listened to by the larger community.

CHAPTER **ELEVEN**

Taming the Resident Monster

Living with the Reality of Television,
Movies, and Videos

Guiding or Controlling Your Child's Viewing

Now that you've seen some of the effects of frightening media fare on children and know some of the ways to predict what will be especially disturbing for your child, let's look at some of the day-to-day techniques that you can use to reduce the chances of negative effects. What *can* you do as a parent who wants to coexist responsibly with television in your home and who wants to make sensible movie and video choices? There are a number of things that can help you.

   Limit the amount of time your child spends watching television, especially around bedtime. Limiting viewing is a good idea for other reasons than reducing your child's exposure to frightening fare. Many studies show that viewing more than one or two hours of television a day interferes with a child's other activities, and the effects can be seen on performance in school as well as in children's social interactions. Recognize that a lot of TV viewing is done out of boredom. To me, one of the most unhealthy aspects of television is that a child can sit in front of the set for long periods of time doing nothing, yet not feeling bored. If the television set suddenly broke down, how long do you think your child would last sitting there on the couch? If some of your child's viewing is prompted by boredom, try getting your child involved in other activities. I realize this is easier said than done, but most kids will stop watching television more willingly if you offer them something else to do rather than simply tell them to stop watching.

Become actively involved in your children's television viewing. This means not only setting up rules for their viewing and guiding their choices of shows but also being aware of what they are watching, sitting down and watching television with them, and having a discussion about what you have seen. By becoming familiar with the different programs your child watches, you can make a more informed judgment about which programs are relatively safe and unlikely to produce fear. In addition, you can be there to monitor the programs you're less sure of. For very young children, you can be ready with the remote to change the channel if the program seems to be veering in a harmful direction. For older children, you can be ready to discuss any troubling issues the program may raise.

There's another benefit to being involved in your child's viewing: Our research on TV ratings and advisories showed that children whose parents watch TV with them and discuss it with them are less likely to choose restricted content when their parents are not around. Those children seem to understand the reasons for their parents' restrictions and are more likely to accept them. As in other areas of child rearing, many children are more likely to accept a restriction if it seems to be arrived at cooperatively and for good reasons, rather than being delivered in an authoritarian fashion. Explaining the reasons for your decisions in a nonjudgmental way is more likely to bring success than simply criticizing the program or your child's taste. You'd do better to say, "We're not going to watch this because it causes nightmares" than to say, "That's garbage—turn it off."

If you can't watch a program or movie in advance or view it with your child, find out as much as you can about the show. Read whatever is available. Many movie reviewers give special attention to things they think might be frightening for young children. I hope that this book will make reviewers more sensitive to some of the specific things that frighten children of different ages, so that reviews will become even more helpful. Talk to the parents of your children's friends as well, checking for any problems their children may have had.

Use whatever information you can get from the rating systems. For movies released in 1995 or later, check the MPAA's web site for content information. For television programs, the amended TV rating system, with all its problems, does give parents advance information that has not been available in the past. In addition to the general age guidelines, there should be an indication (if the rating is done fairly) of the presence of violence, sex, coarse language, and sexual dialogue. This information should permit you to tailor your viewing decisions to your own values and your own concerns about the members of your family. I'll remind you here that much of what frightens children is violent, and there is a great deal of research that shows other harmful effects of viewing violent programs: They can lead to a reduction in empathy for the victims of violence and to the adoption of violent attitudes and behaviors. If you are mainly concerned about your child's exposure to violence, you can be especially wary of children's programs with the FV label and general programming with a V label.

Research also shows that many parents are concerned about their children's exposure to sexual dialogue, sexual situations, and coarse language, and that parents differ in terms of how strongly they worry about the effects of different types of content. If your child's exposure to coarse language concerns you, you can avoid programs with an L; if you feel your child is ready to be exposed to sexual dialogue and innuendo but not to actual depictions of sex, you can avoid programs with an S, but you don't have to worry so much about programs with the designation D. It's up to you.

The V-chip, when available, will allow you to implement your ratings decisions automatically. With a V-chip, you can designate which age-based ratings (for example, TV-14 and up) and content indicators (for example, V or S) are inappropriate for your children, and then all programs with those ratings will be blocked from your set. Only you, or someone else who knows your secret password or code number, will be able to override your decisions. You can think of the V-chip as a sieve over the pipeline that lets television programs into your home. You set the size and shape of the openings to sift out programs whose ratings are unacceptable to you. This gives you an unprecedented form of control over what enters your home through your television. The advantage of the V-chip is that it is mandated, beginning mid-1999, for most new televisions, so it will be much cheaper and more convenient than other devices that are purchased separately.

Look for other blocking technologies beyond the V-chip. The V-chip is not the only way to automatically block programs from entering your home, and it is important to understand the distinction between the V-chip, which is mandated for new television sets, and other blocking technologies that are created on a voluntary basis and will often be sold separately from televisions. Because the V-chip is the result of a governmental mandate, there are limits, politically, to how far it will go. In March of 1998, the FCC approved the technological standard for the V-chip, and few television-set manufacturers are likely to install V-chips that go beyond the FCC's requirements. According to the FCC's mandate, V-chips will be able to read the TV Parental Guidelines and the MPAA ratings, but will not have the capability to read any alternative rating systems that other groups are developing. Moreover, the V-chip will not permit parents the option of blocking unrated programs. Therefore, a family who uses the V-chip will have no protection from news or sports or from any other programs that a channel does not rate.

But what the government *requires* in new TV sets doesn't limit what a manufacturer can produce voluntarily or what a parent can hope to have in other blocking technologies. In terms of technological feasibility, there are many ways blocking devices can go further than the V-chip. Shouldn't you, as an individual parent, have the ability to keep programs out of your home if you're concerned about their effects on your child? One obvious option you should have is the ability to block unrated programs, like the news. The government-mandated V-chip will never block the news because news programs are exempt from ratings. But the news, as we have seen, contains some of the scariest television there is. In early Canadian trials of the V-chip, parents had the option of blocking all unrated programs if they wanted to, and many of them understandably chose that option.

Having read this book, you will also recognize that blocking devices that are based on the TV industry's rating system will be only partially successful in screening out scary material, even in programs that are rated. If TV producers honestly report the contents of their programs, you should be able to block out programs that are explicitly violent by using ratings, but the TV ratings are not sensitive to many of the things that this book has shown are especially scary to preschoolers. Vicious-looking animals, grotesque or deformed characters, and frightening transformations, for example, will not necessarily be captured in the violence codes, so it will be up to you to screen for these scary elements. The OKTV ratings, described at the end of chapter 10, may be helpful in identifying these frightening elements.

Other aspects of television that are left unrated, and that the FCC-mandated V-chip is unable to block, are advertisements and promos for future programs, and as we have seen, promos can be especially frightening for children even though they may be as brief as thirty seconds. Because of this, blocking entire channels may be more useful than blocking by ratings when protecting preschoolers, especially. No matter how many channels your home receives, there are probably only a few that are reasonably safe for young children most of the time. A few channels are sensitive to the needs of young viewers, and they tend not to advertise for scary programs during shows aimed at preschoolers. You might be more at ease, then, if you let in only those channels that you trust when you're not in the room; you can override this blocking when you're there to help with specific selections.

There are several set-top devices available or in development that provide a variety of different program-blocking options. Some simply retrofit a V-chip to older sets to allow you to block on the basis of the TV industry's rating system and the MPAA ratings without having to buy a new TV. But others are likely to provide additional services, and it will be worth the effort to seek out the ones that provide the most effective protection. Look for a device that allows you to block unrated programs in addition to allowing you to block according to rating levels. Not only will this option let you block news and sports, it will turn the entire concept of TV reception upside down. Rather than allowing you only to block programs that have ratings that indicate they might be objectionable, it will put you in the position of inviting into your home only those programs whose ratings are acceptable. With the ability to block unrated programs, you can decide, for example, to let in only programs rated TV-Y. To my mind, this is the way television should be. After all, it is *your* home, and they are *your* children.

Other helpful features to look for are the ability to block entire channels and the ability to block individual programs that you know disturb your own child. Some of

these features may be available in newer TV models. Your
current set may already have them. If not, shop around for
the best blocking features when you buy your set-top box
or your next TV.

If all of these features are not currently available, the
electronics industry will likely produce them if they sense
that there is enough consumer demand. Don't hesitate to
let your local electronics dealer know what would help you.

*Recognize that you will often have to make different
program and movie choices for your different-aged children.* I realize that this may be one of the toughest recommendations to swallow, but the sad fact that this book
reports is that one child's thrill is often his younger
brother or sister's sleepless week. Again and again, the
horror stories I hear involve a younger sibling being exposed to something she never would have chosen herself.
I've included a summary in the appendix of what children
of different ages find disturbing. Be firm with your older
children about not subjecting the younger ones to
trauma, and try to find a way for them to see what's appropriate for their age when the younger ones are off
doing something else. Older kids may need to tape their
shows and watch them later in the evening. When renting
videos, there may be times when you have to rent two.
One for now, and one for after the youngest ones have
gone to bed.

Depend on videos that you already know. One lucky thing about very young children is that they like to watch their favorite videos over and over. There are many wonderful videos that you can buy to have on hand, and there are several newsletters and web sites that review children's videos. You can also tape episodes of good TV programs off the air. When our son was very small, I used to make him tapes of *Sesame Street* and *Mister Rogers' Neighborhood.* What amazed me was how many times he wanted to see the same episodes. For very young children, even these shows are quite complicated, and children seem to enjoy watching them over and over until they become totally familiar with them.

Another tip I've discovered about video viewing is to be certain that your VCR is tuned to a safe channel when your child is viewing a tape. When the tape gets to the end, your television will display whatever channel your VCR is on. If it's PBS or C-SPAN, your child is probably safe. But if it's a major network or a general entertainment cable channel, what your child sees next could be almost anything!

Tape a questionable program and watch it first when your child is not around. If you feel unsure about a program's content despite the ratings systems, previewing it may be the best choice. Also, don't feel that your child has to rush to the theater to see a new movie the first weekend it comes out. By hanging back, you will have much more information at your disposal in making your decision. If you're still not sure, wait for the video. You can screen it first, or at least you can be there when your child sees it. And videos have another advantage: Visual images are not as powerful on the small screen in your well-lit family room as they are on the massive screen of a darkened theater.

And don't forget to be careful about your own TV viewing. Soon after our son was born, we started looking at TV from the perspective of how it would affect our child. What happened first is that we started taping many of our favorite adult-oriented programs for later viewing. But like many other new parents, we found ourselves going to bed earlier and earlier in order to keep up our energy level, and the tapes kept piling up without being viewed. I have gradually come to get less of my entertainment from TV and more from reading, which I can do in the same room as my child without subjecting him to adult fare.

Enlist the cooperation of the parents of your children's friends and the other people who look after your child, including grandparents, baby-sitters, child-care providers, and teachers. Show them this book or tell them about it. Make sure they understand that you're not being silly or overprotective—that your concerns are based on sound research involving data from thousands of children and hundreds of parents. Require child-care providers and schools to obtain parental permission for the showing of entertainment videos.

Don't worry too much. Remember, knowledge is power! The purpose of this book is not to frighten *you!* It's simply to give you better information and tools to guide your child safely through the unpredictable world of television and movies. Just being there and being aware will go a long way toward preventing the types of long-term anxieties and fears we've seen throughout this book. And remember, if your child becomes frightened, there are ways of helping him deal with that fear. If your child stumbles into a disastrous program choice—and that's probably inevitable once in a while—the important thing is to be there for him and help him handle his fears. The fact that you now understand why your child is afraid and know the types of fear-reducing strategies that are most likely to help at your child's age should be greatly reassuring to you and will certainly help you reassure your child.

Making Sure Your Voice Is Heard

Beyond what you can do in your home and for your own family, there are certain steps you can take to help change the television landscape and the media environment we all live in.

First, be sure that your local television station hears your complaints when you think that something inappropriate is on television at a time or in a place that children are likely to be adversely affected by it. During the controversy over the TV ratings, many local stations said they weren't hearing complaints from parents. Perhaps parents had given up, feeling no one was listening to them. If you have time, make your complaint in writing and send a copy to your local paper as a letter to the editor so that other parents may be informed as well. You should also complain when you think a program has been inappropriately rated. Although local stations usually accept the ratings that are provided by the program producers or distributors, they can change ratings that they consider inappropriate. Also, send your complaints to the TV Parental Guidelines Monitoring Board (see the appendix for the address) and the FCC. And be sure that your representatives in Congress know your views. Congress has been extremely responsive to the feelings of parents on this issue.

What we have learned from the controversy over the rating system is that parents do have a voice in these matters, and when the chorus is large, it is heard with resounding clarity. Parents like us can influence how decisions are made in Congress and can force the television industry to be responsive.

There are other things we should be asking the entertainment industry to do to help us protect our children. Here are a few ideas:

Television stations should not air promotional ads for frightening shows and movies during programs with a sizable child audience. Even a promo can cause long-term fears, and parents need more assurance that their child will not be exposed to this type of material when viewing a program that would otherwise be safe.

In general, programmers should agree not to air promos for shows with higher-level ratings in shows with lower ratings. But even if we could get the industry to agree to this, it would not address the fact that many shows are not rated. News and sports, which are not rated, are frequently used to promote other shows. I have received many complaints from parents about the frightening promotions that were aired during recent World Series and Super Bowl telecasts. I realize that one reason networks are willing to pay so much for blockbuster sports events is to promote their other shows. However, networks should be sensitive to the fact that these events are viewed by many children. If a show with controversial content is promoted during a lower-rated or nonrated show, the ad should be designed with a general audience in mind. At the very least, it should exclude the visually frightening elements of the program being promoted.

Movie advertisements and videocassette packages should include the MPAA's reasons for a rating along with the rating. The content that was responsible for the rating a movie received needs to be readily accessible at the time viewing decisions are frequently made—while reading the paper or visiting the video store. And we could really use this type of information for movies rated before 1995. Wouldn't it be helpful if the VCR package for the PG-rated *My Girl* let us know that the movie was about a young girl who is convinced she has contracted a variety of deadly diseases and whose best friend dies from a bee sting? Incidentally, according to the *Motion Picture Rating Directory*, that movie was originally rated PG-13, but the rating was reduced to PG after an appeal.

Family restaurants should not offer toys aimed at preschoolers that tie in with movies that are too scary for that audience. The marketing of *Jurassic Park* was a prime example of a promotional campaign that drew many youngsters to a movie that was clearly too horrifying for them. In an ideal world, the businesspeople making agreements for restaurant tie-ins would show an advance copy of the movie to their own young children before agreeing to promote it to toddlers! But seriously, businesses that cross-promote movies should feel the responsibility to choose the movies they pitch with care.

Let Other People Know When Your Child Has a Negative Emotional Reaction to Something in the Media

This is perhaps the most important thing you can do besides being vigilant about what your children watch. If your child has a fright reaction, you are certainly not alone. Your child is not odd, unstable, or otherwise unbalanced, and there are good reasons why the reaction occurred. Sharing your experience with others will no doubt be therapeutic for you, and it's important to warn other parents about potential effects on their children. If enough parents speak out, we may very well be able to achieve better ratings of programs and movies and more family-friendly programming practices in general.

There are many other changes the entertainment industry could introduce to make television and movies more predictable and less of a minefield for families. Most parents don't want governmental censorship; they don't want adults to be prevented from seeing the adult fare they enjoy. But they do want to protect their children from viewing harmful content—or content they consider inappropriate—without their knowledge in their own homes!

The entertainment industry is extremely well-heeled and its effects are pervasive. But if we communicate with each other and make our needs and wishes known to child advocacy groups, legislators, advertisers, and programmers, we can make the media environment safer for our children. That way, all of us will rest—*and sleep*—easier.

Acknowledgments

I owe so many people so much for helping to make this book a reality that it is difficult to know where to start. But it seems only right that I begin with the person who got me started in research in the first place—Professor Dolf Zillmann of the University of Alabama. It was Dolf who found me as an uncertain first-semester graduate student at the University of Pennsylvania's Annenberg School for Communication and transformed me into an enthusiastic and dedicated researcher. He not only taught me to have high standards as a researcher, but he showed me how much fun and how rewarding the entire research process could be.

Next I want to thank my research collaborators and coauthors who contributed so much to the studies reported here. Special gratitude goes to my first three doctoral advisees, whose contributions during the initial stages of the research were so essential to turning some ideas sketched out in a grant proposal into innovative research procedures and then into influential scholarly publications. To these three most important collaborators, Professor Glenn Sparks (now at Purdue University), Professor Barbara J. Wilson (now at the University of California, Santa Barbara), and Professor Cynthia Hoffner (now at Illinois State University), I owe an enormous debt for assisting me in mapping out the terrain of this program of research. Other important collaborators and coauthors whose work is central to the information and advice given in these pages are Professor Marie-Louise Mares (now at the University of Pennsylvania's Annenberg School for Communication), Professor Mary Beth Oliver (now at Penn. State), Professor Marina Krcmar (now at the University of Connecticut), Dr. Lisa Bruce, and especially Professor Kristen Harrison (now at the University of Michigan) and Dr. Amy Nathanson (now at the University of California, Santa Barbara). I also wish to thank my colleagues at the University of Wisconsin, especially Professor Denise Solomon and Dean Mary Anne Fitzpatrick, for their valuable help and encouragement.

I particularly want to thank Victoria Duran, program director of the National PTA, for her enormous intellectual and moral support of my research on television ratings. Working with her and the leadership of the National PTA has been richly rewarding both personally and professionally, and I have come to appreciate the power of an idealistic and dedicated grassroots organization to affect public policy in a way that benefits America's families.

I have been extremely fortunate to receive the generous financial support that made this research possible. The initial grant from the National Institute of Mental Health was essential to getting my research in this area off the ground. I am also indebted to the University of Wisconsin for generously funding many of these studies and for providing me a supportive work environment for the past two dozen years. Thanks are also due to the Institute for Mental Health Initiatives for helping to fund the parent survey on ratings, to the H. F. Guggenheim Foundation for supporting my research on the attractions of violence, and to the National Cable Television Association for supporting my research on children's reactions to television ratings.

I would also like to thank Linda Henzl for her expert and enthusiastic assistance with the manuscript for this book and so many other projects; Debbie Hanson for her patient handling of all the accounting on my grants; and Paddy Rourke and Dave Fritsch for their generous technical support. I am also very thankful to the many students who helped out in various ways in conducting the research. I am especially indebted to all the children, parents, and college students who participated in my research or told me about their experiences. It is their contributions, after all, that comprise the essence of this book.

I have also benefitted greatly from the encouragement of several people in the fields of communication and mental health, especially Kathryn Montgomery and Jeffrey Chester of the Center for Media Education; Suzanne Stutman of the Institute for Mental Health Initiatives; Ed Donnerstein and Joel Federman of the University of California, Santa Barbara; and Patti Valkenburg of the University of Amsterdam.

With all this support, I still don't know how I would have arrived at a book without the help and guidance of Joan Fischer. It was Joan who helped me get started on this project, collaborating with me on the first proposal for this book, helping me find my own voice as a writer to an audience of parents, and providing valuable support and suggestions all along the way.

I am also deeply indebted to Kate Wendleton, whose advice on getting this book published was crucial; to my agent, Alex Holtz, who immediately made things happen and became a good friend in the process; to Vicki Austin-Smith, my editor at Harcourt Brace, for her unbridled enthusiasm and helpful suggestions; and to Rachel Myers, for her enormously thoughtful and creative copy editing.

Friends and family have also been extremely helpful and supportive, especially my brother Jim Cantor and my sister Mary Hammer, as well as Dorothy Cantor, Sara Larsen, Bonnie Holcomb, and Carol and Jim Lieberman.

Most importantly, I thank the people closest to me: first, my parents, Liz and Chips Cantor, who provided me with a loving home and have always been there when I needed them. Sadly, just as I was completing the manuscript for this book, my mother passed away. Although I miss her enormously, I carry her love and warmth with me every moment, and I am eternally grateful for the ideal role model she has been as a wife, as a mother, and as a woman who contributed her talents and energies for the benefit of the larger community.

And I couldn't have done any of this without my husband, Bob Larsen, and my son, Alex. Bob's love and support fuel everything I accomplish and make life in general so much more rewarding. As for Alex, aside from teaching me, from Day One, the deeper meaning of the words "pride and joy," his presence in my life makes me believe all the more in the critical importance of the work I'm doing.

Problems Frequently Caused by Scary Television and Movies

Immediate Reactions:
- Intense fear
- Crying, clinging, trembling
- Stomach problems (stomach aches, vomiting)

Longer-term Reactions:
- Difficulty sleeping
- Nightmares
- Insistence on sleeping with parents
- Dependence on unusual bedtime rituals
- Refusal to be alone or to be in certain areas of the house
- Refusal to engage in normal activities
- Concern about being hurt or killed
- Unnecessary or unreasonably intense fears
- Long-term aversion to common animals (especially dogs, cats, insects, and spiders)
- Anxiety in specific situations (especially swimming)

The Most Troublesome Content for Different Ages

(Remember, Age Trends Are Approximate)

Two- to Seven-Year-Olds:

- Visual images, whether realistic or fantastic, that are naturally scary: vicious animals; monsters; grotesque, mutilated, or deformed characters
- Physical transformations of characters, especially when a normal character becomes grotesque
- Stories involving the death of a parent
- Stories involving natural disasters, shown vividly

Seven- to Twelve-Year-Olds:

- More realistic threats and dangers that can happen, especially things that can happen to the child
- Violence or the threat of violence
- Stories involving child victims

Age Thirteen and Up:

- Realistic physical harm or threats of intense harm
- Molestation or sexual assault
- Threats from aliens or occult forces

Tips for Helping Frightened Preschoolers

- Remove them from the scary situation.
- Don't belittle or ignore the fear.
- Provide your physical presence, attention, and warmth.
- Try a drink or a snack and a new activity.
- Consider lower doses of the scary image if they want to conquer their fear.
- Go along with reasonable bedtime rituals.
- Recognize the limited effectiveness of logical explanations. (See chapter 8 for adapting them for younger children.)
- Be firm in your resolve to practice prevention.

Tips for Making Explanations Reassuring to Children

For Fantasy Threats:

- For eight-year-olds and over, get them to focus on the impossibility of fantastic happenings.
- For younger children, visually demonstrate the unreal status of fantastic occurrences. (For example, help them apply scary makeup.)

For Real Threats:

- Avoid indicating that a realistic frightening event is possible but unlikely. (Saying "it hardly ever happens" probably won't help.)
- Give them calming, absolute, but limited truthful information. (Saying "It's never happened here" is more likely to succeed.)
- Use their fears as a teachable moment, and offer safety guidelines about how to protect themselves from the threat.
- Talk to them sympathetically about their fears, even when there's nothing particularly reassuring to say.
- Seek professional help if fears are uncontrollable or overpowering.
- Seek your child's cooperation in avoiding future exposure to similar content.

What You Should Know about the Motion Picture Association of America (MPAA) Ratings

G: General Audiences. All ages admitted.

PG: Parental Guidance Suggested. Some material may not be suitable for children.

PG-13: Parents Strongly Cautioned. Some material may be inappropriate for children under 13.

R: Restricted. Under 17 requires accompanying parent or adult guardian.

NC-17: No One 17 and Under Admitted.

- MPAA ratings are decided by majority vote of a committee of parents who judge which rating most parents would find suitable.

- MPAA ratings give age guidelines but don't tell about content.

- Content information for recent movies is now available on the MPAA's web site: www.mpaa.org.

- Only 3 percent of movies rated in 1995 and 1996 were rated G; 14 percent were rated PG; 16 percent were rated PG-13; and 67 percent were rated R.

- 26 percent of PG-rated movies had "bad language" only.

- PG-rated movies (such as *Jaws*) produced before 1984 (when PG-13 was introduced) may be surprisingly intense and scary.

- Even G-rated movies, especially animated adventure features, are often too scary for preschoolers.

A Guide to the Amended TV Parental Guidelines

Children's Programs
  TV-Y: All Children
  TV-Y7: Directed to Older Children
      FV: Fantasy Violence*

*General Programming***
  TV-G: General Audience

  TV-PG: Parental Guidance Suggested
      V: Moderate Violence
      S: Sexual Situations
      L: Infrequent Coarse Language
      D: Some Suggestive Dialogue

  TV-14: Parents Strongly Cautioned
      V: Intense Violence
      S: Intense Sexual Situations
      L: Strong Coarse Language
      D: Intensely Suggestive Dialogue

  TV-MA: Mature Audience Only
      V: Graphic Violence
      S: Explicit Sexual Activity
      L: Crude Indecent Language

*Any intense violence in children's programming is labeled "fantasy violence."

**The most intense level of content determines a program's overall rating. Content existing at lower levels is not displayed.

. . . .

Contacts Regarding TV and Movie Ratings

TV Parental Guidelines Monitoring Board
P. O. Box 14097
Washington, D.C. 20004
E-mail: tvomb@usa.net
web site: www.tvguidelines.org

Classification and Rating Administration
Motion Picture Association of America, Inc.
15503 Ventura Boulevard
Encino, CA 91436-3103
web site: www.mpaa.org

OKTV (Alternative TV Ratings)
c/o Gaffney-Livingstone Consultation Services
59 Griggs Road
Brookline, MA 02146
web site: www.aacap.org (American Academy of Child and
Adolescent Psychiatry)

Federal Communications Commission
1919 M Street, NW
Washington, D.C. 20554
web site: www.fcc.gov/vchip

Notes

·········

A note on these notes: I've included these notes to provide support for the claims I am making by directing your attention to my published research and the writings of others on the topic. But the notes are not meant to be exhaustive in the way the references for a scholarly book would be. More extensive references can be found in many of the academic articles I refer to here.

Preface

p. xv "Recent research on the validity of childhood memories": See C. R. Brewin, B. Andrews, and I. H. Gotlib, "Psychopathology and Early Experience: A Reappraisal of Retrospective Reports," *Psychological Bulletin* 113, no. 1 (1993): 82–98.

Introduction: Is Your Home Really Your Castle?

p. 2 "In fact, research now shows that educational television programming viewed at the preschool level can really improve children's chances for success much later in life": P. A. Collins, et al., "Effects of Early Childhood Media Use on Academic Achievement" (paper presented at Society for Research in Child Development Convention, Washington, D.C., April 1997).

Chapter 1: The Suddenly Crowded Queen-Size Bed

p. 5 and thereafter. All anecdotes presented in this book are real, but the names, when included, have been changed. Some of the reports are based on oral interviews. Most of them (those presented in italics) are from written reports by students or parents and are in their own words. Some are from research participants; others are from class papers. Most of these anecdotes are excerpts of longer descriptions. The only changes from the writer's own words involve deletions to reduce wordiness, or corrections in grammar, punctuation, or spelling. None of these anecdotes have been embellished in any way.

p. 8 "I was amazed by the vividness and emotionality with which they wrote about their experiences": An interesting article in a popular magazine talks about recent advances in the neurobiology of memory, which may help us understand why traumatic events often produce such indelible memory traces: S. S. Hall, "Our Memories, Our Selves," *New York Times Magazine*, February 15, 1998, 26–33, 49, 56–57.

p. 9 "I'll call this the retrospective study": K. Harrison and J. Cantor, "Tales from the Screen: Long-Term Anxiety Reactions to Frightening Movies" (paper presented at the International Communication Association Convention, Chicago, May 1996).

p. 11 "But they have often said that writing about it and learning why it may have happened helped them work through some of their anxieties": In fact, there is evidence that writing about emotional experiences has a profoundly beneficial effect on both psychological and physical well-being. For an important and highly readable book on this topic, see J. W. Pennebaker, *Opening Up: The Healing Power of Expressing Emotions* (New York: Guilford Press, 1997).

pp. 12–13 "a number of psychologists and psychiatrists have claimed that [fright reactions to television and films] may cause children to be plagued by nightmares, sleep disturbances, and bizarre fantasies": for example, J. L. Singer, *Daydreaming and Fantasy* (London: Allen & Unwin, 1975); E. P. Sarafino, *The Fears of Childhood: A Guide to Recognizing and Reducing Fearful States* (New York: Human Sciences Press, 1986).

p. 13 "young people who had to be hospitalized for several days or weeks after watching horror movies such as *The Exorcist* and *Invasion of the Body Snatchers*": J. C. Buzzuto, "Cinematic Neurosis Following *The Exorcist*," *Journal of Nervous and Mental Disease* 161 (1975): 43–48; J. Mathai, "An Acute Anxiety State in an Adolescent Precipitated by Viewing a Horror Movie," *Journal of Adolescence* 6 (1983): 197–200.

p. 13 "two children had suffered from post-traumatic stress disorder": D. Simons and W. R. Silveira, "Post-traumatic Stress Disorder in Children after Television Programmes," *British Medical Journal* 308 (1994): 389–90.

p. 19 "Many of the symptoms . . . are well-known symptoms of both phobias and post-traumatic stress disorder": See "Specific Phobias" and "Post-Traumatic Stress Disorder" in *Diagnostic and Statistical Manual of Mental Disorders,* 4th ed. (Washington, D.C.: American Psychiatric Association, 1994).

p. 20 "my colleagues and I designed a study to observe [spillover effects]": J. Cantor and B. Omdahl, "Effects of Fictional Media Depictions of Realistic Threats on Children's Emotional Responses, Expectations, Worries, and Liking for Related Activities," *Communication Monographs* 58 (1991): 384–401.

p. 20 "*Little House on the Prairie* . . . was among the top-ten fear-producing shows according to a survey of parents my collaborators and I conducted in the early eighties":

J. Cantor and G. G. Sparks, "Children's Fear Responses to Mass Media: Testing Some Piagetian Predictions," *Journal of Communication* 34, no. 2 (1984): 90–103.

p. 23 *"After this incident, I would not go down into our basement":* In a study of the media-induced fright of college students, 10% of males and 68% of females agreed with the statement, "I have sometimes been SO scared of a show or movie that I have actually been afraid to go into certain rooms in my own house." G. G. Sparks, M. M. Spirek, and K. Hodgson, "Individual Differences in Arousability: Implications for Understanding Immediate and Lingering Emotional Reactions to Frightening Mass Media," *Communication Quarterly* 41, no. 4 (1993): 465–76.

p. 25 "To explore more systematically what parents know . . . my colleagues and I recently conducted a phone survey": Some of these findings are reported in J. Cantor and A. Nathanson, "Children's Fright Reactions to Television News," *Journal of Communication* 46, no. 4 (1996): 139–52.

Chapter 2: Through a Child's Eyes

p. 33 "Our retrospective study of college students showed that more than half of those who reported a long-term fright reaction had not particularly wanted to see the program that had caused them to be so upset": K. Harrison and J. Cantor, "Tales from the Screen: Long-Term Anxiety Reactions to Frightening Movies" (paper presented at the International Communication Association Convention, Chicago, May 1996).

p. 39 "Some well-known psychoanalysts have proposed that these stories allow children to work through 'traumas that are seething in the unconscious' ": For example, B. Bettelheim, *The Uses of Enchantment: The Meaning and Importance of Fairy Tales* (New York: Vintage Books, 1975).

Chapter 3: Appearance, Appearance, Appearance

p. 50 "Research shows that very young children respond to things mainly in terms of how they appear": See, for example, R. Melkman, B. Tversky, and D. Baratz, "Developmental Trends in the Use of Perceptual and Conceptual Attributes in Grouping, Clustering, and Retrieval," *Journal of Experimental Child Psychology* 31 (1981): 470–86.

p. 51 "A follower of Piaget noted that young children focus on and react to whatever 'clamors loudest for their attention' ": J. Flavell, *The Developmental Psychology of Jean Piaget* (New York: Van Nostrand, 1963).

p. 52 "The first thing my colleagues and I did to explore this idea was to ask parents which programs and movies had frightened their children the most": J. Cantor and G. G. Sparks, "Children's Fear Responses to Mass Media: Testing Some Piagetian Predictions," *Journal of Communication* 34, no. 2 (1984): 90–103.

p. 55 "my colleagues and I answered the question about

how sensitive to appearance different age groups are by doing a controlled experiment": C. Hoffner and J. Cantor, "Developmental Differences in Responses to a Television Character's Appearance and Behavior," *Developmental Psychology* 21 (1985): 1065–74.

p. 58 "In the survey we conducted in the early eighties, [*The Amityville Horror*] was reported to have scared many more older children than younger ones": J. Cantor and G. G. Sparks, "Children's Fear Responses to Mass Media: Testing Some Piagetian Predictions," *Journal of Communication* 34, no. 2 (1984): 90–103.

p. 59 "When we conducted a random phone survey of parents the night after [*The Day After*] aired": J. Cantor, B. J. Wilson, and C. Hoffner, "Emotional Responses to a Televised Nuclear Holocaust Film," *Communication Research* 13 (1986): 257–77.

p. 64 "Certain types of animals, especially snakes and spiders, more readily evoke fear than other types": See G. S. Hall, "A Study of Fear," *The American Journal of Psychology* 9, no. 2 (1897): 147–249; A. Maurer, "What Children Fear," *The Journal of Genetic Psychology* 106 (1965): 265–77; D. R. Kirkpatrick, "Age, Gender and Patterns of Common Intense Fears Among Adults," *Behavior Research and Therapy* 22, no. 2 (1984): 141–50; R. M. Yerkes and A. W. Yerkes, "Nature and Condition of Avoidance (Fear) in Chimpanzee," *Journal of Comparative Psychology* 21 (1936): 53–66.

p. 64 "A third type of visual image that automatically repels and scares us is physical deformity": See D. O.
Hebb, "On the Nature of Fear," *Psychological Review* 53
(1946): 259–76.

p. 66 "Researchers have identified a small part of the
brain called the amygdala as the center where innately
threatening sights and sounds are received": See J.
LeDoux, *The Emotional Brain: The Mysterious Underpin-
nings of Emotional Life* (New York: Simon & Schuster,
1996); R. J. Davidson and S. K. Sutton, "Affective Neuroscience: The Emergence of a Discipline," *Current
Opinion in Neurobiology* 5 (1995): 217–24; R. J. Davidson, "Affective Style and Affective Disorders: Perspectives from Affective Neuroscience," *Cognition and
Emotion* (1998, in press).

Chapter 4: The Trouble with Transformations

p. 72 "by Piaget's descriptions of how children . . . respond": For a reader-friendly introduction to Piaget,
see D. G. Singer and T. A. Revenson, *A Piaget Primer:
How a Child Thinks* (New York: Plume, 1996). For a
more comprehensive treatment of Piaget's major theoretical principles, see J. Flavell, *The Developmental Psychology of Jean Piaget* (New York: Van Nostrand, 1963).

p. 74 "I soon discovered how frightening young children
found [*The Incredible Hulk*] when I looked at the results of the parent survey we conducted in the spring

of 1981": J. Cantor and G. G. Sparks, "Children's Fear Responses to Mass Media: Testing Some Piagetian Predictions," *Journal of Communication* 34 no. 2 (1984): 90–103.

p. 75 "After finding that young children did indeed find [*The Incredible Hulk*] scary, at least according to their parents, we designed a study to learn more about the reasons for this reaction": G. G. Sparks and J. Cantor, "Developmental Differences in Fright Responses to a Television Program Depicting a Character Transformation," *Journal of Broadcasting & Electronic Media* 30 (1986): 309–23.

p. 82 "in one famous study, children between the ages of three and six were allowed to pet a tame and friendly cat": R. DeVries, *Constancy of Generic Identity in the Years Three to Six*, Monographs of the Society for Research in Child Development, serial no. 127, vol. 34, no. 3 (Chicago: University of Chicago Press for the Society for Research in Child Development, 1969).

Chapter 5: "But It's Only Make-Believe"

pp. 89–90 "Developmental psychologists have noted that children only gradually come to understand the difference between reality and fantasy": For example, P. Morison and H. Gardner, "Dragons and Dinosaurs: The Child's Capacity to Differentiate Fantasy from Reality," *Child Development* 49 (1978): 642–48.

p. 91 "Piaget's take on this situation was to say that pre-school, or preoperational, children do not distinguish play and reality as two distinct realms with different ground rules": J. Flavell, *The Developmental Psychology of Jean Piaget* (New York: Van Nostrand, 1963).

pp. 92–93 "At first children believe that the things they are seeing are actually inside the television set—that if they look inside, they'll find those things and that what's in there might actually be able to come out": J. H. Flavell, et al., "Do Young Children Think of Television Images as Pictures or Real Objects?" *Journal of Broadcasting & Electronic Media* 34, no. 4 (1990): 399–419.

p. 93 "They come to judge whether something on television is real on the basis of whether the things they see in a story actually exist in the real world": P. Morison, H. Kelly, and H. Gardner, "Reasoning about the Realities on Television: A Developmental Study." *Journal of Broadcasting & Electronic Media* 25, no. 3 (1981): 229–41.

p. 95 "In the survey we conducted in the early eighties . . . we categorized the content as either fantasy or fiction": J. Cantor and G. G. Sparks, "Children's Fear Responses to Mass Media: Testing Some Piagetian Predictions," *Journal of Communication* 34 no. 2 (1984): 90–103.

p. 95 "Our more recent survey of parents of children in kindergarten, second, fourth, and sixth grade recon-firmed the importance of the fantasy-reality distinc-tion in what frightens children": Some of these findings are reported in J. Cantor and A. Nathanson, "Children's Fright Reactions to Television News," *Journal of Communication* 46, no. 4 (1996): 139–52.

p. 98 "There are several reasons why we respond so intensely to television shows and movies, even when we know that what we're seeing is fiction": For more discussion of these ideas, see J. Cantor, "Fright Reactions to Mass Media," in *Media Effects: Advances in Theory and Research,* ed. by J. Bryant and D. Zillmann (Hillsdale, N.J.: Erlbaum, 1994): 213–45.

p. 102 "Most scary programs and movies let us know what is going to happen or what might happen, and we become anxious well in advance of the horrifying outcome. Research shows that it's much more frightening this way": J. Cantor, D. Ziemke, and G. G. Sparks, "The Effect of Forewarning on Emotional Responses to a Horror Film," *Journal of Broadcasting* 28 (1984): 21–31; C. Hoffner and J. Cantor, "Forewarning of Threat and Prior Knowledge of Outcome: Effects on Children's Emotional Responses to a Film Sequence," *Human Communication Research* 16 (1990): 323–54.

p. 102 "It seems that music and sound effects dramatically affect our emotional reactions": There is surprisingly little controlled research that supports this claim. One study showed that different musical scores increased or reduced physiological responses to a stressful film but did not affect viewers' ratings of their feelings of anxiety: J. F. Thayer and R. W. Levenson, "Effects of

Music on Psychophysiological Responses to a Stressful Film," *Psychomusicology* 3, no. 1 (1983): 44–52. Another study reported that of three animated cartoons, the one that produced the most anxiety in children was the one that had no violence but had the most "fear-eliciting sound effects": K. Björkqvist and K. Lagerspetz, "Children's Experience of Three Types of Cartoon at Two Age Levels," *International Journal of Psychology* 20 (1985): 77–93. More research is needed on the power of music and sound effects.

p. 104 "Content analyses have shown that in horror movies, attacks against men are usually over and done with quickly, but attacks against women are longer and more drawn out": F. Molitor and B. S. Sapolsky, "Sex, Violence, and Victimization in Slasher Films," *Journal of Broadcasting & Electronic Media* 37, no. 2 (1993): 233–42.

Chapter 6: When Reality Is a Nightmare

p. 112 "A recent study reported that local news is especially violent": "Body Bag Journalism," *Sacramento Bee*, May 22, 1997, sec. B, p. 6.

p. 112 "In the survey we did in the early eighties, in which we asked parents to name the television shows and movies that had frightened their child, television news stories were in the top ten": J. Cantor and G. G. Sparks, "Children's Fear Responses to Mass Media: Testing Some Piagetian Predictions," *Journal of Communication* 34 no. 2 (1984): 90–103.

p. 113 "shortly after the war in the Persian Gulf, almost half of a random sample of parents my colleagues and I contacted said their child had been upset by television coverage of the war": J. Cantor, M. L. Mares, and M. B. Oliver, "Parents' and Children's Emotional Reactions to Televised Coverage of the Gulf War," in *Desert Storm and the Mass Media,* ed. by B. Greenberg and W. Gantz (Cresskill, N.J.: Hampton Press, 1993): 325–40.

p. 113 "in the random survey of parents with children in kindergarten through sixth grade that we did in the spring of 1994, we found that 37 percent said their child had been frightened or upset by a television news story during the preceding year": J. Cantor and A. Nathanson, "Children's Fright Reactions to Television News," *Journal of Communication* 46, no. 4 (1996): 139–52.

p. 115 "Dozens of studies have been conducted in which children have been asked what frightens them, and there is a large consensus regarding age trends in fears": For a review, see J. Cantor, B. J. Wilson, and C. Hoffner, "Emotional Responses to a Televised Nuclear Holocaust Film," *Communication Research* 13 (1986): 257–77.

p. 119 "In our most recent random survey of parents, *Rescue 911* was mentioned more often than any other program (including fantasy and fiction genres) as causing fear in children": Other findings from this survey are reported in J. Cantor and A. Nathanson, "Children's Fright Reactions to Television News," *Journal of Communication* 46, no. 4 (1996): 139–52.

Chapter 7: When Words Won't Work

p. 125 "An early study of children and fear tells the story of the young child who sat down and classified fairy-tale characters as 'real' or 'unreal' ": A. T. Jersild and F. B. Holmes, "Methods of Overcoming Children's Fears," *Journal of Psychology* 1 (1935): 75–104.

p. 125 "When my colleagues and I questioned parents of preschoolers in a survey, most of them said they used that type of explanation when coping with their child's TV fears": B. J. Wilson and J. Cantor, "Reducing Children's Fear Reactions to Mass Media: Effects of Visual Exposure and Verbal Explanation," in *Communication Yearbook 10* (Beverly Hills, Calif.: Sage, 1987): 553–73.

p. 125 "We took a scene from *The Wizard of Oz* that many children find especially scary": J. Cantor and B. J. Wilson, "Modifying Fear Responses to Mass Media in Preschool and Elementary School Children," *Journal of Broadcasting* 28 (1984): 431–43.

p. 126 "When my colleagues and I asked children to indicate how helpful different methods would be in making them feel better if they were scared by something on TV": B. J. Wilson, C. Hoffner, and J. Cantor, "Children's Perceptions of the Effectiveness of Techniques to Reduce Fear from Mass Media," *Journal of Applied Developmental Psychology* 8 (1987): 39–52.

p. 127 "Another experiment my colleagues and I conducted is a case in point. The results surprised us": B. J. Wilson and J. Cantor, "Reducing Children's Fear

Reactions to Mass Media: Effects of Visual Exposure and Verbal Explanation," in *Communication Yearbook 10* (Beverly Hills, Calif.: Sage, 1987): 553–73.

p. 129 "The same preschoolers . . . said that getting something to eat or drink or holding a blanket or cuddly toy would help them the most": B. J. Wilson, C. Hoffner, and J. Cantor, "Children's Perceptions of the Effectiveness of Techniques to Reduce Fear from Mass Media," *Journal of Applied Developmental Psychology* 8 (1987): 39–52.

p. 129 "An interesting experiment was recently reported in which preschoolers watched a scary television movie with or without their older sister or brother": B. J. Wilson and A. J. Weiss, "The Effects of Sibling Co-viewing on Preschoolers' Reactions to a Suspenseful Movie Scene," *Communication Research* 20, no. 2 (1993): 214–48.

p. 132 "Experts differ, sometimes vehemently, on whether [sleeping in a parent's bed] should ever be allowed": Rather than jumping into this controversy, I'll direct you to some differing opinions on the subject: R. Ferber, *Solve Your Child's Sleep Problems* (New York: Simon & Schuster, 1985). This book argues against letting your child sleep with you and has many thoughtful recommendations regarding how to handle children's nighttime fears. R. Wright, "Go Ahead . . . Sleep with Your Children," *APA Monitor* (American Psychological Association) (June 1997): 16. (Also published in *Slate*, www.

slate.com/Code/Reg3/Login.asp?ur/path-Earthling/
97-03-27/Earthling.asp). Wright proposes, using arguments from evolutionary theory, that "the family bed" is
superior to having your baby sleep alone. Both Pene-
lope Leach and T. Berry Brazelton steer a middle
ground, and present the benefits and drawbacks of both
approaches: P. Leach, *Your Baby and Child: From Birth to
Age Five* (New York: Alfred A. Knopf, 1990); T. B. Brazelton, *Touchpoints: Your Child's Emotional and Behavioral Development* (Reading, Mass.: Addison-Wesley, 1992).

p. 135 "exposing themselves to bits and pieces of the program rather than the whole thing. Research shows
that these techniques can actually reduce younger
children's fright while viewing scary programs": B. J.
Wilson, "The Effects of Two Control Strategies on Children's Emotional Reactions to a Frightening Movie
Scene," *Journal of Broadcasting & Electronic Media* 33
(1989): 397–418.

p. 135 "In the experiment we did with *Raiders of the Lost Ark*
we also explored whether we could make the snake
scene less frightening by desensitizing children to the
visual image of snakes": B. J. Wilson and J. Cantor,
"Reducing Children's Fear Reactions to Mass Media:
Effects of Visual Exposure and Verbal Explanation," in
Communication Yearbook 10 (Beverly Hills, Calif.: Sage,
1987): 553–73.

p. 136 "Other researchers have found similar results by allowing children to hold rubber replicas of spiders or

showing them real lizards and worms before they saw scary movies involving these creatures": B. J. Wilson, "Reducing Children's Emotional Reactions to Mass Media Through Rehearsed Explanation and Exposure to a Replica of a Fear Object," *Human Communication Research* 14 (1987): 3–26; B. J. Wilson, "Desensitizing Children's Emotional Reactions to the Mass Media," *Communication Research* 16 (1989): 723–45; A. J. Weiss, D. L. Imrich, and B. J. Wilson, "Prior Exposure to Creatures from a Horror Film: Live Versus Photographic Representation," *Human Communication Research* 20 (1993): 41–66.

p. 136 "My colleagues and I have also taken on *The Incredible Hulk,* using segments of a *Mister Rogers' Neighborhood* episode intended to reduce children's fear of the Hulk": J. Cantor, G. G. Sparks, and C. Hoffner, "Calming Children's Television Fears: Mr. Rogers vs. the Incredible Hulk," *Journal of Broadcasting & Electronic Media* 32 (1988): 271–88.

Chapter 8: Making Explanations Child-Friendly

p. 142 "In the *Wizard of Oz* study, nine- to eleven-year-olds who were told to remember that the witch was not real showed less fear while watching her in a scene": J. Cantor and B. J. Wilson, "Modifying Fear Responses to Mass Media in Preschool and Elementary School Children," *Journal of Broadcasting* 28 (1984): 431–43.

pp. 142–43 "Similarly, other researchers have reported

that seven- to nine-year-olds had their vampire-movie fears reduced by an explanation of how makeup made the vampires look scary, while five- to six-year-olds were not helped": B. J. Wilson and A. J. Weiss, "The effects of two reality explanations on children's reactions to a frightening movie scene," *Communication Monographs* 58 (1991): 307–26.

p. 143 "in a study involving *The Incredible Hulk,* my colleagues and I tried to counteract children's fears by giving them simple explanations of how the Hulk likes to help people, while showing them footage": J. Cantor, G. G. Sparks, and C. Hoffner, "Calming Children's Television Fears: Mr. Rogers vs. the Incredible Hulk," *Journal of Broadcasting & Electronic Media* 32 (1988): 271–88.

p. 143 "For that study, in which we used a scene from the sci-fi thriller *The Blob,* we tried to reassure children by describing the special effects that made the blob look real and letting them create their own 'blobs' out of gelatin and food coloring": J. Cantor and C. Hoffner, "Children's Fear Reactions to a Televised Film as a Function of Perceived Immediacy of Depicted Threat," *Journal of Broadcasting & Electronic Media* 34, no. 4 (1990): 421–42. This technique was used after the study was over, to ensure that children did not leave the experiment with residual feelings of anxiety. Because there was no control condition that did not receive this treatment, we did not collect data to support the treatment's effectiveness as a fear reducer.

pp. 145–46 "In the study involving *The Blob* . . . we explained to a group of five- to eight-year-olds that a
frightening event in a movie could *never* happen anywhere": J. Cantor and C. Hoffner, "Children's Fear Reactions to a Televised Film as a Function of Perceived
Immediacy of Depicted Threat," *Journal of Broadcasting & Electronic Media* 34 (1990): 421–42.

p. 146 "This finding is consistent with research my colleagues and I have done on children's understanding
of concepts related to probability and likelihood":
D. M. Badzinski, J. Cantor, and C. Hoffner, "Children's
Understanding of Quantifiers," *Child Study Journal* 19
(1989): 241–58; C. Hoffner, J. Cantor, and D. M.
Badzinski, "Children's Understanding of Adverbs De-
noting Degree of Likelihood," *Journal of Child Language* 17 (1990): 217–31.

p. 146 "However, research indicates that older children
and even adults also overestimate the likelihood of
outcomes that are intensely threatening, even when
the chances of their happening are infinitesimal": See
P. Slovic, B. Fischhoff, and S. Lichtenstein, "Facts versus Fears: Understanding Perceived Risk," in *Judgment
under Uncertainty: Heuristics and Biases,* ed. by D. Kah-
neman, P. Slovic, and A. Tversky (Cambridge: Cambridge University Press, 1982).

p. 150 "In the study I reported in chapter 1, in which we
showed the schoolhouse burn down in *Little House on
the Prairie,* we ended the session by giving children

basic fire-safety guidelines": J. Cantor and B. Omdahl, "Effects of Fictional Media Depictions of Realistic Threats on Children's Emotional Responses, Expectations, Worries, and Liking for Related Activities," *Communication Monographs* 58 (1991): 384–401.

p. 155 "In fact, I never did make that appointment with the therapist": Some interesting research in interpersonal communication suggests that when you think about a problem with the intention of talking about it, your thoughts become better suited to solving the problem, whether you ultimately have a conversation about it or not. See D. H. Cloven and M. E. Roloff, "Sense-Making Activities and Interpersonal Conflict, II: The Effects of Communicative Intentions on Internal Dialogue," *Western Journal of Communication* 57 (1993): 309–29. By simply thinking about what I would say to a therapist, I was apparently able to put the problem in a more reasonable perspective.

Chapter 9: Why Kids Are Drawn to Scary Entertainment

Many of the ideas in this chapter are distilled from J. Cantor, "Children's Attraction to Violent Television Programming," in *Why We Watch: The Attractions of Violent Entertainment,* ed. by J. Goldstein (New York: Oxford University Press, 1998).

p. 158 "Nielsen ratings consistently show that most of the Saturday-morning programs with the highest child viewership are violent": For example, H. Stipp, "Children's Viewing of News, Reality-Shows, and Other Programming" (paper presented at the Convention of the International Communication Association, Albuquerque, N.M., May 1995).

p. 159 "A second reason we have so many violent programs and movies is that it is more profitable to produce shows that can be exported to foreign countries": S. Stossel, "The Man Who Counts the Killings," *The Atlantic Monthly* 279, no. 5 (1997): 86–104. This claim is attributed to media researcher and activist George Gerbner. The article chronicles Dr. Gerbner's research on the content of television over the past 30 years. Gerbner contends, as I do, that television viewing promotes feelings of anxiety. His work has a different emphasis from mine: He focuses on the cumulative effects of exposure to violent programming on our perceptions of the world as a mean and dangerous place, rather than on the emotional impact of a single frightening program or movie.

p. 161 "when a researcher asked sixth- to eighth-grade children in Milwaukee the question: 'Would you watch a television program if you knew it contained a lot of violence?' 82 percent replied 'yes' ": L. Bruce, "At the Intersection of Real-Life and Television Violence: Emotional Effects, Cognitive Effects, and Interpretive Activities of Children" (PH.D. diss., University of Wisconsin, Madison, 1995).

p. 163 "Some researchers have even argued that it is action (characters moving fast) rather than violence (characters injuring each other) that attracts children's attention to violent television programs": R. Potts, A. Huston, and J. C. Wright, "The Effects of Television Form and Violent Content on Boys' Attention and Social Behavior," *Journal of Experimental Child Psychology* 41 (1986): 1–17.

p. 163 "Many people, and children especially, enjoy violent, scary shows because they like the thrill of being stimulated and aroused by entertainment": For an interesting analysis of the role of arousal in media entertainment, see D. Zillmann, "Television Viewing and Physiological Arousal," in *Responding to the Screen: Reception and Reaction Processes,* ed. by J. Bryant and D. Zillmann (Hillsdale, N.J.: Erlbaum, 1991): 103–33.

p. 164 "Some psychologists believe that this difference is due to the fact that we treat our little boys differently from our little girls": A. Frodi, J. Macaulay, and P. Thome, "Are Women Always Less Aggressive Than Men? A Review of the Experimental Literature," *Psychological Bulletin* 84 (1977): 634–60.

p. 164 "Other psychologists maintain that boys' greater interest in violence is rooted in their hormones, and that biology predisposes them to be more aggressive and to be more interested in aggressive things": J. Goldstein, "Immortal Kombat: War Toys and Violent Videogames," in *Why We Watch: The Attractions of Violent*

Entertainment, ed. by J. Goldstein (New York: Oxford University Press, 1998).

pp. 164–65 "It has also been shown that children who are more violent themselves are more interested in viewing violent programs": For example, C. Atkin, et al., "Selective Exposure to Televised Violence," *Journal of Broadcasting* 23, no. 1 (1979): 5–13.

p. 165 "Viewing violence contributes to children becoming more violent, and children who are violent are more interested in viewing violence": See L. R. Huesmann, "Psychological Processes Promoting the Relation between Exposure to Media Violence and Aggressive Behavior by the Viewer," *Journal of Social Issues* 42, no. 3 (1986): 125–40.

p. 166 "In one study, college students took a six-weeks' heavy dose of action-adventure programs featuring good triumphing over evil": J. Bryant, R. A. Carveth, and D. Brown, "Television Viewing and Anxiety: An Experimental Examination," *Journal of Communication* 31, no. 1 (1981): 106–19.

p. 166 "In one survey of parents, for example, we found that children who had been frightened by television were especially interested in violent programs in which good triumphed over evil": J. Cantor and A. Nathanson, "Predictors of Children's Interest in Violent Television Programming," *Journal of Broadcasting & Electronic Media* 41 (1997): 155–67.

p. 168 "In a study of children in inner-city Milwaukee": L.

Bruce, "At the Intersection of Real-Life and Television Violence: Emotional Effects, Cognitive Effects, and Interpretive Activities of Children" (Ph.D. diss., University of Wisconsin, Madison, 1995).

p. 169 "Research shows that children who watch a lot of violence become less aroused by it over time and that children become less bothered by real interpersonal aggression after watching fictionalized violence": V. B. Cline, R. G. Croft, and S. Courrier, "Desensitization of Children to Television Violence," *Journal of Personality and Social Psychology* 27, no. 3 (1973): 360–65; F. Molitor and K. W. Hirsch, "Children's Toleration of Real-life Aggression after Exposure to Media Violence: a Replication of the Drabman and Thomas Studies," *Child Study Journal* 24, no. 3 (1994): 191–207.

p. 169 "Research also shows that repeated exposure to violence leads to less sympathy for its victims and to the adoption of violent attitudes and behaviors": D. G. Linz, E. Donnerstein, and S. Penrod, "Effects of long-term exposure to violent and sexually degrading depictions of women," *Journal of Personality and Social Psychology* 55 (1988): 758–68; C. R. Mullin and D. Linz, "Desensitization and Resensitization to Violence Against Women: Effects of Exposure to Sexually Violent Films on Judgments of Domestic Violence Victims," *Journal of Personality and Social Psychology* 69 (1995): 449–59; L. R. Huesmann, "Psychological Processes Promoting the Relation Between Exposure to Media Violence and Aggressive Behavior by the Viewer," *Journal of Social Issues* 42, no. 3 (1986): 125–40.

Chapter 10: Ratings Roulette

p. 172 *"We told our son"*: Unlike all the other vignettes that are presented in italics in this book, this anecdote is not a verbatim transcription. It is my re-creation of the story a woman told me when I addressed a group of parents at a local church.

pp. 175–76 "my colleagues and I found that more than one-fourth of [PG-rated movies] had bad language only": J. Cantor, A. Nathanson, and L. L. Henzl, "Reasons Why Movies Received a PG Rating: 1995–1996," Unpublished Report Filed in Comments of Joanne Cantor to the Federal Communications Commission (CS Docket No. 97-55), April 7, 1997.

p. 176 "When my colleagues and I looked at the content of a random sample of movies shown on television, there was only a whisper of a difference between movies rated PG and those rated PG-13": J. Cantor, K. S. Harrison, and M. Krcmar, "Ratings and Advisories: Implications for the New Rating System for Television," in *Television Violence and Public Policy,* ed. by J. T. Hamilton (Ann Arbor: University of Michigan Press, 1998).

p. 177 "one mother who answered a recent nationwide survey of ours": J. Cantor, S. Stutman, and V. Duran, "What Parents Want in a Television Rating System: Results of a National Survey," report released on Capitol

Hill (November 21, 1996), available at www.pta.org/programs/tvrpttoc.htm.

p. 177 "the explanation of the rating supplied by MPAA president Jack Valenti hedges a bit": The excerpt comes from J. Federman, *Media Ratings: Design, Use, and Consequences* (Studio City, Calif.: Mediascope, 1996). This book gives an excellent review of the use of media ratings around the world.

p. 178 "In a story in the *Boston Globe,* one mother complained that the wolves in [*Beauty and the Beast*] had caused her three-year-old daughter to become terrified of dogs": B. F. Meltz, "The Sometimes Terrifying World of Disney," *Boston Globe,* February 20, 1997, sec. F., pp. 1, 5. The woman, Jacquie Sears, who also reported that her daughter started worrying that her parents would die after seeing *Bambi,* has founded "Mothers Offended by the Media" (MOM), and has been crusading for better movie ratings ever since.

pp. 183–84 "I joined with the National PTA and the Institute for Mental Health Initiatives (IMHI) to do a nationwide survey to find out what parents wanted in a rating system": J. Cantor, S. Stutman, and V. Duran, "What Parents Want in a Television Rating System: Results of a National Survey," report released on Capitol Hill (November 21, 1996), available at www.pta.org/programs/tvrpttoc.htm.

p. 186 "This spontaneous comment came from a ten-year-old girl who participated in research my colleagues

and I conducted for the National Television Violence
Study": M. Krcmar and J. Cantor, "The Role of Television Advisories and Ratings in Parent-Child Discussion of Television Viewing Choices," *Journal of
Broadcasting & Electronic Media* 41 (1997): 393–411.

p. 187 "My colleagues and I also did some studies to find
out how these ratings affect kids who make viewing decisions in the absence of their parents": J. Cantor, K. S.
Harrison, and A. Nathanson, "Ratings and Advisories
for Television Programming," in *National Television
Violence Study,* vol. 2, ed. by Center for Communication and Social Policy, University of California, Santa
Barbara (Thousand Oaks, Calif.: Sage Publications,
1997): 267–322.

p. 189 "Jack Valenti had warned critics that he'd see them
in court 'in a nanosecond' if they tried to force any
changes": G. Browning, "No Oscar for Jack," *National
Journal* (August 23, 1997): 1688–91.

Chapter 11: Taming the Resident Monster

p. 195 "Many studies show that viewing more than one or
two hours of television a day interferes with a child's
other activities": For an interesting review of the literature on this topic, see T. M. MacBeth, "Indirect Effects of Television: Creativity, Persistence, School
Achievement, and Participation in Other Activities,"
in *Tuning in to Young Viewers: Social Science Perspectives*

on Television, ed. by T. M. MacBeth (Thousand Oaks, Calif.: Sage Publications, 1996): 149–219.

p. 196 "Our research on TV ratings and advisories showed that children whose parents watch TV with them and discuss it with them are less likely to choose restricted content when their parents are not around": These results come from the National Television Violence Study. J. Cantor and K. S. Harrison, "Ratings and Advisories for Television Programming," in *National Television Violence Study,* vol. 1 (Thousand Oaks, Calif.: Sage Publications, 1996): 361–410; J. Cantor, K. S. Harrison, and A. I. Nathanson, "Ratings and Advisories for Television Programming," in *National Television Violence Study,* vol. 2, ed. by Center for Communication and Social Policy, University of California, Santa Barbara (Thousand Oaks, Calif.: Sage Publications, 1997): 267–322.

p. 197 "Research also shows that many parents are concerned about their children's exposure to sexual dialogue, sexual situations, and coarse language, and that parents differ in terms of how strongly they worry about the effects of different types of content": See the parent survey I did with the National PTA and IMHI: J. Cantor, S. Stutman, and V. Duran, "What Parents Want in a Television Rating System: Results of a National Survey," report released on Capitol Hill (November 21, 1996), available at www.pta.org/programs/tvrpttoc.htm.